Deaf around the World

Deaf around the World

The Impact of Language

EDITED BY

Gaurav Mathur

Donna Jo Napoli

OXFORD

UNIVERSITY PRESS

2011

OXFORD
UNIVERSITY PRESS

Oxford University Press, Inc., publishes works that further
Oxford University's objective of excellence
in research, scholarship, and education.

Oxford   New York
Auckland   Cape Town   Dar es Salaam   Hong Kong   Karachi
Kuala Lumpur   Madrid   Melbourne   Mexico City   Nairobi
New Delhi   Shanghai   Taipei   Toronto

With offices in
Argentina   Austria   Brazil   Chile   Czech Republic   France   Greece
Guatemala   Hungary   Italy   Japan   Poland   Portugal   Singapore
South Korea   Switzerland   Thailand   Turkey   Ukraine   Vietnam

Copyright © 2011 by Oxford University Press, Inc.

Published by Oxford University Press, Inc.
198 Madison Avenue, New York, New York 10016

www.oup.com

Oxford is a registered trademark of Oxford University Press

Library of Congress Cataloging-in-Publication Data
Deaf around the world: the impact of language / edited by
Gaurav Mathur and Donna Jo Napoli.
    p. cm.
Includes bibliographical references and index.
ISBN 978-0-19-973254-8; 978-0-19-973253-1 (pbk.)
1. Sign language. 2. Deaf—Means of communication.
I. Mathur, Gaurav. II. Napoli, Donna Jo, 1948–
HV2474.D43   2010
419—dc22   2009052404

9 8 7 6 5 4 3 2 1

Printed in the United States of America
on acid-free paper

Acknowledgments

The editors thank Leah Geer for help on proofing and formatting the entire manuscript and Dorothy Kuntz for help in technical matters. We thank the William J. Cooper Foundation of Swarthmore College for financial support of the eponymous conference held in spring 2008.

Within their chapters, the authors of the individual contributions to this volume acknowledge those who have helped them. Here we repeat acknowledgments only for reproduction permissions and aid with figures.

For chapter 1, we thank Meir Etedgi for illustrating figure 1.2.

For the response to chapter 4, we thank Connie de Vos for permission to print figure 4R.3, for which she owns the copyright.

For chapter 6, we thank Owen P. Wrigley and the National Association of the Deaf in Thailand for permission to reprint the material in figure 6.14, which is from *The Thai Sign Language Dictionary* (revised and expanded edition), edited by Manfa Suwanarat, Anucha Ratanasint, Vilaiporn Rungsrithong, Lloyd Anderson, and Owen P. Wrigley and published by the National Association of the Deaf in Thailand. In addition, for help in so many ways in procuring that permission, we thank Chip Reilly.

For the response to chapter 6 we thank Ishara Press for permission to reprint figure 6R.1 from Dikyuva and Zeshan's (2008) *Türk İşaret Dili, Birinci Düzey* [Turkish Sign Language, Level One], published in Nijmegen, and from Lutalo-Kiingi's (2008) Possessive Forms and Structures in Ugandan Sign Language, in *Possessive and Existential Constructions in Sign Languages,* Sign Language Typology Series no. 2, edited by Ulrike Zeshan and Pamela Perniss, 105–124, also published in Nijmegen.

For chapter 9, we thank Douglas McLean and Forest Books for permission to print data from Maryland in table 9.1.

For the response to chapter 9, we thank Busisiwe Kheswa for taking the photos in figures 9R1–9R3 and John Meletse and Paul Mokgethi for serving as the models in these photos.

Chapter 10 builds on Karen Nakamura's 2006 article "Creating and Contesting Signs in Contemporary Japan: Language Ideologies, Identity, and Community in Flux" in *Sign Language Studies* 7(1): 11–29. We thank Gallaudet University Press and Project Muse for permission to reprint major parts of that article.

For chapter 11 we thank Wang Ke'nan, principal of Beijing no. 2 School for the Deaf, for permission to use the school gate photo in figure 11.1.

For chapter 12 we thank Gallaudet University Press for permission to reprint the cartoons in figures 12.1–12.5 from *Deaf Culture, Our Way: Anecdotes from the Deaf community,* edited by Roy K. Holcomb, Samuel K. Holcomb, and Thomas K. Holcomb (San Diego: DawnSignPress, 1996).

Contents

Contributors

Yerker Andersson was born deaf and educated in Sweden. He went on to Gallaudet University and Teachers College, Columbia University. He received his PhD in sociology at the University of Maryland in 1981. He taught sociology for thirty years and was chair of the (currently named) Department of American Sign Language and Deaf Studies at Gallaudet University for its initial two years. Since 1950, Dr. Andersson has been involved in international activities. Appointed by President Clinton, he served on the National Council on Disability and was chair of its International Watch. An emeritus professor, he remains active at the international level.

Deborah Chen Pichler is associate professor of linguistics at Gallaudet University. She earned her PhD in Linguistics from the University of Connecticut in 2001, focusing on L1 acquisition of ASL syntax by deaf toddlers. Her current research interests include first, second, and bilingual acquisition of ASL, as well as cross-linguistic comparisons of sign languages. In addition to regular courses at Gallaudet University, Dr. Chen Pichler frequently teaches short courses and workshops on sign acquisition, most recently in Brazil, France, and Croatia. She is a hearing, second language signer of ASL.

Marie Coppola is an assistant professor of psychology and linguistics at the University of Connecticut. She earned her PhD in brain and cognitive sciences at the University of Rochester in 2002, and completed her postgraduate training at the University of Chicago. She conducts fieldwork with deaf children, adolescents, and adults in Nicaragua who are inventing their own homesign systems. She has published scholarly articles and given presentations on her work relating homesign systems to hearing gestures and characterizing the transformation of homesign systems into Nicaraguan Sign Language. She is the founder of Manos Unidas, a nonprofit organization dedicated to enhancing educational and vocational opportunities for deaf people in Nicaragua. She is hearing and has Deaf parents.

Cyril Courtin is a researcher in cognitive sciences at the National Center for Scientific Research at Paris Descartes University. He earned his PhD in cognitive psychology in 1998 and has published several articles and book chapters about the cognitive/metacognitive development of deaf children. In collaboration with Paris 8 University (Vincennes–Saint Denis), he also works on linguistic development in signing deaf children. He is currently on the editorial board of the *Journal of Deaf Studies and Deaf Education*. He is active in the Deaf community and in the French National Federation of the Deaf.

Paul Dudis is assistant professor of linguistics at Gallaudet University. He earned his PhD in linguistics at the University of California at Berkeley in 2004 and has been investigating iconicity in signed language, particularly the ways in which events are depicted. Other interests include cognitive linguistic approaches to signed language morphology, syntax, and discourse. He is director of the Language and Communicative Forms in a Visual Modality Initiative within the National Science Foundation Science of Learning Center: Visual Language and Visual Learning.

Nickson O. Kakiri, a Deaf Kenyan activist, is a mainstreaming disability advisor for VSO/Mongolia and current chair of the Kenya National Association of the Deaf. He advocates for inclusive policies to enable the equal participation of deaf people and people with disabilities in society. He has copresented papers on deaf people in developing countries and consulted with the Kenya Ministry of Education, Liverpool VCT Care and Treatment, and United Disabled Persons of Kenya. The first recipient of the World Deaf Leadership Scholarship (of the Nippon Foundation of Tokyo), he attended Gallaudet University (class of 2005). He is currently working on a master's degree in development studies at the University of Nairobi.

Deborah Karp and her twin sister, Joanna, were born deaf and started learning sign language at seven years of age. She has been deeply involved in the Deaf community ever since. She served as director of the Deaf AIDS Project at Family Service Foundation, Inc., in Landover Hills, Maryland, for four years. She presently works for the Computer Science Corporation in Hanover, Maryland, as a project control analyst. She earned a degree in business at Gallaudet University and one in desktop publishing at the Rochester Institute of Technology.

Adam Kendon studied at Cambridge and Oxford and has held academic positions at Oxford, as well as in the United States, Australia, and Italy. Well known for his work on gesture, he has also published a study of a primary (deaf) sign language used in the Enga province of Papua New Guinea and a book on the alternate sign languages in use among Australian Aborigines. In 2000 he published a translation of an 1832 book about gesture and archaeology in Naples. His book *Gesture: Visible Action as Utterance* was published by Cambridge University Press in 2004. He lives in Philadelphia.

Paddy Ladd is Deaf and a senior lecturer at the Centre for Deaf Studies at the University of Bristol, England, and the author of numerous works, including *Understanding Deaf Culture: In Search of Deafhood*. He completed his PhD in Deaf culture at the University of Bristol in 1998 and in 1999 won the Deaf Lifetime Achievement Award given by the Federation of Deaf People. He is the 2009 recipient of the Laurent Clerc Cultural Fund Edward Miner Gallaudet Award from Gallaudet University. He is currently working with Donna West on *Seeing through New Eyes: Deafhood Pedagogies and the Unrecognised Curriculum*.

Gaurav Mathur is assistant professor of linguistics at Gallaudet University. He earned his PhD in linguistics from MIT in 2000 and did his postdoctoral fellowship in psycholinguistics at the Haskins Laboratories. He has received fellowships from NSF and NIH and published several articles in refereed journals and conference proceedings, as well as given dozens of invited and conference presentations. He has refereed articles for conferences and journals related to sign languages and is presently the review editor for *Sign Language and Linguistics*. He has organized national conferences on sign language linguistics and Deaf academics.

John Meletse is a South African Deaf gay activist working on HIV and lesbian, gay, bisexual, and transgendered (LGBT) issues. He is the first Deaf South African to publicly disclose his HIV status. He has worked for the NGO Gay and Lesbian Memory in Action (GALA) for the past five years on the LGBT Deaf oral history and outreach project. He was part of a team that created an educational comic, "Are Your Rights Respected?" focusing on HIV education for Deaf youth. He has made presentations at local and international conferences, and his life story has appeared in numerous publications.

Leila Monaghan received her PhD in linguistic anthropology from the University of California at Los Angeles in 1996. Her dissertation was on the development of the New Zealand Deaf community. She has coedited several books, including *Many Ways to Be Deaf* and *HIV/AIDS and Deaf Communities*, and has published numerous articles on Deaf cultures, often dealing with the impact of HIV/AIDS on these communities. She is currently a Frison Visiting Scholar in the Department of Anthropology at the University of Wyoming and also works with Deaf and hearing adolescents at the Cathedral Home for Children.

Ruth Morgan is a South African anthropologist. She has a PhD in linguistic anthropology from American University in Washington, D.C., and did her postdoctoral research at the University of the Witwatersrand in South Africa on the life stories of Deaf South Africans. Her work has also focused on life-story research with same-sex sangomas (traditional healers), as well as lesbians and gay men living with HIV. She is coeditor of the book *"deaf me normal": Deaf South Africans Tell Their Life Stories* (2008).

Soya Mori is senior research fellow at the Institute of Developing Economies (IDE-JETRO) and professor of both sign linguistics and development economics at the IDE Advanced School. He has published widely on the analysis of Japanese Sign Language and on the Japanese Deaf community. He is the English-Japanese translator of *Deaf in America* and *Understanding Deaf Culture*. He was the first Deaf president of the Japanese Association of Sign Linguistics (2003–2008) and is now chief editor of *Journal of Disability Studies*, published by the Japan Society of Disability Studies. He is the coordinator of a group of experts in developing countries for the World Federation of the Deaf.

Karen Nakamura is assistant professor of anthropology and East Asian studies at Yale University. Her first ethnography, *Deaf in Japan: Signing and the Politics of Identity* (2006), received a John Whitney Hall Book Prize from the Association for Asian Studies. She has begun working on broader issues in disability in Japan and is currently engaged in fieldwork on mental illness in Japan. Her ethnographic film, *Bethel: Community and Schizophrenia in Northern Japan*, had its world premiere at the 2007 Disabled People's International World Congress in Seoul, South Korea.

Donna Jo Napoli is professor of linguistics at Swarthmore College. She has published widely in theoretical linguistics. In sign studies, she has coauthored several papers on ASL structure and a book comparing ASL and BSL humor and is working on a study of the phonological systems of five languages. She has coordinated one national and one international conference on Deaf issues and is coeditor of two volumes resulting from the first conference. She has coauthored an article on a new method of teaching reading to Deaf children, as well as a storybook and an article on educational ethics and Deaf children.

Angela M. Nonaka is assistant professor of anthropology at the University of Texas, Austin. She earned her PhD in anthropology at the University of California, Los Angeles, and did a postdoctoral fellowship in linguistics at the University of California at Berkeley. With support from the Wenner-Gren Foundation, IIE Fulbright, Rotary International, and the Japanese Ministry of Education, she has lived and worked extensively in Asia, studying sign languages in Thailand, Japan, and Burma. Her research interests in linguistic anthropology include language socialization, language ideologies, discourse analysis, language documentation, and language endangerment.

Carol A. Padden is professor of communication and associate dean of the Division of Social Sciences at the University of California, San Diego. Along with other members of her research group, she has been investigating a new sign language used by a community of deaf and hearing Bedouins in the Middle East. Padden and her colleagues argue that a robust and fully expressive language can develop in two or three generations of users through an interaction of emergent structures and patterns of learning in communities. With Tom Humphries, she has published two books on the culture and community of Deaf people in the United States.

Roland Pfau received his PhD in linguistics from the University of Frankfurt in 2001. He is assistant professor in the Department of General Linguistics of the University of Amsterdam. Since 2007 he has served as editor of the journal *Sign Language and Linguistics*. He has published articles and chapters on various aspects of sign language grammar in journals and books and is a coeditor of *Visible Variation: Comparative Studies on Sign Language Structure* (2007). He has been involved in the organization of a number of international conferences and workshops. Besides sign linguistics, he is interested in speech error research and language typology.

Christian Rathmann is professor of sign linguistics and sign interpreting and chair of the Institut für Deutsche Gebärdensprache und Kommunikation Gehörloser [Institute for German Sign Language and Deaf Communication] at the University of Hamburg. He earned his PhD at the University of Texas in Austin in 2005. His dissertation focuses on event structure in ASL, including aspect and temporal interpretation. His current research includes the study of bilingualism, especially in educational contexts, the interface of sign and gesture, interpreting and corpus linguistics, and, in particular, the morphological and semantic properties of language (including aspect and agreement) from a cross-linguistic and cross-modal perspective.

Russell S. Rosen is assistant professor of education at Teachers College, Columbia University. He earned his AB in anthropology from the University of Chicago and a PhD in education from Columbia University. He is the founder of the Program in the Teaching of American Sign Language as a Foreign Language at Teachers College, Columbia University. He has published numerous peer-reviewed articles in Deaf studies and second language acquisition of ASL, refereed for several academic journals, established ASL programs in secondary and collegiate schools, read for Fulbright Scholarships, and presented papers at many academic conferences.

Paul Scott is British Sign Language development manager for the British Deaf Association based at Cardiff, UK. His poetry demonstrates the beauty and depth of British Sign Language. He has performed his poetry at international conferences held in Rotterdam, Brussels, and Philadelphia, as well as all around the United Kingdom. His poetry has been produced on a DVD, and his second DVD is soon to be released in collaboration with other poets. A native BSL signer, Scott taught Deaf studies and BSL to Deaf children at Elmfield School for Deaf Children in Bristol from 1997 to 2006.

Ann Senghas is associate professor of psychology at Barnard College of Columbia University, where she has taught since 1999. She was introduced to the Nicaraguan Deaf community in 1990 and has been documenting the emergence of Nicaraguan Sign Language ever since. In 1995 she earned her PhD in brain and cognitive sciences from MIT. She then worked as a postdoctoral researcher at the University of Rochester's Sign Language Center and the Max Planck Institute for Psycholinguistics in the Netherlands. Her research is funded by the NIH/NIDCD. She visits Nicaragua almost every summer, and students often accompany her.

Rachel Sutton-Spence is a senior lecturer at the University of Bristol (United Kingdom). She has been researching and teaching sign language linguistics since 1989. She is coauthor (with Bencie Woll) of the award-winning textbook *The Linguistics of British Sign Language* (Cambridge University Press, 1998). Her research interests include sociolinguistic variation in signed languages and sign language creativity and folklore. She has written extensively on sign language poetry (for example, *Analysing Sign Language Poetry*, 2005) and more recently on sign language humor (*Humour in Sign Languages: The Linguistic Underpinnings*, with Donna Jo Napoli, 2009).

Madan M. Vasishta was born in India and became deaf at eleven years of age. He worked as a farmer and a photographer and was involved with the All India Federation of the Deaf. In 1967 Dr. Vasishta came to Gallaudet University and earned his three degrees there. He has worked in education for more than thirty years. He retired as superintendent of the New Mexico School for the Deaf in 2000. He has authored four books and several articles. He divides his time between teaching at Gallaudet and working with organizations in India.

Donna West earned her PhD in the Graduate School of Education at the University of Bristol, where she is now a postdoctoral researcher working with Rachel Sutton-Spence. Her areas of interest include deaf-hearing family life and narrative inquiry. She taught deaf children before moving to CDS to undertake an MSc in Deaf studies. She has worked with Paddy Ladd on a Deafhood pedagogies study, funded by the Leverhulme Trust, titled *Seeing through New Eyes*. She has publications in *Deaf Studies Methodologies*, a textbook (forthcoming, Oxford University Press), and in *Poetic Inquiry: Vibrant Voices in the Social Sciences*, ed. Prendergast, Leggo, and

Sameshima, 2009) and has presented her work at international, qualitative and arts-based conferences.

Amy T. Wilson, PhD, is an associate professor at Gallaudet University and program director for the Master of Arts Degree in International Development in the Department of Educational Foundations and Research. She focuses on the effectiveness of development assistance from federal agencies, nongovernmental organizations, and faith-based groups to people with disabilities and deaf communities in developing countries. Her publications discuss global health care issues for women and children with disabilities, human rights of persons with disabilities, gender equity, and a transformative sociocultural participatory model of research in deaf communities. She has lived and worked in more than thirty countries.

Sandra K. Wood is lecturer in the Department of Psychology and the ASL program at the University of Virginia. She is now finishing her doctoral dissertation in linguistics at the University of Connecticut, Storrs, which focuses on the resilience of language and on universal grammar in homesigned systems and sign language acquisition. Other areas of research include ASL (and Libras) syntax with respect to word order, negation, and *wh*-questions. Wood has presented her work in the United States, Japan, and Brazil and has published articles on both ASL and Libras.

James Woodward received his PhD in sociolinguistics at Georgetown University in 1973. Professor of linguistics and research scientist at Gallaudet University for twenty-six years, he also taught at the Chinese University of Hong Kong (CUHK) and was director of research for Ratchasuda College in Thailand, the first tertiary institution for Deaf people in Southeast Asia. In 2002 he received the Edward Miner Gallaudet Award, which recognizes international leaders who promote the well-being of Deaf people. He is director of the Nippon Foundation Project on Opening University Education to Deaf People in Viet Nam and codirector of the Centre for Sign Linguistics and Deaf Studies at CUHK.

Jun Hui Yang is a lecturer in Deaf studies, School of Education and Social Science, University of Central Lancashire in Preston, UK. She earned a PhD in Deaf education from Gallaudet University in 2006. She has been involved in the sign typology project at the Max Planck Institute for Psycholinguistics, PEN-International research activities for Deaf postsecondary education in China, and the Norway-China SigAm Bilingual Deaf Education Project in Jiangsu, China. She has published several articles and book chapters on Chinese Sign Language and the bilingual education of deaf Chinese children.

Ulrike Zeshan is director of the International Centre for Sign Languages and Deaf Studies at the University of Central Lancashire in Preston, UK. She received a PhD in linguistics from the University of Cologne and then headed the Sign Language Typology Research Group at the Max Planck Institute for Psycholinguistics. She has conducted fieldwork on several sign languages in Asia, and her research focuses on comparative typological studies of sign languages. In addition, Dr. Zeshan is involved in curriculum and materials development with partners in Ghana, Uganda, India, and Turkey and is president of the Deaf Empowerment Foundation.

Deaf around the World

Introduction

Why Go around the Deaf World?

Gaurav Mathur and Donna Jo Napoli

This volume offers work in common areas of inquiry in Deaf studies around the world, both academic and activist. As such, it reaches out to people in multiple fields, including sign language linguistics and the broader area of Deaf studies, drawing on anthropology, psychology, cognitive science, education, medical demography and ethnography, economic development, and other disciplines. Additionally, while the material ranges from technical matters to ordinary topics, the language throughout is accessible to people from all walks of life, consistent with our goal of being a forum for the exchange of ideas between academics and activists and reaching a wide audience.

Why should we need such a forum? Who benefits?

Both of the editors of this volume are involved in linguistics. Work on the linguistics of sign languages is like work on the linguistics of spoken languages. However, not all linguistic communities are equivalent in terms of a researcher's responsibility to the community. If you work on Italian, for example, your linguistic consultants do not necessarily experience problems in daily life due to their language and/or culture. If you work on Haisla (an indigenous language of North America), on the other hand, your linguistic consultants constantly struggle with problems connected to their cultural heritage, including discrimination that (subtly or overtly) threatens their abilities to realize the full range of rights and opportunities that people who are part of the mainstream culture around them enjoy. Furthermore, their language (and, thus, culture) might even be endangered. Common decency demands that the researcher not ignore the plight of the community but instead offer something in return. Many academic linguists who work on endangered languages feel that they should be responsive to the needs and desires of the community in formal arrangements for the dissemination of information, as well as informal commitments to make their work relevant and responsible to community concerns.

Communities of deaf people present the researcher with a more extreme situation. Not only are rights and opportunities at issue, but so is the cognitive faculty of language itself. Because the critical period for first language acquisition does not usually extend beyond childhood, a deaf child who is not exposed to fluent models in an accessible language before that time may not develop complete fluency in any language. (We, along with several of our colleagues, have argued elsewhere for giving the deaf child consistent exposure to both sign and spoken language models from birth to ensure that the faculty of language is properly nourished and to increase the child's chances of realizing full academic, professional, and personal potential.) Denying people a language they feel at home in—a language with which to communicate their hopes, fears, jokes, ironies, affections—is unconscionable. To watch people you are studying (and benefiting from the study of) be denied their civil rights and do nothing about it can be considered unprofessional. Therefore, linguists working on a sign language can and often do get involved in issues of deaf communities in those ways the communities deem helpful and appropriate.

An additional argument can be made for the importance of scholars' understanding a community's concerns: Such understanding improves scholarly work. We use an example from linguistics. Evidence is amassing that linguistic principles alone are inadequate to fully describe, account for, and predict data patterns in languages. Instead, cultural habits and beliefs often influence linguistic structure. The use of formal persons and honorifics (in languages such as Japanese), for example, is clearly culture bound. However, close study has revealed other less obvious instances of culture affecting grammar. One such example is the appropriateness of certain noun phrases in subject position in combination with certain other noun phrases having other grammatical functions in both active and passive sentences depending on whether the referents of the noun phrases are animate or have other semantic properties (in languages such as Navajo). That is, the grammatical and performance patterns of any communication system will reflect the environment it is used in, particularly the environment that children are socialized in. The growing field of "ethnogrammar" cautions us all to pay attention to the communities that use the languages that linguists study. At the heart of all human communication is the creation and interpretation of patterns. Linguists have tended to focus on grammar, and linguistic anthropologists on seeing patterns in performance and community relations. However, activists also point out patterns, the recognition of which (whether the patterns are constructive or destructive) is essential to the ability of a community to thrive. Scholars will be able to do better work if they explore all such patterns and gain a deep understanding and appreciation of the communities they work with.

The activist also benefits from being aware of what the scholars are doing. Early work on sign language among deaf people in France (especially Bébian

1817) and on sign languages among hearing North American Plains Indians in comparison with sign languages of deaf people (Mallery 1881) laid the foundation for scholarly work on deaf community sign languages in the twentieth century. While there was serious work in Europe (Tervoort 1953), it was that of the American William Stokoe (1960) that caught the attention of many, not just in linguistics but also in numerous fields. In fact, Tom Humphries (2008) argues that it was the foundational work of sign linguists that made many deaf people in the United States and Europe and, subsequently, all around the world understand that their language was not some form of gesture inferior to spoken language but instead a bona fide language. Humphries further argues that this realization fueled the Deaf Pride movement of the 1970s and 1980s in the United States and, again, around the globe. The work of linguists was clearly important in helping deaf communities and individuals establish robust identities. The realization that sign languages are natural human languages, with all the cognitive (nonmodally restricted) characteristics of any natural human language, has also been used to critical effect in arguments for legislation that ensures and protects various rights of deaf people, particularly with respect to telecommunications technology and dissemination (as argued in Sonnenstrahl 2008). The increase in commitments to educate deaf children around the world—through the establishment of schools for deaf children and programs within the regular public school system designed specifically to meet deaf children's needs—follows on the heels of the recognition that sign languages are human languages with full "citizenship" so to speak, and the communities that use these languages likewise deserve full citizenship. The price for not having a common communication system (as with isolated deaf people or very small and scattered communities of deaf people) and a coherent community organization is high and evidenced even today when, for instance, deaf people are excluded from conversations about health issues, including HIV/AIDS and high blood pressure. The language decisions of any community impact its economic, educational, medical, cultural, and social life, and deaf activists need to take appropriate action to protect language diversity at the same time that they amass community power to demand their civil rights. If the study of sign languages and their impact on deaf communities has the potential to improve just a single aspect of life in deaf communities, a common forum for activists and scholars is an endeavor well worth pursuing.

It was with this philosophy in mind that, in the spring of 2008, linguistic scholars and activists came together at a conference at Swarthmore College (outside of Philadelphia), funded by the William J. Cooper Foundation, which we hereby thank, and for which all interpreting and computer-assisted, real-time translation (CART) needs were coordinated by Doreen Kelly, whom we also hereby thank. The range of presenters ensured that the audience included people interested in sign languages per se and people interested in the rights of deaf individuals and communities. Scholars and activists exchanged ideas about the many aspects of and situations concerning sign languages and deaf communities in a holistic way. Blinders were lifted, new alliances were formed, and all of the participants had a chance to get others to focus attention on an issue they considered crucial.

The present volume builds on that conference, including some of the papers offered there, as well as new ones that grew from those interactions. While the generosity of the William J. Cooper Foundation allowed that conference to be as global as possible (many participants flew in from various parts of the world), the book in your hands now is even more so. Too little has been published about sign languages and the deeper social situation of deaf communities outside of the United States and Europe; we aim to help remedy that shortage. The contributors to this volume range from people new on the scene to some of our most trusted and experienced leaders in both scholarship and activism. Each chapter examines an issue in detail and is followed by a response chapter that looks at the same issue or a related one in a different context.

The themes that emerged at the conference have led to the two parts of this book, which are tightly linked. The first part focuses on sign languages used in the Deaf world, asking how they are created, how they are used in context, what their form looks like especially in comparison with other sign languages, how they are acquired (as a first language) and learned (as a second language), what factors are involved in their dissemination and in their endangerment, and what they can tell us about the origins of language. The way to address questions of language evolution, whether in the past or occurring right now, is through analysis of present behavior, including not only natural language settings such as indigenous sign communities and creativity in the use of sign but also the patterns developed by children learning Deaf culture. Cross-cultural comparisons are key. This part of the volume includes discussion of sign languages in Europe, North America, the Middle East, Central America, South America, and Asia.

The second part of the volume takes a broader perspective on the Deaf world by examining the social issues that confront it, especially with regard to civil rights, access to education, medical information and care, economic development, and matters of personal and cultural identity, all of which are grounded in sign language use. This part also looks at situations in many places, including Africa, Asia, and Europe.

Language is a fundamental part of how we define ourselves and how others view us. The deaf situation offers us information that studies limited only to spoken language cannot. Because acquiring language is a human right that most people enjoy without struggle, it is hard to imagine the situation of deaf children growing up in hearing families. They often struggle in linguistic isolation before anyone recognizes their right to a language. As a result, feelings about language use in deaf communities run fast and deep. In a deaf community, lexical choices can indicate alignments that deeply reinforce or, alternatively, seriously threaten the identity of individuals. We have a chapter on this—Karen Nakamura's. Additionally, unlike any spoken language situation we know of, deaf people typically learn a sign language whose associated culture is unknown to them (unless they happen to have deaf parents). Thus, new deaf signers are in the unique position of having to learn the culture that is their heritage—not via blood but via their very deafness. We have a chapter on this as well—Paul Scott's. By having the two sides of this volume, the linguistic and the activist, we can approach issues that one side might not even realize exist but that, once recognized, may help them to do a better job in their particular arena.

Before talking briefly about the chapters, we want to point out that many books make a consistent distinction between the term *deaf* with a small *d,* indicating an audiological status, and *Deaf* with a capital *D,* indicating a cultural status. Some of our chapters do that. However, while this distinction can be useful in countries like the United States, it may be blurred or even nonexistent in countries where some (if not all) deaf people are raised in isolation from other deaf people and/or where people use only homesign or village sign, for which there may be few users and the formation of a culture is minimized. Therefore, the reader might find *deaf* used throughout a chapter or in unexpected instances when the author is describing people who live in these other situations. Furthermore, while we are on the topic of conventions, please note that signs used as examples are indicated in small capital letters (CHAIR), whereas spoken words used as examples are italicized *(chair).*

The first part of our book opens with a chapter on "Sign Language geography." Carol Padden describes difficulties in knowing how many sign languages exist and in determining which are genetically related. She compares the situation in North America with that of the Middle East. By looking at the rare remarks about sign languages from a hundred years ago and more, as well as the growth and dissemination of new sign languages (such as Nicaraguan Sign and Al-Sayyid Bedouin Sign Language), we begin to understand how sign languages interact and the extent to which the notion "genetically" related is useful in discussing the relationships among them. Comparisons allow us to see how the pattern of sign language distribution is deeply linked to political, cultural, and social factors that influence how signers have contact with one another.

James Woodward responds in "Some Observations on Research Methodology in Lexicostatistical Studies of Sign Languages" with an overview of how historical linguists classify languages into families. While the comparative method and internal reconstruction are preferable when abundant data are available, the limited data on sign languages indicate that lexicostatistics is the most useful method. This method is made reliable by using the Swadesh word list revised appropriately for sign languages. Languages can have multiple ancestors, that is, languages that have contributed significantly to the daughters (thus, creolization is included). The history of sign languages must be studied in order for it to be understood—it cannot simply be assumed. Finally, an examination of families of signs in Southeast Asia and Central America puts us on alert to the endangered status of indigenous sign languages, often at the hand of ASL.

Gaurav Mathur and Christian Rathmann in "Two Types of Nonconcatenative Morphology in Signed Languages" examine morphological structure in sign languages with an eye toward understanding the kind of morphology that changes the internal properties of a sign. Cross-linguistic comparisons of several languages, including German, Japanese, and American sign languages, reveal that there are two such types of morphological processes. One changes a sign according to fixed forms listed in the lexicon, while the other looks to interaction with gestural space to determine its realization. While both types are subject to language-specific constraints against marked forms, only the latter type is also subject to phonological constraints against moving or twisting a part of the hand or arm. These constraints arise because interaction with gestural space has the potential to result in forms that exceed the limits of the articulations. This latter type of nonconcatenative morphology makes sign languages unique.

Paul Dudis, in "Some Observations on Form-meaning Correspondences in Two Types of Verbs in ASL," continues the discussion of linguistic characteristics unique to sign languages by looking at the structures and conceptual work needed in integrating visual imagery into the proper use of indicating verbs and handling-classifier predicates. Both types of verbs have some unspecified components within their phonological structure that must be elaborated in a way compatible with their semantic structure. The form-meaning correspondences in the indicating verb prompt the signer to direct the movement of the sign toward an appropriate discourse referent—thus filling in location features. On the other hand, these correspondences in the handling-classifier predicate prompt for the depiction of the event that it encodes. Therefore, the phonological features of the handling-classifier predicate filled in by context are not limited to location but, rather, pervade the verb's phonological structure.

In "Sources of Handshape Error in First-time Signers of ASL," Deborah Chen Pichler reports on a study that investigates the phenomenon of "sign accent," or systematic phonological errors made by nonsigners attempting to mimic isolated ASL signs. The study has implications for sign language teaching, where people are learning an unfamiliar language in a modality new to them. Chen Pichler finds two factors relevant to how well nonsigners produce the target handshape. One is markedness; anatomical features of the hand affect dexterity in making a sign, although with qualifications. This general finding is no surprise—studies of acquisition repeatedly show the relevance of phonetic markedness. The other factor, however, is surprising. Chen Pichler finds that transfer of phonological features from gestures hearing people make (with or without accompanying speech) affects the ability to mimic signs.

While Russell Rosen in "Modality and Language in the Second Language Acquisition of American Sign Language" applauds studies of second language learning regarding sign languages, he notes that previous studies concentrate on phonetic phenomena, where the modality difference between spoken and sign languages is most apparent. However, studies of phonological, syntactic, and semantic phenomena where differences are not limited to differences in modality allow us to look more broadly at language differences. For signers whose first language is spoken, the modality difference can affect the acquisition of word-formation processes that are not based on simply adding one meaningful unit after another (as in a word like *unlikely*: [un + like + ly]) but on a nonlinear (nonconcatenative) pattern (such as changing the dynamics or size of a sign). It can also affect nonlinear syntax since this kind of syntax cannot occur in speech given that we have only one speech tract. On the other hand, for signers whose first language is sign, differences in the interface between modality and sign in the two languages are important.

Marie Coppola and Ann Senghas, in "Getting to the Point: The Development of a Linguistic Device in Nicaraguan Signing," pay particular attention to the contribution of generations of child learners, who actively change their language as they inherit it. The researchers consider the fact that, over the past thirty years, deaf Nicaraguans have come together to form a community and in the process created their own new language. The deaf children started with a variety of gestures, called homesigns, to communicate with their families. Together they developed them into the complex linguistic system that is Nicaraguan Sign Language today. Coppola and Senghas follow this process by focusing on a single sign, the humble point, as it transformed from a gesture into a linguistic device.

Roland Pfau responds in "A Point Well Taken: On the Typology and Diachrony of Pointing" by pulling in cross-linguistic observations about the development and use of pointing, whether as a gesture or a sign, from communities that use spoken languages (in Laos, Thailand, Australia, and Latin American Spanish) and from those that use sign languages (in Denmark, Bali, and Germany). He argues that, if we set aside indexicals indicating plurality or time points, subtle changes in the phonological makeup of the remaining pointing signs allow us to distinguish between different functions, considering both manual and nonmanual changes (e.g., eye gaze). He also addresses the issue of grammaticalization and shows how Senghas and Coppola's study adds to our understanding of diachronic change in sign languages.

In "The Acquisition of Topicalization in Very Late Learners of Libras: Degrees of Resilience in Language," Sandra Wood describes the necessary ingredients for learning language, asking what degree of competency is possible for homesigners when they acquire sign language late, especially with different amounts of linguistic input. Homesigners, late learners of Libras (Brazilian Sign Language), and native signers are compared on certain tasks. This study tests people's competence in topicalization, a syntactic construction that is hypothesized to be acquired only after exposure to the target language. Differences are markedly apparent with respect to age and amount of exposure to Libras, as expected. However, this study is of great import not just to linguistics but also to applications in language teaching since it shows that, given proper input, functional mastery of a language can be achieved even after the critical period for language acquisition has passed.

Cyril Courtin fills in the French situation with his response, "A Critical Period for the Acquisition of a Theory of Mind? Clues from Homesigners." He complements Wood's questioning about the linguistic achievement of homesigners by asking whether homesigns are sufficient to help children develop a mature cognition. Several studies on theory of mind in deaf children and adults suggest that language communication (not just gestural communication) is a critical variable in proper cognitive development. Additionally, the age of ten appears to be a significant time—an earlier critical period than Wood's studies found. These findings, while not constant, are relatively persistent regardless of whether children eventually receive hearing aids or cochlear implants (where no difference between the two types of aids is noted).

In "Interrogatives in Ban Khor Sign Language: A Preliminary Description," Angela Nonaka looks at the linguistic process of question formation in a sign language isolate in Thailand that until recently was undocumented and undescribed. Interrogatives are a linguistic feature found in every language, but like other language universals, they vary across languages with respect to several properties. Elucidating these similarities and differences expands our understanding of the extent of linguistic diversity stemming from the human characteristic of and common ability for language. Nonaka shows that yes-no questions in Ban Khor Sign Language have many of the properties of yes-no questions in other sign languages. However, the *wh*-question has some characteristics unique, so far as we know, to this language. There are two *wh*-morphemes, and, while the range of questions for each is similar (*who, what, when,* etc.), the sense of the questions differs, as do their syntactic properties. Nonaka also reports on a mouth morpheme that accompanies other question morphemes but can also be used on its own to indicate interrogativity.

In "Village Sign Languages: A Commentary," Ulrike Zeshan replies that the study of village sign languages is at the forefront of new approaches to developing a typology of languages. Indeed, recent research has shown that the study of village sign disconfirms some of our previously held assumptions about the linguistic structure of sign languages based on the study of the bet-ter-known sign languages of Europe and North America (such as that they all use entity classifiers—Adamorobe Sign Language does not). Further, village sign languages present distinct sociolinguistic contexts that are instructive to study with respect to understanding language contact issues. Finally, the endangered status of these languages raises philosophical questions about the nature of human language.

In "Sign Language Humor, Human Singularities, and the Origins of Language," Donna Jo Napoli and Rachel Sutton-Spence build on the increas-ing evidence for the proposal that sign languages preceded spoken languages, as they present another piece of the jigsaw by exploring the human singular-ities demonstrated in creatively artistic humorous sign language. Using the conceptual integration theory, they argue that what may be seen as "just a funny story in British Sign Language" contains all of the human singularities needed to create the novel mappings and compressions between preexisting conventional cognitive parts and conventionally structured ones that make up human language. While it is arguable that spoken language could do without things like analogy, framing, and the like (though it would be vastly impover-ished), it is entirely impossible for sign language to do so. Thus, the fact that these human singularities emerged at roughly the same time as language makes sense if the first human language were signed.

In "Gesture First or Speech First in Language Origins?" Adam Kendon gives an overview of the debate about whether spoken or sign language came first. He challenges a foundation of the debate: that languages are monomo-dalic. He reports on his study of people describing events. The subjects matched kinesic expressions to the meaning of words and produced kinesic versions of the pronunciations of words, using gestures as schematic devices when describing the shape, location, and size of entities, many of which are conventionalized. Language, then, can be constructed in multiple dimen-sions and modalities simultaneously. The idea that sign languages are unique in being able to express multiple propositions at once is challenged. Kendon conjectures that writing has skewed our idea of how spoken language works since writing, perforce, is concatenative. Probably the earliest languages were multimodal, as today, and made use of whatever fit the circumstance and convenience.

We now move into the second part of the volume. Amy Wilson and Nickson Kakiri, in "Best Practices for Collaborating with Deaf Communities in Develop-ing Countries," highlight some aspects of the best practices of researchers and organizations when collaborating with deaf communities to nurture them in achieving their independence and an enhanced quality of life. The two authors discuss joint work and what brought them to it. Wilson recounts experiences in Brazil that changed her approach to the deaf community from protecting its members to helping to empower them to lead independent lives. Her personal journey reflects a paradigm shift around the world. Nickson describes their joint study to discover how outside funding institutions can aid the economic development of Kenyan deaf communities from the point of view of those communities. Community members identified problems of corruption and misunderstandings of culture that led to the misuse of funding. They recognized the need for community planning, management, and evaluation of projects. They recommended that money from institutions go directly to the communities rather than be funneled through brokers and that deaf Kenyans be trained to help train other deaf Kenyans in what needs to be done. In sum, deaf people must be empowered to make their own changes.

In his reply, "Deaf Mobilization around the world: A Personal Perspective," Yerker Andersson recounts the history of his own work on deafness and development, supporting the call for the establishment of schools and local and national organizations for deaf people, as well as for international organizations to empower deaf communities to meet their goals. Andersson describes how he represented European deaf communities at meetings of international aid institutions after WWII, helping to effect changes in the worldview of deaf people, which led to the establishment of schools for deaf children. Missionaries typically introduced foreign sign languages or the oral method rather than local sign languages. British Sign Language and Swedish Sign Language were often imposed on African and Asian schools, although tribal sign languages not only existed but also continued to be used. Andersson helped bring about the requirement by USAID that the agency's teacher trainers have adequate signing skills. Still, much work remains to be done in raising awareness of Deaf culture and of the validity of sign languages as natural human languages since only a third of the world's countries officially recognize sign language for institutional purposes.

Leila Monaghan and Deborah Karp, in "HIV/AIDS and the Deaf Community: A Conversation," let us eavesdrop on their discussion of the HIV/AIDS epidemic in deaf communities. With respect to these groups, they recommend national rather than local action with regard to HIV/AIDS funding, information dissemination, and information gathering. At the same time they focus on the strengths that the deaf communities bring to this fight, such as peer teaching. They discuss what factors hamper outreach and treatment efforts, including communication barriers, the stigma of AIDS, and the lack of recognition and funding from larger organizations. Karp tells of getting drawn into outreach work by seeing friends become afflicted in greater numbers due to the failure to deliver information to the deaf communities about almost every aspect of the disease—from how it is transmitted, to what a plus symbol really means (i.e., it means something negative regarding the individual's health, whereas in other contexts the symbol indicates something positive), to what is appropriate medical treatment and how to get it. Monaghan explains how the lack of accessible language in outreach organizations has been a major culprit in this confusion.

John Meletse and Ruth Morgan extend this discussion to a different world arena: "HIV AIDS and Deaf Communities in South Africa: A Conversation." They, too, talk about the pernicious effects of lack of access to proper health information, particularly regarding sexual behavior. Meletse is an activist—and was the first Deaf African to self-identify as HIV positive—and Morgan is a linguistic anthropologist. They met in 2000, when he was interviewed for a Deaf culture project, and they have been colleagues and friends ever since. In South Africa even some outreach workers are misinformed and pass on that misinformation. The social stigma associated with HIV/AIDS leads to secrecy, which compounds the problem. National organizations, including disability ones, do not meet their responsibilities to deaf communities, resulting in an ever-escalating number of cases.

In "The Language Politics of Japanese Sign Language (Nihon Shuwa)" Karen Nakamura outlines the difficulties in determining a national sign language by examining language ideologies in a time of transition. She witnessed political fragmentation in Japan as the older generation, represented by the Japanese Federation of the Deaf (JFD), coined and disseminated new signs in order to compete with the national public television service, as well as to fend off criticisms from younger, culturally Deaf members. While everyone agrees new signs are necessary, the JFD is challenged as the guardian of the Japanese Sign Language lexicon both by D-Pro, a group that wants to protect against spoken language influences, and by the television network NHK, which reaches out to all deaf regardless of the extent to which they vocalize or sign and regardless of which variety of sign they use.

Soya Mori responds in "Pluralization: An Alternative to the Existing Hegemony in JSL." Mori has been advising the Myanmar government on policy regarding deaf people. Because Myanmar, like many developing countries, does not have a national deaf community, a national sign language cannot emerge by natural processes. The government wants to develop and promote a standard sign language. However, it did not accept the recommendation that it form a national deaf organization as a first step since that organization would be a power to contend with. The new recommendation is that a Myanmar Sign Language textbook be published, including information about the culture and language of the community. The hope is that the textbook will enlighten both hearing and deaf readers and foster a sense of entitlement to rights, from which a national organization will emerge to advocate for deaf communities. Mori ends with remarks on the changing situation in Japan regarding power with respect to JSL.

In "Social Situations and the Education of Deaf Children in China" Jun Hui Yang presents an overview of the Chinese social situation, where heath care, education, and employment are persistent family concerns. While at least 80 percent of deaf children are now receiving an education, since the country places great emphasis on literacy as a tool for being a useful citizen, many do not use standardized Chinese Sign Language and have little exposure to deaf adults as role models. Although charities and international organizations in cities help some deaf children receive assistive technology and training, most go without. A major goal of the Chinese Disabled People's Foundation is thus to get deaf children placed in local regular schools (not in bilingual-bicultural schools) with rehabilitation and vocational support. On the other hand, recent media attention to sign language has led to sign courses in universities, and a Deaf Pride movement has begun, so Deaf culture is now valued, and several new bilingual-bicultural schools have sprung up.

Madan Vasishta turns our attention to another developing country in "Social Situations and the Education of Deaf Children in India," once again highlighting the two main problems hampering deaf rights: lack of appreciation of Deaf culture and a shortage of successful role models. Having helped develop the first dictionaries of Indian Sign Language (ISL), he moved on to scholarly and activist work with deaf communities. Because Indians tend to hide their deaf children, only 5 percent attend school, and only 10 percent of those are enrolled in programs designed to meet deaf needs, while the rest struggle along without interpreters or other support in regular programs. Few have hearing aids. Most deaf children arrive at school with no language and pick up ISL from other children since most of the teachers know little sign. There are no training programs for interpreters. To date, little research has been done on deaf communities or ISL.

In "Do Deaf Children Eat Deaf Carrots?" Paul Scott shows the effect of his work as exactly the sort of social, cultural, and linguistic role model the preceding chapters argue for. He describes the methods he uses to teach deaf children how to be Deaf. Part of his work is teaching British Sign Language, focusing particularly on characteristics that are typical of sign languages but not of speech, such as the use of space in locating participants in an event. Another aspect is introducing them to Deaf culture. He helps the children to understand that experiences they may have had are typical of deaf people and, as such, make them part of the community. Finally, he educates them about deaf history and famous deaf people in order to instill in them a degree of pride in their cultural heritage.

Donna West and Paddy Ladd close our book with separate responses to Scott's chapter. West worked with Scott educating deaf children before entering academia. She reports on an earlier research project in which she interviewed children about their experiences in Scott's classroom. She gives us the children's responses to her questions, showing through masterfully chosen examples their eloquently expressed appreciation of Scott's instruction. Ladd, instead, uses Scott's chapter as a jumping-off point to talk about deaf education in general. He starts with the value of Deaf educators in the deaf classroom, argues that deaf education is minority education and should be afforded the same attention, urges the inclusion of cultural education, and laments the dominance of medical procedures that threaten Deaf culture. The deaf child in a hearing world needs a safe environment in which to develop a healthy identity that will allow for a strong education and the ability to find a satisfying, productive place in the worlds the child must straddle.

Thirty-one scholars and activists (sixteen deaf, one hearing of deaf parents, and fourteen hearing) have contributed to this volume with the optimistic goal that our joint work will help improve our understanding of both deaf matters and the daily lives of deaf people. The chapters here deal with gestures, sign languages, deaf issues, and deaf communities in Australia, Brazil, China, France, Germany, Great Britain, India, Israel, Italy, Japan, Kenya, Mongolia, Myanmar, Nicaragua, South Africa, Sweden, Thailand, and the United States. While we in no sense cover the entire globe, the picture that emerges shows great similarity and continuity in the Deaf world.

Welcome to our whirlwind tour.

Bibliography

Bébian, Roch-Ambroise Auguste. 1817. *Essai sur les sourds-muets et sur le langage naturel* [Essay on Deaf-mutes and on Natural Language]. Paris: Dent.

Humphries, Tom. 2008. Scientific Explanation and Other Performance Acts in the Reorganization of DEAF. In *Signs and Voices: Deaf Culture, Identity, Language, and Arts*, ed. Kristin A. Lindgren, Doreen DeLuca, and Donna Jo Napoli, 3–20. Washington, D.C.: Gallaudet University Press.

Mallery, Garrick. 1881. *Sign Language among North American Indians: Compared with That among Other Peoples and Deaf-mutes*. Reprint, The Hague: Mouton, 1972.

Sonnenstrahl, Alfred. 2008. A Conversation with Alfred Sonnenstrahl: Focus on Telecommunications. In *Access: Multiple Avenues for Deaf People*, ed. Doreen DeLuca, Irene W. Leigh, Kristin A. Lindgren, and Donna Jo Napoli, 26–37. Washington, D.C.: Gallaudet University Press.

Stokoe, William. 1960. *Sign Language Structure: An Outline of the Visual Communication System of the American Deaf*. Silver Spring, Md.: Linstok.

Tervoort, Bernard. 1953. *Structurele analyse van visueel taalgebruik binnen een groep dove kinderen* [Structual Analysis of Visual Sign Language in a Group of Deaf Children]. Amsterdam: Noord-Hollandse Uitgevers Maatschappij.

Part I

SIGN LANGUAGES: CREATION,
CONTEXT, FORM

CHAPTER 1

Sign Language Geography

Carol A. Padden

INTRODUCTION

We have a fairly good idea of how many spoken languages exist, at least to the nearest thousand. There are websites, encyclopedias, and language atlases that survey known spoken languages based on reports and language surveys; one such source, Ethnologue.com, lists 6,912 known living languages as of 2005. Listing all of the world's spoken languages is on the one hand a classificatory problem: How do we determine that a pair of languages is similar enough to be counted as dialects of one language, not separately as two languages? Conversely, how do we determine that two apparent dialects are more accurately two different languages? On further inquiry, we can investigate whether several languages are genetically related and can be called members of the same language family. A *language family* is defined as a group of languages related by common descent from an ancestor language. Terms such as *dialect, language,* and *language family* denote a history of relationships among speakers and how language change transpires over time. Wars, social upheavals, and migration bring people in contact with one another, with consequences for the languages they speak. As Jean Aitchison reminds us, "[L]anguages are spoken by people, and people move around, sometimes in huge groups. The distribution of languages changes faster than the course of rivers" (Comrie, Matthews, and Polinsky 2003, 7).

We do not have a comparable understanding of how many sign languages there are. Ethnologue.com, which calls itself a reference volume of "the known living languages in the world today," only recently began listing sign languages in its survey of world languages. The 2005 edition lists 121 sign languages. Most entries have general information about the location of the sign language, how many people use it (if known), and whether it might be related to another sign language. Australian Sign Language (Auslan; see the abbreviation list at the end of this chapter), for example, is described in Ethnologue.com as having an estimated fourteen thousand users and as being closely related to British Sign Language (BSL), with some influence from Irish Sign Language (ISL) and American Sign Language (ASL). The entry for ASL, not surprisingly, is longer and more detailed since it is a comparatively well-researched language. An estimated 100–500 thousand users of ASL are reported. Likewise listed are sign language dialects of ASL, such as the Canadian dialect used in English-speaking parts of Canada and Black Sign Language, which has its roots in black deaf schools in the United States.

For cataloguing purposes, Ethnologue.com places all deaf sign languages into a single language family as a way to set them apart from spoken languages. The strategy illustrates the difficulty of coming up with a comparable rubric for sign languages. Included in the Ethnologue.com family of sign languages are languages that cannot have descended from a common ancestor. Ban Khor Sign Language of northeast Thailand, for example, is used by a small community of hearing and deaf signers in a village and has no known history of contact with either ASL or BSL (Nonaka 2007). Furthermore, as is well known, ASL and BSL are unrelated despite the common political history of North America and the United Kingdom.

Based on a flurry of new studies in recent years on village sign languages and young sign languages (Kegl, Senghas, and Coppola 1999; Marsaja 2008; Nonaka 2007; Nyst 2007; Osugi, Supalla, and Webb 1999; Senghas and Coppola 2001; Washabaugh 1986), it is likely that Ethnologue's count of 121 sign languages is on the low side and that there remain yet more undiscovered and unidentified sign languages around the world. Given that deafness has been found in every populated continent, we should expect to find more sign language communities, but how many more? We could make better predictions (and indeed do a better job of categorizing the sign languages we already know) if we knew more about the history of sign languages.

With the recent work on new sign languages, we are now starting to understand how sign languages can begin life and sustain themselves over time. Under what conditions do they appear in spoken language communities? What is the relationship between gestures used by hearing people and the new sign languages that are formed in communities? Once a sign language takes hold, we do not know much about the social conditions under which they have contact with one other. How does one sign language influence another, and how can one replace another? There are cases of signing communities less than one hundred miles apart whose sign languages are as unrelated as two sign languages much farther apart geographically, as I discuss in a later section. Conversely, there are sign languages separated by an ocean of distance, such as French Sign Language (LSF) and ASL, whose vocabularies today still reflect their genetic relationship dating back nearly two hundred years.

Determining relationships between sign languages involves understanding how signers and sign languages move across geographic space and historic time. We know that speakers migrating from one region to another may bring their spoken languages with them or abandon their languages in favor of a more dominant one in the new region. What about signers? Are they compelled to bring or abandon their sign languages when they migrate? Do the same forces that come into play for spoken languages also come into play for sign languages? Unlike spoken languages, sign languages exploit iconicity to some degree. How does the iconic character of sign languages play a role in sign language change over time and under conditions of contact with other sign languages?

Further, under what circumstances do signers bring their language from one geographic location to another? Once signers meet other signers, what happens? What patterns of change take place in the life of sign languages over long periods of time? In terms of scale, sign language communities are far smaller than spoken language societies and almost always coexist within spoken language communities. Sign language communities do not wage wars against each other; signers live among others and within dominant political agendas. The mobility of deaf people and the way in which their languages are transported over space and time should be different from those of other groups of language users, but how? All of these questions figure in an account of sign language geography, that is, the pattern of sign language distribution in various regions of the world and the way in which they change over time as a result of transmission and contact.

To illustrate these special issues, I discuss sign languages and their use in two different regions of the world: North America and the Middle East. In one respect, the regions are alike: A dominant spoken language is used throughout the regions: English in North America and, to a lesser degree, Modern Standard Arabic in the Middle East.[1] These spoken languages play a central role in organizing the political ideology within the respective regions; they are seen as unifying a diverse population across a broad geographic space. However, North America has only a handful of sign languages compared to the Middle East, which has many more small sign languages existing over a region stretching from the Levant in the north to North Africa and the Persian Gulf region in the south. As I will show, juxtaposing the situation in North America with the complex sign language situation in the Middle East brings to light important issues in the description of sign language history that go beyond those of spoken languages. Notably, unlike spoken languages, sign languages may spread from one region to another or be adopted in a new region not only for political and cultural reasons but linguistic ones as well.

HISTORY OF SIGN LANGUAGES

As a class, sign languages are described as young languages for the reason that there is scant evidence of one that is more than two or three hundred years old. Susan Plann (1997) describes the earliest records of deaf education in Spain as dating from about 1550, when monks became tutors for privileged deaf sons of noble families. From the fact that well-known noble families in Spain had more than one deaf child and that the deaf relatives must have communicated within their families and possibly with other deaf people, Plann speculates that they used a sign language, but she could find no description of it or of how easily they were able to communicate with one another.

In her account of an American sign language on Martha's Vineyard, Nora Groce (1985) identified a deaf father and son as among a group of early settlers arriving on Martha's Vineyard around 1714. While tracing the settlers' genealogical history to their ancestors in the Weald of Kent in England, Groce came across a passage in Samuel Pepys's diary, in which he mentions having observed a deaf man communicating by sign with a London politician, Sir George Downing. The date was November 9, 1666. This brief mention by Pepys notes that the deaf man signed fluently and that Downing responded in equal form, but there is no information about the language itself. Peter Jackson (1990) found earlier references to signers and sign language in seventeenth-century Britain, notably a book by John Bulwer written in 1648, *Deafe and dumbe man's friend,* in which Bulwer identifies twenty-five deaf people living in various parts of the country. A chart of the hand alphabet is included in Bulwer's book, but not much else was mentioned about any sign languages in the region at that time.

Jackson argues that there were sign languages in Britain at least a hundred years before the establishment of schools for deaf children in that country around 1760. The evidence is in his favor, but, unfortunately, any descriptions of their form and structure are brief and insubstantial. By the late eighteenth century, however, we begin to see somewhat more useful descriptions. When Europe and North America began building public institutions as arms of the state in the late eighteenth and early nineteenth century, schools for deaf children, as well as schools for blind children, orphanages, and prisons were among the new institutions that represented the state's interest in the well-being of its various populations. As Rothman (1990) notes, these institutions developed new standards of recordkeeping to reflect their belief in the importance of documenting the behavior of those in their care. Very interesting records have survived from these early institutions in Europe, the United States, and Canada. Among the first records of the Pennsylvania Institution for the Deaf and Dumb, one of the first schools for deaf children founded in the United States, were admissions books that listed the names and ages of the deaf children admitted to their care, as well as information about their families. In this book, we see for the first time specific reference to the form of signs. Alongside some of the children's records were notations describing their name signs. Mary Reilly, admitted to the school in 1821, had this description at the bottom of her record: "Sign. The end of forefinger just above the corner of the eyebrow toward the nose with an upward motion." A few pages later, Henry Stehman, who was admitted a few years later, in 1826, had a name sign described thus: "Sign. Pulling the tip of the ear with the thumb and forefinger." Did these name signs accompany the children when they first arrived at the school, or were they assigned to them later? We do not know.

Given that we have evidence that deaf people and signing existed before deaf schools opened, should we describe ASL and BSL as older languages? Probably, but with the small amount of evidence we have, we really do not know how to extrapolate backward from contemporary forms to older signs. What happens when one sign language encounters another? How do signs change, and how does one language absorb grammatical structures from another? We know that French Sign Language (LSF) was imported to the United States when Laurent Clerc came to Hartford, Connecticut, in 1816 to establish the first deaf school there. However, what precisely happened when LSF was introduced to the varieties of sign language already in existence at that time?

Recent work on emerging sign languages may reveal some interesting clues about how they change. Emerging or new sign languages are those that have arisen within the last two or three generations of signers. There are no comparable cases of new spoken languages except for pidgins and creoles, which arise out of contact between two or more existing languages. While pidgins and creoles demonstrate remarkable human creativity in the face of our need to communicate, they are not entirely new languages because the influence of the source languages can still be seen in their vocabulary and structure. However, new sign languages, under the right conditions, can arise without any substantial influence from spoken languages or other sign languages. In such conditions, researchers can observe, in a way not possible with spoken languages, the development of a language from its origin to its contemporary form in only a few decades. New sign languages in various parts of the world and diverse cultural environments are now being described in the sign language literature, allowing us to examine the way in which sign languages develop and how the effects of human interaction and social life exert their influence on them.

CATEGORIES OF EMERGING SIGN LANGUAGES

Meir, Sandler, Padden, and Aronoff (2010) propose distinguishing between emerging sign languages by considering their particular social and linguistic environments. The first category they employ, village sign languages, are those that "arise in an existing, relatively insular community into which a number of deaf children are born." Typically, in such communities we find a genetically transmitted condition of deafness, resulting in a situation in which deaf and hearing signers are related to one another and grow up in the same social and cultural environment. Languages called deaf community sign languages, in contrast, arise when deaf children are brought together from different places (even different cultures) and, once together, form the basis of a community. These signers are typically not related to one another; in fact, signers with deaf relatives or signing hearing relatives are comparatively fewer. What has brought deaf children and adults together is the establishment of a school or some other social institution.

Following a recent observation about the evolution of language (Wray and Grace 2007), how often signers interact with strangers impacts the form and structure of that language. When interacting with relatives, there is a great deal of shared information, but not so when interacting with unknown individuals. When signers are with relatives and members of the same village or community, the context for language is shared, and a common history develops over time. Pointing to a particular location, for example, is easy to do in a village sign language, but when in a large urban center, that location is more likely to be specified by name and not just by pointing. In the case of strangers, communication needs to be more explicit, and shared knowledge cannot always be assumed. When speakers do not know one another, Wray and Grace argue, languages acquire certain kinds of grammars and vocabularies that may differ from those of languages where more is shared. Their basic insight is that cultural practices are implicated in the form and structure of human language.

A historical example of a village sign language is one that developed in Martha's Vineyard from the settlement of the island in the late seventeenth century through the nineteenth century, when the island's population moved off the island and became less insular (Groce 1985).[2] Groce traces deafness on the island back to families from Kent, England, who left for the New World and then subsequently moved to Martha's Vineyard and settled there. The two families carried a recessive condition for deafness, which, after intermarriage on the island, resulted in the birth of a number of deaf children. At one time the number of deaf people born on the island was as high as forty-five, concentrated mainly in the two villages of Tisbury and Chilmark. The use of sign language was amply noted in written records of the island, as well as in the oral recollections of the oldest islanders still alive at the time Groce carried out her research.

In contrast to Martha's Vineyard Sign Language, American Sign Language is an example of a deaf community sign language. When the first American public school for deaf children opened in 1817 in Hartford, Connecticut, deaf children from throughout New England enrolled, and there they met deaf children from other towns and states. Deaf community sign languages are typically organized around the establishment of a school for deaf children, where unrelated signers meet each other. The single largest group of children enrolling in the school during its first several decades came from Martha's

Vineyard (Groce 1985). A large number of other deaf children came from two different signing communities on the mainland. Lane, Pillard, and French (2000) report that between 1817 and 1887 a total of forty-four children enrolled in the Hartford School from Henniker, New Hampshire, and nearby townships. In another settlement of several families in what is today the southeastern part of Maine, twenty-seven deaf children enrolled during the same period. Of the remaining children, many are surmised to have grown up in small towns and rural areas, where they had little or no contact with other deaf people. One of the first deaf students to enroll in the first year of the school's opening was John Brewster Jr., a deaf itinerant painter who is notable in American art history for having produced some of the finest examples of portrait painting from the colonial American period (Lane 2004). Born in 1766, Brewster learned to paint while apprenticed to a master painter. Then, like other portrait painters of that era, he traveled by horseback throughout New England in search of work. Brewster had no deaf relatives and did not live in one of the many towns with deaf residents. According to Lane, the record is not clear as to whether Brewster could sign or, if so, what signing he used. Indeed, how he communicated with those who paid him to do their portraits is unknown (he probably was not literate, so writing is unlikely). What the record does note, however, is that Brewster learned about the school for deaf people in Hartford and enrolled there in 1817, when he was fifty-one years old. Lane speculates that Brewster was one of many who came to the school with little or no knowledge of a sign language; instead, he used homesigns.

How did the different village sign languages in existence in 1817 coalesce with homesign systems (probably several) to create a common sign language? How did LSF enter into this mix? To answer this question, we engage in historical linguistics—of sign languages. We might be able to compare signs from the different village sign languages (if we could find any record of them) with old LSF (from old dictionaries) to see whether we can trace a line of transmission. But doing such a task is not as straightforward as we might think.

SIGN LANGUAGES OF NORTH AMERICA

As one of the most widespread sign languages in the world with a substantial record of description and analysis, ASL may seem like a prototypical sign language, but in many respects it is not. It is unusual in how widely it is used, with generations of ASL signers found throughout North America, from the border between Mexico and the United States to the populated areas of uppermost, English-speaking Canada. Compared to Europe, where many different sign languages are found, ASL has no competing sign languages of similar size. The number of primary users of ASL (i.e., those who use it as a first and dominant language) is estimated at 250,000 signers. With the recent proliferation of

ASL classes in U.S. and Canadian high schools, colleges, and universities over the last three decades, the number of second-language learners and users of ASL surely exceeds the number of primary users. Quebec Sign Language (LSQ), with five to six thousand signers, is the only other widespread sign language in North America, where it is used in the French-speaking areas of Canada. South of the U.S. border lies Mexico, a politically and geographically separate region with its own history of sign languages, including Mexican Sign language (LSM) (Palacios Guerra Currie 1999; Quinto-Pozos 2006; Ramsey and Quinto-Pozos 2010).

How did ASL emerge, and how did it come to replace the various smaller sign languages that once existed in North America? In his meticulous chronicle of deaf society in the United States, Jack Gannon (1981) provides a description of nearly every school for deaf children in the United States, starting with the one in Hartford, Connecticut, in 1817. Gannon's history explains that deaf schools in the United States established later in the nineteenth century were descendants of the first deaf schools, creating an unbroken line of ASL transmission throughout the United States and Canada.

Take, for example, the language history of two of the first deaf schools founded in the United States: the American School for the Deaf in Hartford, Connecticut, and the Pennsylvania Institute for the Deaf and Dumb in Philadelphia. Thomas Hopkins Gallaudet is credited with persuading a signer of LSF to travel from Paris to Hartford in 1817 for the purpose of helping him establish a new school for deaf children in the United States. As the record shows, this cofounder of the school, Laurent Clerc, was instrumentally involved in developing the teaching curriculum at Hartford, through which his native LSF was introduced to the school. Two years later, in 1819, when a scandal involving the head of the Pennsylvania Institute for the Deaf and Dumb threatened to close the new school, the board of directors wrote to Clerc and asked him to assume directorship of the school. Clerc came to Philadelphia and remained there for ten months, at which time a new director was found, enabling him to return to Hartford. Clerc lived out the rest of his life in the United States, providing what must have been a stable presence for the intermingling of LSF and the different sign languages in existence in the early part of the nineteenth century.

On the basis of a lexical comparison of modern LSF and modern ASL, Woodward (1978, 339) speculates that LSF competed with other sign languages of New England that were already in place at the school and argues that these languages subsequently underwent a "massive abrupt change due to creolization" to become what is now known as ASL. If LSF had been imported to the United States and adopted in its entirety as the language of the Hartford school, then the two languages should be more similar. Instead, Woodward finds fewer identical lexical items (about 58 percent of the complete lexicon), compared to a standard 80 percent used by spoken language lexicographers to determine that two related languages are dialects (Gudinschinsky 1964). Woodward finds additional support for the diminishing of LSF in favor of competing sign languages from Clerc's own diary, where he writes about his failure to convey the language of his forebears, the French abbés de l'Épée and Sicard, directly to the American students:

> I see, however, and I say it with regret, that any efforts that we have made or may still be making, to do better than, we have inadvertently fallen somewhat back of Abbé de l'Épée. Some of us have learned and still learn signs from uneducated pupils, instead of learning them from well instructed and experienced teachers. (Clerc 1852, cited in Woodward 1978, 336)

Because so many deaf children in Martha's Vineyard attended the first decades of the Hartford school, it is possible that Martha's Vineyard Sign Language (MVSL) was an important contributor to early ASL, but there is limited evidence from Groce's interviews with elderly people on the island that, like LSF, MVSL did not dominate ASL. When the deaf children returned to the island after having studied at the Hartford school, they were using signs that were not recognized by those who remained behind on the island, suggesting that their MVSL signs had been replaced.

From its beginnings, ASL spread throughout other parts of New England and then into Canada, where Clerc's influence was clearly present. Clerc trained Ronald MacDonald, a hearing man from Quebec, who then established the first Canadian school for deaf children in the city of Quebec in 1831 (Carbin and Smith 1996). Canadian deaf students attended the Hartford school as well, which brought them into contact with the sign language used there. In the United States, Deaf associations formed, including the National Association of the Deaf in 1880 and the National Fraternal Society of the Deaf in 1901, and their membership began meeting nationally at conventions, which brought together signers from various parts of the country. What is notable about North America is how readily signers traveled across great distances, from Massachusetts to what is today the state of Maine, in the eighteenth century (Lane, Pillard, and Hedberg forthcoming) and then across national boundaries into Canada in the early nineteenth century. They then spread to the Midwest and westward to California, arriving by the middle of the nineteenth century. Today, the ASL-using population in North America is enormous compared to that of other sign languages of the world and spans a very large geographic area.

Groce (1985) suggests that more historical research might uncover the contributions of the different sign languages in existence before the Hartford school and how they came to shape ASL. In recent work using dictionaries and films from the early 1900s, Ted Supalla (2004) compares early ASL forms with modern ones to show the pattern and direction of morphological change.

He gives examples of phrasal compounds in older ASL (WATER~FLOW = RIVER) that have become single signs over time (RIVER), leading him to conclude that compounding is a common source of lexical development in ASL and probably in many other sign languages. Research of this type has the potential of guiding historical analyses of early ASL and its vocabulary by suggesting what forms older ASL signs may have had and in what direction they have changed over time.

SIGN LANGUAGES OF THE MIDDLE EAST

A different approach looks at modern research on sign languages in other areas of the world and observes the ways in which the social and cultural forces there shape the ways in which the sign languages of those places meet and interact. One such region is the Middle East, which turns out to be significantly different from the United States and Europe in a number of respects. First, the different pattern of schooling for deaf children in the Middle East affects the ways in which these youngsters meet each other. Second, political boundaries in this region have changed significantly in the last two centuries, influencing how groups of individuals travel within the region. Third, compared to North America and Europe, this region has more cases of genetically transmitted deafness because of the common cultural practice of consanguineous marriage (marriage to close relatives). The combination of these factors has resulted in a quite different pattern of sign language use and transmission that may actually help us understand the distribution of sign languages in other parts of the world. This pattern may also help us imagine what sign language transmission and use might have been like in Europe and North America in its earlier history.

I begin with an account of the state's relationship with deaf children and adults who live within its boundaries in the Middle East. In Arab countries, the first deaf school was established in Jordan in 1964. A deaf school in Beirut, Lebanon, was founded only a few years before it—in 1957. Generally, then, a recorded history of deaf schools, at least in the European or North American sense of providing public education for large groups of deaf children, did not appear in the Middle East until the twentieth century. More generally, government institutions that remove individuals from their families and communities and place them in orphanages, schools for deaf or blind people, asylums for people with mental illness, are either not present in this region or have been only recently introduced. Deaf children and children with disabilities have typically remained with their families. In Israel, the first deaf school was founded in 1932 in Jerusalem, followed by another in Tel Aviv in 1941 and one in the northern part of Israel, in Haifa, in 1949 (Meir and Sandler 2008). Bedouin children, deaf and hearing, generally did not attend school until after

1980. Consequently, many deaf Bedouin children did not leave their villages to attend schools for deaf students until after this time.

Second, travel in the Middle East is complicated by political and ethnic boundaries. Citizens of Jordan do not need a visa to travel to Syria or Lebanon, but they do if they travel south to Saudi Arabia, Qatar, or Yemen. Depending on one's ethnic background, a visa can be hard to obtain. A Palestinian from Jordan may not be able to travel to Israel or the West Bank. A Bedouin with Israeli citizenship can visit Jordan, but such travel is infrequent unless one has family members in Jordan. For Bedouin women, travel is even more limited than for men: Some women are unable to leave their village unless accompanied by a husband or a male relative. The political landscape of the Middle East is highly complicated and changing even from decade to decade, thus restricting the mobility of groups of people, including deaf people, in any number of ways.

With respect to the incidence of deafness in this region, childhood diseases are one cause, but genetically transmitted deafness is much more common than in many other areas of the world. Endogamy, or marriage within the limits of a local community, clan, or tribe, is widely practiced and encouraged in Arab communities, including Bedouins. For Bedouins, marriage between cousins is an accepted means of confirming strong family ties and sharing land inheritance within their village. Marriage between cousins also increases the chances of the parents' sharing their genetic inheritance. If a community has carriers of a genetic condition that results in deafness (importantly, not every community does), then deaf children can be born into that community. Shahin et al. (2002, 284) report that "prelingual hereditary hearing impairment occurs in the Palestinian population at a frequency of approximately 1.7 per 1,000 and is higher in some villages." They compare this figure with the global average reported by Nadol (1993) as 1 per 1,000, making the incidence of deafness in Palestinian areas at least 70 percent higher overall.

Nonetheless, even though these factors are common among users of Arab sign languages, they are not exclusive to them. Consanguinity and genetic factors have also played a role in the development of a sign language used in a Jewish enclave in Ghardaia, Algeria (Briggs and Guède 1964; Lanesman and Meir 2007). When the Jewish settlers left Ghardaia in 1966 and immigrated to Israel and France, deaf and hearing signers brought their language with them to Israel, where it exists today as a minority sign language. These three factors—endogamy, recent introduction of schooling, and restricted mobility—taken together describe a region quite unlike North America and Europe politically, historically, and culturally. As it turns out, the distribution of sign languages in this region reveals a markedly different pattern.

The description of genetic relationships between languages, or the study of language classification in spoken languages, uses three types of comparisons: (1) basic vocabulary, (2) sound correspondences, and (3) patterned grammatical agreements. As a first and partial measure of sign language similarity and diversity in this region, Al-Fityani and Padden (2010) compare the basic vocabularies of five selected sign languages in the Arab world: Jordanian Sign Language (LIU), Kuwaiti Sign Language (KSL), Libyan Sign Language (LSL), Palestinian Sign Language (PSL), and Al-Sayyid Bedouin Sign Language (ABSL).[3] These languages were selected in part because each had published sign language dictionaries large enough for a vocabulary comparison. In terms of categories of sign languages discussed earlier, four of the sign languages in our comparison set are deaf community sign languages. They are used in the major city centers of each country, and the vocabulary items in their dictionaries are recognized (by some community standard) as general to the country. The last sign language, ABSL, is a village sign language, used by a closed, insular community of Bedouins in southern Israel (Sandler et al. 2005). Moreover, ABSL is a new sign language, having first appeared about seventy-five years ago, when deaf children were born into the community. At present there are about 125 deaf children and adults in a community of thirty-five hundred.

With the exception of ABSL, which does not yet have a dictionary, vocabulary items used for the analysis were drawn from published dictionaries of the sign languages. For ABSL, vocabulary items were elicited through videotaped interviews with signers. As a baseline, we compared LIU vocabulary with lexical items from a sixth, unrelated sign language, ASL. Because there is no history of contact between ASL and LIU, we expected to find the lowest number of similar signs compared to the other sign languages, all

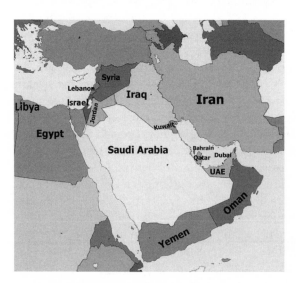

Figure 1.1. Map of the Middle East

of which may have had more contact simply because they are in the same region.

The analysis was performed on vocabulary that could be retrieved from the dictionaries of the five sign languages. This method somewhat constrained the size of the vocabularies used for comparison because we were dependent on whatever vocabulary was included in a given dictionary (table 1.1). The PSL dictionary, for one, included more academic vocabulary than the other dictionaries. For more detail about which vocabulary items were selected for the analysis and how similarities were recorded across vocabularies, see Al-Fityani (2007) and Al-Fityani and Padden (2010).

On the basis of political and ethnic history and a shared border, we expected the vocabularies of LIU and PSL to show some similarity, and our analysis supports the prediction, with about 58 percent of their vocabularies showing similarity. In our analysis, the comparison was not with all of the known vocabulary items in the two sign languages but with vocabulary items that the two dictionaries have in common that had previously been identified as not indexic or directional.[4] Next ranked in terms of similarity were LIU and KSL, at 40 percent. There is a history of contact between Jordan and Kuwait among both hearing and deaf people when job opportunities became available for Jordanians in Kuwait in the last couple of decades.

Crowley (1992) defines two spoken languages as dialects of a common ancestor if 80 percent or more of their vocabulary items are identical or highly similar. In order to determine whether any of the sign languages of the Middle East are dialects, we would need cultural and social evidence of sustained contact between signers of different communities, as well as further linguistic evidence. At present, we have only vocabulary comparisons, not other evidence more readily available to spoken languages, such as sound correspondences and patterned grammatical agreement. The vocabularies of KSL, PSL, and LIU have some level of shared vocabulary, but it would be difficult to argue that they are dialects on the basis of basic vocabulary alone. Libya is in the North African area of the Middle East, geographically more distant from Jordan, and as expected, the two vocabularies are mostly dissimilar, sharing only 34 percent of their items. In addition, ABSL, a village sign language that is geographically close to Jordan, shows the lowest degree of similarity, at 24 percent. Only ASL is more dissimilar, at about 18 percent.

Table 1.1. Number of Vocabulary Items Used for Comparison between LIU and PSL, KSL, LSL, ABSL, and ASL

| Total signs | 167 | 183 | 267 | 165 | 410 |

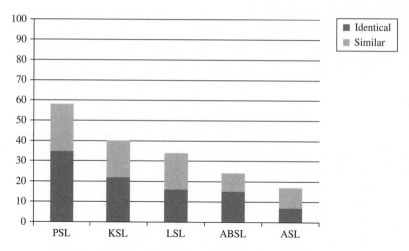

Figure 1.2. Cognates between LIU and other sign languages

These figures reflect patterns of mobility and political geography in the region. Since 1948, Palestine and Jordan have shared a border that has alternately tightened and loosened, depending on the political situation, but in general, Palestinians cross the border at Jordan with some difficulty. A Jordanian who wishes to travel to Kuwait or Libya must have a visa, which can make travel difficult, at least more so than travel to Syria or Lebanon.

In Al-Sayyid, as in many other Bedouin villages, community ties are especially strong; marriage is encouraged among village members rather than with outsiders. Strong in-group ties among Bedouins led to the emergence of a village sign language that exists apart from other sign languages despite the geographic proximity of Al-Sayyid to the deaf community sign languages of Israel and Jordan. Because some Bedouins in Israel have family members in Jordan, they can travel between the countries, but they do not make the difficult trip frequently.

Given the restrictions on mobility, how is it that apparently unrelated sign languages such as LIU, LSL, KSL, and ABSL have any sign vocabulary in common (20–30 percent)? Furthermore, why does LIU have any vocabulary similar to ASL, a sign language from a different and more distant continent? The fact that there is residual similarity between the vocabularies of any two sign languages could point to unknown contact between the languages (say, through the media), but more likely it demonstrates that the visual-gestural modality inherent in sign languages predisposes their vocabulary to similarity. Time and again we have heard reports that ABSL "looks like" LIU or even ASL. Such impressions are often based on seeing a single short video clip with one or two sentences. Clearly the iconicity of sign languages is compelling, and the fact that any kind of similarity exists between them immediately prompts comparisons. This is both a problem and an opportunity in the historical study of sign languages.

Take, for example, one of two signs that are used in Al-Sayyid for the word "fish." The first looks similar to the one-handed ASL sign FISH, and it shows the movement of a prototypical fish. (On close examination, they are not exactly alike; the ASL sign involves only hand movement, while the ABSL sign involves arm movement.) The other sign used by some ABSL signers is two handed, with the thumbs rotating (figure 1.3). The latter form is also found in Indo-Pakistani Sign Language (Zeshan 2000) and Ghardaia Sign Language (Lanesman and Meir 2007). Does this mean that the three sign languages have some history of contact? Opportunities for Bedouin signers from southern Israel to meet Pakistani or Jewish Algerian signers from Ghardaia are highly unlikely. Instead, it is more likely that the same sign was created independently in three different places in the world.

In another comparison of vocabularies of related and unrelated sign languages, Currie, Meier, and Walters (2002) have compared the vocabulary of the sign languages of Mexico, Spain, and Japan and found a residual amount of similarity (23 percent) despite the fact that Mexican Sign Language and Japanese Sign Language have no history of contact. They argue that the visuospatial modality may allow different sign languages to create similar iconic forms by accident.

The presence of iconicity in sign languages confounds historical analysis to some extent, but it also suggests a different approach to understanding how they evolve. New sign languages can simply create new vocabulary instead of borrowing items from other sign languages. If it is the case that ASL was not greatly influenced by either MVSL or LSF, then it must have created a large number of new vocabulary items instead of

Figure 1.3. Illustration of FISH in ABSL. Similar forms appear in Pakistani Sign Language and Ghardaia Sign Language.

borrowing to a great extent from input sign languages. Whether sign languages are more likely to create or borrow new vocabulary can be tested by looking at village sign languages that come into contact with each other or cases in which several village sign languages develop into a deaf community sign language.

SIGN LANGUAGE GEOGRAPHY IN A GLOBAL PERSPECTIVE

As in North America, there is a common spoken language used throughout the Middle East, but with respect to sign languages, the two regions are very different. Whereas one sign language dominates in most of North America, the Middle East has many more distinct and smaller sign languages. In addition to the Arab sign languages mentioned earlier, there is also Israeli Sign Language. Looking at the two countries in the region that share a border, Israel and Jordan, for example, we see that the sign languages on either side are very different. Al-Sayyid, a Bedouin village in the Negev, is only about eighty miles from Amman, the capital of Jordan, but LIU and ABSL are almost as dissimilar as LIU and ASL, although Bedouins live on both sides.

North America has no known village sign languages, though at least two existed in the twentieth century: Martha's Vineyard Sign Language, now extinct, and Maritime Sign Language from Nova Scotia, which has some elderly signers but is dying (Carbin and Smith 1996). As explained earlier, the fact that schools for deaf children have only recently been introduced in the Middle East and that schooling was made compulsory only recently most likely accounts for the continued existence of village sign languages in this region. From the Middle Eastern example, we begin to see how schooling, incidence of deafness, and political geography can interact to create quite different languages and linguistic situations.

From contemporary examples such as ABSL, we can imagine how the village sign languages of Martha's Vineyard and Henniker, New Hampshire, might have developed. By observing the development of a new deaf community sign language in Israel, formed when Israel became a state in 1948, and more recently in Nicaragua, we can speculate in useful ways about how the different sign languages of the nineteenth century came together to create what is now modern ASL.

In the end we may finally be able to determine whether the notion of "language family" can be usefully adopted to describe genetic relationships between sign languages, as well as their evolution and transmission. We will then be much closer to understanding why and how signed and spoken languages are fundamentally alike—or different.

Abbreviations

ABSL	Al-Sayyid Bedouin Sign Language
ASL	American Sign Language
Auslan	Australian Sign Language
BSL	British Sign Language
KSL	Kuwaiti Sign Language
LIU	Jordanian Sign Language
LSF	French Sign Language
LSL	Libyan Sign Language
LSM	Mexican Sign Language
LSQ	Quebec Sign Language
MVSL	Martha's Vineyard Sign Language
PSL	Palestinian Sign Language

Notes

The research for this work was made possible by support from NIH/NIDCD, R01DC006473. I thank Meir Etedgi for his skill with the illustrations of ABSL signs. I also thank David Perlmutter, Kinda Al-Fityani, Wendy Sandler, Irit Meir, and Mark Aronoff for comments, ideas, and corrections, all of which I have strived to incorporate here.

1. Modern Standard Arabic is used in written language and formal speech. With respect to vernacular or colloquial Arabic, a number of different varieties are used throughout the region, some of which have been described as separate languages of the Arabic family.

2. Typically, village sign languages are spontaneously created. In the case of Martha's Vineyard, the sign language used on the island may have been created earlier and elsewhere. An early settler on the island was a deaf man from Kent, England, who may have brought a sign language with him from his country of origin. However, absent a description of the sign language as it was used on the island, we cannot know for sure.

3. By no means do these languages represent an exhaustive list of sign languages in this region. There are many more not mentioned here (e.g., those in Saudi Arabia, Yemen, Syria, Qatar, Egypt, and Morocco).

4. We did not compare signs involving pointing to locations on the body (eyes, head, ears, etc.), nor did we compare indexic signs of direction and position, such as up, down, this, or that.

Bibliography

Al-Fityani, Kinda. 2007. Arab Sign Languages: A Lexical Comparison. *Center for Research in Language Technical Reports* 19(1): 3–13.

———, and Carol A. Padden. 2010. Sign Language Geography in the Arab World. In *Sign Languages,* ed. Diane Brentari, 433–450. New York: Cambridge University Press.

Briggs, Lloyd C., and Norina L. Guède. 1964. *No More for Ever: A Saharan Jewish Town*. Cambridge: The Museum.

Carbin, Clifton F., and Dorothy L. Smith. 1996. *Deaf Heritage in Canada: A Distinctive, Diverse, and Enduring Culture*. New York: McGraw-Hill Ryerson.

Comrie, Bernard C., Stephen M. Matthews, and Maria P. Polinsky. 2003. *The Atlas of Languages: The Origin and Development of Languages throughout the World*, rev. ed. New York: Facts on File.

Crowley, Terry. 1992. *An Introduction to Historical Linguistics*, 2d ed. New York: Oxford University Press.

Currie, Anne-Marie, Richard Meier, and Keith Walters. 2002. A Cross-linguistic Examination of the Lexicons of Four Signed Languages. In *Modality and Structure in Signed and Spoken Language*, ed. Richard P. Meier, Kearsy Cormier, and David Quinto-Pozos, 224–236. New York: Cambridge University Press.

Gannon, Jack R. 1981. *Deaf Heritage: A Narrative History of Deaf America*. Silver Spring, Md.: National Association of the Deaf.

Groce, Nora E. 1985. *Everyone Here Spoke Sign Language: Hereditary Deafness on Martha's Vineyard*. Cambridge, Mass.: Harvard University Press.

Gudinschinsky, Sarah G. 1964. The ABCs of Lexicostatistics. In *Language in Culture and Society*, ed. Dell Hymes, 612–623. New York: Harper and Row.

Jackson, Peter. 1990. *Britain's Deaf Heritage*. Edinburgh: Pentland.

Kegl, Judy, Ann Senghas, and Marie Coppola. 1999. Creation through Contact: Sign Language Emergence and Sign Language Change in Nicaragua. In *Language Creation and Language Change: Creolization, Diachrony, and Development*, ed. Michael DeGraff, 179–237. Cambridge, Mass.: MIT Press.

Lane, Harlan L. 2004. *A Deaf Artist in Early America: The Worlds of John Brewster, Jr.* Boston: Beacon.

———, Richard Pillard, and Mary French. 2000. Origins of the American Deaf-world: Assimilating and Differentiating Societies and Their Relation to Genetic Patterning. *Sign Language Studies* 1: 17–44.

Lanesman, Sara, and Irit Meir. 2007. The Sign Language of Algerian Immigrants in Israel. Talk presented at the Cross-linguistic Research and International Cooperation in Sign Language Linguistics workshop. April 9–14. Nijmegen, the Netherlands.

Marsaja, I. Gede. 2008. *Desa Kolok: A Deaf Village and Its Sign Language in Bali*. Nijmegen: Ishara.

Meir, Irit, and Wendy Sandler. 2008. *A Language in Space: The Story of Israeli Sign Language*. New York: Taylor and Francis.

———, Carol Padden, and Mark Aronoff. 2010. Emerging Sign Languages. In *Oxford Handbook of Deaf Studies, Language, and Education*, vol. 2, ed. Marc Marschark and Patricia E. Spencer. 267–280. New York: Oxford University Press.

Nadol, Joseph B. 1993. Hearing Loss. *New England Journal of Medicine* 329: 1092–1102.

Nonaka, Angela M. 2007. Emergence of an Indigenous Sign Language and a Speech/sign Community in Ban Khor, Thailand. PhD diss., University of California at Los Angeles.

Nyst, Victoria. 2007. *A Descriptive Analysis of Adamarobe Sign Language (Ghana)*. Utrecht: Lot.

Osugi, Yutaka, Ted Supalla, and Rebecca Webb. 1999. The Use of Word Elicitation to Identify Distinctive Gestural Systems on Amami Island. *Sign Language and Linguistics* 2(1): 87–112.

Palacios Guerra Currie, Anne-Marie. 1999. A Mexican Sign Language Lexicon: Internal and Cross-linguistic Similarities and Variation. PhD diss., University of Texas at Austin.

Plann, Susan. 1997. *A Silent Minority: Deaf Education in Spain, 1550–1835.* Berkeley: University of California Press.

Quinto-Pozos, David. 2006. Contact between Mexican Sign Language (LSM) and American Sign Language (ASL) in Two Texas Border Areas. *Sign Language and Linguistics* 7(2): 215–219.

Ramsey, Claire, and David Quinto-Pozos. 2010. Transmission of Sign Languages in Latin America. In *Sign Languages: A Cambridge Survey,* ed. Diane Brentari, 46–73. New York: Cambridge University Press.

Rothman, David. J. 1990. *The Discovery of the Asylum: Social Order and Disorder in the New Republic,* rev. ed. Boston: Little, Brown.

Sandler, Wendy, Irit Meir, Carol Padden, and Mark Aronoff. 2005. The Emergence of Grammar: Systematic Structure in a New Language. *Proceedings of the National Academy of Sciences* 102(7): 2661–2665.

Senghas, Ann, and Marie Coppola. 2001. Children Creating Language: How Nicaraguan Sign Language Acquired a Spatial Grammar. *Psychological Science* 12(4): 323–328.

Shahin, Hashem, Tom Walsh, Tama Sobe, Eric Lynch, Mary-Claire King, Karen B. Avraham, and Molen Kanaan. 2002. Genetics of Congenital Deafness in the Palestinian Population: Multiple Connexin 26 Alleles with Shared Origins in the Middle East. *Human Genetics* 110(3): 284–289.

Supalla, Ted. 2004. The Validity of the Gallaudet Lecture Films. *Sign Language Studies* 4(3): 261–292.

Washabaugh, William. 1986. *Five Fingers for Survival.* Ann Arbor: Karoma.

Woodward, James. 1978. Historical Bases of American Sign Language. In *Understanding Language through Sign Language Research,* ed. Patricia Siple, 333–348. New York: Academic Press.

Wray, Alison, and George W. Grace. 2007. The Consequences of Talking to Strangers: Evolutionary Corollaries of Socio-cultural Influences on Linguistic Form. *Lingua* 117: 543–578.

Zeshan, Ulrike. 2000. *Sign Language in Indo-Pakistan: A Description of a Signed Language.* Amsterdam: Benjamins.

Some Observations on Research Methodology in Lexicostatistical Studies of Sign Languages

James Woodward

INTRODUCTION

Historical linguistics includes a wide variety of topics, including the study of areas such as the historical origins and the genetic relationships of language varieties, internal changes that occur over time in the phonology, morphology, syntax, semantics, and lexicon of language varieties, borrowings from one language to another, and language genesis due to creolization.

Since the purposes of this work are limited to the classification of languages into language families, I begin with a discussion of the subgrouping or classification of languages into language families.

THE SUBGROUPING OR CLASSIFICATION OF LANGUAGES INTO LANGUAGE FAMILIES

Historical linguists use three primary techniques in the subgrouping or classification of languages into language families, largely depending on the amount of data available on the language varieties to be grouped or classified: the comparative method, internal reconstruction, and lexicostatistics. Some historical linguists also use an additional technique called glottochronology.

If there are large amounts of data on two or more languages, the comparative method is typically used. The comparative method has been successfully used to classify Indo-European languages into several language families. If there are large amounts of data only on one language and there are no other known existing languages in the family, as is the case with Japanese and Basque, the technique of internal reconstruction is typically used.

On the other hand, when there are limited amounts of data on two or more languages, the technique of lexicostatistics is ordinarily chosen. Lexicostatistics has normally been the technique of choice for unwritten languages that have been previously undescribed or underdescribed. Lexicostatistics has been especially useful in the classification of 959 distinct, underdescribed Austronesian spoken languages and 250 distinct, underdescribed Australian spoken languages (Lehmann 1992).

Glottochronology, while related to lexicostatistics, is essentially a separate technique used to determine how long language varieties have been separated. Because it attempts to assign dates to language change, it is the most controversial of the four techniques. However, glottochronology has been used in an interesting way by some linguists to argue that a given language has developed from more than one ancestor and is the result of the mixing of two or more languages, usually through hybridization or creolization.

With these very general explanations in mind let's look at how these four techniques in historical linguistics have (or have not) been applied to sign languages.

THE COMPARATIVE METHOD AND INTERNAL RECONSTRUCTION IN SIGN LANGUAGE LINGUISTICS

Since the linguistic study of sign languages is so young, there are not yet enough data from several related sign languages to perform the types of comparative studies commonly found in the historical study of spoken languages. Furthermore, because of the short history of sign language linguistics, there are not even enough data on any one sign language to perform the meticulous types of internal reconstruction studies done on languages like spoken Japanese.

Despite the lack of data and additional problems, one hopes that a time will come in which ways to profitably use the comparative method or internal reconstruction will be devised. Readers who wish to familiarize themselves with how linguists have used the comparative method and/or internal reconstruction are encouraged to read the excellent treatments in Crowley (1992) and Lehmann (1992).

LEXICOSTATISTICS IN SIGN LANGUAGE LINGUISTICS

As discussed earlier, standard articles and books on historical linguistics (Crowley 1992; Gudschinsky 1964; Lehmann 1992) point out that lexicostatistics is often used for determining relationships across unwritten spoken languages that are underdescribed or undescribed and for which relatively limited amounts of data are available.

Given the facts that most sign languages are unwritten, most are underdescribed or undescribed, and there is limited data on most sign languages, it is not surprising that a number of lexicostatistical studies of sign languages have been done (e.g., Currie, Meier, and Walters 2002; McKee and Kennedy 2000; Padden this volume; Vasishta, Woodward, and Wilson 1978; Woodward 1978, 1991, 1992, 1993a, 1993b, 1996, 2000, 2003).

The reason that lexicostatistics is such an appropriate technique for underdescribed languages is that it allows a linguist to determine the relative degree of relationship between languages by comparing a small number of basic lexical items in the languages and determining the degree of similarity between them. These basic lexical items are chosen from what is often referred to as core vocabulary, which is relatively stable and resistant to change from borrowing. Core vocabulary includes items such as pronouns, numerals, body parts, terms for nuclear family members, geographical features, basic actions, basic colors, and basic states. Lexicostatistics is reliable only when basic core vocabulary is compared, not when general vocabulary is compared (Crowley 1992; Gudchinsky 1964; Lehmann 1992). Gudschinsky (1964, 613) points out, "The contrast between the basic core vocabulary and general vocabulary may be seen in the following illustration of French loan words in English: 'As against perhaps 50 percent of borrowed correspondences between English and French in the general vocabulary, we find just 6 percent in the basic vocabulary' (Swadesh 1951a, p. 13)." (Note: In the bibliography here this is given as Swadesh 1951.) In other words, if linguists compared general vocabulary of French and English, they would be forced to incorrectly conclude that French and English belong to the same language family, while if the same linguists compared the basic core vocabulary, they would conclude correctly that French and English belong to different language families.

It is unfortunate that some lexicostatistical studies of sign languages (e.g., Currie, Meier, and Walters 2002; Padden this volume) have not followed standard procedure in lexicostatistics and have compared general vocabulary rather than core vocabulary, which has resulted in higher than expected rates of cognates (e.g., a 23 percent rate of cognates in basic vocabulary between Japanese Sign Language and Mexican Sign Language). Until such studies do lexicostatistical comparisons of core vocabulary, their findings must be considered at best tentative because the data can lead to unjustified conclusions—just like the earlier example from Swadesh, comparing general vocabulary in French and English.

Almost all historical linguists working with spoken languages tend to use the two-hundred-word Swadesh list, named for Morris Swadesh, the historical linguist who devised this list. When as many words as possible have been elicited, recorded, and transcribed from each language to be studied, the linguist then compares the words between every pair of languages, identifies the cognates by determining which lexical items could have been derived from the same common lexical item by normal phonological processes, counts the number of cognates, and then calculates the percentages of cognates by dividing the total number of cognates by the total number of lexical items examined.

Linguists working on the lexicostatistics of spoken languages will classify two forms as cognates only if the application of plausible rules can derive form A from form B, form B from form A, or both form A and form B from some other form that once existed or continues to exist in related languages. Such phonological rules can be rules of assimilation, dissimilation, deletion, epenthesis, coalesence, metathesis, and/or some other phonological process recognized by modern linguistics.

Some sign language linguists have proposed counting how many of the five parameters (handshape, orientation, location, movement, and nonmanual expression) are similar and then using that number to determine whether the signs are cognate (Currie, Meier, and Walters 2002). Nothing like this has been done for lexicostatistical studies of spoken languages, and there is little linguistic reason to propose it for sign languages.

Linguists working on lexicostatistics of sign languages should classify two forms as cognates using the same standards employed by linguists working on spoken languages, that is, only if the application of plausible rules can derive form A from form B, form B from form A, or both form A and form B from some other form that once existed or continues to exist in related languages. Such phonological rules can be rules of assimilation, dissimilation, deletion, epenthesis, coalesence, metathesis, maximal differentiation, centralization, and/or some other phonological process in sign languages recognized by modern linguistics. (See Frishberg 1975, 1976 and Woodward 1976, as well as Johnson and Liddell 1989 and Sandler 1989 for a more recent treatment of these phonological processes.)

Based on the percentages of cognates, the linguist will group or classify the languages into categories. According to the most commonly used lexicostatistical guidelines for subgroupings, dialects of the same language should have an 81–100 percent rate of cognates, and languages belonging to the same language family should have a 36–80 percent rate of cognates.

A particular advantage to lexicostatistics that is not shared by the comparative method is that lexicostatistics does not assume that languages in the same language family necessarily came from one common ancestor—merely that something has influenced these languages so that they have become similar to each other. This something could be a common ancestor, or it could be extensive borrowing, hybridization, and/or creolization.

Another advantage of lexicostatistics is that it is easily and almost completely transferable to sign language research. The one important exception is the word list used for elicitation. As pointed out earlier, it is common to use the original two-hundred-word Swadesh list (shown in table 1R.1) to compare for cognates in basic vocabulary across spoken languages.

Table 1R.1. Original Swadesh Word List

1. all	46. few	91. liver	136. sit
2. and	47. fight	92. long	137. skin
3. animal	48. fire	93. louse	138. sky
4. ashes	49. fish	94. man	139. sleep
5. at	50. five	95. many	140. small
6. back	51. float	96. meat	141. smell
7. bad	52. flow	97. mother	142. smoke
8. bark	53. flower	98. mountain	143. smooth
9. because	54. fly	99. mouth	144. snake
10. belly	55. fog	100. name	145. snow
11. big	56. foot	101. narrow	146. some
12. bird	57. four	102. near	147. spit
13. bite	58. freeze	103. neck	148. split
14. black	59. fruit	104. new	149. squeeze
15. blood	60. give	105. night	150. stab
16. blow	61. good	106. nose	151. stand
17. bone	62. grass	107. not	152. star
18. breathe	63. green	108. old	153. stick
19. burn	64. guts	109. one	154. stone
20. child	65. hair	110. other	155. straight
21. cloud	66. hand	111. person	156. suck
22. cold	67. he	112. play	157. sun
23. come	68. head	113. pull	158. swell
24. count	69. hear	114. push	159. swim
25. cut	70. heart	115. rain	160. tail
26. day	71. heavy	116. red	161. that
27. die	72. here	117. right	162. there
28. dig	73. hit	118. right (direction)	163. they
29. dirty	74. hold/take	119. river	164. thick
30. dog	75. how	120. road	165. thin
31. drink	76. hunt	121. root	166. think
32. dry	77. husband	122. rope	167. this
33. dull	78. I	123. rotten	168. thou
34. dust	79. ice	124. rub	169. three
35. ear	80. if	125. salt	170. throw
36. earth	81. in	126. sand	171. tie
37. eat	82. kill	127. say	172. tongue
38. egg	83. know	128. scratch	173. tooth
39. eye	84. lake	129. sea	174. three
40. fall	85. laugh	130. see	175. turn
41. far	86. leaf	131. seed	176. two
42. fat/grease	87. left	132. sew	177. vomit
43. father	88. leg	133. sharp	178. walk
44. fear	89. lie	134. short	179. warm
45. feather	90. live	135. sing	180. wash

Table 1R.1. (continued)

181. water	186. where	191. wind	196. wood
182. we	187. white	192. wing	197. worm
183. wet	188. who	193. wipe	198. ye
184. what	189. wide	194. with	199. year
185. when	190. wife	195. woman	200. yellow

Let's examine what happens when we use the Swadesh list to compare for cognates in basic vocabulary of American Sign Language (ASL) and three sign language varieties in Costa Rica. This information was collected in 1990 in Costa Rica (see Woodward 1991, 1992). One of these sign language varieties (New Costa Rican Sign [NCRSL] or Modern Costa Rican Sign Language) is used by younger signers (in 1990, under the age of twenty-eight); one (Original Costa Rican Sign Language [OCRSL]) is used by older signers (in 1990, over the age of forty-four) in San Jose, Costa Rica; and one (Bribri Sign Language [BrSL]) is used in a small group of hearing and deaf Bribris in the southern part of Costa Rica. At the time of data collection the researcher believed that the younger signing should show direct influence from ASL but that neither the older signing nor the Bribri signing should show do so. It was, however, possible that the older signing would show some similarity to ASL because of possible earlier influence of Spanish Sign Language on the older forms of Costa Rican signing. (French Sign Language [LSF] is known to have influenced ASL and Spanish Sign Language—see Pinedo Peydró 1987.)

Table 1R.2 shows the results of comparisons for cognates using the original Swadesh word list.

The standard groupings for lexicostatistics using the original Swadesh word list would classify these four language varieties as four separate languages that belong to the same language family, as shown in figure 1R.1.

However, since we know that BrSL is used in a very isolated community with no known direct contact with any of the other three sign languages, the lexicostatistic results are unexpected.

Table 1R.2. Results of Lexicostatistical Analysis Using the Original Swadesh Word List

	Bribri SL	OCRSL	NCRSL	ASL
Bribri SL	X	36%	38%	36%
Original Costa Rican SL		X	55%	47%
New Costa Rican SL			X	73%
American SL				X

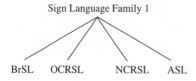

Figure 1R.1. Family relationships according to original Swadesh word list

If we go back and examine the original Swadesh list carefully, we can see that it contains many items, such as body parts and pronouns, which are represented indexically (i.e., simply by pointing) in many sign languages. The comparison of such indexic signs might result in a number of false potential cognates. In addition, the list contains certain nouns that are no longer commonly used in many Deaf communities, such as "spears," which may no longer have a commonly used sign and may be represented gesturally in a more iconic manner than other sign translations for the Swadesh list.

A modified list with many such problematic items omitted and with a few basic items added to make an even one hundred words has been developed and used by sign language linguists interested in lexicostatistics. This modified list is shown in table 1R.3.

Table 1R.3. Modified Swadesh List for Sign Language Research

1. all	26. grass	51. other	76. warm
2. animal	27. green	52. person	77. water
3. bad	28. heavy	53. play	78. wet
4. because	29. how	54. rain	79. what
5. bird	30. hunt/look for	55. red	80. when
6. black	31. husband	56. right/correct	81. where
7. blood	32. ice	57. river	82. white
8. child	33. if	58. rope	83. who
9. count	34. kill	59. salt	84. wide
10. day	35. laugh	60. sea	85. wife
11. die	36. leaf	61. sharp	86. wind
12. dirty	37. lie (tell a)	62. short (time)	87. with
13. dog	38. live	63. sing	88. woman
14. dry	39. long	64. sit	89. wood
15. dull	40. louse	65. smooth	90. worm
16. dust	41. man	66. snake	91. year
17. earth	42. meat	67. snow	92. yellow
18. egg	43. mother	68. stand	93. full
19. grease	44. mountain	69. star	94. moon
20. father	45. name	70. stone	95. brother
21. feather	46. narrow	71. sun	96. cat
22. fire	47. new	72. tail	97. dance
23. fish	48. night	73. thin	98. pig
24. flower	49. not	74. tree	99. sister
25. good	50. old	75. vomit	100. work

Table 1R.4. Results of Lexicostatistical Analysis Using the Modified Word List

	BrSL	OCRSL	NCRSL	ASL
BrSL	X	~~14%~~	~~10%~~	~~7%~~
OCRSL		X	42%	~~27%~~
NCRSL			X	63%
ASL				X

Note: Strikethroughs indicate that the languages are members of different language families.

Figure 1R.2. Family relationships in Costa Rica according to modified Swadesh word list

Now let's examine what happens when we use the modified Swadesh list to compare for cognates in basic vocabulary of ASL and the same three sign language varieties in Costa Rica. Table 1R.4 shows the results.

The standard groupings for lexicostatistics using the modified Swadesh word list would classify these four language varieties as four separate languages that belong to three separate language families, as seen in figure 1R.2.

The results of using the modified Swadesh word list conform to general expectations, given the historical information available on the language varieties. We can see that BrSL, which is used in a very isolated community with no known direct contact with any of the other three sign languages, belongs to a completely separate language family from the other languages. We can also see that ASL and OCRSL do not share a sufficient number of cognates to be classified in the same language family—they belong in different language families. However, NCRSL appears to belong to two language families; that is, it comes from two (or more) ancestors. This would be expected only if there were a hybridization of two languages or a creolization involving more than two languages.

PATTERNS IN THE ORIGINS OF MODERN SIGN LANGUAGES

The situation in Costa Rica is far from unique. The effect of the introduction of American signs into Thailand by well-meaning educators has also had profound effects upon original sign languages in Thailand. Lexicostatistical studies of Modern TSL (Woodward 1996, 2000) show that 52 percent of basic vocabulary in Modern TSL is cognate with American signs, while less than 30 percent is cognate with Original Chiangmai Sign Language (29 percent) or with Original Bangkok Sign Language (26 percent). (OCSL and OBSL demonstrate a 65 percent cognate rate in basic vocabulary.)

The standard groupings for lexicostatistics using the modified Swadesh word list would classify these four language varieties into four separate languages that belong to two separate language families, as in figure 1R.3.

We can see that ASL and Modern TSL share sufficient cognates to be classified as members of the same language family. Moreover, OCSL and OBSL share sufficient cognates to be classified as members of the same language family. However, even though Modern TSL and the original sign languages in Thailand have been separated by only fifty-four years, they no longer belong in the same family (as a glottochronology analysis shows—not included here since my focus is lexicostatistics).

Ironically, even though the direct influence of ASL is less in Thailand (52 percent) than it is in Costa Rica (63 percent), the net result is that Modern TSL has moved much further away from the original sign languages in Thailand (26–29 percent) than NCRSL has moved away from the original sign languages in Costa Rica (42 percent). The net effect of this is that the original sign languages in Thailand are even more endangered than those in Costa Rica. Until 1996 many young Deaf people in Thailand had no idea that there had been earlier, original signs for DOG, NAME, and so on other than the ones they used. Thanks to basic training in sign language linguistics for Thai Deaf people since 1997, more and more Thai Deaf people are becoming aware of their linguistic history and the importance of the original sign languages. A growing number of younger Deaf users of Modern TSL are striving to get more training in linguistics and are making efforts to at least document the original sign languages in Thailand before they die out in the next forty or so years. They are also seeking ways to try to revive these languages as second languages among interested Deaf people in Thailand.

So far, we have seen that the origins of Modern ASL, NCRSL, and Modern TSL have many parallels. Each of these languages has been formed

Figure 1R.3. Family relationships in Thailand according to modified Swadesh word list

through a mixture of original sign language(s) and an outside, usually foreign sign language introduced into the educational system. The creation of the new sign language, while offering new educational opportunities for Deaf people, has endangered the existing original sign languages. Deaf people have not been able to maintain the original sign languages in many countries because of the small numbers of Deaf people with Deaf parents. With little transmission of sign language from parent to child and massive transmission of sign language from child to child in an educational setting, any foreign sign language imported into an educational system is bound to have a strong influence on local sign language varieties.

The pattern of origin for Modern ASL, NCRSL, and Modern TSL has been found through lexicostatistical studies in a number of other countries and areas, including Hong Kong (Woodward 1993b) and Viet Nam (Woodward 2000). It has also been posited in other countries where there are no completed lexicostatistical studies to back up the hypothesis, such as the Philippines (ASL and original sign languages in the Philippines), Malaysia and Singapore (ASL and original local sign languages), Laos (Modern TSL and original sign languages existing in Laos), to name a few. This may be the regular pattern of the origin of modern sign languages in Asia. It could also be a pattern in much of Central and South America if Costa Rica is a typical case, but this cannot be known until there are more lexicostatistical studies in Central and South American countries. In these countries, there is a possibility of finding mixtures of Spanish, Portuguese, French, Italian (Argentina), and/or American Sign Language varieties with local original sign languages, but it is impossible to say until appropriate historical linguistic information is gathered on site. In some countries, such as Costa Rica, some original sign languages will still be present; in other countries, any original sign languages may be extinct. This will depend to a large extent on when the foreign sign language was introduced into the country.

The origin of modern sign languages on the African continent remains largely unstudied. Clearly, there have been some original sign languages in Africa; Adamorobe Sign Language in Ghana is a clear example, where one of every seven persons is reported to be deaf from birth or to have become deaf at an early age (Frishberg 1987). Clearly ASL and LSF have been promoted in various parts of Africa. From what we know about other parts of the world, it seems inconceivable that there would not have been original sign languages in a number of countries in Africa and not just limited to Ghana.

However, until the historical linguistic work is done in a lot more countries, we can only speculate on the history of many sign languages. Still, whenever we speculate, we need to incorporate the findings of current studies into our model.

THE NEED TO START INCORPORATING HISTORICAL LINGUISTICS
INTO ALL SIGN LANGUAGE RESEARCH

Before one begins research on any new sign language, it is important to do preliminary lexicostatistical studies. For example, if we know nothing about the sign language situation in Viet Nam, our first question should not be "What does the structure of Vietnamese Sign Language look like?" Rather, it should be "How many sign languages are there in Viet Nam?"

In Viet Nam there are three major sign languages: Ho Chi Minh City Sign Language (HCMCSL), Ha Noi Sign Language (HNSL), and Hai Phong Sign Language (HPSL). There may be other smaller sign languages as well. Lexicostatistical studies of the three major sign languages in Viet Nam (Woodward 2000, 2003) indicate a 54–58 percent rate of cognates in their basic vocabulary, a bit less similar than LSF and ASL and a bit more similar than Modern TSL and ASL. Researchers cannot by any stretch of the imagination say that they are studying Vietnamese Sign Language. They can say they are studying sign languages in Viet Nam or even Vietnamese sign languages, but one should be very careful to include the word-final -s.

Not only is it necessary to do preliminary lexicostatistical studies of new sign language situations, but it may also be necessary to do some lexicostatistical studies on various sign languages we think we already know about. For example, a number of studies discuss Chinese Sign Language. In fact, it appears that many of these studies are actually studies of Hong Kong Sign Language (HKSL) varieties. Lexicostatistical studies of HKSL have shown that HKSL and Shanghai Sign Language (SSL) share less than 80 percent cognates in basic vocabulary (Woodward 1993a). This would indicate that HKSL and SSL are different languages. Since this is the case, we know that there is more than one sign language in China, but we do not have any idea how many. This is because no one has ever done any comparisons of either HKSL or SSL with sign language varieties in other parts of China with the Swadesh list modified for sign language research. There may well be a group of Chinese sign languages, just like there are several Vietnamese sign languages in Viet Nam.

Every bit of information we have on Deaf education in Hong Kong indicates that Deaf people from Shanghai brought Shanghai signs to Hong Kong after World War II ended in 1945 and introduced them into the schools for Deaf people that they started.

Now if Shanghai signs have been in Hong Kong only since 1945, they have had only a limited amount of time to change. It is likely that Hong Kong Sign Language is a mixture of original sign language varieties used in Hong Kong with foreign Shanghai signs that were brought by Shanghai Deaf people who became the first educators of Deaf people in Hong Kong.

All of this brings us to an inescapable fact: We cannot assume we know anything at all about the history of sign languages until we have studied their histories explicitly. In addition, we cannot assume we can explain the findings of sign language historical research based on what we know either about spoken language in given countries or about the histories and cultures of groups of hearing people from the given countries. We must instead turn to the unique histories and cultures of Deaf people in the given countries (see Woodward 2003).

DEAF HISTORIES AND DEAF CULTURES AS EXPLANATORY TOOLS IN SIGN LANGUAGE HISTORICAL LINGUISTICS

One of the clearest examples of the importance of Deaf histories and Deaf cultures as explanatory tools in the historical linguistic study of sign languages is the case of the relationships between certain sign languages in Thailand and Viet Nam (see Woodward 2000, 2003).

Let's begin by reviewing what I have already said about sign languages in Thailand and Viet Nam. We have considered three sign languages in Thailand (OBSL, OCSL, and Modern TSL) that belong to two different language families (Modern TSL belongs to a different family from the two original sign languages in Thailand). We have also discussed three different sign languages in Viet Nam (HNSL, HPSL, and HCMCSL) that belong to one language family. We might assume that there is no need to compare sign languages in Thailand and sign languages in Viet Nam for cognates and that these six sign languages would ultimately belong to three different language families.

However, what would happen if we compared the three sign languages from Thailand and the three sign languages from Viet Nam for cognates? Could there be any historical relationships here? Table 1R.5 shows the results of such a comparison (Woodward 2000, 2003).

This explicit lexicostatistical comparison does indicate historical relationships between the sign languages in the two countries. According to table 1R.5, the six sign languages should be classified into two language families, as shown in figure 1R.4.

Table 1R.5. Cognates in Selected Sign Languages in Thailand and Viet Nam

	OCSL	OBSL	HPSL	HNSL	HCMCSL	Modern TSL
OriginalCM SL	X	65%	46%	33%	23%	29%
OriginalBK SL		X	48%	31%	25%	26%
HP SL			X	54%	54%	40%
HN SL				X	58%	45%
HCMC SL					X	39%
Modern Thai SL						X

Note: Strikethroughs indicate that the languages are members of different language families.

We now have to try to answer some interesting questions:

1. Why doesn't Modern TSL, which is used in Thailand, belong to a language family that includes other sign languages from Thailand? Why does it belong to a language family that appears to be made up of sign languages used only in Viet Nam?
2. How can HPSL, which is used in Viet Nam, belong to two separate language families, especially when one of the families appears to include only original sign languages in Thailand?

The answers to these questions can be found in the histories of the Deaf people who use these languages.

1. Because Modern TSL was greatly influenced by American signs, it is not related to the original sign languages in Thailand, which were not influenced by ASL. The relationship of Modern TSL to sign languages in Viet Nam is not a result of direct but indirect contact. Furthermore, HNSL, HPSL, and HCMCSL all show strong influences from LSF, which was introduced into the first school for deaf people in Viet Nam in 1886. Modern TSL has been extensively influenced by ASL, which is closely related to LSF. The influence of ASL on Modern TSL and the influence of LSF on sign languages in Viet Nam result in a large number of shared cognates in Modern TSL and sign languages in Viet Nam.

2. While it is true that HNSL, HPSL, and HCMCSL have all three been influenced by LSF, Hai Phong signers, perhaps because of their relative isolation from Ha Noi and Ho Chi Minh City, have managed to preserve more original Southeast Asian signs than signers in Ha Noi and Ho Chi Minh City. Even when HPSL has borrowed a French sign for a vocabulary item, Hai Phong signers have sometimes kept the original Southeast Asian sign along with the French one. This has resulted in pairs of cognates for a number of words. One sign in the cognate pair is cognate with original sign languages in Southeast Asia and one with LSF. Examples of this are signs such as WIFE, HUSBAND, and PIG. Because of these pairs, HPSL shows strong similarities to Southeast Asian sign languages that have not been influenced by LSF or ASL (OCSL and OBSL) and also shows strong similarities to Southeast Asian sign languages that have been influenced either by LSF (HNSL, HCMCSL) or by ASL (Modern TSL).

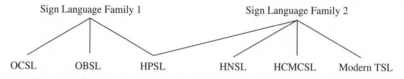

Figure 1R.4. Family relationships in Thailand and Viet Nam together, according to modified Swadesh word list

Some lexicostatistical studies of sign language have taken the very strict, limited position that unless two sign languages have come into direct contact, they cannot be related and should not show much similarity. For example, Currie, Meier, and Walters (2002) say that Japanese Sign Language and Mexican Sign Language should not show as much similarity as was found because these two sign languages have no history of contact.

Before going any further, it should be again noted that the lexicostatistical data used for the comparison of Japanese Sign Language and Mexican Sign Language consisted of general vocabulary, not core vocabulary. We should therefore examine the issue with a stronger theoretical base.

If the Swadesh list modified for sign language research is used and we have valid and reliable data, can there be a significant lexicostatical relationship between an Asian and a Latin American sign language that have no history of contact?

The answer to this question is yes. The two sign languages are Modern TSL and NCRSL. These two languages have never been in direct contact, yet they have a 44 percent rate of cognates in basic vocabulary, meaning that they should be classified in the same language family. This family would also include ASL, which shares a 52 percent rate of cognates with Modern TSL (Woodward 1996, 2000) and a 63 percent rate of cognates with Modern CRSL (Woodward 1991, 1992). It is because ASL mixed or creolized with Modern TSL and because ASL mixed or creolized with Modern CRSL that Modern TSL and Modern CRSL are so closely related lexicostatistically that they should be classified in the same language family. It is clear that we have to be aware that some sign languages (as do some spoken languages) have more than one ancestor. As stated earlier, a particular advantage to lexicostatistics that the comparative method does not have is that lexicostatistics does not assume that languages in the same language family necessarily come from one common ancestor—merely that something has influenced these languages so that they have become similar. This something could be a common ancestor, or it could be extensive borrowing, hybridization, and/or creolization.

SUMMARY

Historical linguistics is the study of language differences that occur over time. All languages are constantly changing. Changes may occur in the lexicon or in any component of the grammar: phonetics, phonology, morphology, syntax, semantics.

Since lexicostatistics is primarily used for languages that are unwritten, underdescribed, or undescribed, it has frequently been used in sign language historical linguistics. A fundamental rule of lexicostatistical research methodology is that general vocabulary cannot be used for comparisons for cognates.

The use of general vocabulary instead of core vocabulary results in higher than expected rates of cognates because general vocabulary is more subject to change than core vocabulary. Most lexicostatistical studies have used a modified version of the two-hundred-word Swadesh list since the original list results in a slight overestimation of the relationship of closely related sign languages, moderate overestimation of that of loosely related sign languages, and great overestimation of that of historically unrelated sign languages.

The historical linguistic study of sign languages has shown that, contrary to popular opinion, many countries have more than one sign language. In addition, historical sign linguistics has demonstrated that we cannot assume we know anything at all about the history of sign languages until we have actually taken the time to study their histories. In addition, we cannot assume we can explain the findings of sign language historical research from what we know about spoken language in given countries or about the histories and cultures of groups of hearing people from those countries. We must instead turn to the unique histories and cultures of Deaf people in those regions.

Bibliography

Crowley, Terry. 1992. *An Introduction to Historical Linguistics.* New York: Oxford University Press.

Currie, Anne-Marie, Richard Meier, and Keith Walters. 2002. A Cross-linguistic Examination of the Lexicons of Four Signed Languages. In *Modality and Structure in Signed and Spoken Language,* ed. Richard Meier, Kearsy Cormier, and David Quinto-Pozos, 224–236. New York: Cambridge University Press.

Frishberg, Nancy. 1975. Arbitrariness and Iconicity: Historical Change in American Sign Language. *Language* 51: 696–719.

———. 1976. Some Aspects of the Historical Change in American Sign Language. PhD diss., University of California at San Diego.

———. 1987. Ghanaian Sign Language. In *The Gallaudet Encyclopedia of Deaf People and Deafness,* ed. John V. Van Cleve, vol. 3, 78–79. New York: McGraw Hill.

Gudschinsky, Sarah. 1964. The ABCs of Lexicostatistics (Glottochronology). In *Language in Culture and Society,* ed. Dell Hymes, 612–623. New York: Harper.

Johnson, Robert, and Scott Liddell. 1989. American Sign Language: The Phonological Base. *Sign Language Studies* 18(64): 195–227.

Lehmann, Winfred. 1992. *Historical Linguistics: An Introduction.* New York: Routledge.

McKee, David, and Graeme Kennedy. 2000. Lexical Comparison of Signs from American, Australian, British, and New Zealand Sign Languages. In *The Signs of Language Revisited: An Anthology in Honor of Ursula Bellugi and Edward Klima,* ed. Karen Emmorey and Harlan Lane, 49–76. Mahwah, N.J.: Erlbaum.

Pinedo Peydró, Félix-Jesús. 1987. Sign Languages: Spanish. In *Gallaudet Encyclopedia of Deaf People and Deafness,* ed. John V. Van Cleve, vol. 3, 108–109. New York: McGraw-Hill.

Sandler, Wendy. 1989. *Phonological Representation of the Sign.* Dordrecht: Foris.

Swadesh, Morris. 1951. Diffusional Cumulation and Archaic Residue as Historical Explanations. *Southwestern Journal of Anthropology* 7(1): 1–21.

Vasishta, Madan, James Woodward, and Kirk L. Wilson. 1978. Sign Language in India: Regional Variation in the Deaf Population. *Indian Journal of Applied Linguistics* 4(2): 66–72.

Woodward, James. 1976. Signs of Change: Historical Variation in American Sign Language. *Sign Language Studies* 10: 81–94.

———. 1978. Historical Bases of American Sign Language. In *Understanding Language through Sign Language Research,* ed. Patricia Siple, 333–348. New York: Academic Press.

———. 1991. Sign Language Varieties in Costa Rica. *Sign Language Studies* 73: 329–346.

———. 1992. Historical Bases of New Costa Rican Sign Language. *Revista de filología y lingüística de la Universidad de Costa Rica* 18(1): 127–132.

———. 1993a. Lexical Evidence for the Existence of South Asian and East Asian Sign Language Families. *Journal of Asian Pacific Communication* 4(2): 91–106.

———. 1993b. The Relationship of Sign Language Varieties in India, Pakistan, and Nepal. *Sign Language Studies* 78: 15–22.

———. 1996. Modern Standard Thai Sign Language, Influence from ASL, and Its Relationship to Original Sign Language Varieties in Thailand. *Sign Language Studies* 92: 227–252.

———. 2000. Sign Languages and Sign Language Families in Thailand and Viet Nam. In *The Signs of Language Revisited: An Anthology in Honor of Ursula Bellugi and Edward Klima,* ed. Karen Emmorey and Harlan Lane, 23–47. Mahwah, N.J.: Erlbaum.

———. 2003. Sign Languages and Deaf Identities in Thailand and Viet Nam. In *Many Ways to Be Deaf,* ed. Leila Monaghan, Constance Schmaling, Karen Nakamura, and Graham Turner, 282–301. Washington, D.C.: Gallaudet University Press.

CHAPTER 2

Two Types of Nonconcatenative Morphology in Signed Languages

Gaurav Mathur and Christian Rathmann

CREATING WORDS

Morphology, the study of words, has recognized two ways to create words out of other words. First is the concatenative way, in which an affix is attached to a stem. The English words *walks, walking,* and *walked* share the same stem, *walk,* but have different affixes (i.e.,*–s,–ing,* and*–ed,* respectively). Both stems and affixes are considered morphemes, the smallest meaningful units of a language. They can be stored in a mental dictionary, or lexicon, as a list of pairs of meaning and form, as in table 2.1. To identify a morpheme, one must identify both its meaning and its form, each of which must remain more or less consistent in all of its appearances.

The other way to create words from other words is nonconcatenative. Instead of attaching an affix to the stem, part of the stem or the whole stem undergoes a process. Possible processes include stem-internal changes, like those seen in the past-tense forms of *see, run,* and *lie* (as in *lie down*): *saw, ran,* and *lay.* In these cases, the vowel quality of the stem changes to convey past tense. It is less obvious how to divide such words into a stem and an affix that can be listed separately in the lexicon. One solution, in the distributed morphology approach of Halle and Marantz (1993), is to associate a particular meaning with a list of possible forms. Thus, past tense is associated with the affix*–ed,* as well as with a process that changes the vowel quality for a certain set of words. Table 2.2 illustrates this approach.

In addition to stem-internal changes, nonconcatenative morphology includes processes that apply to (a part of) the stem, such as reduplication, as well as templatic morphology, seen in Semitic languages like Hebrew and Arabic. List (1) provides a brief example of templatic morphology *(binyan)* in Arabic, taken from McCarthy (1982) and cited in Spencer (1991, 135). In this language, some roots consist of three consonants; specific vowels are inserted among the consonants depending on the particular meaning. As

Table 2.1. A Subset of the English Lexicon

Meaning	Form
move on foot at regular pace	walk
move up incline with feet/hands	climb
carry out activity as part of job	work
third-person singular present tense	+ s
progressive aspect	+ ing
past tense	+ ed

Table 2.2. Another Subset of the English Lexicon

Meaning	Form
perceive through the eyes	see
move on foot at a quick pace	run
be prone	lie
past tense	(i) change vowel quality in X where X = {see, run, lie . . . } (ii) + ed for other verbs

the following example shows, morphemes do not have to be combined in a linear manner:

List (1) Nonconcatenative Morphology in a Spoken Language (Arabic)

a.	katab	perfective active	('have written')
b.	kutib	perfective passive	('has been written')
c.	aktub	imperfective active	('is writing')
d.	uktab	imperfective passive	('is being written')

Signed languages are no different in using concatenation and nonconcatenation to create words. Table 2.3 lists stems in American Sign Language (ASL) that can be combined concatenatively with another sign glossed as PERSON to create a new word (e.g., TEACH combines with PERSON to create a word meaning *teacher*). For more discussion of the PERSON morpheme, see Supalla (2004).

Signed languages display nonconcatenative morphology as well (Klima and Bellugi 1979; Liddell and Johnson 1986; Sandler 1989, among others). In the case of signed languages, nonconcatenative morphology includes processes that change at least one of the parameters of the stem, such as handshape, orientation, location, or movement. For example, numeral incorporation changes the handshape of some signs to indicate a numerical quantity up to a certain point. Thus, the handshape of DAY or WEEK can be replaced with the

Table 2.3. A Subset of the ASL Lexicon

Meaning	Form
show/explain how to do something	TEACH
gain knowledge of something	LEARN
continent in northern hemisphere	EUROPE
study of the human mind	PSYCHOLOGY
person who does or is affiliated with x where x is meaning of stem	+ PERSON

handshape of TWO to indicate the meaning of *two days* or *two weeks*. As with the example of stem-internal changes in English, there is not a straightforward way to represent this process in the lexicon. A free stem has phonological specifications for all of its parameters. The process of numeral incorporation does not affix a sign with a complete set of phonological specifications to the stem. Rather, it changes one of the stem's parameters. If the approach of Halle and Marantz (1993) is followed, numeral incorporation can be listed as a process, as in table 2.4.

The concatenative way seems more common in spoken languages, while signed languages favor the noncatenative way. According to Fernald and Napoli (2000, 5):

> ASL morphology does not make significant use of concatenative affixation (an observation also made by others), but it does make rampant use of alternation of phonological parameters. That is, one mechanism (alternation of phonological features) exploited in relatively limited ways in spoken languages is embraced by signed languages, whereas another mechanism (concatenation) found frequently in spoken languages is practically eschewed by signed languages.

Aronoff, Meir, and Sandler (2005, 303) similarly note that "sign-language morphology . . . seems to comprise two radically different types. One is rich, complex, and simultaneous [= nonconcatenative], and the other is sparse, relatively simple, and sequential [= concatenative]."

Klima and Bellugi (1979), Fernald and Napoli (2000), Rathmann and Mathur (2002), Aronoff, Meir, and Sandler (2005), and Sandler and

Table 2.4. Another Subset of the ASL Lexicon

Meaning	Form
period of time lasting twenty-four hours	DAY
period of time lasting seven days	WEEK
quantity of two	(i) TWO
	(ii) change handshape to 2 in X
	where X = {DAY, WEEK, MONTH . . . }

Lillo-Martin (2006), among many others, already debate the question of why each language modality prefers a particular way of creating words. This chapter goes beyond that question by focusing on nonconcatenative morphology and argues that there are two types, one of which is unique to signed languages.

TWO TYPES OF NONCONCATENATIVE MORPHOLOGY

Nonconcatenative morphology separates into two types based on how the morphemes are realized. In one type, all of the morphemes in a word have a fixed phonological realization. This type has been illustrated with numeral incorporation. According to Liddell's (1996) analysis, TWO+WEEK (where the plus symbol indicates numeral incorporation) in ASL, as shown in figure 2.1, can be broken down into two morphemes: the bound form of TWO, which has a phonological specification for handshape only, and the bound form of WEEK, which has a phonological specification for location, orientation, and movement. These morphemes are combined to create a well-formed sign (i.e., a sign with a complete set of specifications for all of the parameters). While each morpheme cannot stand alone on account of an incomplete set of phonological specifications, they still have some phonological content specified in the lexicon.

In the other type of nonconcatenative morphology, at least one of the morphemes in a word does not have lexically specified phonological content. Verb agreement is one such example. In ASL, a sign meaning 'I asked her' is made in such a way that the palm of the hand faces the area of signing space (henceforth called 'gestural space') associated with the referent of *her*. In contrast, the sign for 'she asked me' is made with the opposite palm orientation: The palm faces the signer. See figure 2.2 for an illustration of the first form.

There is extensive literature on how to analyze this phenomenon, for example, Meier (1982, 1990, 2002), Padden (1983), Liddell (1990, 1995, 2000,

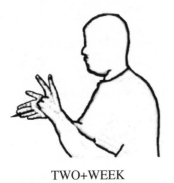

TWO+WEEK

Figure 2.1. Example of first type of nonconcatenative morphology. The example from ASL involves numeral incorporation and means *two weeks*.

I+ASK+HER

Figure 2.2. Example of second type of nonconcatenative morphology. The example from ASL involves verb agreement and means *I asked her.*

2003), Lillo-Martin (1986, 1991, 2002), Meir (1998, 2002), Mathur (2000), Rathmann and Mathur (2002), and Aronoff, Meir, and Sandler (2005). According to one analysis by Rathmann and Mathur (2008b), the process of verb agreement changes the orientation of the stem so that the palm faces an area specified by an agreement morpheme. The agreement morpheme for a first-person object specifies an area near the signer's chest, but the corresponding morpheme for a non-first-person object is a zero morpheme; that is, the lexicon does not specify phonological content for this morpheme and so does not specify any particular area toward which to orient the palm. Rather, that morpheme is realized through interaction with gestural space. If a signer envisions the referent of *her* as being on the right side of gestural space, the morpheme will be realized as an area on the right side. (See Rathmann and Mathur [2002] for a discussion of why that is so. In short, to solve the problem of listing a potentially infinite number of forms in the lexicon, it is proposed that an interface exists between the linguistic system and gestural space and that the realization of the non-first-person morpheme occurs in this interface.)

This second type of nonconcatenative morphology differs from morphology that simply involves phonologically null morphemes. Morphemes of this second type, while specified as phonologically empty in the lexicon, do become realized through interaction with gestural space. They are thus different from other phonologically null morphemes. Depending on the theory of morphology that is assumed, spoken languages can be said to have morphemes that lack phonological content. In English, the morpheme for first-person singular, present tense (and in fact for all combinations of person and number features in the present tense except third-person singular) is a phonological zero, symbolized by in the following examples: *I walk+*, *you walk+*, *we walk+*, *you all walk+*, *they walk+*.

Signed languages have analogous morphemes. In ASL, plural number for a large class of nouns is expressed by a phonological zero. The ASL sign for the singular form of FATHER is the same as that for the plural form. This sign is made with an open hand, all fingers spread, touching the forehead on the tip of the thumb. Other elements in the context, such as verbal inflection or quantifiers, provide clues to the number of the entity. (See Pfau and Steinbach [2006] for further discussion of strategies for pluralization in signed languages.) Unlike the morphemes in the second type of nonconcatenative morphology, the zero morphemes in English *I walk* and ASL FATHER 'fathers' are never realized.

To sum up, the distinction between the two types of nonconcatenative morphology in signed languages lies in the source of a morpheme's realization. In the first type, the realization of all of the morphemes comes from the lexicon exclusively. This type includes the past-tense forms of English *see* and *run*, as well as ASL numeral incorporation, because all of their phonological specifications come from the lexicon. The examples of English *I walk* and ASL FATHER 'fathers' also fall under this type because the zero morphemes in these examples are specified as phonologically null in the lexicon and are not realized. On the other hand, in the second type, at least one morpheme is specified as phonologically null in the lexicon but is realized through interaction with gestural space. The example of verb agreement in ASL falls under this type.

The second type of nonconcatenative morphology is unique to signed languages. It is difficult to imagine a morpheme in a spoken language that is specified as phonologically null in the lexicon but is realized as pointing in gestural space. Granted, speakers gesture while speaking, and some gestures may be aligned with certain morphemes, as McNeill (2000), Kendon (2004), and Liddell (2000), among others, have pointed out. Thus, a speaker may utter *I want this* and point to a particular book while uttering *this*. However, the word *this* is still realized by specific phonological content, and the optional gesture is seen as adding to the meaning of *this* rather than realizing its form.

The distinction between the two types of nonconcatenative morphology is not a trivial one inasmuch as it shows up in each type's interaction with phonology. It comes as no surprise that nonconcatenative morphology has a tight interaction with phonology since it alters the phonological form of a stem in some way. This chapter argues that each type interacts with phonology in a different way.

In the first type, it is assumed that the realization of a morpheme originates in its lexical specification and is subject to phonological constraints that are language internal and language specific (e.g., phonotactic constraints against the combination of certain phonological properties in a morpheme). For example, some cases of numeral incorporation in a given language do not occur because overlaying the properties of a numeral with those of a sign leads to a marked form of movement that, while physically possible, is not

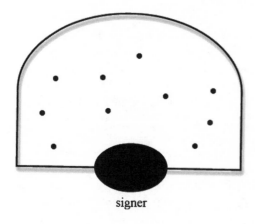

signer

Figure 2.3. Gestural space with an infinite number of points that can be used to refer to entities

tolerated in that language. Here, these constraints are referred to as phonological constraints on the complexity of articulation.

In the second type, the realization of at least one morpheme comes from the interface with gestural space. Gestural space is in principle infinite and allows an infinite number of possible realizations, as illustrated in figure 2.3. One can point to a book close by or to a mountain that is far away or, in a more extreme case, to a star. The infinite number is limited only by what one's articulators can do physically. The length of one's articulators constrain the extent of pointing to those areas of gestural space that are reachable. A person then uses one of the reachable areas to refer to the intended mountain or star. Similar constraints apply to pointing to referents that cannot be pointed to directly, such as entities that are not present in the immediate environment or those that are intangible, like abstract ideas. Similarly, some forms of verb agreement are not realized because they require twisting the arm at an awkward angle in order for the palm to face a particular area in gestural space. Such constraints are rooted in the physiological limits of the articulators and come into play when realization in gestural space exceeds these limits. Henceforth, these kinds of constraints are referred to as phonological constraints on the degree of articulation.

Perlmutter (2006), in response to Mathur and Rathmann (2006), has argued that it is not necessary to postulate phonological constraints in ruling out certain forms of verb agreement. He suggests that it is sufficient to let phonetic factors like the physiological limits of the articulators rule out the unattested forms. A pilot study of second language acquisition of verb agreement in ASL reveals, however, that late learners of ASL produce agreement forms that are not produced by native signers, including ones that Perlmutter would have ruled out due to physiological limits, suggesting that the limits need to be internalized and systematized as phonological constraints (Rathmann and Mathur 1999).

The bulk of the present chapter makes a case for the distinctiveness of the two types of nonconcatenative morphology by showing that each type interacts with phonology differently. The next section uses numeral incorporation as a case study for the first type and demonstrates that it interacts primarily with phonological constraints on the complexity of articulation. The succeeding section focuses on verb agreement as an example of the second type and illustrates how it interacts with phonological constraints on the degree of articulation, in addition to constraints on the complexity of articulation. To provide further support for the typology of nonconcatenative morphology, this chapter shows briefly how other morphological processes fit one of the two types. In the end, we present a revised picture of morphology in signed languages.

NUMERAL INCORPORATION

Numeral incorporation illustrates the type of nonconcatenative morphology in which all of the morphemes are realized according to their lexical specification. This section first outlines what numeral incorporation looks like in a number of signed languages and then homes in on three cases in which numeral incorporation is not fully realized, thereby revealing a number of phonological constraints on this morphological process. These constraints are shown to involve the complexity of articulation. They are language specific and language internal. They have analogues in spoken languages and in that sense are not necessarily modality specific.

Numeral Incorporation in Various Signed Languages

Rathmann and Mathur (2008a) conducted a preliminary survey of numeral incorporation in three signed languages: German Sign Language (DGS), American Sign Language (ASL), and Japanese Sign Language (Nihon Shuwa). For each one, they consulted two native or near-native Deaf signers. Due to the range of sociolinguistic factors present with any language, the survey focused on patterns within each individual. Thus, the data are not necessarily representative of the signed language as a whole. Given the limitations of the data, the aim of the survey was not so much to establish a comprehensive paradigm of numeral incorporation in each signed language as it was to understand the constraints that the data reveal.

The following data were elicited from each signer through nonverbal stimuli (i.e., Arabic numerals and images), which were presented in PowerPoint:

List (2) Stimuli Used for Survey of Numeral Incorporation

  (i) numerals: 1 through 20, 100, 200 . . . 900, 1,000

(ii) units of quantity:

'second'	'minute'	'hour'
'day'	'week'	'month'
'year'	'age'	'cent' (or equivalent)
'currency' (e.g., 'euro')	'grade/class'	'rank'
'ordinal'		

(iii) numerals combined with units of quantity

One author coded the data for the phonological parameters of handshape, orientation, location, and movement. The coder also noted whether numeral incorporation occurred and, if so, which numerals incorporate and which parameters change. (The other author coded 40 percent of the tokens with 97 percent agreement.)

The data reveal that signed languages vary with respect to the signs that incorporate numerals. For example, in DGS, the signs for 'ordinal,' 'currency,' 'hour,' 'week,' 'month,' 'year,' and 'age' incorporate numerals, while ASL incorporates numerals in all of the signs in (1) except for 'grade/class,' and Nihon Shuwa incorporates numerals in 'hundred,' 'rank,' 'minute,' 'hour,' 'day,' 'week,' and 'year.' It should be kept in mind that many other signs in these languages, which have not been included in the survey, may also incorporate numerals. Signed languages also vary with respect to the range of incorporated numerals. In DGS and Nihon Shuwa, most of the signs incorporate a range of numerals between 1 and 10 (so some signs may incorporate only up to 4 or 5, while others may incorporate up to 10), while in ASL, signs incorporate a range of numerals between 1 and 9 (that is, some signs may incorporate up to a certain number below 10 but rarely more than 9).

The schema for numeral incorporation is presented in figure 2.4 and follows the formalism of Fernald and Napoli (2000). The abbreviations *HS*, *Loc*, and *Mvt* stand for the parameters of handshape, location, and movement, respectively. For ease of presentation, orientation is not shown in figure 2.1. The subscripts indicate whether the parameters have different values. Thus, HS_a and HS_b refer to different handshapes. Figure 2.4 illustrates schematic representations of three signs: a numeral (such as DREI 'three' in DGS), a sign (such as WOCHE 'week'), and a sign incorporating the numeral (such as DREI+WOCHE 'three-week'), as illustrated in figure 2.5. The numeral DREI and the sign WOCHE have different values for all of the parameters, as indicated by the different subscripts. The sign with the incorporated numeral takes its handshape from the numeral DREI (indicated by the subscript *a*) and its location and movement from the sign WOCHE (indicated by the subscript *b*).

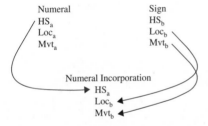

Figure 2.4. Complete numeral incorporation. The handshape of the numeral is substituted for the handshape of the sign.

When Numeral Incorporation Does Not Occur

As mentioned earlier, signed languages vary in whether they allow numeral incorporation for particular signs or numerals. The cross-linguistic variation reveals many cases where numeral incorporation is expected, given its appearance in other languages, but does not occur. For example, the sign for 'day' incorporates numerals in ASL and Nihon Shuwa but not in DGS. The sign for 'currency' incorporates numerals in DGS and ASL but not in Nihon Shuwa. Then, signs that allow numeral incorporation do so for numerals up to ten in DGS and Nihon Shuwa but only up to five or nine in ASL. If numeral incorporation does not occur, the numeral is usually signed in its entirety and is followed by the sign, or vice versa (e.g., DREI TAG 'three day' in DGS vs. *DREI+TAG 'three-day' and TEN DAY in ASL vs. *TEN+DAY; see figure 2.6).

The schema for these cases is presented in figure 2.7, which lists the parameters for the numeral separately from those of the sign. In contrast to the schema in figure 2.4, here there is no representation of a sign with an incorporated numeral.

In addition, the data reveal more complex cases: partial numeral incorporation. This phenomenon occurs when a numeral involves a sequence of two handshapes. Then only one part of the numeral is incorporated into the sign. A clear example comes from Nihon Shuwa: JUUNI+JIKAN 'twelve-hour' (figure 2.8a).

DREI+WOCHE

Figure 2.5. Example of numeral incorporation in DGS. The example means *three weeks*.

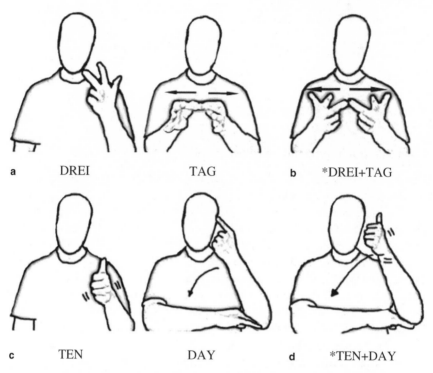

a	DREI	TAG	b	*DREI+TAG
c	TEN	DAY	d	*TEN+DAY

Figure 2.6. Examples of cases in DGS and ASL where numeral incorporation does not occur. The example (a) shows the correct form in DGS for *three days* as opposed to the incorrect form in (b). Likewise, the example (c) shows the correct form in ASL for *ten days* as opposed to the incorrect form in (d).

The numeral JUUNI 'twelve' has a sequence of two handshapes: an extended index finger bending and then extending back along with the middle finger. The sign JIKAN 'hour' has a sequence of two movements: the hand, palm down, rotates in a small circle above the nondominant wrist and then moves down to touch the wrist. In the incorporated form, the entire first part of the numeral is executed in its entirety, and then the second handshape of the numeral JUUNI, with the palm facing up, is incorporated into the location and movements of the sign JIKAN (figure 2.9). The subscripts and the arrows clarify which parts of the numeral and the sign are mapped into the incorporated form.

Numeral	Sign	
HS_a	HS_b	**Figure 2.7.** Absence of numeral incorporation. The
Loc_a	Loc_b	parameters of the numeral remain separate from
Mvt_a	Mvt_b	the parameters of the sign.

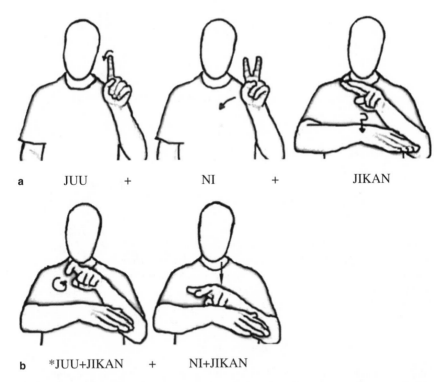

a   JUU   +   NI   +   JIKAN

b   *JUU+JIKAN   +   NI+JIKAN

Figure 2.8. Example of partial numeral incorporation in Nihon Shuwa. The example (a) shows the correct form in Nihon Shuwa for *twelve hours* as opposed to the incorrect form in (b).

While both the numeral and the sign have a sequence of two movements in the Nihon Shuwa example, only the fact that the numeral had two movements is relevant to our discussion of the partial numeral incorporation in JUUNI+JIKAN. Now we turn to an example of partial numeral incorporation where the relevant fact is that the sign rather than the numeral has a sequence of two movements. This case is exemplified by ASL TWO+YEAR (figure 2.10). The sign YEAR involves a sequence of two handshapes (the extended index finger and the closed fist) spread over two movements (a twist made from the radioulnar part of the arm overlaid with a closing of the fingers, followed by downward movement to the nondominant hand, which is a closed fist). The handshape of the numeral TWO (extended index and middle fingers) is incorporated into only the first movement of YEAR.

These examples from Nihon Shuwa and ASL contrast with the earlier examples of numeral incorporation (e.g., DGS DREI+WOCHE 'three-week'), in which the handshape of the numeral persists throughout the entire length of the sign.

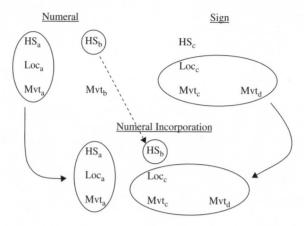

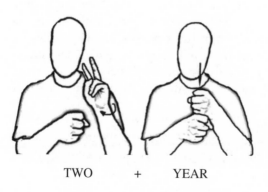

Figure 2.9. Partial numeral incorporation. The numeral has a sequence of two handshapes mapped onto two movements. The sign has one handshape and one location mapped onto two movements. In the incorporated form, the entire first part of the numeral is preserved, while the second handshape of the numeral is mapped onto the location and movement of the sign.

Phonological Constraints on Numeral Incorporation

Several cases have been identified in which numeral incorporation does not occur although it is expected, for example, DGS *DREI+TAG 'three-day' (figure 2.6b) and ASL *TEN+DAY (figure 2.6d). Examples of partial numeral incorporation have also been presented (e.g., Nihon Shuwa JUUNI+JIKAN 'twelve hour'). The next question is why complete numeral incorporation does not occur in these cases. Each example is discussed in turn. The following discussion is based on Rathmann and Mathur (2008a). For an alternative view of similar examples, see Liddell (1996), who treats numeral incorporation along with its gaps as "schemas that fall below the threshold of being able to sanction new expressions" (221).

TWO   +   YEAR

Figure 2.10. Example of partial numeral incorporation in ASL. The form means *two years.*

In the DGS example, TAG 'day' uses both hands in the same F handshape (all fingers extended and spread except for the index finger, which touches the thumb). The two hands initially touch each other at the index-thumb and then move away from each other. The lexical specification for this handshape is apparently fixed and cannot be rewritten by a morphological process such as numeral incorporation. This proposal is supported by another DGS example that has the same handshape as TAG and also does not incorporate numerals: MINUTE 'minute.' This one-handed sign is produced between the mouth and the cheek. Thus, one plausible reason for the absence of numeral incorporation is that the language requires that the lexical specification of the sign be preserved. One way to encode this requirement is to do so in the lexicon: Some signs are marked as allowing numeral incorporation. Those that are not marked as such do not allow it.

Another plausible reason is that TAG is a two-handed symmetric sign, and numeral incorporation does not seem to be available for two-handed symmetric signs. Indeed, none of the numeral-incorporating signs in our data are two-handed symmetric signs. Incorporating the numeral on both hands would appear redundant, and incorporating the numeral on just one hand would disrupt the symmetry of the sign. The first scenario (incorporating on both hands) could be barred by a constraint against redundancy, while the other scenario (incorporating on one hand) could be prevented by a constraint that preserves the lexical property of two-handed symmetry.

Determining which signs undergo numeral incorporation can depend on the iconicity of the sign. In Nihon Shuwa, YEN '(Japanese) currency' does not incorporate numerals at all, unlike DGS and ASL. The Nihon Shuwa sign YEN is iconic because it evokes the rectangular shape of the bill (more specifically the upper and lower edges of the bill) by moving the curved thumb and index finger, extended apart, through neutral space; that is, it builds on a size-and-shape-specifier (SASS) classifier. If the handshape of the sign were replaced with the handshape of a numeral, the iconicity would be lost. In this signer's idiolect, the preference to preserve the iconicity of the sign overrides the process of numeral incorporation. Preservation of iconicity can be argued to be a special case of preservation of a lexical specification on the assumption that iconic aspects are encoded through lexical specification of the values of certain parameters. It turns out that Nihon Shuwa uses another sign with the same meaning of YEN that is not as iconic and does incorporate numerals (personal communication, Soya Mori, June 2009). Furthermore, ASL has a comparable scenario: DOLLAR does not incorporate numerals, but ASL has another sign with the same meaning that involves twisting the radioulnar part of the arm and does allow numeral incorporation.

Now consider the ASL example *TEN+DAY. Why does DAY allow the incorporation of numerals up to nine but not of ten and above? DAY is made by moving the dominant hand, palm facing the body, downward to contact the flat, nondominant arm. The numerals ONE through NINE involve presenting a hand configuration in the neutral area (i.e., not on the face or body). The numeral TEN is different, however: In addition to presenting a specific hand configuration in the neutral area (closed fist with extended thumb pointing up), it also involves a trilled movement in the form of twisting the radioulnar part of the arm repeatedly. The trilled movement is a distinctive part of the numeral TEN and cannot be sacrificed when it is incorporated into another sign. However, overlaying the trilled movement with the movement required by DAY leads to a complex movement that, while physically possible, is not tolerated in the frozen lexicon. Thus, a phonological constraint against complex movement seems to rule out forms like *TEN+DAY. The constraint also explains why signs like DAY do not incorporate numerals above TEN since, in ASL, all of these numerals involve complex movement as well. In contrast, the numerals ONE through NINE do not involve a trilled movement or any other lexically specified movement that must be preserved, with the result that the constraint does not apply to them when they are incorporated into DAY and other signs.

The proposal of this constraint receives support from further evidence in DGS, which allows the incorporation of numerals up to ten. The numerals in this language are different in a crucial way from those in the other signed languages discussed here. For example, EIN 'one' is made with the extended thumb of a fist, and SECHS 'six' is made with both hands: The nondominant hand extends all fingers while the dominant hand extends the thumb. ZEHN 'ten' is made with both hands extending all fingers. These numerals do not have any special type of movement other than a slight straight movement in the neutral area. Therein lies the difference: TEN in ASL has a trilled movement that prevents it from being incorporated, but ZEHN 'ten' in DGS does not and thus can be incorporated. Numerals above ten in DGS, however, have a complex movement and are not incorporated due to the very same phonological constraint that bars ASL TEN and above from being incorporated.

The last example under consideration, Nihon Shuwa JUUNI+JIKAN 'twelve-hour,' involves partial incorporation (figure 2.8a). Recall that JUUNI 'twelve' has two parts: an extended index finger (accompanied by bending) and then extended index and middle fingers. The first part may correspond to JUU 'ten,' and the latter part to NI 'two.' The incorporated form has three parts: The first part shows the handshape and movement of JUU; the second part shows the handshape of NI (palm up) and the first half of the movement for JIKAN 'hour' (circular movement above the nondominant wrist); the third part continues with the handshape of NI and the second half of the movement for JIKAN (downward to the wrist). Theoretically, the handshape of JUU could be incorporated into the first half of the movement for JIKAN, and then the handshape of NI could be incorporated into the second half (figure 2.8b). That is, the first handshape of JUUNI could be mapped onto the first movement of JIKAN, and the second handshape of JUUNI could be mapped onto the second movement of JIKAN. This putative form would incorporate both handshapes of the numeral JUUNI into the sign JIKAN and be more similar to the cases of complete numeral incorporation. However, this form does not occur; rather, only the second handshape of the numeral is incorporated into the entire movement sequence of JIKAN. An examination of JUU explains why. The numeral involves a bending movement that is lexically specified and must be preserved in order to distinguish it from the sign ICHI 'one,' which has the same handshape. Incorporating JUU into the first half of JIKAN would result in complex movement, violating the same phonological constraint that rules out some cases of numeral incorporation in DGS and ASL. To avoid violating that constraint, the language prefers a form that presents JUU separately and then incorporates NI, with palm orientation up, into JIKAN.

Thus far, two kinds of phonological constraints explain why complete numeral incorporation does not always occur. First, a constraint that preserves lexical specifications (such as marked handshape) prevents some signs from incorporating numerals at all. Second, a constraint against the complexity of movement prevents some numerals with special movement from being incorporated. These two cases exemplify different kinds of constraints: The first is akin to faithfulness constraints in the sense of Optimality Theory (Prince and Smolensky 1993; McCarthy and Prince 1993), which preserve properties of the lexical input, while the second is analogous to markedness constraints, which ensure that the structure of the word is well formed. While the particular content of the phonological constraints may differ from those seen in spoken languages due to different articulatory systems, the general nature of these constraints is remarkably similar to those in spoken languages, suggesting that numeral incorporation is a familiar type of nonconcatenative morphology that is subject to the usual language-internal constraints.

VERB AGREEMENT

In the second type of nonconcatenative morphology, at least one of the morphemes is realized through interaction with gestural space. The present section illustrates this type with verb agreement. After describing the nature of verb agreement in several signed languages, the section presents three cases in which the target form of verb agreement is not realized. These cases suggest a number of phonological constraints on the morphological process of verb agreement, some of which are shown to relate to the degree of articulation. It is difficult to imagine analogues in spoken languages since the constraints are triggered only when there is potential to exceed the limits of the articulatory system due to interaction with gestural space, and it is this interaction that is unique to the signed modality.

Verb Agreement in Signed Languages

Using similar methodology as that of the survey of numeral incorporation, in Mathur and Rathmann (2006) we examine verb agreement in four signed languages: DGS, ASL, Nihon Shuwa, and Australian Sign Language (Auslan). Again, we consulted two native or near-native Deaf signers for each signed language. The same caveat applies here: The individual signers' patterns do not necessarily generalize to the signed language as used by the community.

To elicit relevant data, we (2006) drew on a master list of seventy-nine verbs with different meanings (as encoded by English glosses) that we originally compiled in Mathur and Rathmann (2001, 26). With the assistance of a consultant in some cases, signs were collected in each language that came close to the meaning of the English glosses in the master list. This methodology allows comparison of agreement forms in verbs with similar meaning in a number of signed languages. Visual aids were used to elicit several agreement forms for each verb. Figure 2.11 shows an example of a visual aid that is designed to elicit an agreement form marking a first-person singular subject and a non-first-person singular direct object, as in *I asked her* (figure 2.2).

For each verb, five agreement forms were elicited. Their schematic forms are illustrated in figure 2.12. The agreement form in figure 2.12a (roughly meaning 'she [left]-to-him [right]' or, more formally, marking non-first-person singular subject and non-first-person singular direct object) requires a significant change in the hand orientation that could clash with the phonological form of the verb. Note in the visual aid that the arrow goes from left to right from the signer's perspective. The direction of the arrow indicates that the area on the left is to be associated with the referent of the subject (*she*) and the area on the right is to be associated with the referent of the direct object (*him*). The associations between the areas of gestural space and the referents usually occur in discourse, but during the elicitation the participants were asked to assume the associations pictured in the visual aid. Thus, the arrow is intended to trigger a specific interaction with gestural space. (Note that the arrow is not intended to indicate the direction of the hand movement.)

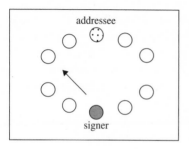

Figure 2.11. Example of a visual aid used for elicitation of an agreement form. One circle, marked in color, represents the signer, while another circle, marked in a different color, represents the addressee. The other circles, which lack color, represent other individuals. The arrow indicates the requested agreement form, for example, a form for a first person singular subject and a non-first person singular direct object.

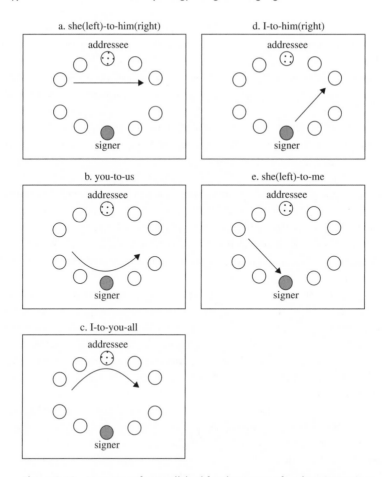

Figure 2.12. Agreement forms elicited for the survey of verb agreement.

Sometimes a verb does not realize a particular agreement form. There are two possible reasons. There could be a morphological gap in the paradigm of the verb, or there could be a phonological/phonetic reason. To rule out the possibility of a morphological gap, we investigated whether the verb can realize two other similar forms: (i) the form shown in figure 2.12d ('I-to-him [right]' or, formally, first-person singular subject and non-first-person singular direct object), and (ii) the form shown in figure 2.12e ('she [left]-to-me' or non-first-person singular subject and first-person singular direct object). If a verb can realize a form marking a non-first-person singular direct object and a form marking a non-first-person singular subject, the verb should also realize a form marking both (i.e., the 'she-to-him' form), so if such a form is absent, the explanation is likely phonological or phonetic rather than morphological. At the same time, it should be kept in mind that the realization of verb agreement, even if it is phonologically or phonetically possible, is not always required but rather optional and often dependent on discourse-related factors (see Rathmann 2000; Rathmann and Mathur 2008b).

The next agreement form (figure 2.12b) is used for 'you-to-us' cases (i.e., for a non-first-person singular subject and a first-person plural direct object). The plural number is indicated by an arc in the visual aid, which is located near the signer since the direct object is first person. The arc may interact with the lexical movement of the verb in certain ways. In addition, the palms must be oriented to face the signer in order to mark the first-person feature of the object. Changing the hand orientation and adding an arc movement may result in a complex phonological form. The controls for this form are the 'she (left)-to-me' (figure 2.12e) and the 'I-to-you-all' (figure 2.12c) forms (the latter is described later). If a verb can realize these two forms, then it is morphologically able to modulate for a non-first-person singular subject, a first-person object, and a plural object (i.e., the 'you-to-us' form).

Another agreement form (figure 2.12c) occurs in an 'I-to-you-all' context (formally, a first-person singular subject and non-first-person plural direct object). This form is included in the survey because the plural number of the direct object is realized by an arc movement in the area associated with the referent of the direct object. This arc movement, notated in the visual aid by an arc located near the addressee, has the potential to interact with the lexical movement of the verb in phonologically interesting ways. The controls for this form are the form for 'I-to-him' (figure 2.12d) and the form for 'you-to-us' (figure 2.12b and discussed earlier). If a verb realizes both forms but not the 'I-to-you-all' form, the absence is probably due to phonological or phonetic factors rather than morphology.

The data were coded as follows. We split the data between us and recorded the handshape(s), orientation, location, manner, direction, and path shape of the verb movement. Then we noted whether the verb showed the expected agreement form. If it did not, we put down the form that was used instead. There was high intercoder reliability (96 percent agreement in half of the data from ASL).

The data reveal two general patterns. First, many verbs in all of the signed languages show some or all of the agreement forms in figure 2.12. This pattern suggests that the agreement forms are not specific to one signed language and appear to be common across several signed languages. It is well possible that the uniformity of the signed languages with respect to the realization of the agreement forms is tied to interaction with gestural space, which they all have in common and which is required for the realization of some agreement forms. At the same time, there is another pattern: Some verbs fail to realize an agreement form when it is otherwise predicted by the morphological paradigm, as well as cross-linguistic comparison with other signed languages. These cases vary from one signed language to another depending on the particular verb and the particular agreement form, suggesting that the absence of an agreement form is tied to phonological or phonetic properties within the language.

When Verb Agreement Does Not Occur

This section presents three cases in which an agreement form is semantically and morphologically expected but not realized. The first case involves the agreement form for 'she (left)-to-him (right).' The DGS verb FRAGEN 'ask' realizes this form: For a right-handed signer, the right hand is in the F handshape (index finger contacts the thumb, with the other fingers extended and spread) and moves from left to right in the gestural space. Figure 2.13a illustrates the corresponding form for a left-handed signer. This verb realizes the agreement form through the direction of movement of the hands, which matches the arrow in the form. Some verbs in other signed languages also realize the form fully (e.g., ASL SHOW, Auslan ANSWER, and Nihon Shuwa CHUUI SURU 'advise'). (For more examples, see Mathur and Rathmann 2006, who also provide further examples for the cases discussed later.) In contrast, the ASL verb ASK must realize agreement forms through a change in palm orientation along with a change in the direction of movement of the hands. To realize the 'she (left)-to-him (right)' form of the verb, right-handed signers would have to twist their arm and hand awkwardly so that the hand in the shape of an extended finger is situated at the left, with the palm facing the right, and then moves toward the right as the extended finger bends into a crooked finger (figure 2.13b). The angle of the arm is so awkward that the signer opts to drop this form in favor of one that is easier to produce: The right palm faces the right area but is now

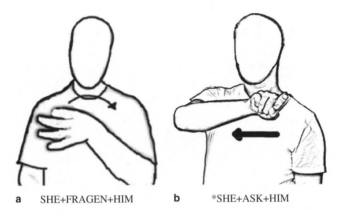

a   SHE+FRAGEN+HIM   b   *SHE+ASK+HIM

Figure 2.13. Examples of the *she*+VERB+*him* agreement form that either occur or do not occur. The example (a) shows a form from DGS that means *she asks him (something)*, whereas (b) shows the corresponding form in ASL that does not occur.

placed near the signer, such that the form no longer marks the non-first-person singular feature of the subject. That is, the right hand does not move across the gestural space from the contralateral to the ipsilateral side but instead is located near the signer's body to start with and moves rightward. The other signed languages have examples that behave like ASL ASK: DGS VERSPOTTEN 'tease,' Auslan CONTACT, and Nihon Shuwa DAMASU 'deceive.'

Now let's turn to the second case, which concerns the agreement form for 'you-to-us.' The same example from ASL, SHOW, is able to realize this form completely: The right hand touches the upright palm of the left hand—facing right—on the fingertip of the extended index finger, and the two hands move as a unit in an arc near the addressee (see figure 2.14a). Other signed languages have examples that work similarly in principle: DGS GEBEN 'give' and Auslan ANSWER. (The plural number is not attested in the data that we have on Nihon Shuwa.) Yet, other verbs do not realize the form completely. One example is ASL ANALYZE (figure 2.14b). This two-handed sign is symmetrical: The two arms are raised, the index and middle fingers are spread and crooked (while the other fingers are closed), and the hands move down in sync as the fingers wiggle. To realize the 'you-to-us' form, the palms would have to face the signer and move in an arc toward the signer. This places a strain on the nondominant arm, which has to twist at an awkward angle at the beginning of the arc. Instead, some signers choose to realize the form in a simpler way by dropping the arc and just having the palms face the signer and then using context (e.g., pronouns) to clarify the plural feature of the direct

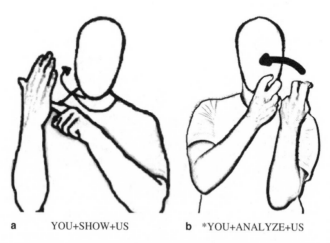

a   YOU+SHOW+US   b   *YOU+ANALYZE+US

Figure 2.14. Examples of the *you*+VERB+*us* agreement form that either occur or do not occur. The example (a) shows a form from ASL that means *you show us (something)*, whereas (b) shows the same form that does not occur in ASL, meaning *you analyze us*.

object. Other examples that work similarly are DGS VERSPOTTEN 'tease' and Auslan ABANDON.

The last case relates to the agreement form for 'I-to-you-all.' One example that realizes the form is ASL TEST, which looks like ASL ASK with two differences: (i) It is two handed and symmetrical, with both palms facing the addressee, and (ii) the fingers crook repeatedly as they move downward (in contrast, in ASK, the hands move away from the signer in the uninflected form). The repetition of downward movement is preserved in the 'I-to-you-all' form: The hands move up and down repeatedly as they proceed along an arc toward the addressee (figure 2.15a). Other similar examples are DGS VERSPOTTEN 'tease' and Auslan CONTACT. However, ASL ASK realizes the form somewhat differently. With the palm facing the addressee, the extended index finger is crooked once as it is moved in an arc toward the addressee. In theory, the index finger could have crooked repeatedly while moving along the arc, like in TEST, but this is not attested in the particular form under discussion. There is a preference for crooking the finger just once over the arc rather than repeatedly even when the latter option is seen in other verbs like TEST (figure 2.15b). Examples that realize the form without repeated movement include DGS GEBEN 'give' and Auslan ANSWER.

These cases show that for all of the signed languages in the survey, some verbs do not realize certain agreement forms when they are predicted to do so, suggesting that there are phonological or phonetic constraints in place on the realization of agreement.

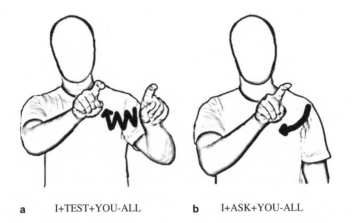

a   I+TEST+YOU-ALL   b   I+ASK+YOU-ALL

Figure 2.15. Examples of the *I+VERB+you-all* agreement form that either involve repeated movement or do not. The example (a) shows a form with repeated movement from meaning means *I tested you all*, whereas (b) shows an example of the same form without repeated movement in ASL, meaning *I asked you all*.

Phonological Constraints on Verb Agreement

Let's consider the nature of the phonological or phonetic constraints on the realization of agreement in each case, starting with the 'she-to-him' form. Some verbs in each of the signed languages do not realize this form because it would require pronating the arm at an awkward angle so that the palm faces the left area of gestural space (see figure 2.13b for an example from ASL). Here, pronation refers to twisting the forearm (the part of the arm between the elbow and the wrist) so that the thumb side of the right palm faces left. There is then a phonological/phonetic constraint against pronating the arm so far (roughly, more than ninety degrees if zero degrees refers to the state in which the right palm faces to the left). The constraint is rooted in the degree of articulation, that is, how far an articulator can be pronated, which in turn depends on the physiological limits of the articulator itself.

A similar kind of constraint applies to the realization of the 'you-to-us' form. In the example given, ASL ANALYZE (figure 2.14b), the nondominant arm is supinated at an awkward angle in order for the palm to face the signer and initiate an arc movement. Supination is the opposite of pronation and means that the forearm twists in such a way that the thumb side of the right palm faces right. This case suggests a phonological/phonetic constraint against supination that exceeds the physiological limits of the articulator. The limits seem to be same as in the constraint on pronation: approximately no more than ninety degrees in the opposite direction if zero degrees is taken to be the state in which the right palm faces to the left.

A different kind of constraint applies to the 'I-to-you-all' form of ASL ASK (figure 2.15b). Recall that the finger crooking happens just once instead of multiple times throughout the arc movement. The single instance of finger crooking seems to indicate a preference to keep the movement as minimal as possible. That is, in the absence of any lexical specification, the movement should consist of a single action of the arm, which may be overlaid with a single movement of the fingers. The constraint may be overridden if there is a lexical specification for movement that must be preserved, as in the case of TEST, which involves a repeated downward movement along with the finger crooking. The example of TEST shows that the constraint is not absolute and that its application depends on the lexical properties of the morphemes. This type of constraint is not rooted in the physiological limits of the articulatory system but rather ensures production with the minimal possible movement of language-specific properties encoded in the lexicon. The example of ASK then illustrates that the realization of verb agreement is subject to constraints on the complexity of articulation, just like the realization of numeral incorporation. However, there is an important difference: The realization of verb agreement is also constrained by the degree of articulation, whereas the realization of numeral incorporation does not seem to interact with such constraints.

The constraints on supination and pronation look similar enough that they may well be collapsed into a more general constraint on the rotation of the arm in any direction. This constraint could fall under a family of constraints that have a common basis in the degree of articulation. The constraints would pertain to movements of the hand/arm in general, including not only rotation but also extension and flexion. There is further evidence for this family of constraints from examples marking the plural number of the direct object by an arc movement (e.g., the 'you-to-us' and 'I-to-you-all' forms). Imagine an audience facing a signer. The signer could sign 'I ask you all' by signing a large arc movement that traces the entire audience. However, the signer can sign only so large an arc movement. Suppose the audience is in a circular auditorium. The signer is now facing just half of the audience but is still talking to the entire audience. The signer cannot flex and extend her arm so much so that the arc movement traces the entire audience in a circle around her. The signer would need to adopt a different strategy and perhaps simply turn to face the other half of the audience and repeat the arc movement.

Constraints on degree of articulation receive cross-linguistic support. They appear in all of the signed languages studied. The universality of the constraints follows from their roots in the limits of the articulatory system, which is common to all of the signed languages. Moreover, the interaction of such constraints with morphological processes seems unique to signed languages. It is difficult to construct analogous examples in spoken languages where the application of a morphological process is directly constrained by the physiological limits of the articulatory system. On the other hand, in signed languages, morphological processes like verb agreement sometimes require interaction with gestural space for their realization. This interaction, which is modality specific, allows such a wide range of possibilities that the morphological realization is necessarily constrained by the limits of the articulatory system.

The interaction with gestural space explains the difference between two types of nonconcatenative morphology in signed languages. One type, exemplified by numeral incorporation, does not require interaction with gestural space and is thus not affected by constraints on degree of articulation. The other type, illustrated by verb agreement, requires interaction with gestural space for the most part and is consequently subject to degree constraints.

OTHER MORPHOLOGICAL PROCESSES

Other morphological processes in signed languages fall into one of the two types outlined in earlier sections, supporting our proposed typology of nonconcatenative morphology in signed languages. In particular, aspectual modulations belong to the same type as numeral incorporation since they do not require interaction with gestural space for realization, while some classifier constructions pattern with verb agreement owing to the fact that they can be realized in a potentially infinite number of ways due to their interaction with gestural space.

Klima and Bellugi (1979) conducted the first extensive analysis of aspectual modulations in ASL. In Rathmann's (2005) follow-up study of the aspectual system in ASL and other signed languages, six aspectual morphemes are recognized, five of which are bound morphemes in that they affect the manner of movement of the verb. For example, the continuative morpheme often lengthens or stretches the movement of the verb, while the iterative morpheme reduplicates it, and the hold morpheme truncates it. This is a preliminary description. The actual realization of an aspectual morpheme depends on the lexical properties of a verb, so that there may be several phonological variants of the morpheme (i.e., allomorphs). Rathmann (2005) focuses on the semantic and syntactic properties of the morphemes, leaving their precise phonological characterization open to future research. It would be worthwhile to examine the phonological and phonetic constraints on the realization of aspectual morphemes. For example, the continuative morpheme lengthens the movement of some stems by repeating the movement in a circular pattern. What happens if the verb already has a repeated movement of its own, like ASL WALK? In this example, instead of repeating the movement in a circular pattern, the timing of each repeated movement is lengthened. Since the realization of aspectual morphemes affects the manner of movement and does not depend on interaction with gestural space, it is predicted that they will pattern like numeral incorporation and that constraints on their realization will concern complexity, not degree, of articulation.

While numeral incorporation and aspectual morphology are both predicted to belong to the same type of nonconcatenative morphology, one difference between the two processes deserves mention. Numeral incorporation seems comparable to compounding processes in their evolution. First, there are cases in which no numeral incorporation occurs; instead, a sign and a numeral are concatenated, just as the ASL compound TOMATO might have originally been signed as RED+SLICE-ROUND-OBJECT. Then there is partial numeral incorporation, as in the Nihon Shuwa example of JUUNI+JIKAN 'twelve-hour,' which is reminiscent of (partial) phonological fusion and only partly concatenative. Analogously, in a latter variant of the compound TOMATO, the first sign may assimilate its palm orientation to that of the second sign. Finally, there is full phonological fusion of the numeral's handshape with the sign's other parameters, which process may be considered as nonconcatenative and analogous to some current forms of TOMATO that have lost their resemblance to the original form by assimilating the handshape of the second sign to that of the first. The overall point is that numeral incorporation seems to be a case of nonconcatenative morphology that has arisen from concatenative morphology.

In contrast, it is not obvious how aspectual morphology might have originated from concatenative morphology. Rather, it is possible that some of aspectual morphology has iconic roots. Rathmann (2005, 66) raises the possibility that "the aspectual morphemes involving reduplication are originally rooted in ideophones." For example, the iterative morpheme involves reduplicating the movement of the verb stem, which mirrors the meaning of the morpheme (that an event has occurred repeatedly). Nevertheless, while numeral incorporation and aspectual morphology may spring from different sources, they still fall under the type of nonconcatenative morphology that does not draw on gestural space.

With respect to several types of classifier constructions, we expect them to fall under the same type of nonconcatenative morphology as verb agreement (i.e., nonconcatenative morphology that draws on gestural space). If that is the case, there should be classifier-construction examples that exhibit constraints on degree of articulation, and there seem to be many.

One such example is the use of entity classifiers to describe the spatial relationship between two vehicles. In ASL, the two hands are in the 3 handshape (i.e., the thumb, the index finger, and the middle finger are extended, and the other fingers are closed). They have a midway palm orientation (i.e., the top side of the index finger is above the bottom side of the pinky). This combination of handshape and orientation marks the vehicle class in ASL. The hands can be placed in different positions in gestural space to indicate the spatial relationship of the vehicles. For example, the palms can face each other to show that two vehicles are parked side by side, as in a parking lot. The right hand can be placed in front of the left hand to signify that one vehicle is parked in front of the other one, say, on a narrow street. Gestural space in fact offers infinitely many ways to locate the two hands relative to each other depending on the intended meaning. However, as with verb agreement, the possibilities are restricted by the limits of the articulatory system. If a signer wishes to describe two vehicles whose rear bumpers are touching, the two hands would have to be oriented at an awkward angle so that the heels of the hands are touching. A constraint against excessive pronation would rule out this form and favor another strategy such as orienting the hands in a different but more comfortable way that still depicts the same scenario, for example, by having the right fingertips point forward and the left fingertips point toward the signer and making the heel of the right palm touch the base of the back of the left hand. This example suggests that classifier constructions are subject to constraints on degree of articulation and thus fall under the second type of nonconcatenative morphology.

REVISITING SIGNED LANGUAGE MORPHOLOGY AND PHONOLOGY

This chapter has argued that there are two types of nonconcatenative morphology in signed languages. This claim can be broadened to say that there are two types of morphology. One type interacts with gestural space and includes a narrow set of morphological processes that appears only in signed languages. The other type includes the rest of morphology: nonconcatenative morphology in signed languages that does not interact with gestural space, concatenative morphology in signed languages, and all morphology in spoken languages, including both nonconcatenative and concatenative. It is interaction with gestural space that sets apart the two types of morphology. This interaction, by allowing infinitely many possibilities, triggers constraints on the degree of articulation. Since such interaction is unique to signed languages, the application of constraints on degree of articulation is specific to the signed modality. Constraints on the complexity of articulation apply to both types and appear in both modalities.

One issue remains open for future study. Why do the phonetic and phonological constraints under discussion look similar across signed languages? Granted, there are phonotactic constraints governing possible combinations of handshapes, locations, and movements that are language specific. At the same time, this chapter has demonstrated a constraint on the degree of articulation that appears in all of the signed languages studied. It has also shown a constraint on the complexity of articulation, specifically on complex movement, that appears in these languages. It is possible that the constraints have emerged to balance the many degrees of freedom offered in a signed language morphology. First, interaction with gestural space allows a large number of possibilities that are limited by the articulatory system and are encoded in constraints on degree of articulation. Second, the articulatory system itself allows many ways to create a sign: The large inventory of handshapes, locations, and movements results in an even larger set of possible combinations that can become physiologically unwieldy to use. Constraints on the complexity of articulation help to refine the set into one that can be easily produced and understood.

Bibliography

Aronoff, Mark, Irit Meir, and Wendy Sandler. 2005. The Paradox of Sign Language Morphology. *Language* 81: 301–344.

Fernald, Ted, and Donna Jo Napoli. 2000. Exploitation of Morphological Possibilities in Signed Languages. *Sign Language and Linguistics* 3: 3–58.

Halle, Morris, and Alec Marantz. 1993. Distributed Morphology and the Pieces of Inflection. In *The View from Building 20: Essays in Linguistics in Honor of Sylvain Bromberger*, ed. Kenneth Hale and Samuel Jay Keyser, 111–176. Cambridge, Mass.: MIT Press.

Kendon, Adam. 2004. *Gesture: Visible Action as Utterance*. New York: Cambridge University Press.

Klima, Edward, and Ursula Bellugi. 1979. *Signs of language*. Cambridge, Mass.: Harvard University Press.

Liddell, Scott. 1990. Four Functions of a Locus: Re-examining the Structure of Space in ASL. In *Sign Language Research: Theoretical Issues*, ed. Ceil Lucas, 176–198. Washington, D.C.: Gallaudet University Press.

———. 1995. Real, Surrogate, and Token Space: Grammatical Consequences in ASL. In *Language, Gesture, and Space*, ed. Karen Emmorey and Judy Reilly, 19–42. Hillsdale, NJ: Erlbaum.

———. 1996. Numeral Incorporating Roots and Non-incorporating Prefixes in American Sign Language. *Sign Language Studies* 92: 201–226.

———. 2000. Indicating Verbs and Pronouns: Pointing Away from Agreement. In *The Signs of Language Revisited: An Anthology to Honor Ursula Bellugi and Edward Klima*, ed. Harlan Lane and Karen Emmorey, 303–320. Mahwah, NJ: Erlbaum.

———. 2003. *Grammar, Gesture, and Meaning in American Sign Language*. New York: Cambridge University Press.

———, and Robert Johnson. 1986. American Sign Language Compound Formation Processes, Lexicalization, and Phonological Remnants. *Natural Language and Linguistic Theory* 4: 445–513.

Lillo-Martin, Diane. 1986. Two Kinds of Null Arguments in American Sign Language. *Natural Language and Linguistic Theory* 4: 415–444.

———. 1991. *Universal Grammar and American Sign Language: Setting the Null Argument Parameters*. Dordrecht: Kluwer Academic.

———. 2002. Where Are All the Modality Effects? In *Modality and Structure in Signed and Spoken Languages*, ed. Richard Meier, Kearsy Cormier, and David Quinto-Pozos, 241–262. New York: Cambridge University Press.

Mathur, Gaurav. 2000. Verb Agreement as Alignment in Signed Languages. PhD diss., Massachusetts Institute of Technology.

———, and Christian Rathmann. 2001. Why Not GIVE-US: An Articulatory Constraint in Signed Languages. In *Signed Languages: Discoveries from International Research*, ed. Valerie Dively, Melanie Metzger, Sarah Taub, and Anne-Marie Baer, 1–26. Washington, D.C.: Gallaudet University Press.

———. 2006. Variability in Verbal Agreement Forms across Four Signed Languages. In *Papers from Laboratory Phonology VIII: Varieties of Phonological Competence*, ed. Louis Goldstein, Catherine T. Best, and Doug Whalen, 285–314. The Hague: Mouton.

McCarthy, John. 1982. *Formal Problems in Semitic Phonology and Morphology*. New York: Garland.

———, and Alan Prince. 1993. Prosodic Morphology I: Constraint Interaction and Satisfaction. Ms., University of Massachusetts at Amherst and Rutgers University, New Brunswick, NJ.

McNeill, David. 2000. *Language and Gesture: Window into Thought and Action*. New York: Cambridge University Press.

Meier, Richard. 1982. Icons, Analogues, and Morphemes: The Acquisition of Verb Agreement in American Sign Language. PhD diss., University of California at San Diego.

———. 1990. Person Deixis in American Sign Language. In *Theoretical Issues In Sign Language Research*. Vol. 1, *Linguistics*, ed. Susan Fischer and Patricia Siple, 175–190. Chicago: University of Chicago Press.

———. 2002. The Acquisition of Verb Agreement: Pointing Out Arguments for the Linguistic Status of Agreement in Signed Languages. In *Directions In Sign Language Acquisition*, ed. Gary Morgan and Bencie Woll, 115–141. Amsterdam: Benjamins.

Meir, Irit. 1998. Thematic Structure and Verb Agreement in Israeli Sign Language. PhD diss., Hebrew University of Jerusalem.

———. 2002. A Cross-modality Perspective on Verb Agreement. *Natural Language and Linguistic Theory* 20: 413–450.

Padden, Carol. 1983. Interaction of Morphology and Syntax in American Sign Language. PhD diss., University of California at San Diego.

Perlmutter, David. 2006. Some Current Claims about Sign Language Phonetics, Phonology, and Experimental Results. In *Papers from Laboratory Phonology VIII: Varieties of Phonological Competence*, ed. Louis Goldstein, Catherine T. Best, and Doug Whalen, 315–338. The Hague: Mouton.

Pfau, Roland, and Markus Steinbach. 2006. Pluralization in Sign and Speech: A Cross-modal Typological Study. *Linguistic Typology* 10: 135–182.

Prince, Alan, and Paul Smolensky. 1993. Optimality Theory: Constraint Interaction in Generative Grammar. Ms., Rutgers University, New Brunswick, NJ, and the University of Colorado at Boulder.

Rathmann, Christian. 2000. The Optionality of Agreement Phrase: Evidence from German Sign Language. Qualifying paper, University of Texas at Austin.

———. 2005. Event Structure in American Sign Language. PhD diss., University of Texas at Austin.

———, and Gaurav Mathur. 1999. The Linguistic Status of Joint-based Constraints in Signed Languages. Paper presented at the thirty-fifth annual meeting of the Chicago Linguistic Society (CLS 35), University of Chicago, April 1999.

———. 2002. Is Verb Agreement Different Cross-modally? In *Modality and Structure in Signed and Spoken Languages*, ed. Richard P. Meier, Kearsy Cormier, and David Quinto-Pozos, 370–404. New York: Cambridge University Press.

———. 2008a. Constraints on Numeral Incorporation in Signed Languages. Invited presentation at the first SignTyp Conference at the University of Connecticut, Storrs, June 2008.

———. 2008b. Verb Agreement as a Linguistic Innovation in Signed Languages. In *Signs of the Time: Selected Papers from TISLR 2004*, ed. Josep Quer, 191–216. Hamburg: Signum.

Sandler, Wendy. 1989. *Phonological Representation of the Sign*. Dordrecht: Foris.

———, and Diane Lillo-Martin. 2006. *Sign Language and Linguistic Universals*. New York: Cambridge University Press.

Spencer, Andrew. 1991. *Morphological Theory*. Oxford: Blackwell.

Supalla, Ted. 2004. The Validity of the Gallaudet Lecture Films. *Sign Language Studies* 4(3): 261–292.

CHAPTER 2 RESPONSE

Some Observations on Form-Meaning Correspondences in Two Types of Verbs in ASL

Paul G. Dudis

INTRODUCTION

This chapter describes observations of a feature that is potentially unique to signed languages. It is related to the one discussed in Mathur and Rathmann (chapter 2, this volume; henceforth M&R), that is, the required use of gestural space by agreement verbs. The feature of interest is more directly associated with *visual imagery* (a term used in DeMatteo 1977 and explicitly reintroduced in Liddell and Vogt-Svendsen 2007). Because visual imagery is manifested in the gestures of nonsigners, and gesture and language are generally viewed as distinct systems, one might think that direct ties to imagery determine the non-linguistic status of a component of a given expression. The present chapter discusses how this might not necessarily be the case. Many signed language expressions that would be analyzed as instances of nonconcatenative morphology (M&R and others) exhibit manifestations of visual imagery. Such imagery is exhibited by all classifier predicates, which are generally viewed as being at least in part linguistic, typically with full linguistic status accorded to the classifier handshape. It is also exhibited in some ASL aspectual constructions (Dudis 2004b), which can have as a component a sign that does not manifest imagery.

Later I describe a version of Liddell's analysis of indicating verbs (termed "agreement verbs" or "agreeing verbs" in other analyses, including M&R's), whose characteristic directionality can be described as arising from a correspondence between components in the phonological and semantic structures. This correspondence is in large part what makes indicating verbs unique to signed languages. I then describe different correspondences underlying various types of visual imagery and discuss how this type of correspondence makes the structure of classifier predicates and aspectual constructions unique to signed languages as well.

VISUAL IMAGERY AND DEPICTION

Visual imagery is prevalent in signed languages and is often associated with what are popularly known as role-shifting and classifier predicates. It can be described as arising via correspondences between components of a situation being described and components within the signer's immediate circumstances, which include the body and space. For example, during a description of what people do on amusement park rides, the signer could raise both arms in the air and wear a certain facial expression. Here the signer is representing the actions of riders using not just the arms and face but much of the body as well, and, therefore, via a body-for-body correspondence (see Taub 2001 for an overview of various iconic correspondences). The representation is understandable to anyone who has had experience with roller-coasters and the like, the motivation of this form-meaning pairing assumedly being so apparent that one need not rely very heavily on context to decipher it.

For various reasons, the representation just described is an example of an expression that would likely be judged to not have the status of a linguistic unit. It might be described as constructed action (Winston 1992; Metzger 1995) or even imagistic gesture (McNeill 1992). As such, visual imagery is not unique to signed languages. However, what seems unique is that some linguistic units in signed languages are tied to visual imagery.

Analysis of the conceptual work underlying visual imagery in signed languages has been conducted by Liddell (1998, 2003) using Fauconnier and Turner's (1994, 2002) conceptual blending framework. The basic analysis has components of different conceptual domains, one of which is associated with the signer's perception of immediate circumstances (termed "real space" in Liddell 1995) integrated into a third domain. A simplified blending analysis of the representation of the rider described earlier would include the concepts of 'rider' and 'car' within the frame of amusement park riding, which is part of the domain created during discourse to describe the event. These concepts are mapped onto the signer's body and certain portions of the surrounding space, respectively. Projection of these concepts into a third domain, the blend, creates "signer as rider" and "space as amusement park ride environment."

A variety of cues indicate the activation of this blend, including eye gaze, facial expression, and other bodily actions, all of which demonstrate (in the sense of Clark and Gerrig 1990) the rider's actions. As Dudis (2007) discusses, bringing to the analysis other real-space elements in addition to the signer/ body and space allows for greater precision in the identification of several varieties of real-space blends. As a result, it is possible to distinguish between blends created to describe settings and those created to describe events. The basis for this distinction is the essential role in the latter of temporal components within the domains, including real time, that is, the progression of time (Dudis 2004b). This is discussed further later on.

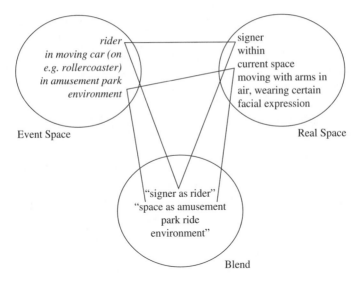

Figure 2R.1. A simplified blending analysis of the representation of a rider experiencing an amusement park ride

Finally, visual imagery has been associated with gesture but not language per se (McNeill 1992 and others). Since certain linguistic units in signed languages are proposed here to be associated with visual imagery, this compels a term that is neutral as to the linguistic status of the expression in question or the components within it. I have adopted "depiction" as a term that describes any act that results in the type of imagery discussed earlier.

DIRECTIONALITY OF INDICATING VERBS

In this section the description of directionality in indicating verbs is largely based on the monomorphemic analysis of indicating verbs in Liddell (2003) and uses additional notions from cognitive grammar (Langacker 1987). The analysis here is compatible with that proposed by M&R. Both analyses agree that these verbs interact with space and that they do not specifically prompt the signer to produce depiction.

The indicating verb analysis described here views the use of indicating verbs as involving, in cognitive grammar terms, the elaboration of schematic components in both phonological and semantic structures. First, for the indicating verb, most of the content within the phonological structure—for example, handshape, movement—is specified (with the exception of at least one feature pertaining to location). Unlike for plain verbs, which have fully specified phonological content, it is necessary to elaborate on (i.e., provide content for) this feature. Many of the possible loci within the signer's reach can do this.

This act of elaboration is of course more than merely an issue of form. The directionality of the movement is guided by a particular correspondence between the schematic phonological component and the event participant within the semantics of the verb. If the latter is, say, a recipient (necessarily schematic), then the signer would need to direct the sign toward either (a) an actual, present entity that is the specific recipient in question or (b) a depiction of the recipient (more on the latter in the next section). Given the form-meaning correspondence, directing the sign toward an entity simultaneously elaborates two schematic components. The elaboration of the direction features specifies the event participant within the verb's semantic structure or, in Liddell's terms, maps the entity onto the relevant component within the semantic structure. As for the schematic phonological content, the elaboration can be regarded as more of a by-product rather than a direct consequence of the directionality. This phenomenon in no way detracts from the sign's status as a verb but is to be seen as an additional feature that makes indicating verbs unique to signed languages (Liddell 2003, 139).

This correspondence between the schematic location in the phonological structure and an event participant within the semantic structure is not one that results in the existence of a depictive component within the verb. There may be other form-meaning correspondences between the two structures of the verb, as evident from the iconicity of the hand in the ASL indicating verb GIVE^{-y} (the superscript in this gloss signifies that the sign is directed toward an event participant other than the agent). Depiction does not arise from these correspondences, either. Indicating verbs have just a requirement to point. How the signer satisfies this requirement varies. Producing depiction is one option, but this is not stipulated by the verb.

THE INDICATING VERB AND TYPES OF DEPICTION

Some linguistic units in ASL, in contrast, do seem to stipulate depiction. As discussed later, this is sufficient grounds to consider this as another feature unique to signed languages, in addition to the requirement of indicating verbs to point. This section makes the overall point that, while indicating verbs as signs can be directed to a depiction of a referent or are part of an utterance depiction itself, they do not have the ability to depict events other than utterances. Then the section offers reasons for this.

As described earlier, the indicating verb as a sign can be directed toward present entities. If this entity is the addressee, then the signer directs the sign toward that person. If the entity is someone else in the interlocutor's physical environment, then the signer directs the sign toward that individual. In cases where no relevant entity is present, the signer necessarily produces one of the following types of depiction.

It is possible to produce a life-sized depiction of an individual within a setting, and this type of depiction is what Liddell (1995) calls a surrogate space. Within the conceptual structure underlying this depiction are several correspondences between the individual and the setting being depicted on the one hand and the signer's environment on the other. An indicating verb as a sign can be directed toward the individual imagined as present, who is not visible because a portion of space rather than a person's body is used as the goal of movement. Other types of depiction are more abstract, such as tokens (Liddell 1995), which take up small portions of space in front of the signer, beginning with either side of the signer. Often tokens are produced on the fly; indicating verbs are sometimes the only source informing us that a token has been created. Finally, a fingertip of a list buoy (Liddell 2003) can be used as an abstract depiction of the recipient and also be the location toward which the form of the indicating verb can be directed. For example, the tip of the thumb could be used to represent the eldest of several siblings, and GIVE^{-y} could be directed toward that tip to elaborate the schematic components of the verb. Regardless of whether the form of the indicating verb is directed toward actual or depicted entities, elaborations of schematic components occur.

Earlier I also described indicating verbs as not stipulating depiction. A different stipulation is evident, however, when the verb is produced as part of event depictions: Their use would be possible (perhaps only) if they are understood to be part of a depiction of an utterance.

The depiction of an utterance, which is generally known in signed language research as constructed dialogue (Tannen 1986; Roy 1989), has a set of correspondences between the utterance being described and the signer's utterance itself. Because creations of utterances are actions, the depiction of an utterance could also be considered constructed action (Metzger 1995, who also cites Winston 1991, 1992, discussing a similar point) in which a correspondence holds between the interlocutor of the event being described and the signer. In many cases, it is not just the bodies that are linked; otherwise, the resulting depiction would be about an object (e.g., the body itself) rather than an event. There is additionally a correspondence that enables the depiction of an individual's state of mind or subjective take on an event that is occurring. In such cases, the depiction of facial expression, for instance, is intended not to demonstrate the physical act itself (i.e., the manipulation of muscles) but rather the depicted individual's state of mind, of which facial behavior is one index.

These correspondences suggest that the signer-as-individual and the hands used in the depiction of an utterance are unitary. That is, along with the head, face, torso, and arms, they contribute to the depiction of a single entity, namely, the individual.

This contrasts with other event depictions where the hands and the rest of the body are used to represent distinct entities. One example detailed in Dudis (2004a) has two simultaneous depictions occurring, a signer-as-motorcyclist and a classifier predicate that describes a motorcycle going uphill. Through the former, the signer demonstrates the actions of the animate event participant, and through the latter, the signer depicts the uphill climb with one hand as figure and the other as ground. This simultaneity is possible in part from the ability to conceptually partition certain parts of the body for the purpose of depicting different aspects of the situation being described. In the motorcycle-riding demonstration, the hands are partitioned to produce the classifier predicate, while much of the rest of the body depicts the action of the motorcyclist.

Depictions of most, if not all, actually produced utterances do not require such body partitioning because what is being depicted is typically just a person—or a nonhuman speaker via anthropomorphism (Sutton-Spence and Napoli 2010), consciously and physically engaged in communicative activity, using the body and the manual and nonmanual articulators of signed languages. The articulator-for-articulator correspondence is not distinct from the signer-as-interlocutor correspondence. They are both part of a general mapping between the depicted interlocutor and the signer. Linguistic units used during utterance depictions are then analyzed as depicting the physical act of utterance creation, which is part of the overall depiction of one's experience of interacting communicatively with another person. The ability to use indicating verbs in utterance depictions is then not linguistically stipulated but is an instance of a broader ability to use various linguistic and nonlinguistic materials for the purpose of depiction.

Why does it not seem possible for at least the canonical indicating verbs (e.g., GIVE^{-y}, TELL^{-y}, SHOW^{-y}) to be part of depictions of events other than utterance creation? This restriction is apparent in any depiction of two events occurring in immediate sequence. For example, in the first event, an individual inquires whether he has given his interlocutor a business card. This is followed by the first individual's taking out a card and handing it to the second person. GIVE^{-y} can be used in the depiction of the first action, the utterance (e.g., something like PRO-1 FINISH GIVE^{-y} BUSINESS CARD? 'Have I ever given you my business card?'), but not of the latter, the actual handing over of the business card. The handling classifier predicate that depicts the handing of a flat object to someone would be used instead. If the signer wishes to use GIVE^{-y} instead to describe the latter event, the depiction of the first person's experience would need to cease. However, the rest of the depiction would necessarily remain intact; this allows a description of the actual handing of the business card by directing GIVE^{-y} toward where the second interlocutor is conceptualized to be.

We can look to correspondences between the depicted situation and components of the signer's immediate experience to explain this restriction on indicating verbs. Later I give several examples of correspondences and then return to the restriction on indicating verbs. The life-sized setting depictions and event depictions described in this chapter are, in Liddell's terms, surrogate spaces. In any surrogate space, a correspondence may exist between the depicted individual and the signer. In setting depictions, there are two possibilities. There may be a correspondence between vantage points, allowing the signer to depict the setting from a particular viewpoint. Additionally, a correspondence between bodies is also possible, as seen in a depiction using the signer's chest to demonstrate the path of the slice (and not the slicing event itself) to be performed on a salmon as part of cooking preparations (example from Liddell 2003).

Then there are correspondences between actions. It is possible to, say, wrinkle one's nose to demonstrate a conventional gesture, perhaps as part of a response to the question "What is one way to nonverbally express a negative reaction to a situation?" This demonstration of a physical act (i.e., manipulation of muscles) is quite different from a depiction of an individual reacting to a situation. In both cases, a physical act is demonstrated, but in the latter there is also a depiction of the (signer's construal of) an individual's state of mind. As noted earlier, depiction of physical indexes produced on the face are often more about inner experience than about the manipulation of facial muscles. For example, a facial expression of skepticism could be depicted not to demonstrate one's outward reaction, which might not be appropriate in front of a task-delegating authority figure, but rather to indicate one's take on a situation. This is comparable to the depiction of inner speech, which is accessible only to actual addressees but not the depicted participants. These illustrate how physical reenactments can differ, depending on what correspondences are attended to: solely a movement-for-movement correspondence or, additionally, a set of correspondences that in part enable one to depict inner experience.

There are also depictions of events that do not involve human participants. A depiction of the big bang, for example, would not likely include a depiction of a human eyewitness, and so certain correspondences would not exist. Yet they can still be distinguished from setting depictions. There are cues, at least within an extended version that has a duration of, say, a couple of seconds, that suggest that it has correspondences that define event depiction. These cues may be somewhat nuanced, but they are essential to event depiction. Onomatopoetic-like forms produced (silently) via oral articulators depict effects arising as a result of physical interaction (e.g., a boom associated with explosions). Facial muscles (e.g., those involved in squinting one's eyes or pursing one's lips) can be employed to depict components that are directly or indirectly associated with the event (e.g., the squinting can contribute to the depiction by indicating perhaps the intensity of the explosion). Finally, the ASL classifier predicate that depicts an event that involves expansion can be used here, with the fingers wiggling as the hands move away from each other. These cues point to a set of correspondences that involve temporal components. Specifically, the temporal progression of the depicted event corresponds to the one the signer immediately experiences or continually keeps track of.

Now that I have illustrated several kinds of depictions, I am in a position to explain the restriction on indicating verbs. When used within event depiction, particularly the depiction of an actor performing a physical act, the indicating verb would necessarily be understood to be part of a depiction of the sign (or speech) production of an event participant. Otherwise, it does not seem possible for this verb to be used as part of event depictions. This is because the indicating verb by itself lacks the temporal correspondences of event depictions. The assumption here is that temporal correspondences exist within event depiction (and not in other types of depiction). These correspondences constrain the use of signs. There are two ways a sign can be produced within event depictions. They need to also have similar temporal correspondences, or they need to be understood to be the manual actions of the signer-as-individual who is producing an utterance.

CORRESPONDENCES WITHIN VERBS THAT DEPICT HANDLING EVENTS

In contrast to indicating verbs, handling classifier predicates have the ability to depict other events in addition to utterance events. It is worth considering some of the factors underlying this difference, which seem to have to do with the distinct structures of the two types of verbs.

One characteristic that both handling classifier predicates and indicating verbs have in common is the way in which the elaboration of their schematic phonological content is guided by its correspondences with semantic content. Recall that the verb glossed as GIVE^{-y} is analyzed by Liddell (2003) as having only one schematic component within its phonological structure, the final location of the sign. This component corresponds with the recipient of the event encoded by the verb.

The verb that depicts the event of handling a flat object also appears to have schematic components. However, in contrast to the situation with indicating verbs, a straightforward analysis is not readily apparent for this (type of) verb. One explanation involves the possible movements that can be produced. GIVE^{-y} is very limited in this regard, having a specific movement complex that employs primarily the wrist and often the elbow as well. In contrast, the depicting verb can be moved using the elbow alone or in combination with the wrist, shoulder, and sometimes the torso. As a consequence, a wide variety of movement permutations is possible, and there are many more possible loci at which the depicting verb arrives than are available for indicating verbs. Thus, the movement complex within the depicting verb's phonological structure is more fully schematic as compared with that of GIVE^{-y}.

The schematic movement complex within the depicting verb's phonological content corresponds to the schematic movement complex within the verb's semantics. The existence of a form-meaning correspondence alone, however, is not sufficient for conferring the status of a depicting sign on the handling classifier predicate. Recall that the handshape of GIVE^{-y} corresponds to a hand configuration typically produced to grasp and transfer a flat object to someone. Yet this handshape in and of itself does not depict anything, as it is possible to use the sign to talk about transferring objects that are too large or heavy to be held. Thus, there must be something other than a basic hand-for-hand correspondence that distinguishes the two types of verbs, but given space limitations, this issue will have to await an in-depth examination.[1]

Nevertheless, the description of the two types of verbs here may be sufficient for my main purpose, which is to suggest that the indicating verb and the verb depicting a handling event have form-meaning correspondences that are unique to each verb type. The correspondences in the indicating verb only prompt the signer to direct the sign toward an appropriate entity, whether a referent that is present or a depiction of the referent. The correspondences in the handling classifier predicate prompt for the depiction of the event that it encodes. The phonological content that these correspondences involve for the handling classifier predicate is not limited to location, as it is for the indicating verb, but rather pervades the verb's phonological structure.

There is another correspondence that event-depicting verbs, by definition, have. This is the correspondence between temporal components of the phonological and semantic structures of these verbs. One should, at the very least, be able to explain how it is possible to depict the rate at which the depicted event occurs, but, as the following section suggests, there is a critical factor without which this examination would be incomplete. What is essential is that signers keep track of this depiction of temporal progression. If the agent of the handling classifier predicate is also depicted, then we additionally have a depiction of the experience this agent has while creating the manual action. This point is relevant to the claim being developed pertaining to certain aspectual constructions in ASL, which I now turn to.

DEPICTION AND THE ASL UNREALIZED-INCEPTIVE ASPECT CONSTRUCTION

In the preceding discussion of the depicting verb, I have avoided the question of its morphological complexity. There are views that such expressions are generally multimorphemic (e.g., Supalla 1986), but a monomorphemic analysis appears possible. Due to space limitations, it suffices to simply suggest that the essential form-meaning correspondences are central to either analysis, particularly so within a cognitive linguistic approach. It is worthwhile, however, to present a cognitive grammar–guided glimpse of how these correspondences figure in an expression that is a clearer example of nonconcatenative morphology, the unrealized-inceptive aspect construction (Liddell 1984). Much of the approach described here can be undertaken with other aspectual constructions in ASL that are also proposed to have depictive components (Dudis 2004b).

The unrealized-inceptive aspectual construction enables one to talk about a situation in which one was about to do something, but just when the event was about to commence, the event was prevented from occurring, either by one's own volition or not.[2] For example, an individual, upon learning special information, becomes determined to bring it to someone else's attention, but at the moment the information is to be divulged, the individual decides not to do so.

Liddell (1984) details the phonological process by which these expressions are produced (for an abbreviated description see Liddell 2003). He describes the process as involving a phonological unit labeled as a frame. To summarize in cognitive grammar terms, this unit has several components that are fully specified. They include a particular movement complex that can be generally described as a backward arc. Additionally, a set of nonmanual behaviors is specified, which includes a slight mouth opening and a certain movement of the torso.

Schematic components, particularly the hand configurations, are also part of the frame. These components are elaborated by the specific handshape components within the verb that participates in the frame process (Liddell describes this elaboration as feature insertion). In the expression described earlier, the two-handed verb that is the second component of the construction is one whose meaning is more or less equivalent to the English verb *inform* and is glossed accordingly. INFORM has two handshapes. The first one is the closed handshape similar to that in GIVE^{-y} (and this similarity is not coincidental: See Taub 2001 for an analysis of the sign as being the result of iconic and metaphorical mappings). The second handshape is an open and spread version of the first. The unrealized-inceptive aspectual construction requires that this handshape precede the first in the composite (in other words, going against the iconicity of the nonaspectual verb form). The location components, which are tied to the handshape, are also schematic within the frame and are elaborated by the verb. Thus, the spread handshapes are produced directly in front of the signer as per the verb—but initially rather than finally (in contrast to the order in the nonaspectual form of the verb). These hands close as they quickly move in a downward arc closer to the signer, the dominant hand touching the forehead as per the verb. During this movement, the signer produces the nonmanual components specified by the frame.

Iconicity is evident in this expression even though it is not the same as in the nonaspectual form of the verb. The phonological structure preceding the final segment corresponds to the buildup to the inception of the event. The final segment corresponds to the point where the inception of the event would occur. There also appears to be an extended hold here. This, in combination with how the components of the first segment of INFORM elaborate the schematic components of the final segment, is where the iconicity is probably the most apparent in the manual portion of the expression.

As discussed earlier, that a component within an expression is iconic does not necessarily mean that it is also depictive. Since there are instances where INFORM behaves similarly to GIVE⁻ʸ where event depiction is concerned, I consider INFORM to be an indicating verb and thus nondepictive. However, I consider the unrealized-inceptive form of INFORM to be depictive. This is determined by its ability to produce the form simultaneously with the signer-as-individual to depict an event other than an utterance. The unrealized-inceptive form can be preceded by, say, a depiction of an individual who is learning sensitive information (using a depicting verb of looking) and responding to it (e.g., "Yikes!"). The individual and his experience of the situation are continually depicted throughout and potentially beyond the production of the aspectual form (e.g., in a debate with himself about whether to divulge the information). Given that the aspectual form can be produced within this event depiction for a purpose other than utterance depiction, we can confer on the expression the status of an event-depicting sign.

Since the source of the depiction in the unrealized-inceptive form is not the verb INFORM itself, the frame is a candidate source of the prompt for depiction. This prompt contrasts with one made by indicating verbs, which simply prompt the signer to direct the sign toward an appropriate location. At the very least, one can propose that the prompt for event depiction arises in part from a particular correspondence, one that is more than simply iconic, between the temporal components of the phonological and semantic structures of the frame.

SUMMARY

This chapter has considered some of the form-meaning correspondences that distinguish between the two categories of verbs in ASL, indicating verbs and event-depicting verbs. The phonological structure of the two types of verbs examined here has both specified and schematic (i.e., unspecified) components that correspond to components of their semantic structure. Schematic components of the sign's form need to be elaborated (i.e., specified). Elaborating them simultaneously elaborates the semantic components that they correspond to. The structure of indicating verbs prompts the signer to direct them toward an entity appropriate to the discourse content at hand. Doing so elaborates locative features of the verb, as well as of the event participant (e.g., the recipient). The phonological content of event-depicting verbs has multiple schematic components that need elaboration. However, unlike the indicating verbs, the structure of event-depicting verbs prompts visual imagery. While the two prompts arise in part from form-meaning correspondences, the structure of the two types of verbs and the conceptual work necessitated by their usage are sufficiently distinct from what we find in spoken languages to incline us to consider them as two features unique to signed languages. The brief examination of the unrealized-inceptive aspectual construction in ASL suggests that it also prompts visual imagery. This conclusion seems plausible within a certain view of grammar implicit in this discussion, one that views verbs and constructions as form-meaning pairings (Langacker 1987).

Notes

This research was supported in part by the National Science Foundation under grant number SBE-0541953. Any opinions, findings, and conclusions or recommendations expressed are mine and do not necessarily reflect the views of the National Science Foundation.

    1. See Padden (1990), among others, who also talks about the distinction between indicating verbs and handling classifier predicates (as exemplars of spatial verbs) on morphological and syntactic grounds.

    2. See also Rathmann (2005), who groups this construction with another one labeled "delayed completive" by Brentari (1998) under the broader notion of "conative."

Bibliography

Brentari, Diane. 1998. *A Prosodic Model of Sign Language Phonology.* Cambridge, Mass.: MIT Press.

Clark, Herbert, and Richard Gerrig. 1990. Quotations as Demonstrations. *Language* 66(4): 764–805.

DeMatteo, Asa. 1977. Visual Imagery and Visual Analogues in American Sign Language. In *On the Other Hand: New Perspectives on American Sign Language,* ed. Lynn A. Friedman, 109–136. New York: Academic Press.

Dudis, Paul. 2004a. Body Partitioning and Real-space Blends. *Cognitive Linguistics* 15(2): 223–238.

———. 2004b. Depiction of Events in ASL: Conceptual Integration of Temporal Components. PhD diss., University of California at Berkeley.

———. 2007. Types of Depiction in ASL. Manuscript, Gallaudet University.

Fauconnier, Gilles, and Mark Turner. 1994. Conceptual Projection and Middle Spaces. Cognitive Science Technical Report. University of California at San Diego.

———. 2002. *The Way We Think: Conceptual Blending and the Mind's Hidden Complexities.* New York: Basic Books.

Langacker, Ronald W. 1987. *Foundations of Cognitive Grammar.* Stanford: Stanford University Press.

Liddell, Scott K. 1984. Unrealized-inceptive Aspect in American Sign Language: Feature Insertion in Syllabic Frames. In *Papers from the 20th Regional Meeting of the Chicago Linguistic Society,* ed. Joseph Drogo, Veena Mishra, and David Teston, 257–270. Chicago: University of Chicago Press.

———. 1995. Real, Surrogate, and Token Space: Grammatical Consequences in ASL. In *Language, Gesture, and Space,* ed. Karen Emmorey and Judy Reilly, 19–41. Hillsdale, NJ: Erlbaum.

———. 1998. Grounded Blends, Gestures, and Conceptual Shifts. *Cognitive Linguistics* 9(3): 283–314.

———. 2003. *Grammar, Gesture, and Meaning in American Sign Language.* New York: Cambridge University Press.

———, and Marit Vogt-Svendsen. 2007. Constructing Spatial Conceptualizations from Limited Input: Evidence from Norwegian Sign Language. In *Gesture and the Dynamic Dimension of Language,* ed. David McNeill, Susan D. Duncan, Justine Cassell, and Elean T. Levy, 173–194. Philadelphia: Benjamins.

McNeill, David. 1992. *Hand and Mind: What Gestures Reveal about Thought.* Chicago: University of Chicago Press.

Metzger, Melanie. 1995. Constructed Dialogue and Constructed Action in American Sign Language. In *Sociolinguistics in Deaf Communities,* ed. Ceil Lucas, 255–271. Washington, D.C.: Gallaudet University Press.

Padden, Carol. 1990. The Relation between Space and Grammar in ASL Verb Morphology. In *Sign Language Research: Theoretical Issues,* ed. Ceil Lucas, 118–132. Washington, D.C.: Gallaudet University Press.

Rathmann, Christian. 2005. Event Structure in American Sign Language. PhD diss., University of Texas at Austin.

Roy, Cynthia B. 1989. Features of Discourse in an American Sign Language Lecture. In *The Sociolinguistics of the Deaf Community,* ed. Ceil Lucas, 231–251. San Diego: Academic Press.

Supalla, Ted. 1986. The Classifier System in American Sign Language. In *Noun Classes and Categorization: Proceedings of a Symposium on Categorization and Noun Classification, Eugene, Oregon, October 1983.* Typological Studies in Language 7, ed. Colette Craig, 181–214. Philadelphia: Benjamins.

Sutton-Spence, Rachel, and Donna Jo Napoli. 2010. Anthropomorphism in Sign Languages: A Look at Poetry and Storytelling with a Focus on British Sign Language. *Sign Language Studies* 10(4): 442–475.

Tannen, Deborah. 1986. Introducing Constructed Dialogue in Greek and American Conversational and Literacy Narratives. In *Direct and Indirect Speech,* ed. Florian Coulmas, 311–332. New York: de Gruyter.

Taub, Sarah F. 2001. *Language from the Body: Iconicity and Metaphor in American Sign Language.* New York: Cambridge University Press.

Winston, Elizabeth. 1991. Spatial Referencing and Cohesion in an American Sign Language Text. *Sign Language Studies* 73: 397–410.

———. 1992. Space and Involvement in an American Sign Language Lecture. In *Expanding Horizons: Proceedings of the Twelfth National Convention of the Registry of Interpreters for the Deaf,* ed. Jean Plant-Moeller, 93–105. Silver Spring, Md.: RID Publications.

CHAPTER 3

Sources of Handshape Error in First-Time Signers of ASL

Deborah Chen Pichler

INTRODUCTION

There is a popular assumption among proficient signers of American Sign Language (ASL) that the concept of accent applies to sign languages just as it does to spoken languages and poses the same challenge to second language learners as any spoken language does. A casual Google search for "sign language accent" turns up postings from chat room exchanges, including statements such as those in the following excerpts, in which participants discuss second language learner accent with respect to sign languages:

(1) [A] native user of BSL [British Sign Language] who learned ASL would undoubtedly retain a BSL intonation or "accent." . . . [A] native signer can usually (though not invariably) recognize a hearing person by the slightly halting quality of their signing and the way they use their face and body: "Oh, you sign with a hearing accent!" (Thedeafway n.d.)

(2) I know I still sign with a "hearing accent," but I'm always trying to lose it. This book will give you the worst hearing accent you can imagine. (Customer 2004)

These two short quotes are enough to illustrate a few interesting assumptions about accent in the signing community: (a) that a "hearing" accent is different from a "foreign" accent, (b) that accent in sign is characterized by a variety of non-targetlike formational features, and (c) that an accent can diminish or increase through exposure. The last assumption, if true, provides good motivation for research in second language ASL phonology, with the goal of eventually informing ASL pedagogy. The first assumption is an intriguing one that I have only recently begun to explore (cf. Chen Pichler 2008, a presentation on preliminary data at the Swarthmore conference on which this volume is largely based), although I do not discuss it here. My focus for this chapter is assumption (b), that accent in sign is characterized by a variety of non-targetlike formational features. To test this assumption, I examine the handshape errors that occur in the imitation of ASL signs by individuals who have no previous experience with that language, meant to represent the very beginning stage of ASL acquisition as a second language. I argue that handshape errors are potentially caused by a variety of factors, including markedness and transfer, both familiar from the literature on L2 accent in spoken languages.

In the sections that follow, I first summarize the existing literature on second language acquisition of sign and then introduce the central concepts of markedness and transfer, arguing that both are applicable to sign, as well as to spoken, data. Next I discuss data collected as part of a pilot project conducted on hearing subjects exposed to ASL for the first time. Finally, I close with some thoughts on modifications for future studies in this area and applications of this research in the ASL classroom.

Before I begin, a note about terminology is in order. In my research comparing handshape errors of hearing nonsigners with those of native signers of non-ASL sign languages, I restrict the label "L2 learner" to the latter group. For these learners, both their L1 and their L2 reside in the same modality, parallel to the case of native speakers learning a second spoken language. In contrast, learners with a native spoken language who learn a sign language as their second language might plausibly experience difficulties imposed by the new modality on top of the regular second language effects that are typically studied. For this reason, I refer to such learners as M2 or "second modality learners" (thanks to Martha Tyrone, Richard Meier, and others for this label). Even though this chapter does not discuss foreign signers, I adopt this terminology for the sake of consistency and refer to the hearing, first-time signers in this study as M2 signers.

PREVIOUS WORK ON ASL AS AN M2

Although second language acquisition is an area of intense investigation for spoken languages, there is very little published research on either M2 or L2 signing. Among the earliest studies are Kantor (1978) and Budding et al. (1995), both of which focus on the perception of sign accent by various groups of ASL users. Kantor (1978) tested signers' ability to determine nativeness and hearing status from watching video-recorded narratives by native-Deaf, native-hearing (CODA), L2-Deaf (which she defines as orally raised Deaf who learned ASL only after puberty, as either an M2 or a late L1), and M2-hearing signers. Budding et al. (1995) asked subjects to rate ASL narratives by Deaf signers who had learned Quebec Sign Language (LSQ) as their L1 and ASL as their L2. Both studies asked raters to identify the features of ASL that were inaccurately reproduced by the signers they had judged as nonnative. Raters cited a broad spectrum of features including movement, handshape, vocabulary choice, classifier choice, and non-manual expression. More recent work on perception has since been carried out by Goeke (2005), who focuses only on the contribution of handshape on signers' perceptions of accent. Goeke's data indicate that inaccuracies in handshape elicit a nonnative rating by beginner, advanced, and native raters (defined according to the number of years' experience with ASL) and also that accuracy in handshape does not necessarily guarantee a nativelike or even near-native rating. She concludes that although handshape error does contribute to nonnative accent in sign, other features such as movement are possibly more significant.

Studies focusing on M2 sign production are slightly more recent than the perception studies, including a study of M2 development of nonmanuals by McIntire and Reilly (1988), a report on proximalization of movement in M2 signing by Mirus, Rathmann, and Meier (2001), and a study on the use of various narrative elements of ASL by M2 signers by Taub et al. (2008). Thompson and colleagues have also recently used eye-tracking methodologies to investigate eye gaze patterns for grammatical purposes among native and novice signers (Thompson 2006; Emmorey et al. 2008; Thompson et al. 2009). The most recent M2 sign production study dealing specifically with handshape accuracy is Rosen (2004), a discussion of the phonological errors he observed in the output of his first-level ASL students at Columbia University. Rosen categorizes the students' phonological errors within his cognitive phonology model, according to which errors stem primarily from either faulty perception or lack of dexterity, where dexterity is defined simply as the "anatomical ability to align fingers, hands and faces" (Rosen 2004, 37) to match a target sign. As exposure to ASL increases, learners' perception of the linguistically relevant categories for ASL become more accurate; also, as learners receive more and more practice using their hands to sign, their dexterity improves, and their sign production becomes more accurate.

With respect to handshape accuracy, Rosen reports numerous errors that he attributes to poor manual dexterity, resulting in incorrect handshapes or sequences of handshape changes. For instance, he reports that some students produced YEAR with two A handshapes rather than the target S handshapes. Others substituted the open-8 handshape for the target 1 handshape for the nondominant hand of SHOW. Still others switched the order of two handshape sequences within a single sign (e.g., producing THROW with a 5-handshape-to-S-handshape sequence, when the target is actually an S-handshape-to-5-handshape sequence). Such errors could also be due to faulty perception of the target, although Rosen does not classify them as such. He limits the possible effects of perception errors on handshape to either deletion or addition of handshape segments, neither of which occur in his data.

Two additional sources of handshape error that Rosen (2004) does not pursue are transfer from the L1 and markedness, both of which play an important role in nonnative accent in spoken L2, as I discuss in the following sections. Rosen argues that these two factors are not as relevant in the discussion of M2 signing because there can be no transfer between a spoken L1 and a signed M2 due to modality differences, and also because the new signers in his class are adults, who have fully developed motor and cognitive capabilities and thus presumably follow different developmental paths than young children learning ASL as an L1. In contrast, I argue that both transfer and markedness are relevant to second language acquisition across modalities and should be considered in a comprehensive investigation of M2 sign phonology.

MARKEDNESS IN SPEECH AND SIGN

With respect to spoken language, perception of nonnative accent can result from a wide spectrum of errors in phonology, as well as (less typically) errors in lexical choice, syntax, discourse, and other linguistic features. Phonological aspects of accented speech have been extensively studied for a variety of L1/L2 combinations, producing a well-established body of literature (see Major 2001 for a good overview). Regardless of the particular L1 and L2 involved, both markedness of the target form and transfer from the native language (L1) are repeatedly observed to exert important influences on L2 phonology.

Cross-linguistically, unmarked elements are more widely attested than their marked counterparts and are generally mastered earlier in L1 acquisition. For instance, in spoken languages, voiceless stops (e.g., [p], [t], [k]) are less marked than their voiced counterparts ([b], [d], [g], respectively). Voiceless stops occur in all spoken languages that we know of, while voiced stops do not. This forms a one-way implicational hierarchy: Any language that includes the latter also includes the former, but the opposite is not necessarily true (Jakobson 1968). With respect to acquisition, unmarked forms are predicted to be acquired earlier than marked forms for both L1 and L2 learners. Additionally, certain markedness hierarchies may be universal and are thus predicted to exert an effect regardless of the learner's particular L1 and/or L2 (Eckman 1977).

Markedness is a familiar concept in the L1 acquisition of handshape, and several markedness hierarchies have been proposed in the recent sign language literature. Most, such as Boyes Braem (1990) and Ann (2006), determine markedness based on the anatomy of the human hand. Ann (2006) computes ease of articulation scores for handshapes in Taiwan Sign Language (TSL, the object of her investigation) using an algorithm based on five anatomical criteria (such as amount of muscle opposition in joint configurations, spreading of fingers, opposition of the thumb). Depending on the resulting scores, handshapes are classified as easy (unmarked and frequently occurring), difficult (marked and infrequently occurring), or impossible. Boyes

Braem (1990) proposes a similarly anatomically informed model based on handshapes from ASL rather than TSL. She observes that the fingers of the hand are successively bound by ligaments into several autonomous and semi-autonomous bundles, such that certain combinations of fingers are more difficult to manipulate than others. The thumb and the index finger are the most independent of the digits and as such are easy to manipulate individually. In contrast, the ring finger is the least independent digit because it is bound by a ligament to the middle and the pinky fingers. These three fingers are relatively easy to move as a group but difficult to manipulate individually. From this anatomical fact, Boyes Braem predicts that a handshape such as L (in which all three fingers in this bundle are closed) is less marked than the 3 handshape, which requires the middle finger to dissociate from the other two fingers in its bundle.

In addition to pure anatomical reasons for markedness, Boyes Braem proposes secondary factors that increase articulatory complexity, such as the crossing of fingers for R or the insertion of fingers for T and N or the opposition of the thumb for S and 1. She also notes factors such as the availability of different types of feedback or the overall complexity of the sign in which the handshape occurs (cf. also Meier 2006), which plausibly affect handshape accuracy in child signing. Taken together, these factors predict a hierarchy of handshape complexity that Boyes Braem divides into four stages (plus A as the maximally unmarked handshape) (table 3.1). The predictions made by

Table 3.1. Boyes Braem (1990) Hierarchy of Handshape Markedness

Maximally unmarked handshape	A	closest to the shape of a hand at rest
Stage I	S, L, bO, G/1, 5, C	involves manipulation of hand as a whole OR radial group of fingers only
Stage II	B, F, O	only the highly independent digits are able to move separately (thumb and index)
Stage III	(I, Y) (D, P, 3, V, H) W	begins to differentiate individual fingers, to inhibit or activate specific groups of fingers
Stage IV	(8, 7), X, R, (T, M, N)	learns to activate and inhibit ulnar fingers independently; applies 2° features *cross* and *insertion*

the Boyes Braem hierarchy have been tested on naturalistic output by young children acquiring ASL as their L1 (Boyes Braem 1990; McIntire 1977) and have generally been found to be consistent with child production data.

Boyes Braem's (1990) hierarchy and Ann's (2006) analysis of handshapes have not, to my knowledge, been applied to M2 signing. As mentioned in the previous section, Rosen (2004) dismisses markedness as being more relevant to L1 sign development than to M2 since M2 learners (mostly adults) have fully developed motor skills and are less likely than young children to struggle with the anatomical demands of marked handshapes. However, as Mirus, Rathmann, and Meier (2001) rightly point out, a fully developed motor system does not guarantee flawless motor skills in all physical domains. Most adults faced with unfamiliar motor tasks, such as skiing or signing, execute them awkwardly until they have enough practice to maintain effective motor control in these new domains. During this period of adjustment, markedness may affect adult M2 production of handshape in the same way it does child L1 production. In fact, Rosen (2004) acknowledges that many of his students' handshape errors, such as substituting the A handshape for the S handshape in YEAR, are compatible with markedness hierarchies such as that proposed by Boyes Braem (1990).

TRANSFER IN SPEECH AND SIGN

Unlike markedness, which is often assumed to apply universally regardless of the learner's L1 and L2, phonological transfer is a language-specific phenomenon. Transfer is said to be *positive* when learners correctly perceive a target form as being identical to a form in their L1. The learners can then transfer that form into the L2 without having to learn it. On the other hand, transfer is said to be negative when learners fail to perceive a difference between the target form in the L2 and a similar (but not identical) form in the L1. For instance, L1 French speakers learning L2 English often mistakenly perceive the English phonemes /I/ (the lax vowel sound in the English word *sit*) as equivalent to the French phoneme /i/ (similar to the vowel sound in the English word *seat*). Because of their perceptual assimilation of English /I/ to French /i/ to, these learners pronounce *seat* and *sit* identically, contributing to a French accent.

In contrast, when the L2 target phoneme differs more dramatically from the closest L1 equivalent (e.g., English vowel /u/ as in *moon*, versus French vowel /y/ as in *sucre* "sugar"), learners perceive it as an uncategorizable speech sound (Best 1995), leading to the establishment of the target phoneme as a new category in their phonetic inventory. Thus, a persistent foreign accent, perhaps contrary to intuition, stems more from the mispronunciation of target forms that are highly similar to familiar forms in L1 than from forms that are completely

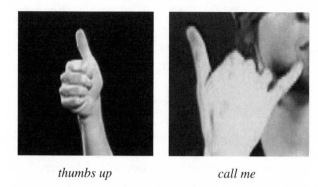

thumbs up   *call me*

Figure 3.1. Conventionalized gestures common in the United States

foreign to the learner (Best 1995; Flege 1995). Once the learner recognizes a phoneme as a new form, acquisition of that phoneme is predicted to take place according to the normal developmental path, subject to universal developmental factors such as markedness (Major 2001). Thus, markedness and transfer not only exert individual effects on accent but also interact with each other.

With respect to M2 acquisition of sign by native users of spoken language, I agree with Rosen (2004) that modality differences preclude the transfer of phonological features from learners' L1 English to their M2 ASL. However, I question the assumption that nonsigners have no previous experience with handshapes found in formal sign languages. There are a large number of common, conventionalized gestures (emblems) in the American hearing community that are widely used and understood, such as *thumbs up* and *call me* (figure 3.1). I am not aware of any phonetic analysis of the handshapes employed by these gestures, but popular guides to American gesture such as Axtell (1997) and Armstrong and Wagner (2003) refer to a set of plain-English handshape labels in their descriptions of gestures, such as *fist* or *point* or *V shape*, suggesting that these handshapes are reasonably similar among users. Many of these handshapes look identical or similar to those found in ASL, raising the possibility that ASL learners might (at least initially) transfer them to their M2 signing. This is based on the assumption that nonsigners recognize handshape as a discrete unit at some level. This assumption is adopted in this chapter for the purpose of guiding the initial investigation into the phenomenon of M2 sign phonology.

RESEARCH QUESTIONS

As Kantor (1978) and Budding et al. (1995) note, nonnative signing is characterized by a wide variety of features that range from non-targetlike phonological features to inappropriate lexical choice. Although a comprehensive understanding of M2 ASL will require investigation of all of these features, the current study focuses only on handshape for two main reasons. First, handshapes fall into relatively discrete categories, compared to movements and nonmanual expressions, and thus are easier to classify. Second, as I mentioned in the previous section, there are plausible similarities between handshapes used in ASL and those observed in conventional hearing gestures, providing a possible source of transfer into M2 ASL.

With respect to markedness, the prediction for this study is that, all else being equal, subjects will accurately reproduce unmarked handshapes more often than marked ones. With respect to transfer, the prediction is that subjects will substitute (transfer) a handshape used in a conventional gesture for a target sign handshape whenever the two are perceived as being the same. Transfer will result in an accurate response when the two handshapes are in fact identical (positive transfer); it will result in an error when the two handshapes are similar but not identical (negative transfer).

METHODOLOGY

In an attempt to control for the wide variability typical of M2 acquisition, my students and I recruited four hearing, nonsigning subjects for this pilot study as opposed to students already enrolled in an ASL class. Age of exposure to a second language, the environment in which it is learned, the type and amount of exposure learners receive, the attitude and motivation they bring to the task, and so on all affect development. The net result of these factors is that, even within the same classroom, individual students can progress at vastly different rates. By testing subjects with no previous experience with sign languages, we hoped to mimic the initial stage of acquisition before learner variability becomes too pronounced. Also, since our experiment constituted the subjects' first and only input to ASL, we had a high degree of control over their exposure to the target language. The trade-off, of course, is that our subjects are not true learners of ASL, and it is quite possible that some of the patterns noted in our data may not occur in an actual classroom environment.

We developed stimuli that included ten common American gestures and 38 signs from ASL (the full list of stimuli is given in the appendix at the end of this chapter). Following the Boyes Braem hierarchy, both marked handshapes (4/10 gestures and 16/38 signs) and unmarked handshapes (6/10 gestures and 22/38 signs) were represented. Among the stimuli were also signs with handshapes potentially identical or very similar to handshapes used in conventional gesture (26/38 signs), as well as signs with handshapes clearly distinct from any used in gestures (12/38 signs). We tried to minimize confounding effects of other phonological factors by selecting signs that had relatively unmarked location (either chest, chin, or neutral space) and movement (mostly contact movements or a shake/trill) and no more than a single handshape throughout the sign (i.e., no signs with sequences of multiple handshapes). The resulting 38 ASL signs and 10 conventionalized gestures were presented in random order in two trials. The signs were modeled by a native signer from our class, whom we filmed from two angles, such that the subjects saw each stimulus three times: first from head on, then from the side, and finally from head on again in order to give as clear a view of each sign as possible.

Subjects were instructed to focus on the model's hands as they watched the stimuli on a computer screen. In their reproduction of each stimulus, they were asked to copy the model's hand activity as faithfully as they could. Their production was videotaped and coded for handshape accuracy. A reproduced sign handshape was coded as accurate if it was the same as that used by the model; it was coded as inaccurate if it differed from that of the model in thumb opposition, position of unselected fingers, and/or degree of splay of extended fingers. These criteria were also used in determining (a) whether gestures matched the model's and (b) whether the two trials of a given gesture matched for each subject.

PRELIMINARY FINDINGS

Because only ten gestures were elicited in this pilot study, I discuss all of them here. However, for the sake of brevity, I focus on a subset of six target handshapes from the elicited signs: S, 1, B dot, Y, W, and open 8. The first three handshapes are classified as unmarked, according to the Boyes Braem (1990) hierarchy, while the last three are classified as marked. Similarly, Ann (2006) classifies S and 1 as easy and Y, W, and open 8 as difficult. The only relevant handshape for which the BoyesBraem (1990) and Ann (2006) classifications diverge is the B dot handshape, which Ann (2006) somewhat reservedly classifies as difficult, citing the fact that the fingers are held together (adducted), whereas fingers have a natural tendency to spread apart (abduct). For the purposes of this study, I assume the Boyes Braem (1990) classification of B dot as unmarked.

Given that this experimental task represented the subjects' first experience with sign language, my students and I had anticipated a fair degree of physical awkwardness in their production. We were thus surprised by the subjects' overall accuracy. Nevertheless, they still produced many errors, with plausible etiologies ranging from markedness to transfer to dexterity or perception issues. Once again I must emphasize that none of the subjects in this pilot had any knowledge of ASL, so their only experience with the language was what they saw on the computer screen. When a subject reproduced a stimulus that did not match what the subject was shown, I refer to this as an error. My use of this term is in no way an attempt to dictate universal standards of right or wrong handshape in ASL signs; it is limited only to right or wrong within the context of this particular experiment.

I discuss the results of this study from several perspectives. First, I briefly report the results of the subjects' reproduction of the elicited gestures to determine the degree to which the subjects were consistent with the model and within their own production. Next, I turn to a subset of the elicited signs to investigate whether handshape markedness affected accuracy. Finally, I explore the conditions under which handshape transfer occurs from conventional gesture to target sign.

Handshape Accuracy for Elicited Gestures

For the two sets of elicited gestures, the subjects produced handshapes that matched the model 58–92 percent of the time, as shown by the white bars in figure 3.2. With respect to individual gestures, only two of the ten elicited gestures (*thumbs up* and *call me*) matched the model for all four subjects in both trials. One interpretation of these results is that despite the subjects' attempts to reproduce as faithfully as possible the gestures they saw on screen, these two gestures were the only ones that all of the subjects were able to copy accurately.

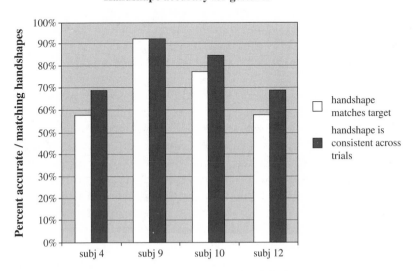

Figure 3.2. Handshape accuracy in elicited gestures

An alternative interpretation is that the divergence of the subjects' gesture handshapes from the model reflects their idiosyncratic forms for these gestures. Under this interpretation, as soon as the subjects recognized a gesture on screen, they automatically produced their own habitual form of that gesture rather than copying the model faithfully as they had been instructed. This interpretation is supported by the fact that the percentage of matching handshapes within a single subject's production was consistently higher than (or as high as, in the case of subject 9) the percentage of handshapes matching the model, as shown by the black bars in figure 3.2. Also, the subjects often smiled as they produced the gestures, suggesting recognition (and relief), in stark contrast to the expressions of concentration many of them wore while reproducing the sign stimuli. As for the gestures *thumbs up* and *call me*, these may have particularly stable forms for American gesturers, such that all four subjects happened to produce them with the same handshapes as the model.

Handshape Accuracy for Elicited Signs: Effects of Markedness

Figure 3.3 presents a visual summary of the subjects' percentage of accuracy in reproducing the six target handshapes discussed in this chapter. The handshapes are grouped visually by shading pattern: unmarked handshapes (S, 1, B dot) are represented by solid shading, while marked handshapes (Y, W, open 8) appear in patterned shading (checked or striped). An absent bar represents a 0 percent accuracy rate for that particular handshape. The small number of data points shown in figure 3.3, as well as the fact that the stimuli were not balanced with respect to both independent variables in this study (markedness and handshape/gesture similarity), means that these data do not generally lend themselves to meaningful statistical analysis. I thus focus more on patterns that emerge for individual subjects or handshapes than on statistical trends or overall patterns in the full data set.

The prediction for this study with respect to markedness was that, all else being equal, the subjects would reproduce unmarked handshapes more accurately than marked ones. Applied at the level of overall performance for each subject, this prediction appears to be true only for subject 9, whose production is overall more accurate for unmarked handshapes than for marked ones. In this case, the negative correlation between markedness and accuracy is strong enough to reach statistical significance (by the one-tailed Fisher's exact test; $p = .0012$). This is not so for any of the other subjects, however, least of all for subject 4, who shows a statistically significant *positive* correlation between markedness and accuracy ($p = .0002$).

However, examination of the data with respect to specific handshapes rather than overall subject performance reveals plentiful evidence that markedness

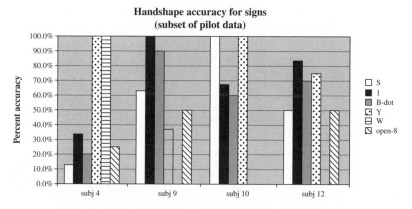

Figure 3.3. Handshape accuracy in elicited signs

should still be considered as an influential factor affecting M2 handshape accuracy. For instance, all subjects but subject 4 were able to reproduce unmarked 1 and B dot handshapes at least 60 percent of the time. Conversely, the highly marked handshapes W and open 8 posed serious problems for all of the subjects. With the exception of subject 4, none of them correctly reproduced the W handshape in any of the sign stimuli (0/4 items). As for open 8, subjects 9 and 12 reproduced the handshape accurately in half of the sign stimuli (2/4 items), subject 4 in a quarter of the stimuli (1/4 items), and subject 10 in none of the stimuli (0/4 items). The examples in figures 3.4 and 3.5 illustrate the errors with target handshapes open 8 and W, respectively. For each example, the target stimulus viewed by the subjects appears at the top.

The open 8 handshape is predicted to be very marked by the Boyes Braem hierarchy and does not occur in any conventionalized American gesture, as far as we know. It is thus unfamiliar to the subjects and predicted to be acquired according to normal developmental patterns (i.e., subject to universal factors such as markedness). Errors with this handshape generally involved placement of the nonselected fingers (thumb, index, ring finger, and pinky), the fingers that do not make contact with the chest. Errors with the W handshape, in contrast, tended to involve the selected fingers (pinky and thumb): Subjects 9 and 10 produced this handshape with the nail of the pinky pinned under the thumb rather than touching pad-to-pad with the thumb. Again, although this appears to be a handshape variant permitted in ASL, we coded it as an error since it did not match the handshape in the stimulus that these subjects received. Subject 12 touched the wrong finger (ring finger) with the thumb. Errors with the W handshape for at least one subject may be explained by transfer (discussed in the next subsection).

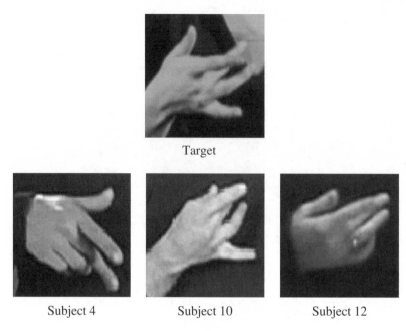

Target

Subject 4   Subject 10   Subject 12

Figure 3.4. Errors with target open-8: FEEL

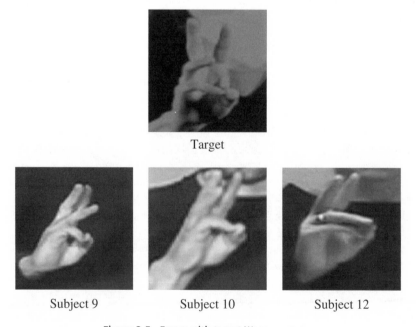

Target

Subject 9   Subject 10   Subject 12

Figure 3.5. Errors with target W: SIX-YEARS-OLD

The subjects also made many substitutions of a less marked handshape for one that is more marked. For instance, subjects 4 and 9 substituted the A handshape for target S in SENATE. Because S requires opposition of the thumb, it is more marked than A, a secondary feature predicted by Boyes Braem (1990) to increase handshape complexity. Since these substitutions are made in the direction of less marked forms, such errors are still compatible with the prediction that markedness exerts a negative influence on accuracy. In the case of subject 4, her particular pattern of substitution could alternatively be analyzed as the result of transfer, as I detail in the next subsection.

Finally, subject 4 was highly successful with marked handshapes W and Y, reproducing them accurately in 100 percent of the sign stimuli. This result is unexpected from the viewpoint of the Boyes Braem (1990) hierarchy. One feature that the W and Y handshapes have in common, in contrast to the open 8 handshape, which subject 4 reproduced poorly, is that the index, middle, and ring fingers share the same configuration (i.e., all open or all closed). These three fingers are not bound by any ligament into a bundle in the same way that, for instance, the middle, ring, and pinky fingers are. Thus a strictly anatomical/production explanation fails to account for this particular accuracy pattern. Instead, the movement of the inside three fingers as a single block in opposition to the pinky and thumb may improve the perceptual saliency of W and Y for subject 4, leading to successful reproduction (thanks to Gaurav Mathur and Donna Jo Napoli for this observation).

Handshape Accuracy for Elicited Signs: Effects of Transfer

The second prediction for this pilot study was that the subjects would accurately reproduce handshapes that are identical to those they use for conventional gestures (positive transfer) but commit transfer errors for target handshapes that are very similar but not identical to those they use for conventional gestures (negative transfer). We considered two handshapes to be very similar but not identical if they differed only in the position of the thumb or unselected fingers and/or the degree of splay of the extended fingers, the same features we used to determine the accuracy of handshape reproduction. Of the handshapes analyzed here, only open 8 has no similar gestural counterpart. The other five handshapes are all similar or identical to handshapes found in common American gestures (see appendix).

In cases where (a) the model produced sign stimuli with the same handshape that she used in a gesture stimulus and (b) the subjects accurately reproduced that target handshape for both gesture and sign stimuli, it is impossible to determine whether accuracy was due to positive transfer or to the subjects' cognitive and motor abilities (or both). Transfer is easier to identify in cases

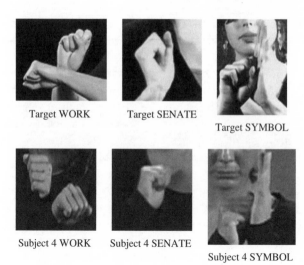

Target WORK   Target SENATE

Target SYMBOL

Subject 4 WORK   Subject 4 SENATE

Subject 4 SYMBOL

Figure 3.6. Subject 4 errors in S-handshape

where the subjects produce a nontarget sign handshape that matches a hand-shape they also use in a gesture. Our data include several cases of such negative transfer, almost all involving the unmarked handshapes S and 1. Subject 4 substituted a fist with unopposed or partially opposed thumbs for the target S handshape (fully opposed thumb) in several signs (WORK, SENATE, SYMBOL), as illustrated in figure 3.6. As mentioned in the previous subsection, marked-ness might be a factor in this substitution pattern since the S handshape is considered to be slightly more marked than the A handshape. However, mark-edness alone does not provide a satisfying explanation for these errors. Both the A and the S handshape lie at the unmarked extreme of the markedness hierarchy, which should render them relatively easy to execute, especially for adults with fully developed motor abilities. More likely some other factor has led subject 4 to perceive the S handshape incorrectly as the A handshape in these stimuli.

Close examination of subject 4's production of the gesture *Yes!* (two fists raised in the air in victory) provides a possible explanation for her handshape errors described earlier. While the model produced this gesture with two S handshapes, subject 4 reproduced it with unopposed or partially opposed thumbs (figure 3.7). This makes a compelling case for negative transfer since the same nontarget handshape occurs in both gesture and sign stimuli that target the S handshape. I speculate that subject 4's handshape inventory includes a handshape that we can call the *fist* handshape. When she sees signs or gestures with the A or the S handshape, she perceptually assimilates them (Best 1995) to the *fist* category she already possesses. This leads her to repro-duce signs targeting the A and S handshapes with her particular version of the

Target gesture *Yes!*

Subject 4 gesture *Yes!* (trial 1)

Subject 4 gesture *Yes!* (trial 2)

Figure 3.7. Subject 4's production of the S-handshape in gesture

fist handshape, which involves an unopposed or partially opposed thumb. For signs that target the A handshape, this transfer results in accurate reproduction (at least with respect to thumb position), as seen in the sign ATHLETE in figure 3.8. For signs targeting the S handshape, transfer results in an error despite the fact that the S handshape is very unmarked.

A negative transfer account is also plausible for errors in subject 4's production of the target handshape 1. The sign stimulus WHERE requires full thumb opposition but is reproduced by subject 4 in both trials with an unopposed thumb. Subsequent analysis reveals that this subject's gesture for *wait a minute* is also produced with the unopposed thumb version of the 1 handshape (figure 3.9). The same variant of the 1 handshape occurred in subject 4's production of DIFFERENT, but only on the dominant hand.

Target ATHLETE   Subject 4 ATHLETE

Figure 3.8. Subject 4's production of the A-handshape

Target WHERE   Subject 4 WHERE   Subject 4 WHERE
                        (trial 1)   (trial 2)

Target *Wait a minute*   Subject 4 *Wait a minute*

Figure 3.9. Subject 4's production of target handshape 1

In the present data, almost all instances of negative transfer occurred with unmarked handshapes. The only exception was the case of W, mentioned in the previous subsection. This highly marked handshape (or something like it) exists in conventional American gesture, namely in the gesture for *three* (not to be confused with ASL THREE). In the stimuli, our signing model demonstrated this gesture with the tip of her pinky pinned under the pad of her thumb. In contrast, for both sign stimuli using the W handshape, our signing model did not use her thumb to pin down her pinky but either placed it beside the thumb (WATER) or pressed its pad against the pad of the thumb (SIX-YEARS-OLD). Subject 10 pinned his pinky under the thumb for both instances of the gesture *three*, as well as for all four sign tokens calling for the W handshape. This pattern suggests that subject 10 is perceptually assimilating the model's W handshapes to an existing handshape category in which the tip of the pinky is pinned under the thumb, resulting in negative transfer. A comparison of subject 10's handshapes with those of the sign model is shown in figure 3.10.

Finally, negative transfer from gesture did not occur in all of the predicted cases. For instance, the target Y handshape in our sign stimulus WRONG differs from the handshape in our target gesture *call me* in the degree to which the thumb and the pinky are splayed. The two handshapes

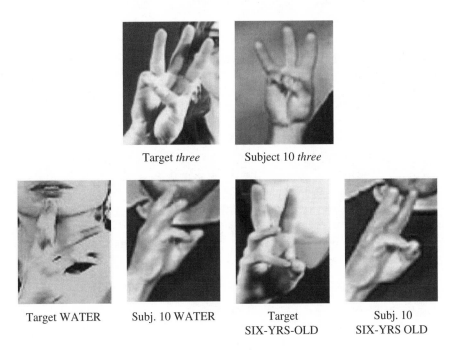

Target *three*   Subject 10 *three*

Target WATER   Subj. 10 WATER   Target   Subj. 10
                                         SIX-YRS-OLD   SIX-YRS OLD

Figure 3.10. Sign model and subject 10 handshapes for *three*, WATER, SIX-YEARS-OLD

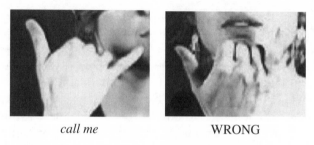

call me   WRONG

Figure 3.11. Target handshape for *call me* and WRONG

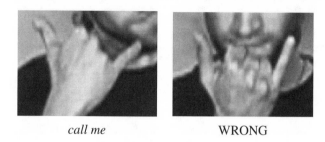

call me   WRONG

Figure 3.12. Subject 10 handshape for *call me* and WRONG

are otherwise very similar, and one might expect subjects to transfer their handshape from the *call me* gesture to signs requiring the Y handshape. However, this did not occur. As mentioned earlier, all four subjects accurately reproduced the *call me* gesture, with the pinky and thumb splayed widely. They also accurately reproduced sign stimuli targeting the Y handshape, such as WRONG, in which the pinky and thumb are not widely splayed (figures 3.11 and 3.12). Subjects 4 and 10 produced target Y handshape accurately 100 percent of the time (8/8 items), and subject 12 did so 75 percent of the time (6/8 items).

In this case I agree with Rosen (2004) that marked handshapes do not necessarily pose the same production challenges for M2 learners as they do for L1 child learners, whose motor skills are still developing. After all, even a complete ASL novice such as subject 10 was able to accurately reproduce the ASL handshape in WRONG after seeing it for the first time. Nevertheless, comparison of this case of nontransfer with those of transfer documented for subject 4 earlier suggests that markedness actually exerts a subtle influence in *both* cases. While subject 4 was able to perceptually extract the unmarked handshapes 1 and S from the sign stimuli and recognize them as being part of her existing gestural inventory, the highly marked handshape Y apparently did not trigger this same kind of recognition for subject 10. Thus, I argue that, despite subject 10's successful reproduction of WRONG, the marked status of the Y handshape may still be influencing his perception and categorization of this handshape. Markedness remains a factor that affects handshape accuracy even in cases of correct reproduction and should be considered seriously in studies of M2 signing.

FUTURE DIRECTIONS

Although this pilot study was not intended to paint a comprehensive picture of M2 handshape production, it draws attention to areas begging for study. As I have emphasized throughout this chapter, the data presented here are preliminary, and the conclusions drawn from them must now be subjected to further testing. Ideally, the intriguing patterns suggested by these limited data will inspire research on M2 handshapes well beyond my own research team and lead to a clearer understanding of the factors that influence the accurate formation of signs. For those wishing to pursue research in this area, I briefly note some insights that my students and I gained while running this pilot study that should be considered in future investigations.

First, this study presupposes that subjects generally perceived the stimuli handshapes accurately, but this is not necessarily the case. Subjects in both the current study and in Rosen's (2004) study produced errors that were clearly due to faulty perception of the stimuli. The most convincing of these were "mirror" errors, in which the subjects reproduced signs from their own perspective rather than from that of the model. In light of these observations, the selection of stimuli for future experiments should be informed more extensively by studies of subjects' perception and discrimination of handshapes (e.g., Baker 2002; Emmorey, McCullough, and Brentari 2003; Mathur and Best 2007).

Second, this pilot highlights for us the need for more information on handshape variation in both conventional American gesture and signs in ASL, as well as a consistent phonetic system for notating this variation (discussed in more detail below). My students and I were often surprised to find that some of the M2 handshapes we had initially categorized as errors were actually very faithful reproductions of the model's handshapes, which varied from what we had assumed to be standard. This discovery triggered a period of intensive observation and analysis of other signers around us, reminding us of the considerable variation in handshape that occurs even among native signers of ASL. Fortunately, our study was designed so that the model's signs were the only ones the subjects had ever been exposed to, so we could still confidently apply a standard of accuracy based on the model's production. Nonetheless, in a wider context, a better understanding of how much handshape variation exists in the signing population is clearly crucial for the accurate identification of handshape errors committed by M2 signers who are exposed to this hand-shape variation.

Third, my students and I realize in retrospect that, despite our efforts to control for complicating effects of movement, location, and other phonological factors in the stimuli, the effects of these factors were still very much in evidence. For instance, two-handed signs are automatically more complex than one-handed ones, particularly when two different handshapes are required (cf. Meier 2006). The subjects also displayed poor thumb and pinky control, a tendency that Boyes Braem (1990) noted in her observation of child L1 signing. While these factors do not necessarily preclude the inclusion of two-handed target signs or signs that require manipulation of the thumb or pinky in future experimental stimuli, researchers should be aware of the additional complexity these factors contribute and control for them accordingly. Careful balancing of these and other factors across the stimuli should allow for the meaningful application of statistical analysis and result in stronger results than this small pilot was able to achieve.

Fourth, any study of handshape requires a consistent notational system capable of capturing the fine details of handshape variation. Although this study analyzes handshapes with respect to certain features such as thumb opposition and finger splay, these are only two of many features that potentially distinguish a learner's handshape from the target. Using a notational system that comprehensively represents handshapes by their formational subfeatures, such as that presented by Johnson and Liddell (forthcoming), greatly increases the accuracy with which handshape data can be analyzed. Readers interested in how adoption of such a notational system affected the analysis presented in the current chapter are referred to Chen Pichler (2009).

Finally, although our study did not target movement, my students and I noted very striking movement errors in our data, including proximalization errors of the type described by Mirus, Rathmann, and Meier (2001). Clearly, future research on nonnative sign accent should include a thorough analysis of non-targetlike movement. One such study is currently under way by Goeke (forthcoming), but this area of investigation is sufficiently complex to warrant many studies in order to understand how non-targetlike movement contributes to sign accent.

APPLICATION TO SIGN LANGUAGE TEACHING

Studies of second language acquisition provide important insights into how humans perceive and categorize input in a new language and open a window into the workings of the human brain. They also inform classroom practice by suggesting ways to maximize the effectiveness of formal instruction. Although the existing research on M2 signing is still quite limited, it nevertheless offers some preliminary insight that may be useful to sign language instructors. For example, both Rosen (2004) and the current study emphasize the important influence of perception on production. A failure to perceive a phonetic distinction between two handshapes (such as the difference between the S and A handshapes) can lead to a failure to distinguish them in production. In such cases, explicitly drawing students' attention to important distinguishing features such as thumb opposition may help them establish separate perceptual categories for distinct handshapes. Studies of spoken L2 acquisition have reported encouraging results from explicit perception training, wherein speakers learn how to hear distinctions between L2 phonemes that they had previously perceived as a single category (Bradlow 2008). The fact that the main articulators for sign language (the hands) are readily visible could render explicit perception training in sign particularly effective.

Moreover, not all the errors produced by the subjects in this and other experimental studies will necessarily occur in the natural environment of the sign language classroom. For example, we noted a learning effect for many of our subjects, wherein certain signs that were reproduced incorrectly in the first set of stimuli were produced correctly in the second set. Many of these errors in our pilot data involved location and orientation rather than handshape, but they are a reminder that the artificial setting of laboratory experiments sometimes induces errors that do not occur in real life. Alternatively, some of these errors may occur only at the initial stages of exposure to ASL but be so ephemeral as to disappear within the first few days of sign instruction and then cease to cause further problems. The only way to know for sure would be to carry out this line of research in a longitudinal format and test actual ASL students enrolled in an ASL class as they progress in their learning. This would give us a more realistic picture of the patterns of handshape errors that M2 signers produce, as well as provide an opportunity to test the effects of markedness, transfer, dexterity, and perception proposed by laboratory studies of M2 signing.

CONCLUSIONS

My wording of the predictions motivating this study refer to markedness and transfer as independent factors that affect handshape accuracy in M2 signers. The limited pilot data presented here provide some support for individual effects of transfer (e.g., if the A handshape represents the subject's version of the fist, this handshape is transferred to signs also perceived as involving a fist) and markedness (e.g., unmarked B dot and 1 handshapes tend to be reproduced consistently, while marked open 8 is not). The markedness analysis is not incompatible with Rosen's (2004) assessment of handshape errors as being largely due to the limited dexterity of M2 signers; by nature, marked handshapes are difficult to produce and would thus be expected to pose difficulties for those with limited experience with language in the visual/ gestural modality.

These preliminary data also suggest that the effect of markedness and transfer on M2 handshape accuracy is interactive as well as individual, in that transfer (both positive and negative) is in some cases blocked for highly marked handshapes or for handshapes that combine with a marked location or movement pattern. In the terminology of speech perception models such as that advanced by Best (1995), markedness appears to be a factor that can prevent learners from perceptually assimilating certain handshapes to similar handshapes that they use in gestures and for which they already have an established handshape category. I propose that in such cases subjects approach the target sign as an unfamiliar bundle of handshape, movement, and location features that they must do their best to replicate in a short period of time. Their adult cognitive skills are sufficient to ensure accurate reproduction in some cases (e.g., the Y handshape in WRONG for subject 10) but not in others (e.g., the W handshape in WATER for subject 4), where they make errors reminiscent of those observed in the L1 ASL of young signers.

Of course, markedness and transfer alone cannot account for all the handshape errors that M2 signers produce. Our full set of data includes many examples of marked handshapes that were reproduced with higher accuracy than expected, even when these were distinct from those used in common American gestures and were therefore assumed to be novel for our subjects. In these cases, I agree with Rosen (2004) that the cognitive abilities of adult learners sometimes prevail over markedness and allow for the accurate reproduction of the target handshape where a child learner might typically fail. This should be a reminder of the fundamental complexity of second language acquisition in general: Each adult learner brings a unique combination of linguistic experience, aptitude, and motivation to the task of a new language; thus, no two learners will follow the same developmental path. When the new language also happens to involve a modality different from that of the learner's native language, additional challenges may arise. The most effective approach to M2 sign phonology will be one that recognizes both a variety of factors that influence accuracy and the complex ways in which they interact.

APPENDIX

Sign (in small capitals) and gesture (in lowercase letters) stimuli; the stimuli analyzed for this chapter are shown in **bold type** in table 3.2. Note: For two-handed signs in which both hands form the same handshape, each hand was counted separately in calculations of accuracy.

Table 3.2. Comprehensive List of Pilot Stimuli for Signs and Gestures

Highly unmarked handshapes	
A	Gesture: none
	Signs: ATHLETE, AUSTIN
A dot	Gesture: *thumbs up*
	Signs: NUT, PATIENCE, CONTINUE
S	**Gesture: *Yes!***
	Signs: WORK, SENATE, SYMBOL
I	**Gesture: *one/wait a minute***
	Signs: DIFFERENT, WHERE
5	Gesture: *five*
	Signs: MOVIE
claw	Gestures: *none*
	Signs: RAIN, BALL
Moderately unmarked handshapes	
B	Gesture: none
	Signs: SATISFIED, BLUE
B dot	**Gesture: *Stop!***
	Signs: MINE, YOURS, SCHOOL, PLEASE
F	Gesture: *A-OK*
	Signs: SIMPLE, PREACH, NOTHING-TO-IT
Moderately marked handshapes	
D	Gesture: none
	Signs: DENVER, DATE
V	Gesture: *peace/victory*
	Signs: LOOK-UP-AND-DOWN, VANILLA, STUCK
Y	**Gesture: *Call me***
	Signs: SAME, MEASURE, WRONG
W	**Gesture: *three***
	Signs: WATER, 6-YEARS-OLD
Highly marked handshapes	
open 8	**Gesture: none**
	Signs: MEDICINE, FEEL
R	Gesture: *Keep your fingers crossed*
	Signs: RULE, READY
N	Gesture: none
	Signs: NURSE, NEUTRAL

Note

This work was funded by a grant from the Gallaudet Research Institute. I would like to extend thanks to our ASL model and to subjects from the Gallaudet University and Georgetown University communities. Many thanks also to audience members at the Swarthmore 2008 conference and to students in my 2005, 2006, and 2007 LIN 812 classes for their help in data collection and discussion. I appreciate their excellent feedback and intuitions; all errors in the current report are mine.

Bibliography

Ann, Jean. 2006. *Frequency of Occurrence and Ease of Articulation of Sign Language Hand-shapes: The Taiwanese Example*. Washington, D.C.: Gallaudet University Press.

Armstrong, Nancy, and Melissa Wagner. 2003. *Field Guide to Gestures: How to Identify and Interpret Virtually Every Gesture Known to Man*. Philadelphia: Quirk.

Axtell, Roger E. 1997. *Gestures: The Do's and Taboos of Body Language around the World*. New York: Wiley.

Baker, Stephanie A. 2002. The Perception of Handshape in American Sign Language. PhD diss., University of Delaware.

Best, Cathi. 1995. A Direct Realist View of Cross-language Speech Perception. In *Speech Perception and Linguistic Experience: Issues in Cross-language Research*, ed. Winifred Strange, 171–204. Baltimore: York.

Boyes Braem, Penny. 1990. Acquisition of Handshape in American Sign Language. In *From Gesture to Sign Language in Hearing and Deaf Children*, ed. Virginia Volterra and Carol J. Erting, 107–127. Berlin: Springer.

Bradlow, Ann R. 2008. Training Non-native Language Sound Patterns. In *Phonology and Second Language Acquisition*, ed. Hansen J. Edwards and Mary L. Zampini, 287–308. Amsterdam: Benjamins.

Budding, Carlos, Rob Hoopes, Monica Mueller, and Karen Scarcello. 1995. Identification of Foreign Sign Language Accents by the Deaf. In *Gallaudet University Communication Forum*, vol.4, ed. Laura Byers, Jessica Chaiken, and Monica Mueller, 1–16. Washington, D.C.: Gallaudet University Press.

Chen Pichler, Deborah. 2006. Handshape in L2 ASL: Effects of Markedness and Transfer. Presented at the Ninth Congress on Theoretical Issues in Sign Language Research (TISLR), Florianópolis, Brazil, December 6–10.

———. 2008. Signing with an Accent: Second Language (L2) ASL Phonology. Presented at the Around the Deaf World in Two Days conference, Swarthmore College, February 29–March 1.

———. 2009. Sign Production by First-Time Hearing Signers: A Closer Look at Handshape Accuracy. *Cadernos de Saúde*, Special volume on sign languages, 2:37–50.

Customer. 2004. Review of *The Art of Sign Language* by Christopher Brown. Pocket Guide series. http://www.amazon.com/gp/product/customer-reviews/1592230571/sr=1–2/qid=1173985135/ref=cm_cr_dp_pt/104–5459912–5565530?ie=UTF8&n=283155&s=books&qid=1173985135&sr=1–2 (accessed November 30, 2006).

Eckman, Fred R. 1977. Markedness and the Contrastive Analysis Hypothesis. *Language Learning* 27: 315–330.

Emmorey, Karen, Stephen McCullough, and Diane Brentari. 2003. Categorical Perception in American Sign Language. *Language and Cognitive Processes* 18: 21–45.

Emmorey, Karen, Robin Thompson, and Rachael Colvin. 2008. Eye Gaze during Comprehension of American Sign Language by Native and Beginning Signers. *Journal of Deaf Studies and Deaf Education* 14: 237–243.

Flege, James E. 1995. Second Language Learning: Theory, Findings, and Problems. In *Speech Perception and Linguistic Experience: Issues in Cross-language Research,* ed. Winifred Strange, 233–237. Baltimore: York.

Goeke, Amber. 2005. The Effect of Handshape Error on the Perception of Non-native Accent in L2 ASL. Manuscript, Gallaudet University.

———. Forthcoming. Production of Movement in Users of American Sign Language and Its Influence on Being Identified as Non-native. PhD diss., Gallaudet University.

Jakobson, Roman. 1968. *Child Language, Aphasia, and Phonological Universals.* The Hague: Mouton.

Johnson, Robert E., and Scott Liddell. Forthcoming. A Phonetic Notation System for Sign Languages. Manuscript, Gallaudet University.

Kantor, Rebecca M. 1978. Identifying Native and Second Language Signers. *Communication and Cognition* 11(1): 39–55.

Major, Roy C. 2001. *Foreign Accent: The Ontogeny and Phylogeny of Second Language Phonology.* Mahwah, N.J.: Erlbaum.

Mathur, Gaurav, and Catherine Best. 2007. Three Experimental Techniques for Investigating Sign Language Processing. Presented at the twentieth annual CUNY Conference on Human Sentence Processing, La Jolla, Calif., March 29–31.

McIntire, Marina. 1977. The Acquisition of American Sign Language Hand Configurations. *Sign Language Studies* 16: 247–266.

———, and Judy S. Reilly. 1988. Nonmanual Behaviors in L1 & L2 Learners of American Sign Language. *Sign Language Studies* 61: 351–375.

Meier, Richard P. 2006. The Form of Early Signs: Explaining Signing Children's Articulatory Development. In *Advances in Sign Language Development by Deaf Children,* ed. Marc Marschark, Brenda Schick, and Patricia E. Spencer, 202–230. New York: Oxford University Press.

Mirus, Gene R., Christian Rathmann, and Richard P. Meier. 2001. Proximalization and Distalization of Sign Movement in Adult Learners. In *Signed Languages: Discoveries from International Research,* ed. Valerie Dively, Melanie Metzger, Sarah Taub, and Anne Marie Baer, 103–119. Washington, D.C.: Gallaudet University Press.

Rosen, Russell S. 2004. Beginning L2 Production Errors in ASL Lexical Phonology. *Sign Language and Linguistics* 7: 31–61.

Taub, Sarah, Dennis Galvan, Pilar Piñar, and Susan Mather. 2008. Gesture and ASL L2 Acquisition. In *Sign Languages: Spinning and Unraveling the Past, Present, and Future from TISLR9,* ed. Ronice Müller de Quadros, 639–651. Petropolis, Brazil: Editorar Arara Azul.

Thedeafway. n.d. http://www.thedeafway.net/html_files/faqsbot.htm#4 (accessed November 30, 2006).

Thompson, Robin. 2006. Eye Gaze in American Sign Language: Linguistic Functions for Verbs and Pronouns. PhD diss., University of California, San Diego.

Thompson, Robin, Karen Emmorey, and Robert Kluender. 2009. Learning to Look: The Acquisition of Eye Gaze Agreement during the Production of ASL Verbs. *Bilingualism: Language and Cognition* 12: 393–409.

Modality and Language in the Second Language Acquisition of American Sign Language

Russell S. Rosen

If the past decade provides any guide, the field of second language acquisition (SLA) of ASL is small but growing. A handful of published studies, especially those by Mirus, Rathmann, and Meier (2001), Rosen (2004), and Chen Pichler (this volume), have focused on how individuals learn ASL as a second language.

The studies examine both the ability of L2 learners to articulate the phonological properties of signs and the phonological errors they make in producing lexical items. One parameter, movement, as produced by L2 adult learners and nonnative signers, was studied by Mirus, Rathmann, and Meier (2001), who found an order in the mastery of the articulation of the movement parameter: The L2 signers in their study first used proximal joints, or articulators, such as shoulder and elbow, before they used distal joints such as wrists. They also substituted proximal for distal articulators.

Another parameter, handshape, is studied by Chen Pichler (this volume). Chen Pichler examines the errors made in imitating signs by the adult participants in her study. Using Boyes-Braem's order of acquisition of handshapes for L1 child learners of ASL as a point of comparison, Chen Pichler found that the participants substituted certain handshapes for others. In particular, handshapes that were acquired early by the L1 children were substituted for those that they acquired later. In addition, in Chen Pichler's study the adult L2 learners made errors in imitating handshapes of gestures not commonly used in the community. Chen Pichler proposes that the sources of production errors are markedness of handshapes, as well as the transfer of gestures used within the community.

Phonological errors in lexical production by L2 adult users of ASL were studied in Rosen (2004). Rosen found that the learners made two types of errors. They either signed the lexical items in a mirror depiction of the input source or failed to align their hands and fingers properly for the lexical items they were trying to produce. For instance, when they signed QUEEN, they moved the Q handshape in a diagonal line from the ipsilateral side of the chest to the contralateral side of the waist rather than in a diagonal line from the contralateral side of the chest to the ipsilateral side of the waist. When they signed CLASS, they signed it either with spread fingers (instead of fingers touching each other) or with thumbs placed inside the hand (against the palm). In the case of QUEEN, the learners made errors based on not putting themselves in the place of the model. Their perception and, hence, their production of the sign were therefore the mirror image of what they should have been. In the case of CLASS, they exhibited poor manual dexterity (due perhaps not so much to physical inability as to poor attention to the articulators, particularly distal ones). In other words, the learners exhibited poor cognitive control over manual dexterity and poor perceptual acuity of sign formations. Rosen (2004) proposed a cognitive phonology model to account for the L2 acquisition of ASL phonology.

These studies focus on one component of the grammar; they look mainly at articulatory phonetics. They suggest that, particularly for adult learners of ASL, the formation of articulatory handshape features is a cognitive process of creating and manipulating body schemas for linguistic purposes. In addition, these studies demonstrate that articulatory phonetics in sign language is distinct from phonology, just as the two systems are distinct in spoken language. Phonology in sign language is concerned with linguistic symbols that make up lexemes, and articulation in sign language involves processes that translate these linguistic symbols into motor control of the articulators.

The selection of articulation as the main topic in these studies may be due to the researchers' fascination with the modality-language issue in sign language acquisition. They were intrigued by how hearing individuals, primarily those who use spoken English as their first language, can learn the principles of a language in a different modality. The nature and production of the phonological parameters bring to light the nature and source of language in general and of sign language in particular. That the phonological parameters carry articulatory (binary) and segmental information for the construction of sign language is evidence that signed languages should be classified with spoken languages as natural human languages. That the actual features of the articulation system for spoken and signed languages differ enormously, however, distinguishes them as occurring in different modalities.

In other words, articulation is modality specific, whereas phonology (that is, the rules that govern how the various parameters can be combined) belongs to that thing we know as language, which is independent of modality. Here's the issue: The modality differences between, say, English and ASL, have, unfortunately, limited researchers from seeing the bigger picture regarding what is involved in the learning of ASL as a second language. The focus has typically been on modality differences, particularly for learners whose L1 languages are spoken. It's time to refocus on language as a whole.

The study of articulation alone does not sufficiently represent everything involved in the SLA of ASL. There are other components of language the learner must master as well, such as syntax. There is a need for the field of SLA studies to move forward and examine the syntactic constructions made by learners of ASL, for example. For this reason I take the opportunity here to move beyond research of the sort Chen Pichler and others have done and focus on the state of the field as a whole.

Learners of ASL as an L2 need to make linguistic sense of the visual input, connecting visual information about an action, the participants in it, and its location, for example, to a verb, various noun phrases, and locative phrases, respectively. Thus, any adequate theory of SLA for L2 learners of ASL must take into account the differences between sounds produced by the speech tract and perceived by the auditory tract versus manual shapes and movements produced by muscles and joints from the shoulder to the knuckles and perceived (typically) by vision. In addition, an adequate theory of SLA for L2 learners of ASL must look at grammatical units and take into account the many ways all languages (signed or spoken) are similar: They all use lexical categories (noun and verb, for example) and functional categories (number and temporal aspect, for example).

Even a brief consideration of the following question, which is among the most basic of questions for a syntax acquisition study, reveals the hopelessness of trying to disentangle these two foci of modality and language:

> What is the chronological order of acquisition of ASL syntax by L2 learners, particularly of lexical phrases such as those headed by noun, verb, adjective, and preposition, and of functional categories such as tense, temporal aspect, number, and others (many of which are conveyed by the nonmanual parameter)?

To see another difficulty in a single-focus approach to the study of SLA, consider the fact that ASL has concatenative (that is, linear) and nonconcatenative operations, both morphological and syntactic. Concatenative operations of ASL include producing signs (including compounds) and phrases by simply ordering one lexical item after another without modification of the internal structure of each item. Nonconcatenative operations of ASL include producing signs and phrases by altering the internal structure of lexical items (that is, by changing their phonological parameters). These operations involve modality-specific actions. Nonconcatenative operations are seen in noun and verb inflections, nonmanual contributions, classifier constructions, numeral incorporation, and the like. Nonconcatenative operations, perforce, must be governed by both the modality and linguistic principles of ASL, while it might be possible to argue that the concatenative properties are governed solely by the latter. As such, the acquisition of both concatenative and nonconcatenative operations of ASL needs to take into consideration its modality and language characteristics.

What we need to do is develop a theory of language acquisition that builds upon the relationship between modality and language. Such a theory must consider the gesture-sign interfaces in language acquisition. In this spirit, I offer the following proposal for consideration by future SLA of ASL researchers regarding the L2 acquisition of ASL syntax by learners whose L1 languages are spoken.

I contend that L2 learners of ASL, particularly those whose L1 languages are spoken, initially rely on their visual and manual abilities to understand and produce lexical items. There is no influence from L1 languages; indeed, learners cannot use any of the phonological structures in their L1 languages to help them learn ASL phonology.

In the intermediate stages, learners rely also on their linguistic knowledge of L1 word and phrase structure. If a grammatical structure in L1 appears in L2 as well, then the learner may have little trouble mastering that structure in L2. However, if L2 has structures that do not appear in L1, learners may have trouble mastering them.

Similarity in L1 and L2 structures expedites the acquisition of ASL concatenative syntactic operations (as well as concatenative morphological operations) since learners can rely on their linguistic knowledge of L1 to help them learn the linguistic structures in ASL. In general, there is full transfer of concatenative syntactic operations from L1 to L2 (Vainikka and Young-Scholten 1998; Clahsen and Felser 2006).

The transfer of nonconcatenative syntax, however, is complicated for learners of ASL as an L2 by the fact discussed earlier: Both modality principles and language principles come into play in nonconcatenative operations in ASL. With respect to spoken English as L1 and ASL as L2, L2 has nonconcatenative syntactic operations (as well as nonconcatenative morphological ones) that are not found in L1. Indeed, spoken English has at most minimal nonconcatenative syntax (and morphology), so there can be no influence from L1 on the acquisition of ASL nonconcatenative syntax. In this case, learners acquire nonconcatenative syntactic operations in L2 typically in the later stages of language acquisition. That is, before learners can acquire ASL's nonconcatenative syntactic structures, it appears they need to first acquire its concatenative syntactic structures. Here we have learning of L2 without transfer from L1 to L2.

This proposal is a work in progress and will undoubtedly be modified as new studies (my own and those of others) inform me. Nonetheless, it is clear that modality and language both interact and are profoundly involved in the learning of ASL as a second language for speakers whose L1 has a different modality. When L1 and L2 share the same modality, different interfaces between modality and language might be in play in second language acquisition.

Bibliography

Clahsen, Harald, and Claudia Felser. 2006. Continuity and Shallow Structures in Language Processing. *Applied Psycholinguistics* 27: 107–126.

Mirus, Gene R., Christian Rathmann, and Richard P. Meier. 2001. Proximalization and Distalization of Sign Movement in Adult Learners. In *Signed languages: Discoveries from International Research,* ed. Valerie L. Dively, Melanie Metzger, Sarah Taub, and Anne Marie Baer, 103–119. Washington, D.C.: Gallaudet University Press.

Rosen, Russell S. 2004. Beginning L2 Production Errors in ASL Lexical Phonology: A Cognitive Phonology Model. *Sign Language and Linguistics* 7(1): 31–61.

Vainikka, Anne, and Martha Young-Scholten. 1998. The Initial State in the L2 Acquisition of Phrase Structure. In *The Generative Study of Second Language Acquisition,* ed. Suzanne Flynn, Gita Martohardjono, and Wayne O'Neil, 17–34. Mahwah, N.J.: Erlbaum.

Getting to the Point

How a Simple Gesture Became a Linguistic Element in Nicaraguan Signing

Ann Senghas and Marie Coppola

INTRODUCTION

If you have ever watched people communicating in a sign language you didn't know, you most likely remember seeing many unfamiliar signs—too many to follow the conversation. But sprinkled among them you also may have noticed some familiar movements, including nods, facial expressions, and even local hand gestures. They probably looked a lot like the gestures that hearing people make when they are talking. In the hands of Deaf people, many such gesticulations are, in fact, signs. As signs, they have a different meaning from the identical gesture and can be combined with other signs in a way that a gesture cannot.

Why is this the case? First, it seems pretty clear that many signs originally came from gestures, which were the raw materials that deaf people used when they first created sign languages. Then, as the gestures became coordinated with each other to form a language, their meanings and their linguistic functions changed.

For basic vocabulary, the historical path is the most obvious. If there is a local gesture that means 'drink,' it can easily be adapted into a sign that means 'drink.' A gesture commonly used by beggars to ask for money can become a sign for 'beg.' Gestures can be reshaped into linguistic elements, too (Casey 2003; Newport and Supalla 2000; Wilcox 2004), and here the gap between the gesture and the sign is greater. However, it is often still possible to trace the link from a modern sign back to its gesture. A sign in Jordanian Sign Language that marks events as not yet completed likely originated as a common Jordanian gesture that means 'wait a second' (Hendriks 2004). A future marker in American Sign Language (ASL) probably started out as a French gesture that means 'go' (Janzen and Shaffer 2002). Even facial expressions can become linguistic elements. Conditional expressions in ASL, as in "If I were president . . ." are linguistically marked by a raising of the eyebrows; this linguistic element probably originated in a similar, brow-raising facial gesture that English speakers make when they produce conditional expressions (Pyers and Emmorey 2008).

Sign languages aren't the only languages that change over time and develop new linguistic elements. All languages do. It's not unusual for old words to be reshaped into new linguistic elements (Hopper and Traugott 1993; Traugott and Heine 1991). For example, the word *will* in English used to mean 'want.' It can still have that meaning, but today it more often marks future tense. So, in modern English, *Ritchie will run* says nothing about whether Ritchie wants to run; it tells us only that the running will take place in the future. What is unusual in the case of sign languages is that they use the visual-manual modality, as gestures do. As a result, sign languages have more than old words at their disposal—they can use gestures, too, even those like facial expressions that were never produced alone (that is, without speech) (Janzen and Shaffer 2002; Pfau and Steinbach 2006; Rathmann and Mathur 2008; Wilcox 2004).

How, exactly, do gestures become linguistic elements? There are likely to be several steps in the process, with every step taking a form further from its gestural roots. Because changes happen as languages are passed down from one generation to the next, we propose that children are responsible. The skills that children have for learning language may be the creative force behind language change as well. By capturing the precise steps in the process, we can learn about the nature of that creative ability.

In this chapter we take a single, humble gesture—the point—and follow its transformation into a linguistic element. This basic gesture often accompanies speech to indicate real-world locations and objects that surround a speaker. As it is taken up by signers and transformed into a sign, we see an increase in its use to identify the participants in events rather than locations or real-world objects. With this shift, points take on new linguistic functions, including indicating the subject of a verb and serving as a pronoun.

To catch the very earliest stages of such a transformation, we turned to a young language—Nicaraguan Sign Language (NSL). Because NSL is only thirty years old, the pioneering generation that created it, those who really got their hands dirty sculpting gestures into signs, are around today and are able to show us what the earliest Nicaraguan signing looked like.

FROM NICARAGUAN HOMESIGNS TO NICARAGUAN SIGN LANGUAGE

The Nicaraguan Deaf community and its language have existed only since the late 1970s (Kegl and Iwata 1989; Kegl, Senghas, and Coppola 1999; Polich

2005; Richard Senghas 2003). Before that time, deaf Nicaraguans had few opportunities to meet each other. Most deaf people stayed at home most of the time, where they came into contact only with neighbors and family members who were not deaf. The few day schools and clinics available for deaf children served very small numbers of children for short periods, with no contact outside school hours (Polich 2005). As a result, deaf children had minimal contact with each other and no contact with deaf individuals older than themselves. It is quite clear, when you meet deaf adults who grew up before the 1970s, that the conditions then were insufficient for a sign language to develop. Very few of those in their late forties and older socialize with other deaf people, and they do not have a sign language even today.

Deaf children in this situation often develop homesigns to communicate with the hearing people around them (Goldin-Meadow 2003; Morford 1996). Homesigns are systems of gestural communication that are typically used only with family members and close neighbors. Homesign systems developed by young children in places as different as the United States and Taiwan have been found to include certain common, fundamental language characteristics, including a basic vocabulary, consistent word order frames that allow recursion (Goldin-Meadow 1982), and the ability to discuss referents displaced in space and time from the here and now (Morford 1993).

When homesigners continue to use their systems into adulthood, their signing becomes more complex. An examination of the homesign systems used by three different Nicaraguan adults found that each had developed a way to indicate the grammatical subject of a sentence (Coppola and Newport 2005). However, homesign lexicons, sentence patterns, and use of the signing space, while internally consistent, are idiosyncratic and vary widely from one deaf homesigner to another (Coppola 2002; Coppola and So 2005). The fact that homesigners are not part of a larger signing community and are therefore unable to pass their system along to new learners seems to limit the complexity of homesign systems.

For a sign language to develop beyond homesigns requires a community in contact, both among peers and across generations. For deaf Nicaraguans, the critical change occurred with the rapid expansion of special education programs in the late 1970s. A new center for special education opened in 1977, with classes in deaf education offered from preschool through grade six. Initially, approximately fifty deaf students enrolled, increasing to one hundred within the first few years (Polich 2005). Although language instruction aimed to teach students to lip-read and to speak Spanish (with little success), the children spontaneously used gestures to communicate with each other, and they did so with enthusiasm whenever they had the chance—on the buses, during recess, even behind the teachers' backs in class. These interactions served as the starting point of a new sign language and a new social community. What started as a hodgepodge of different homesign systems must have begun to reshape itself at this time, eventually converging into a single, common system. In 1981 a vocational center for adolescents with disabilities opened, and many of the alumni of the primary school program enrolled. In 1983 the two centers were serving more than four hundred deaf students altogether (Polich 2005).

Every year since then, a new wave of children has entered school (typically at the preschool level) and learned to sign by socializing naturally with the older children there. Graduates of these programs have maintained social contact into adulthood, establishing social and athletic programs for deaf adults, celebrating major holidays together, even marrying other deaf people and starting new families together. Today members of the community range in age from birth to forty-five and number more than a thousand. They communicate in Nicaraguan Sign Language (NSL), the language that emerged from their social contact, and most of them have used it as their primary (indeed, only) language throughout their lives.

Because children entered this group steadily throughout the 1980s and 1990s, the community today provides a snapshot of a continuum of language experience. Recall that those who arrived in its earliest years encountered a fledgling system of signing, while those who arrived more recently encountered a richer, more developed language. This social situation has led to an unusual language community in which the richest, most fluent signers are the youngest members. It provides us with a rare opportunity to track the historical development of a new language by comparing different age cohorts of signers, progressing forward in time from older to younger signers.

To capture different periods in the emergence of the language, we have found it convenient to group members of the community into cohorts based on the period in which they first arrived. Those children who arrived in the late 1970s and early 1980s (now adults) form the first cohort, those who arrived in the mid- to late 1980s (now adolescents) form the second cohort, and those who arrived in the 1990s (now children) form the third cohort. In the study that we describe here, we compared signed stories narrated in NSL by four deaf signers from each of these three cohorts. All of them are fluent signers who have been using NSL as their primary language all of their lives—since they were five or younger.

To go one level deeper in the fossil record, we compared these NSL signers to four deaf homesigners who never entered the programs in Managua. As adults, these homesigners have had at most sporadic contact with signers of NSL; none of them has a regular communication partner who signs NSL, none uses NSL vocabulary (aside from those signs that share forms with common Nicaraguan gestures), and none has even rudimentary knowledge of NSL grammar. The homesigners ranged from twenty to thirty years of age at the time their narratives were elicited. They give us a view of the communication systems of deaf Nicaraguans before NSL developed.

To collect comparable language samples from all of the participants, we showed them each an animated cartoon titled "Canary Row," involving the familiar characters Sylvester the cat and Tweety Bird. This cartoon has been used extensively in previous research on sign languages and gesture. (For a full description see McNeill 1992.) Participants watched the cartoon a few times on a monitor and then told the story to someone else. The NSL signers told the story to a peer from the same cohort, and the homesigners told the story to a communication partner familiar with their homesign system. All of the narratives were videotaped for later analysis.

FOLLOWING A FORM

For many reasons, pointing gestures are good candidates to be taken up and integrated into a new sign language. People use points all the time. They have been found in the gestures that accompany speech (Kendon 2004; Kita and Özyürek 2003; McNeill 1992; and many others), in mature sign languages (Sandler and Lillo-Martin 2006), and in homesign (Coppola 2002; Fusellier-Souza 2006; Goldin-Meadow and Mylander 1984; Morford 1996). Points are generally made with an extended finger or an open hand directed away from the body, though you can also point with other parts of the body, such as by jutting an elbow or pursing the lips in the direction of the intended referent (Kegl 2002; Kita 2003). Both hearing children (Bates et al. 1979) and deaf children (Bellugi and Klima 1982; Hoffmeister 1978) start producing points at a very young age, along with their very first utterances.

Points are so pervasive that it is easy to overlook their complexity and the mental machinery required to interpret them. Even the most basic use of a point—to direct someone's attention to an object in the immediate environment—requires that both communication partners understand that the person who produces the point intends to refer to something. Try producing a point for your cat, and you will find the cat is more likely to sniff your finger than follow its trajectory across the room. Most of the time, when people point, they are speaking at the same time, and the timing and movement of the point are coordinated with their speech (McNeill 1992, 2005). To understand such pointing, a listener must coordinate it with the spoken words and the greater context of the conversation. Among other uses, such cospeech points often provide information about the location or identity of a referent, as in points that accompany expressions like *over there* or *that tablecloth*. Even if you can't hear the speech, you can often infer the intended places and objects in the world to which such points refer. For this reason, it is perhaps unsurprising that points can be used in sign languages for the same function. Researchers have proposed that pointing entered the grammar of sign languages as a marker of location (Pfau and Steinbach 2006), though their use in mature sign languages has expanded to include many other functions, to which we now turn.

POINTING IN SIGN LANGUAGES

Pointing movements accomplish a range of tasks in sign languages around the world. They indicate the participants of events and their roles by linking verbs to nouns to make it clear who does what to whom (Engberg-Pedersen 1993; McBurney 2002; Meier 1990; Padden 1988; and others). They can serve as determiners by combining with nouns to indicate that a referent is either a specific one that has been mentioned before, a generic one, or a new referent (Bahan et al. 1995; Zimmer and Patschke 1990). They are also used to describe the locations of objects and events (Emmorey 2002; Padden 1988; Shepard-Kegl 1985). (Some recent accounts propose that these uses of points are not linguistic and should be considered a gestural component of the language (Liddell 1995; Liddell and Metzger 1998).)

Of course, points in sign languages can be used to draw attention to things in the immediate environment, just as in co-speech gesture (Liddell 1996). However, when the referent is not in the immediate here and now, the use is a more abstract one. The particular use depends partly on the form of the point. Within each particular sign language, different types of points can carry out different functions. For example, in ASL, a point with the index finger can show the subject or object of a verb, like *he* or *him*, while an open palm shows possession, like *his* or *yours*.

Sign languages make extensive use of the three-dimensional space in front of the signer in an integrated system that includes much more than just pointing. In many sign languages, locations in the signing space can become associated with particular referents (Klima and Bellugi 1979; Meier 2002; Meir 1998; Padden 1988; Supalla 1982). The signer can then incorporate a location into other signs in order to refer to its referent and to link other signs with it. For example, a signer might associate a man with a location on the right and later produce the sign PAY toward the right, indicating that the man was paid. In this way, signers can use locations in the signing space to link characters to their roles in certain events, or objects with their traits. Locations in the signing space can also be associated with particular places, or with points along a timeline (Frishberg and Gough 2000; Taub 2001). All mature sign languages that have been documented take advantage of the signing space for these kinds of functions, though the specific uses differ from language to language. Any use of pointing must be compatible with the other devices of a language. When they have been used to assign meaning to certain locations in the signing space, points to those locations can then take on meaning themselves.

Some of the uses of pointing that are common to sign languages have been documented in homesigns as well. Deaf homesigning children in many countries, including the United States, Taiwan, Nicaragua, and Spain, all use a point to refer to objects and locations (Goldin-Meadow 2003). Two elderly Japanese sisters who are homesigners were also found to use points for these functions and to indicate nonpresent persons and objects. They also used points as prosodic markers for phrases and clauses (Torigoe 2000). Previous work with four adult homesigners in Nicaragua found that each had developed a way to indicate nonpresent participants and their roles in simple events; these devices included points to the chest to indicate the agent of an event, points to other people who were present, points to fingers to represent participants in events, and points to empty spatial locations to indicate both locations and persons (Coppola and So 2005).

PICKING OUT THE POINTS IN NICARAGUAN NARRATIVES

We decided to follow a single element, the point, as it developed from a gesture to a linguistic form. To accomplish this, we systematically compared the points produced by participants situated at four different moments along a continuum of language emergence: adult homesigners who never acquired a conventional sign language, as well as NSL signers who acquired the language at three successive periods during its emergence, that is, first-, second-, and third-cohort signers. How do the form and the function of pointing change as we progress along this continuum?

We reviewed the narratives that we had videotaped from each signer and picked out every instance of a point made with a finger, hand, or even an outward movement of the arm. We set aside those few instances (ten altogether) that were directed toward some aspect of the immediate real-world environment, such as a nearby object or the communication partner. The remaining points were the focus of our analyses. Some of them were directed at a part of the signer's body (typically the chest), and the large majority pointed to an empty space.

We then determined the meaning and function of the point within the narrative. To do this, we looked at the context of the narrative to see what the point referred to. We categorized the points into two types: those that referred to locations (such as 'overhead' or 'to the left') and those that referred to persons or objects (such as Tweety Bird or the cage). We refer to these functions as locative and nominal uses.[1]

Note that both of these types of use entail a displacement of the referent from the real world and real objects. This kind of displacement is a fundamental symbolic characteristic of language that allows reference to entities and locations that are not part of the here and now (Hockett 1966). As the points took on this symbolic function, we also examined whether they combined with other signs to form phrases. The ability to combine and recombine elements is another fundamental characteristic of language. It enables the creation of new expressions with even a limited set of symbols. These were the kinds of changes we set out to capture as pointing gestures became integrated into the emerging grammar of NSL.

FROM LOCATIVE TO NOMINAL POINTS

As we counted up the locative and nominal uses of points, we wanted to be sure to take into account the variation in signing rate and the length of the narratives of the signers in our different groups. To do this, we computed how often each kind of point appeared per one thousand signs for each signer. Specifically, we first counted the locative and nominal points produced by each participant in the eight stories that make up the Canary Row narrative. These were our numerators. We then calculated the signing rate of each participant for the fifth story. We used this calculation to estimate the number of signs produced in the entire narrative. By using this second figure in the denominator, we effectively controlled for variation in the signing rate and length of narratives. We then multiplied this proportion by one thousand. This adjusted amount is reported in the following results. (However, we see a similar pattern of results when we plot the raw number of points instead.)

We found many locative uses of points in the narratives. An example is given in figure 4.1, in which a homesigner points above his own head to refer to a location above the head of the cat in the story. Note that his eye gaze follows the point. This use of eye gaze with a locative is highly typical for all four groups, and may even be obligatory.

We also found several nominal uses of points. An example is shown in figure 4.2, in which a first-cohort signer points to her left to refer to Tweety Bird. The nominal points are quite different in appearance from the locative points. They are signed more quickly and with a smaller movement or no movement at all. Eye gaze, in these cases, does not follow the point. In figure 4.2 the signer closes her eyes as she points to the left.

The most striking difference between the locative and nominal points is how often they are produced. We discovered that this frequency depends on language group. Specifically, the nominal uses—and not the locative— increase dramatically across the continuum of groups. This development can be seen in figure 4.3. For each group, the first bar represents the locative points, that is, the points used to refer to locations. As you look across the groups, you can see that these points are frequently produced by all of the groups and at a relatively constant rate. A linear regression analysis did not detect any change across the groups.

Figure 4.1. Example of a locative point. A homesigner points above his own head to refer to the location above the cat. Note that his eye gaze follows the point.

The second bar for each group refers to the nominal points, that is, the points that refer to characters and things. As you look across the groups, you can see that each one uses this type of point more than the last, from the homesigners through the three cohorts of NSL signers. A linear regression analysis revealed a significant increase across the groups: $F (1,14) = 10.2$, $p = 0.006$.

COMBINING POINTS WITH VERBS TO FORM COMPLEX EXPRESSIONS

The fact that nominal points are being used with greater frequency in more recent versions of NSL suggests that they are being used differently from before. To examine this question more closely, we counted how often points

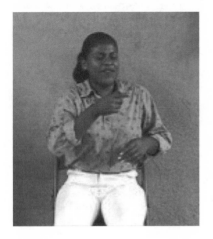

Figure 4.2. Example of a nominal point. A first-cohort signer points to her left to refer to the bird, which has been previously associated with that locus. Note that the movement is constrained within the signing space, and that her eye gaze does not follow the point.

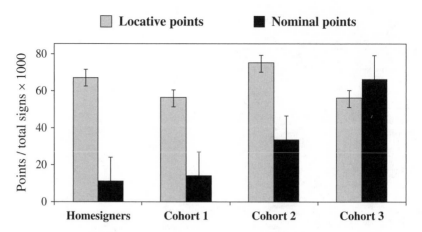

Figure 4.3. Points with locative and nominal uses. In contrast to locative points, which do not differ systematically across groups, nominal points increase across the language continuum, reflecting the emergence of a new function for these forms.

were combined with another sign to form a phrase. We then computed, for each group, how frequently the points combined with a noun, as in POINT + BOOKCASE (figure 4.4), or a verb, as in POINT + TALK (figure 4.5). (We defined *verbs* here to include all verbal elements, including plain verbs, classifier constructions, and constructed action sequences.) When we considered how often nominal points were combined with verbs, a very clear pattern emerged. As you can see in figure 4.6, this combination increases dramatically across the continuum. A linear regression analysis again revealed a significant increase across the groups: $F (1,14) = 5.9$, $p = 0.03$.

No such pattern emerged when we counted up how often nominal points were combined with nouns. There was also no such pattern for locative points in combination with either nouns or verbs. Apparently something is special about the combination of nominal points with verbs. They appear to reflect a change in function, in which points are increasingly being used in a pronoun-like way to indicate the subjects and objects that need to be associated with verbs. In this way, signers can show who is doing what to whom without repeating nouns or the names of characters. For a long time, homesigners and signers have been combining nouns with verbs to form basic sentences. The pattern of change shown here suggests that nominal points replace many of the nouns in these sentences.

GESTURE IN, GRAMMAR OUT

As we look at the development of signing in Nicaragua from its origins in home-signs through three age cohorts of NSL signers, we see a shift in the use of the

point-loc

bookcase-a

bookcase-b

bookcase-c

Figure 4.4. An example of a locative point combined with a noun, produced by a first-cohort signer. He produces a point to the upper right, followed by a three-part sign for BOOKCASE, meaning, "There is a bookcase up off to the right side."

point-nom

talk-a

talk-b

Figure 4.5. An example of a nominal point combined with a verb, produced by a third-cohort signer. She produces a point to her left, followed by the sign TALK, meaning, "He (Sylvester the cat) talks."

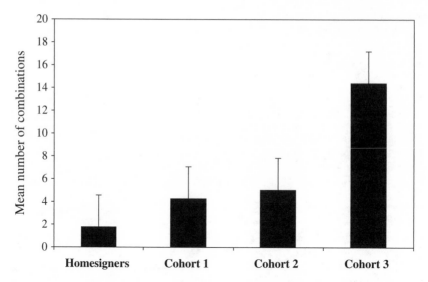

Figure 4.6. Combinations of nominal points with verbs. The number of combinations of nominal points with verbs increases across the language continuum, reflecting the integration of this new function for pointing into the syntax.

manual point. What started out with a mostly universal, concrete, locative meaning that is close to its gestural roots has taken on a more symbolic, abstract, and displaced nominal (and possibly pronominal) function. Over the same period, pointing signs have become reduced phonetically and lost some or all of their movement across space. Throughout this process, they are being integrated into the linguistic system of NSL and becoming part of its grammar. The new points participate in constructions that give them a more categorical, languagelike, less context-bound flavor than the co-speech forms that are their origin.

Other changes in NSL include a similar repurposing of the signing space. For example, in earlier work, one of us proposed that concrete uses of space (such as describing where people are sitting) were a precursor to more abstract uses (such as indicating that signs are coreferent) (Ann Senghas 2003). The interesting change in both of these cases is that signing space loses spatial meaning. In the case of pointing, the locative piece must be separated from a holistic package that includes the immediate physical context (the here and now), leaving its form and a bit of associated semiotic content. Once the point has been segmented in this way, it can be combined with other linguistic elements to form phrases and sentences. (See Senghas, Kita, and Özyürek [2004] for a description of this segmentation process in the domain of path and manner of movement.)

Researchers who study how space is used by sign languages often argue about whether these uses are part of a linguistic system or are gestural (and, by implication, less linguistically integrated). One thing is clear to us: The use of pointing and space that we have found here differs strikingly from that of gestures that accompany speech. Indeed, the more these uses develop, the less they show the spatial meaning associated with typical pointing gestures. Apparently, a crucial step in the transformation of pointing gestures into forms that can be used as abstract, recombinable linguistic elements seems to be the loss of their locative content. This is why, as we move along the continuum from the earliest to the most developed form of NSL, we find more and more points to locations that refer not to locations but to entities.

Because we know the history of NSL, we can deduce who is responsible for these changes: children, waves of new children and more children, learning and relearning the language, transforming it into something different from what it was. This same process most likely is responsible for historical changes in all languages as they are passed from one generation to the next, each generation tweaking the system before passing it on. In this extreme case, where much of the system was still very close to its holistic and unanalyzed gestural roots, the process of learning results in more than tweaks—it leads to the creation of linguistic structure. As children learned their language, they also created it.

By focusing our attention on pointing, we have captured a small part of this creative process. Over a period of only thirty years, a holistic, spatial gesture used to draw attention to real-world objects and their locations has been transformed into an abstract point at empty air, referring to some nonpresent referent at some nonpresent time. With its new status, it can combine with other elements and draw meaning from the structure of the sentence. This new use is more abstract, more displaced from the here and now, and more linguistic in function. This is the transformative power of human language acquisition.

Note

1. All of the data were coded by the second author; a subset of the data was coded by the first author to ensure reliability of the coding categories. Intercoder reliability for locative versus nominal reference was 0.95.

Bibliography

Bahan, Benjamin, Judy Kegl, Dawn MacLaughlin, and Carol Neidle. 1995. Convergent Evidence for the Structure of Determiner Phrases in American Sign Language. In *FLSM VI: Proceedings of the Sixth Annual Meeting of the Formal Linguistics Society of Mid-America.* Vol. 2, *Syntax II and Semantics/Pragmatics,* ed. Leslie Gabriele, Debra Hardison, and Robert Westmoreland, 1–12. Bloomington: Indiana University Linguistics Club.

Bates, Elizabeth, Laura Benigni, Inge Bretherton, Luigia Camaioni, and Virginia Volterra. 1979. *The Emergence of Symbols: Cognition and Communication in Infancy.* New York: Academic Press.

Bellugi, Ursula, and Edward Klima. 1982. From Gesture to Sign: Deixis in a Visuogestural Language. In *Speech, Place, and Action: Studies in Deixis and Related Topics,* ed. R. J. Jarvella and Wolfgang Klein, 279–313. New York: Wiley.

Casey, Shannon. 2003. "Agreement" in Gestures and Signed Languages: The Use of Directionality to Indicate Referents Involved in Actions. PhD diss., University of California at San Diego.

Coppola, Marie. 2002. The Emergence of the Grammatical Category of Subject in Home Sign: Evidence from Family-based Gesture Systems in Nicaragua. PhD diss., University of Rochester.

———, and Elissa L. Newport. 2005. Grammatical Subjects in Home Sign: Abstract Linguistic Structure in Adult Primary Gesture Systems without Linguistic Input. *Proceedings of the National Academy of Science* 102: 19249–19253.

———, and Wing Chee So. 2005. Abstract and Object-anchored Deixis: Pointing and Spatial Layout in Adult Homesign Systems in Nicaragua. In *BUCLD 29: Proceedings of the 29th Annual Boston University Conference on Language Development,* ed. Manuella R. Clark-Cotton, Alejna Brugos, and Seungwan Ha, 144–155. Somerville, Mass.: Cascadilla.

Emmorey, Karen. 2002. *Language, Cognition, and the Brain: Insights From Sign Language Research.* Mahwah, N.J.: Erlbaum.

Engberg-Pedersen, Elisabeth. 1993. *Space in Danish Sign Language: The Semantics and Morphosyntax of the Use of Space in a Visual Language.* Hamburg: Signum.

Frishberg, Nancy, and Bonnie Gough. 2000. Morphology in American Sign Language. *Sign Language and Linguistics* 3(1): 103–131.

Fusellier-Souza, Ivani. 2006. Emergence and Development of Signed Languages: From a Semiogenetic Point of View. *Sign Language Studies* 7: 30–56.

Goldin-Meadow, Susan. 1982. The Resilience of Recursion: A Study of a Communication System Developed without a Conventional Language Model. In *Language Acquisition: The State of the Art,* ed. Eric Wanner and Lila R. Gleitman, 51–77. New York: Cambridge University Press.

———. 2003. *The Resilience of Language: What Gesture Creation in Deaf Children Can Tell Us about How All Children Learn Language.* Essays in Developmental Psychology. New York: Psychology Press.

———, and Carolyn Mylander. 1984. Gestural Communication in Deaf Children: The Effects and Noneffects of Parental Input on Early Language Development. *Monographs of the Society for Research in Child Development* 49.

Hendriks, Bernadet. 2004. *An Introduction to the Grammar of Jordanian Sign Language.* Salt, Jordan: Al-Balqa University.

Hockett, Charles Francis. 1966. The Problem of Universals in Language. In *Universals of Language,* ed. Joseph H. Greenberg, 1–29. Cambridge, Mass.: MIT Press.

Hoffmeister, Robert J. 1978. The Development of Demonstrative Pronouns, Locatives, and Personal Pronouns in the Acquisition of ASL by Deaf Children of Deaf Parents. PhD diss., University of Minnesota.

Hopper, Paul J., and Elizabeth Closs Traugott. 1993. *Grammaticalization.* Cambridge Textbooks in Linguistics. New York: Cambridge University Press.

Janzen, Terry, and Barbara Shaffer. 2002. Gesture as the Substrate in the Process of ASL Grammaticalization. In *Modality and Structure in Signed and Spoken Languages,* ed. Richard P. Meier, Kearsy Cormier, and David Quinto-Pozos, 199–223. New York: Cambridge University Press.

Kegl, Judy. 2002. Language Emergence in a Language-ready Brain: Acquisition. In *Directions in Sign Language Acquisition,* ed. Gary Morgan and Bencie Woll, 207–254. Amsterdam: Benjamins.

———, and Gail Iwata. 1989. Lenguaje de Signos Nicaragüense: A Pidgin Sheds Light on the "Creole?" ASL. In *Proceedings of the Fourth Annual Meeting of the Pacific Linguistics Conference,* ed. Robert Carlsson, Scott DeLancey, Spike Gildea, Doris Payne, and Anju Saxena, 266–294. Eugene, Ore., May.

Kegl, Judy, Ann Senghas, and Marie Coppola. 1999. Creation through Contact: Sign Language Emergence and Sign Language Change in Nicaragua. In *Language Creation and Language Change: Creolization, Diachrony, and Development,* ed. Michel DeGraff, 179–237. Cambridge, Mass.: MIT Press.

Kendon, Adam. 2004. *Gesture: Visible Action as Utterance.* New York: Cambridge University Press.

Kita, Sotaro. 2003. Pointing: A Foundational Building Block of Human Communication. In *Pointing: Where Language, Culture, and Cognition Meet,* ed. Sotaro Kita, 1–8. Mahwah, N.J.: Erlbaum.

———, and Asli Özyürek. 2003. What Does Cross-linguistic Variation in Semantic Coordination of Speech and Gesture Reveal?: Evidence for an Interface Representation of Spatial Thinking and Speaking. *Journal of Memory and Language* 48:16–32.

Klima, Edward, and Ursula Bellugi. 1979. *The Signs of Language.* Cambridge, Mass.: Harvard University Press.

Liddell, Scott K. 1995. Real, Surrogate, and Token Space: Grammatical Consequences in ASL. In *Language, Gesture, and Space,* ed. Karen Emmorey and Judy Snitzer Reilly, 19–41. Hillsdale, NJ: Erlbaum.

———. 1996. Spatial Representations in Discourse: Comparing Spoken and Signed Language. *Lingua* 98: 145–167.

———, and Melanie Metzger. 1998. Gesture in Sign Language Discourse. *Journal of Pragmatics* 30: 657–697.

McBurney, Susan L. 2002. Pronominal Reference in Signed and Spoken Language. In *Modality and Structure in Signed and Spoken Languages,* ed. Richard P. Meier, Kearsy Cormier, and David Quinto-Pozos. New York: Cambridge University Press.

McNeill, David. 1992. *Hand and Mind: What Gestures Reveal about Thought.* Chicago: University of Chicago Press.

———. 2005. *Gesture and Thought.* Chicago: University of Chicago Press.

Meier, Richard P. 1990. Person Deixis in American Sign Language. In *Theoretical Issues in Sign Language Research,* ed. Susan Fischer and Patricia Siple, 175–190. Chicago: University of Chicago Press.

———. 2002. The Acquisition of Verb Agreement: Pointing Out Arguments for the Linguistic Status of Agreement in Sign Languages. In *Current Developments in the Study of Signed Language Acquisition,* ed. Gary Morgan and Bencie Woll, 115–141. Amsterdam: Benjamins.

Meir, Irit. 1998. Syntactic-semantic Interaction in Israeli Sign Language Verbs: The Case of Backward Verbs. *Sign Language and Linguistics* 1: 3–37.

Morford, Jill Patterson. 1993. Creating the Language of Thought: The Development of Displaced Reference in Child-generated Language. PhD diss., University of Chicago.

———. 1996. Insights to Language from the Study of Gesture: A Review of Research on the Gestural Communication of Non-signing Deaf People. *Language and Communication* 16: 165–178.

Newport, Elissa L., and Ted Supalla. 2000. Sign Language Research at the Millennium. In *The Signs of Language Revisited: An Anthology to Honor Ursula Bellugi and Edward Klima*, ed. Karen Emmorey and Harlan L. Lane, 103–114. Mahwah, N.J.: Erlbaum.

Padden, Carol. 1988. *Interaction of Morphology and Syntax in American Sign Language.* New York: Garland.

Pfau, Roland, and Markus Steinbach. 2006. Modality-independent and Modality-specific Aspects of Grammaticalization in Sign Languages. *Linguistics in Potsdam* 24: 3–98. Potsdam, Germany: Institute of Linguistics. http://www.ling.uni-potsdam.de/lip/.

Polich, Laura. 2005. *The Emergence of the Deaf Community in Nicaragua: "With Sign Language You Can Learn So Much."* Washington, D.C.: Gallaudet University Press.

Pyers, Jennie E., and Karen Emmorey. 2008. The Face of Bimodal Bilingualism: Bilinguals Produce ASL Grammar While Speaking English. *Psychological Science* 19: 531–536.

Rathmann, Christian, and Gaurav Mathur. 2008. Verb Agreement as a Linguistic Innovation in Signed Languages. In *Signs of the Time: Selected Papers from TISLR 8*, ed. Josep Quer, 191–216. Hamburg: Signum.

Sandler, Wendy, and Diane C. Lillo-Martin. 2006. *Sign Language and Linguistic Universals.* New York: Cambridge University Press.

Senghas, Ann. 2003. Intergenerational Influence and Ontogenetic Development in the Emergence of Spatial Grammar in Nicaraguan Sign Language. *Cognitive Development* 18: 511–531.

———, Sotaro Kita, and Asli Özyürek. 2004. Children Creating Core Properties of Language: Evidence from an Emerging Sign Language in Nicaragua. *Science* 305: 1779–1782.

Senghas, Richard J. 2003. New Ways to Be Deaf in Nicaragua: Changes in Language, Personhood, and Community. In *Many Ways to Be Deaf: International, Linguistic, and Sociocultural Variation,* ed. Leila Monaghan, Karen Nakamura, Constanze Schmaling, and Graham H. Turner, 260–282. Washington, D.C.: Gallaudet University Press.

Shepard-Kegl, Judy. 1985. Locative Relations in ASL Word Formation, Syntax, and Discourse. PhD diss., MIT.

Supalla, Ted. 1982. Structure and Acquisition of Verbs of Motion and Location in American Sign Language. PhD diss., University of California at San Diego.

Taub, Sarah. 2001. *Language from the Body: Iconicity and Metaphor in American Sign Language.* New York: Cambridge University Press.

Torigoe, Takashi. 2000. Grammaticalization of Pointings and Oral Movements in a Home Sign. Presented at the Seventh International Congress on Theoretical Issues in Sign Language Research, Amsterdam, July 23–27.

Traugott, Elizabeth Closs, and Bernd Heine. 1991. *Approaches to Grammaticalization.* Typological Studies in Language, vol. 19, 1–2. Philadelphia: Benjamins.

Wilcox, Sherman. 2004. Gesture and Language: Cross-linguistic and Historical Data from Signed Languages. *Gesture* 4: 43–73.

Zimmer, June, and Cynthia G. Patschke. 1990. A Class of Determiners in ASL. In *Sign Language Research: Theoretical Issues,* ed. Ceil Lucas, 201–210. Washington, D.C.: Gallaudet University Press.

CHAPTER 4 RESPONSE

A Point Well Taken

On the Typology and Diachrony of Pointing

Roland Pfau

INTRODUCTION

For attentive observers, the claim that pointing is ubiquitous in everyday inter-action will not come as a surprise. A brief lecture on the distribution and form of pointing gestures will probably also convince them that pointing can be considered a foundational building block of human communication (Kita 2003b). First, pointing appears to be species specific; chimpanzees, for instance, do not point—at least not with their index finger (Povinelli and Davis 1994; but cf. also Leavens, Hopkins, and Bard 1996). Based on a wealth of cross-cultural studies, it has been suggested that pointing is a universal human behavior attested in cultures around the world. Second, in babies, point-ing to nearby objects emerges early on at an average age of eleven months (Butterworth and Morissette 1996). Moreover, research indicates that the com-bination of single-word utterances and pointing gestures may function as a transitional bridge between one- and two-word speech (Goldin-Meadow and Butcher 2003). Third, to a certain extent, the use of pointing gestures seems to be rule based and tightly linked to the accompanying speech (Kendon 2004). What is more, some utterances simply cannot be interpreted without taking into account the accompanying pointing gestures.

In their original and insightful study, Senghas and Coppola (chapter 4, this volume; hereafter S&C) investigate the use and distribution of pointing signs in Nicaraguan Sign Language (NSL), a sign language that emerged—under the advertent eye of linguists—at a Deaf school in Managua in the past thirty years (Kegl, Senghas, and Coppola 1999; Polich 2005). In their chapter S&C focus on locative points (i.e., adverbials such as 'there') and nominal points (i.e., demonstratives/determiners and personal pronouns) and analyze data from homesigners and from three distinct cohorts of NSL users, where cohort membership is determined by the period in which an individual entered the school. Every group included four subjects. In a nutshell, they find that the use of locative points does not differ significantly across the groups, while the use of nominal points clearly increases. They conclude that in the course of only thirty years a shift in the use of pointing signs has occurred. From a gestural input, the second- and third-cohort signers developed linguistic elements that have "a more categorical, languagelike, less context-bound flavor than the co-speech forms that are their origin."

This chapter is meant as a commentary—albeit a somewhat loosely related one—on S&C's intriguing findings. I add to the picture some cross-linguistic observations on the development and use of pointing gestures/signs in both spoken and signed languages, and I point out possible implications for their study. In the next section I start by looking at variation in pointing gestures as described for spoken languages. Phonological variation in the use of indexical signs in sign languages is the topic of the subsequent section. In the context of variation I point out some further potential complexities in the articulation of pointing signs that were outside the scope of the S&C study but which open up potential avenues for future research. Finally, in the section titled "On the Grammaticalization of Pointing: Speculations and Some Evidence," I address the issue of grammaticalization and show how the S&C study adds to our understanding of diachronic change in sign languages.

POINTING AS COSPEECH GESTURE

Kita (2003b, 1) defines the prototypical pointing gesture as "a communicative body movement that projects a vector from a body part. This vector indicates a certain direction, location, or object." Hence, even when used as a cospeech gesture, pointing can fulfill (at least) a locative function ('there') and a nominal function ('that,' 'she/he')—that is, the two functions that are also the center of attention in the S&C study. Often the pointing sign is necessary to disambiguate the meaning expressed by a vocal utterance. Consider, for instance, the utterance in (1). Clearly, the statement could not be interpreted without paying attention to the simultaneous cospeech gestures, both of which are articulated with an extended index finger.

(1) This   is my friend Mark, and over there   is his wife.
    [point forward left]   [point forward right, arm extended]

In (1), pointing gestures accompany first a demonstrative pronoun, then a locative (distal) adverb. The description of these gestures is simplified, but their execution clearly differs with respect to height and movement trajectory.

Pointing gestures are commonly articulated with the hand(s). Across cultures, the handshape that is most frequently used is most certainly the 1-handshape (i.e., a handshape with extended index finger). For the reader's convenience, the handshapes referred to throughout this chapter are provided in figure 4R.1 together with their labels.

Povinelli and Davis (1994) claim that the predominance of this gesture results from morphological features (in the biological sense) of the human hand since the index finger is extended relative to the other digits in the resting state of the hand (the same is not true for chimpanzees, and, therefore, index finger pointing does not typically emerge in chimpanzees; also see Povinelli, Bering, and Giambrone [2003]). However, other handshapes may also be used for pointing—for instance, the extended thumb handshape (A-hand) and the flat hand with all fingers extended (B-hand). Analyzing data from England (Northamptonshire) and Italy (Campania), Kendon (2004) and Kendon and Versante (2003) find that different handshapes tend to be used in different contexts. They observe, for instance, that the 1-handshape is most likely to be used when "a speaker singles out an object which is to be attended to as a particular individual object" (Kendon 2004, 205). Typically, this handshape is accompanied by a deictic word. In contrast, in all cases in which the B-handshape is used, "the object being indicated is not itself the primary focus or topic of the discourse but is something that is linked to the topic" (Kendon 2004, 208). Interestingly, deictic words are less frequently observed in the accompanying speech when the B-handshape is used. In addition to handshape, the palm orientation also seems to play a role; for the 1-handshape and the B-handshape, relevant distinctions are palm vertical and palm down (see the studies mentioned earlier for details). Finally, use of the A-handshape can be explained at least partially by anatomical factors. Generally, the objects pointed to with this handshape are either to the side or to the rear of the speaker. Moreover, the thumb seems to be used when the exact location or identity of the object is not important.

Wilkins (2003) challenges the common view that the index finger is universally privileged in pointing by showing that in some cultures (e.g., the Barai of Papua New Guinea), index finger pointing is not used at all (instead, lip pointing is used; see later discussion), while in others, pointing with the index finger appears not to be the most dominant form. Based on an analysis of data from speakers of Arrernte, a central Australian (Pama-Nyungan) language, he

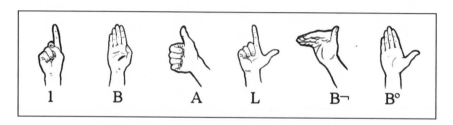

Figure 4R.1. Pointing handshapes and handshape labels

proposes a hierarchical system of pointing ("orienting behaviors") that distinguishes six different handshapes that are used for different purposes. Within this system, the canonical index point (palm down) is treated as an allomorph of the one-finger point. Note that besides the 1-handshape and the B-handshape, the pointing handshapes distinguished by Wilkins include the "middle finger point" and the "wide hand point."

Finally, besides manual pointing gestures, nonmanual pointing is also attested. Lip pointing, for instance, is a fairly widespread form of deictic gesture that is attested in Southeast Asia (Enfield 2001), Australia (Wilkins 2003), Latin America (Sherzer 1973), and Africa. Actually, as Enfield (2001, 186) points out, " 'lip-pointing' is not an ideal label" since protrusion of the lip(s) is almost always accompanied by a "quick raising of the head and chin, and orientation of gaze towards the referent." Focusing on speakers of Lao (Laos and Thailand), Enfield shows that lip pointing exhibits consistent conventions of both form and function. It is important to note that the use of lip pointing does not exclude the use of manual pointing. Rather, lip pointing may be complemented by and coordinated with manual gestures. Unlike manual pointing, however, lip pointing "only occurs when the identity or location of the referent is the focus of the speaker's utterance" (Enfield 2001, 195), for instance, as answers to "Where?" and "Which one?" questions. In the data from Arrernte speakers, Wilkins (2003) observed not only lip pointing but also eye pointing. Before pointing with the eye, the speaker first has to be sure of the interlocutor's attention. The speaker then shifts the eye "noticeably within the socket toward a particular referent. There is typically no accompanying head movement" (Wilkins 2003, 187). It is probably the latter feature that distinguishes eye pointing from eye gaze toward a location. The use of eye pointing reflects a conspiratorial mood; it is used to exclude third parties from being privy to what or who is being talked about (see Kita 2009 for further discussion of cross-cultural variation in cospeech gestures).

POINTING SIGNS: PATTERNS OF VARIATION

Just like spoken discourse, signed discourse abounds with pointing signs. Based on the analysis of Danish Sign Language discourse from four signers, Engberg-Pedersen (2003, 271), for instance, estimates that "on the average, almost every fourth sign in signed discourse is a pointing sign." For Kata Kolok, a village sign language of Bali, de Vos (2008) reports that one out of six signs is a pointing sign.

In the literature, various functions of pointing signs have been identified. Assigning an unambiguous function to a given pointing sign, however, is not always straightforward and may at times even be impossible. First of all, pointing signs may indicate the location of an object or event. Locative points may combine with nouns ('the house over there') or may be used predicatively ('the house is over there'). Second, within a noun phrase (NP), pointing may also function as a definite determiner ('the house') or a demonstrative pronoun ('this/that house') (Zimmer and Patschke 1990; MacLaughlin 1997). What complicates matters is the fact that NP internally, a point may also be used to associate a nonpresent referent with an arbitrary location in the signing space. For some sign languages, it has been suggested that within the NP (or determiner phrase, DP), the position of the pointing sign vis-à-vis the head noun may distinguish between various functions (MacLaughlin 1997), while for others it has been argued that at least demonstratives may occur pre- or postnominally (Zhang 2007). Third, pointing—be it to present referents or to loci that have previously been established in the discourse—may also be used anaphorically. That is, points may function as personal pronouns, thereby indicating the participants of events and their roles in the event (Lillo-Martin and Klima 1990; Meier 1990; Engberg-Pedersen 1993, 2003; McBurney 2002; also see Sandler and Lillo-Martin 2006).

For the purpose of their study, S&C distinguish between locative points and nominal points. In order to determine the meaning and function of pointing signs within the elicited narratives, they look at the context of a particular pointing sign to see what the point referred to. Points "that referred to locations (such as 'overhead' or 'to the left')" were classified as locative; those "that referred to persons or objects (such as Tweety Bird or the cage)" were considered nominal points. Importantly, S&C's notion of a nominal point covers NP-internal, as well as pronominal, uses of pointing signs (see the next section, "On the Grammaticalization of Pointing: Speculations and Some Evidence," for further discussion).

In the present section I discuss cross-linguistic evidence suggesting that subtle changes in the phonological makeup of pointing signs might help us distinguish different functions. To that end I consider manual (movement, handshape, and orientation) and nonmanual (eye gaze) properties of pointing signs. However, before addressing the issue of phonological variation, I want to briefly point out further uses of indexical signs that are not considered in the present context. These include indexicals with plural meaning (multiple locations or referents) that are marked by the addition of an arc-shaped movement on the horizontal plane; specialized grammatical functions such as the reflexive and the possessive, which may be marked by a change in handshape (Sandler and Lillo-Martin 2006); and pointing signs that refer to time (e.g., a B-handshape pointing directly overhead for NOON in Kata Kolok) (Marsaja 2008).

Movement

The first phonological parameter that may distinguish between different uses of pointing signs is the parameter of movement. Among the features that play a role are the length and shape of the movement trajectory and the tenseness of movement. In the following, all of the pointing signs are glossed as INDEX with further specification of function.

Within the group of locative adverbials, movement may distinguish between proximal ('here') and distal ('(over) there') meanings. Consider the German Sign Language [Deutsche Gebärdensprache, DGS] examples in (2). In (2a), the pointing sign is articulated in front of the signer's body with the fingertip pointing down. A short downward movement is executed either by the lower arm or by the wrist joint. The proximal adverbial is illustrated in figure 4R.2a (the bold curved line represents the torso of the signer). Note that, due to articulatory constraints, the index finger is not fully extended but bent (Van der Kooij 2002).

(2) a.
			top			
INDEX-PROX$_{front-of-body}$	ZUVOR	INDEX$_1$	NIE		ANWESEND	
here	before	I	never		be.present	

     'I have never been here before.'

 b.
ZUVOR	POSS$_1$	BRUDER	WOHN	INDEX-DIST$_{far-right}$
before	my	brother	live	(over) there

     'My brother used to live (over) there.'

 c.
INDEX$_1$	ENTSCHEID	BUCH	INDEX-DEM$_{forward-right}$	KAUF
I	decide	book	that	buy

     'I decided to buy that book.'

Example (2b) exemplifies the use of the distal adverbial. As figure 4R.2b shows, this pointing sign is articulated higher in the signing space (at shoulder height) and with a long, arc-shaped movement. Figures 4R.2a and 4R.2b illustrate two extremes; intermediate realizations are also possible. Finally, the demonstrative in example (2c) also shows a forward movement, but this movement is short, tense, and often repeated; see figure 4R.2c (here I neglect the distinction between proximal ('this') and distal ('that') demonstratives). In both the distal adverbial and the demonstrative, palm orientation is usually down. Obviously, the illustrations in figure 4R.2 are rough sketches. They are meant only to illustrate movement and handshape characteristics, while the orientation features are not accurately represented—at least not for a right-handed signer. As far as direction and length of movement are concerned, pronominal pointing signs pattern with demonstratives. In contrast to demonstratives, however, the movement is less tense and not repeated (except when used contrastively). Except for the first-person singular pronoun, the palm is usually oriented downward. For Danish Sign Language (DSL), Engberg-Pedersen (2003) describes the use of verb forms that are related to pointing signs and can be modified for loci in signing space (e.g., the verb GO-TO). Just like the distal adverbial (figure 4R.2b), GO-TO is made with an arclike (or straight) movement toward a previously established locus, the palm facing downward (see the later subsection on orientation).

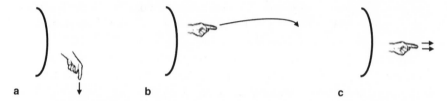

Figure 4R.2. Movement characteristics of proximal adverbial (a), distal adverbial (b), and demonstrative (c)

According to S&C, differences with respect to movement are also attested in the NSL pointing signs they found. Based on their observations, they conclude that nominal points contrast with locative points in that the former "are signed more quickly and with a smaller movement or no movement at all." However, their label "nominal point" collapses NP- and VP-internal uses of pointing signs, that is, signs that function as determiners or demonstratives and signs that function as pronouns. In future analysis, it would be interesting to address the question of whether different nominal uses can be distinguished on the basis of manner of movement.

When analyzing movement patterns, one has to keep in mind the fact that the number of movements may be influenced by prosodic factors. For Israeli Sign Language, Sandler (1999) observes that repetitions may be added in prosodically strong positions (e.g., the end of an intonational phrase) or deleted in prosodically weak positions. In other words, repetition of movement in pointing signs—which often occupy a phrase-final position—is not necessarily always indicative of a specific function.

Handshape

As mentioned previously, in the present context I do not focus on the handshape modulations commonly observed in possessive pronouns (e.g., use of B-handshape) and reflexive pronouns (e.g., use of A-handshape). From the available descriptions, it can be concluded that the 1-handshape is by far the most frequently used handshape in pointing signs across sign languages. However, similar to the cospeech pointing gestures introduced in the section "Pointing as Cospeech Gesture," the B-handshape and the A-handshape are also attested. Unfortunately, only little is known about potential specialized functions associated with these two forms.

In her discussion of person deixis in Brazilian Sign Language [Língua de Sinais Brasileira, LSB or Libras], Berenz (2002) points out that, in pronominalization, the B-handshape is used as a polite form. She even speculates that the extension of all fingers might convey a plural meaning, similar to the use of honorific pronouns in spoken languages, where they are often homonymous with plural pronouns (e.g., French *vous*, which is also the second-person plural pronoun, and German *Sie*, which is homonymous with the third-person plural pronoun). In Kata Kolok, the first-person singular pronoun (ICANG) has two variants, the 1-handshape and the B-handshape. Marsaja (2008, 177) observes that "[t]he former is used more frequently than the latter, even though they have the same function and meaning." In contrast, the second- and third-person pronouns have only the index finger configuration. Similarly, Woodward (1978) suggests that in Providence Island Sign Language, flat hand pointing occurs when the location pointed to is on the signer's body.

From informal observations of Sign Language of the Netherlands [Neder-landse Gebarentaal, NGT] and DGS, it seems that factors similar to those described earlier for cospeech gesture motivate the use of the A-handshape, that is, articulatory factors. This handshape may be used, for instance, when a right-handed signer points to a discourse participant located directly to the signer's right. Further research is needed to verify this claim. Note that in both NGT and DGS, the A-handshape is attested in lexicalized temporal deixis, for instance, in the signs YESTERDAY and TOMORROW.

Besides the previously mentioned handshapes, Alibašić Ciciliani and Wilbur (2006) describe the use of the L-handshape in Croatian Sign Language [Hrvatski Znakovni Jezik, HZJ], which they consider a variant of index finger pointing. They also investigate the possibility that different handshapes are used for case marking (i.e., to mark the case that would be used in the equiva-lent Croatian sentence). It turned out, however, that there was no systematic correlation between handshape and case. The 1- and the L-handshapes were attested in all case environments; variants of the flat hand (B, B°, and B¬) were observed mostly, but not exclusively, in accusative environments.

Although S&C remark that "points are generally made with an extended finger or an open hand directed away from the body," in their analysis of the NSL data, they do not distinguish between different handshapes. However, given the nature of their data elicitation (i.e., the retelling of an animated cartoon), it seems unlikely that a non-1-handshape would be used for one of the reasons mentioned earlier. First, with the possible exception of role shift, there would be no need to use a first-person pronoun (see Pyers and Senghas [2007] for the use of indexical points to self in NSL role shift). Second, the use of honorific forms seems highly unlikely in the elicitation setting. Third, for the most part, there was no discourse participant sitting on the dominant-hand side of the signer, that is, in a position that might trigger use of the L-hand. Still, in principle, one cannot exclude the possibility that different handshapes signal other functions that have yet to be determined.

As with the movement characteristics discussed in the previous subsection, it has to be noted that additional factors may influence the handshape of point-ing signs in certain environments. As noted by Corina (1990) and Sandler (1999), among others, the handshape of a pronoun may assimilate to that of a preceding or following content sign. Corina, for example, describes an instance in which a first-person pronoun is signed with a B¬-handshape, thereby anticipating the handshape of the following verb, KNOW. Sandler (1999) claims that, from a prosodic point of view, handshape assimilation may be indicative of cliticization.

Orientation

In the following discussion of the role of orientation in pointing signs, I distinguish two palm orientation values: palm vertical and palm down. In the literature (e.g., Engberg-Pedersen 2003; Van der Kooij, Crasborn, and Ros 2006), these orientations are sometimes also referred to as "palm neutral" and "palm prone," respectively.

Marsaja (2008) and de Vos (2008) observe that, in Kata Kolok, all pointing signs (including lip pointing) are directed to real-world locations, such as locations in the village or referents present in the discourse. That is, pointing in Kata Kolok employs an absolute frame of reference (Levinson 2003). However, different functions of pointing signs are consistently distinguished by the parameter of palm orientation. According to de Vos (2008), vertical palm orientation is characteristic of nominal points, that is, pointing for reference to persons and objects. In contrast, locative points (predication: 'located at x') are typically signed with the palm oriented down. This distinction is illustrated in figure 4R.3. Similarly, Marsaja (2008, 163) observes palm down (or up) in locative pointing signs. For pronominal pointing, however, he reports that the palm is also facing down. While this statement is made in the text (177), the accompanying pictures on the same page indicate that the palm is indeed oriented vertically, in line with what is reported by de Vos (2008).

Interestingly, Engberg-Pedersen (2003, 278) reaches the same conclusion for DSL. In her data, "the pronoun, determiner and proform are normally made with a neutral hand orientation [i.e., palm vertical] and the verb with the

Figure 4R.3. Nominal point (reference) and locative point (predication) in Kata Kolok

hand pronated [i.e., palm down]." Consequently, "neutral hand orientation seems to indicate the referential aspect of the pointing signs, whereas pronation indicates the locational aspect."

Orientation variation in pointing signs is also reported in a study on NGT conducted by Van der Kooij, Crasborn, and Ros (2006). It appears, however, that all of the pointing signs they consider are nominal points. The authors stress the fact that the attested variation cannot be predicted on the basis of articulatory factors (phonetic simplicity), as it can, for instance, in the first-person singular pronoun INDEX$_1$, which is never realized with palm down. They distinguish two types of indexicals, INDEX(prone), that is, a palm-down pointing sign, and INDEX(var), which has a variable palm orientation. Their data indicate that the former is always used for specific referents and that it may be repeated (cf. figure 4R.2c). It might therefore be interpreted as a determiner or demonstrative. In addition, referents may be localized by means of INDEX(prone). In contrast, INDEX(var) is used to refer to locations that have previously been established in discourse, but not for the introduction of new locations in signing space. INDEX(var) is never repeated. Hence, in the hypothetical NGT example in (3), the nonpresent referent JONGEN ('boy') would be localized by INDEX(prone). Subsequently, when referring to location 3a, INDEX(var) would be used. Based on the interpretation of facts by Van der Kooij, Crasborn, and Ros, it seems tempting to explain the attested orientation variation in information structure terms (e.g., new/old information, specificity).

(3) JONGEN INDEX(prone)$_{3a}$ BLIJ   OMDAT   INDEX(var)$_{3a}$ TIEN   EURO   VIND
      boy   index   happy because he   ten   Euro   find
      'The boy is happy because he found ten Euro.'

In their analysis S&C do not include the parameter of palm orientation. Clearly, a reconsideration of the NSL pointing signs in light of these findings might yield interesting results. Is palm orientation in NSL variable to the extent that it cannot be linked to a specific function, or are different types of points consistently distinguished by means of orientation? Furthermore, if the latter is the case, does NSL follow the pattern previously described for Kata Kolok and Danish Sign Language?

Nonmanuals: Eye Gaze

The role of eye gaze in the context of pointing signs has been investigated in a number of studies involving different sign languages (Meier 1990; Bahan and Supalla 1995; Berenz 2002; Engberg-Pedersen 2003; Alibašić Ciciliani and Wilbur 2006). According to S&C, eye gaze may distinguish between nominal and locative points in NSL. In particular, they observe that the "use of eye gaze with a locative is highly typical for all four groups and may even be obligatory." In contrast, in nominal points, the eye gaze does not follow the point (see their figures 4.1 and 4.2). It may be a coincidence, but it is still worth pointing out that the opposite eye gaze pattern can be seen in the Kata Kolok examples in figure 4R.3 in this chapter: Eye gaze follows the nominal point (reference) but does not align with the locative point (predication).

While S&C find that locative and nominal points in NSL are distinguished by means of eye gaze, other authors report that eye gaze may also play a distinctive role in the realm of pronominalization, that is, within the group of nominal pointing signs. Based on an analysis of eye gaze accompanying pronominal signs in LSB, Berenz (2002) challenges Meier's (1990) claim that sign languages distinguish between only first- and non-first-person within their pronominal systems (thereby violating a proposed universal). She finds that, at least in LSB, eye gaze consistently aligns with second-person pronouns but not with third-person pronouns. Along similar lines, Alibašić Ciciliani and Wilbur (2006) argue for a distinction between grammatical second- and third-person pronouns in HZJ. They observe that in indicating a "nonpresent or present second person referent, the hand, gaze and head line up," while "for pronominal reference to the nonpresent or present third person, disjunction of head, gaze and hand occurs" (Alibašić Ciciliani and Wilbur 2006, 130). It is possible that, in S&C's data, all of the nominal points have third-person referents (animate participants or objects from the cartoon). Further research on NSL pointing should reveal whether eye gaze not only distinguishes locative from nominal points but, within the latter group, also marks the distinction between second- and third-person pronouns (see Kita [2003a] for the alignment of the hand with torso rotation and eye gaze in cospeech pointing gestures and Engberg-Pedersen [2003] for eye gaze behavior and head/body rotation in DSL discourse).

ON THE GRAMMATICALIZATION OF POINTING: SPECULATIONS AND SOME EVIDENCE

Sign languages, just like spoken languages, are subject to diachronic change. On the one hand, changes at the lexical and syntactic level may be caused by external factors, such as language contact (Fischer 1975; Brentari 2001) and standardization (Schermer 2003). On the other hand, changes at the phonological and lexical level may also be triggered by internal factors, such as ease of articulation and perception (Frishberg 1975) and grammaticalization.

It is the last of these phenomena, grammaticalization, that is the center of attention in this section. Simplifying somewhat, grammaticalization can be defined as the development of functional (grammatical) elements from lexical elements, such as the development of prepositions from nouns (e.g., 'face > front') and of tense (or time) markers from verbs (e.g., 'go > future'). It has been shown that common grammaticalization pathways that have been described for spoken languages (Hopper and Traugott 1993; Heine and Kuteva 2002) are also attested in sign languages (Sexton 1999; Pfau and Steinbach 2006). In addition, however, sign languages have the unique possibility of developing functional elements from manual (Janzen and Shaffer 2002; Wilcox 2004, 2007) and nonmanual gestures (Janzen 1999; McClave 2001).

The following discussion of the grammaticalization of pointing builds on facts and hypotheses first reported in Pfau and Steinbach (2006). This study provides an overview of modality-independent and modality-specific aspects of grammaticalization in sign languages. As for the grammaticalization of manual gestures, it is argued that these gestures may skip the lexical stage; that is, they may enter the linguistic system as functional elements. However, once they are integrated into the grammar of a given sign language, their further development generally follows well-known, modality-independent paths. For indexicals in sign languages, Pfau and Steinbach (2006, 61) suggest the grammaticalization pathway in figure 4R.4. Pfau and Steinbach propose that pointing entered the grammar of sign languages as a marker of location (step ① in figure 4R.4). Remember that the locative function, that is, pointing to nearby objects, also appears very early in the cospeech gesture of hearing children. Pointing to locations is concrete in that a location does not represent anything other than itself, and therefore the act of pointing appears closest to its gestural root. From that stage onward, the use of locations may become more and more abstract. As S&C assert, "a crucial step in the transformation of pointing gestures into forms that can be used as abstract, recombinable linguistic elements seems to be the loss of their locative content."

In the subsections to follow I focus on steps ②, ③, and ⑤ in the pathway in figure 4R.4 (also see Coppola and Senghas 2010 for discussion). Due to the scarcity or even nonavailability of historical data, it is notoriously difficult to make statements about the diachronic development of sign languages. Essentially, the claims made by Pfau and Steinbach (2006) are speculations based on

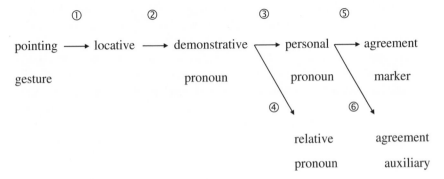

Figure 4R.4. Suggested grammaticalization path for sign language indexicals

comparative spoken language data that take into account two important points: In most cases, the source and the target of the grammaticalization process are coexistent, and grammaticalization is usually hypothesized to be a unidirectional process. Crucially, the developments we observe in the NSL data analyzed by S&C constitute the first direct supporting evidence for at least some of the assumptions concerning the grammaticalization of pointing made in figure 4R.4. Hence, the value of their results cannot be overestimated.

From Locative Adverbial to Demonstrative Pronoun

In his thorough study on the form, function, and grammaticalization of demonstratives, Diessel (1999) subsumes under the term "demonstrative" not only demonstrative pronouns but also locational adverbs. Here I keep these two notions separate due to the observation that, cross-linguistically, locational adverbs are a common source of demonstrative pronouns. Not surprisingly, proximal demonstratives ('this') are derived from proximal locatives ('here'), while distal demonstratives ('that') are based on distal locatives ('there'); see Heine and Kuteva (2002) for examples. Based on these observations, Pfau and Steinbach (2006) tentatively claim that, in sign languages, the demonstrative use of the pointing sign also developed from its locative use. In principle, however, an alternative scenario might be suggested according to which both the demonstrative and the locative developed from the pointing gesture (i.e., the leftmost arrow in figure 4R.4 would be branching).

Let us now consider the extent to which the data collected by S&C might turn out to be informative in this respect. First, the NSL data from different cohorts clearly show that all of the signers, irrespective of cohort, make frequent use of locative points (approximately 6.0–7.5 per 100 signs; see their table 4.4a). Second, a comparable number of locative points is attested in the gesture systems used by the homesigners (ca. 6.7 percent). From this we may conclude that pointing gestures, once they enter a language system, do indeed start out as locative points, as indicated in figure 4R.4. In contrast, the use of nominal points increases dramatically across cohorts, from approximately 1.4 percent (cohort 1) to 3.2 percent (cohort 2) to 6.7 percent (cohort 3). Cohort 3 signers even use nominal points more frequently than locative points. As for the development of demonstratives from locatives, we have to keep in mind that S&C subsume demonstrative and personal pronouns under the label "nominal point." Therefore, the figures in their table 4.4a are not informative in this respect. In a further analysis, however, they distinguish between nominal points that combine with nouns (e.g., POINT BIRD) and nominal points that combine with verbs (e.g., POINT CLIMB), where the former would likely fulfill a demonstrative function and the latter a pronominal function. It turned out that only the combination of nominal points with verbs increased across cohorts (see their table 4.4b). It therefore appears that the demonstrative use of nominal points, which remained constant across cohorts, is the more basic one and is available to signers at an earlier stage in the development of the language. Taken together, the data from homesigners and from NSL signers of different cohorts support the claim that the locative use of pointing signs intermediates between the gestural source and the demonstrative use of pointing signs.

From Demonstrative Pronoun to Personal Pronoun

Having established that the NSL data provide evidence of the grammaticalization of demonstrative pronouns from locatives, I now turn to step ③ on the grammaticalization pathway in figure 4R.4, the grammaticalization of personal pronouns from demonstratives. This diachronic process is fairly common in spoken languages. English *he,* for instance, originates from the Proto-Indo-European demonstrative *ei-s,* and the French third-person singular (masculine) pronoun *il* is derived from the Latin demonstrative *ille.* However, in spoken languages, first- and second-person singular pronouns are not grammaticalized from demonstratives. Rather, they usually originate from nouns denoting social relations (Lehmann 1995). The Indonesian first-person singular pronoun *saya,* for instance, is derived from the noun *sahaya* 'servant,' while the Spanish honorific pronoun *usted* is a contracted form of *vuestra merced* 'your grace.' In contrast to that, all sign language pronouns have a common source, that is, a pointing gesture.

   In the previous section I pointed out that a very clear pattern emerged when S&C considered how often nominal points were combined with verbs. The frequency of this combination increases only slightly from cohort 1 to cohort 2, from a mean of 4 to a mean of 5 combinations per signer. Comparing cohort 2 and 3, however, S&C observe a significant increase in the number of combinations: The four signers of cohort 3 produced a mean of more than fourteen combinations of nominal points with verbs. I agree with S&C in their note that this striking pattern appears to reflect a change in the function of nominal points, which "are increasingly being used in a pronounlike way to indicate the subjects and objects that need to be associated with verbs." In contrast, the homesigners, as well as the signers from cohorts 1 and 2, combine nouns with verbs to form basic sentences. The fact that nominal points frequently replace nouns suggests that we witness the grammaticalization of personal pronouns from demonstratives. In other words, the NSL data provide evidence for step ③ in the grammaticalization chain in figure 4R.4. The NSL pointing signs have taken on a more symbolic, abstract function and have lost much of the concrete spatial meaning associated with typical pointing gestures.

From Pronoun to Agreement Marker

Before concluding this chapter, I want to add a few comments on step ⑤ in the grammaticalization pathway in figure 4R.4, the development of bound agreement markers from pronouns (see Steinbach and Pfau [2007] for discussion of step ⑥). Evidence from spoken languages suggests that pronouns are indeed the most common source of verbal subject agreement markers. For the most part, the source pronouns are third-person singular pronouns.

As is well known, the locations in signing space that pointing signs target also play a crucial role in sign language verb agreement by defining the beginning and the endpoint of the movement (Padden 1988; Meir 2002). We may therefore speculate that agreement markers in sign languages developed from pronouns. Applying this admittedly somewhat speculative scenario to NSL, one would expect that the use of personal pronouns precedes the spatial modulation of verb signs for the expression of agreement. While S&C do not address this issue, the development of spatial grammar is the topic of previous studies conducted by Senghas and Coppola. In a production study (retelling of a cartoon) with first- and second-cohort signers, Senghas and Coppola (2001) found that cohort membership, as well as age of first exposure to NSL, had an influence on the frequency of spatially modulated verb forms. First, within both groups, early exposed signers produced more spatial modulations than late-exposed signers. Second, early-exposed signers of the second cohort produced such modulations significantly more often than early-exposed signers of the first cohort. Third, the higher prevalence of spatial modulations in the second cohort resulted from indications of shared reference, that is, from establishing a grammatical link between two signs (e.g., a verb-object combination) by using a common location (see Senghas [2003] for supporting evidence from a perception study). Senghas and Coppola (2001, 327) conclude "that the youngest members of the second cohort, as children, surpassed their input, taking a partially developed language and systematizing it in a specific way."

While this intriguing result suggests that in NSL a system of grammatical agreement (shared reference) emerged in the group of second-cohort signers (who entered the community between 1985 and 1990), it is not informative with respect to a possible grammaticalization pathway from pronouns to agreement. Recall from the subsection "From Demonstrative Pronoun to Personal Pronoun" that frequent use of nominal points in combination with verbs was attested only in the third cohort, which did not participate in the study discussed earlier. However, it might still turn out that the use of nominal points with verbs (i.e., pronouns) is a prerequisite for the use of spatially modified verbs. In other words, all NSL signers who use spatially modulated verbs are also expected to use pronominal forms, whereas the opposite is not true. Reconsideration of the available data seems necessary to verify this claim.

CONCLUSION

The evidence discussed in this chapter indicates that pointing is a multifarious task, the complexity of which is easily overlooked. Vocal utterances are commonly accompanied by manual and nonmanual pointing gestures to real-world locations that, for the most part, the speaker produces unconsciously. In a similar fashion, homesigners employ pointing in their self-styled gestural communication systems. The NSL data presented by S&C show that these gestural points may be integrated into a developing language system; that is, a gesture may transform itself into a linguistic element. As S&C point out, "There are likely to be several steps in the process, with every step taking a form further from its gestural roots." In this response I have investigated possible diachronic shifts in the use of pointing signs along a largely modality-independent grammaticalization chain. Some of the shifts proposed for the pointing sign are supported by the NSL data because we observe "an increase in its use to identify the participants in events rather than locations or real-world objects." Also, I have explored the possibility that some of the function shifts are marked by subtle phonological changes.

Earlier I suggested that the crucial first step, that is, the transition from gesture to language, may be modality-specific. This characterization may not be fully accurate, however. In fact, there is an ongoing debate on whether spoken language originated in gesture alone or in gesture and vocalization together (see Corballis [2003] for an overview; also see Napoli and Sutton-Spence, this volume, and the response by Kendon). Hewes (1981) makes specific reference to pointing and suggests that pointing gestures were a critical stepping-stone in the evolution of language.

Whatever position one takes concerning the role of gestures in the evolution of spoken languages, it is the merit of S&C's study to have shown that, in NSL, a humble pointing gesture has been integrated into the linguistic system of the language. I conclude that this is indeed a point well taken.

Note

Figure 4R.3 is copyrighted by Connie de Vos and reprinted here with her permission, for which I am grateful.

Bibliography

Alibašić Ciciliani, Tamara, and Ronnie B. Wilbur. 2006. Pronominal System in Croatian Sign Language. *Sign Language and Linguistics* 9: 95–132.

Bahan, Ben, and Samuel J. Supalla. 1995. Line Segmentation and Narrative Structure: A Study of Eyegaze Behavior in American Sign Language. In *Language, Gesture, and Space*, ed. Karen Emmorey and Judy Reilly, 171–191. Hillsdale, N.J.: Erlbaum.

Berenz, Norine. 2002. Insights into Person Deixis. *Sign Language and Linguistics* 5: 203–227.

Brentari, Diane, ed. 2001. *Foreign Vocabulary in Sign Languages: A Cross-linguistic Investigation of Word Formation*. Mahwah, N.J.: Erlbaum.

Butterworth, George E., and Paul Morissette. 1996. Onset of Pointing and the Acquisition of Language in Infancy. *Journal of Reproductive and Infant Psychology* 14: 219–231.

Coppola, Marie, and Ann Senghas. 2010. Deixis in an Emerging Sign Language. In *Sign Languages (Cambridge Language Surveys)*, ed. Diane Brentari, 543–569. Cambridge: Cambridge University Press.

Corballis, Michael C. 2003. From Hand to Mouth: The Gestural Origins of Language. In *Language Evolution*, ed. Morten Christiansen and Simon Kirby, 201–218. New York: Oxford University Press.

Corina, David P. 1990. Handshape Assimilations in Hierarchical Phonological Representation. In *Sign Language Research: Theoretical Issues*, ed. Ceil Lucas, 27–49. Washington, D.C.: Gallaudet University Press.

Diessel, Holger. 1999. *Demonstratives: Form, Function, and Grammaticalization*. Amsterdam: Benjamins.

Enfield, Nick. 2001. Lip Pointing? A Discussion of Form and Function with Reference to Data from Laos. *Gesture* 1: 185–212.

Engberg-Pedersen, Elisabeth. 1993. *Space in Danish Sign Language: The Semantics and Morphosyntax of the Use of Space in a Visual Language*. Hamburg: Signum.

———. 2003. From Pointing to Reference and Predication: Pointing Signs, Eyegaze, and Head and Body Orientation in Danish Sign Language. In *Pointing: Where Language, Culture, and Cognition Meet*, ed. Sotaro Kita, 269–292. Mahwah, N.J.: Erlbaum.

Fischer, Susan. 1975. Influences on Word Order Change in ASL. In *Word Order and Word Order Change*, ed. Charles N. Li, 1–25. Austin: University of Texas Press.

Frishberg, Nancy. 1975. Arbitrariness and Iconicity: Historical Change in American Sign Language. *Language* 51: 696–719.

Goldin-Meadow, Susan, and Cynthia Butcher. 2003. Pointing toward Two-word Speech in Young Children. In *Pointing: Where Language, Culture, and Cognition Meet*, ed. Sotaro Kita, 85–107. Mahwah, N.J.: Erlbaum.

Heine, Bernd, and Tania Kuteva. 2002. *World Lexicon of Grammaticalization*. New York: Cambridge University Press.

Hewes, Gordon W. 1981. Pointing and Language. In *The Cognitive Representation of Speech*, ed. Terry Myers, John Laver, and John Anderson, 263–269. Amsterdam: North Holland.

Hopper, Paul, and Elizabeth C. Traugott. 1993. *Grammaticalization*. New York: Cambridge University Press.

Janzen, Terry. 1999. The Grammaticization of Topics in American Sign Language. *Studies in Language* 23: 271–306.

———, and Barbara Shaffer. 2002. Gesture as the Substrate in the Process of ASL Grammaticization. In *Modality and Structure in Signed and Spoken Languages,* ed. Richard P. Meier, Kearsy A. Cormier, and David G. Quinto-Pozos, 199–223. New York: Cambridge University Press.

Kegl, Judy, Ann Senghas, and Marie Coppola. 1999. Creation through Contact: Sign Language Emergence and Sign Language Change in Nicaragua. In *Language Creation and Language Change: Creolization, Diachrony, and Development,* ed. Michael DeGraff, 179–237. Cambridge, Mass.: MIT Press.

Kendon, Adam. 2004. *Gesture: Visible Action as Utterance.* New York: Cambridge University Press.

———, and Laura Versante. 2003. Pointing by Hand in "Neapolitan." In *Pointing: Where Language, Culture, and Cognition Meet,* ed. Sotaro Kita, 109–137. Mahwah, N.J.: Erlbaum.

Kita, Sotaro. 2003a. Interplay of Gaze, Hand, Torso Orientation, and Language in Pointing. In *Pointing: Where Language, Culture, and Cognition Meet,* ed. Sotaro Kita, 307–328. Mahwah, N.J.: Erlbaum.

———. 2003b. Pointing: A Foundational Building Block of Human Communication. In *Pointing: Where Language, Culture, and Cognition Meet,* ed. Sotaro Kita, 1–8. Mahwah, N.J.: Erlbaum.

———. 2009. Cross-cultural Variation of Speech-accompanying Gesture: A Review. *Language and Cognitive Processes* 24: 145–167.

Kooij, Els van der. 2002. *Phonological Categories in Sign Language of the Netherlands: The Role Of Phonetic Implementation and Iconicity.* Utrecht: LOT.

———, Onno Crasborn, and Johan Ros. 2006. Manual Prosodic Cues: PALM-UP and Pointing Signs. Poster presented at the Ninth Congress on Theoretical Issues in Sign Language Research (TISLR 9), Florianópolis, December.

Leavens, David A., William D. Hopkins, and Kim A. Bard. 1996. Indexical and Referential Pointing in Chimpanzees *(Pan troglodytes). Journal of Comparative Psychology* 110: 346–353.

Lehmann, Christian. 1995. *Thoughts on Grammaticalization.* Munich: LINCOM.

Levinson, Stephen. 2003. *Space in Language and Cognition: Explorations in Cognitive Diversity.* New York: Cambridge University Press.

Lillo-Martin, Diane, and Edward S. Klima. 1990. Pointing Out Differences: ASL Pronouns in Syntactic Theory. In *Theoretical Issues In Sign Language Research.* Vol.1, *Linguistics,* ed. Susan Fischer and Patricia Siple, 191–210. Chicago: University of Chicago Press.

MacLaughlin, Dawn. 1997. The Structure of Determiner Phrases: Evidence from American Sign Language. PhD diss., Boston University.

Marsaja, Gede. 2008. *Desa Kolok: A Deaf Village and Its Sign Language in Bali, Indonesia.* Nijmegen: Ishara.

McBurney, Susan. 2002. Pronominal Reference in Signed and Spoken Language: Are Grammatical Categories Modality Dependent? In *Modality and Structure in Signed and Spoken Languages,* ed. Richard P. Meier, Kearsy A. Cormier, and David G. Quinto-Pozos, 329–369. New York: Cambridge University Press.

McClave, Evelyn Z. 2001. The Relationship between Spontaneous Gestures of the Hearing and American Sign Language. *Gesture* 1: 51–72.

Meier, Richard P. 1990. Person Deixis in American Sign Language. In *Theoretical Issues in Sign Language Research.* Vol.1, *Linguistics,* ed. Susan D. Fischer and Patricia Siple, 175–190. Chicago: University of Chicago Press.

Meir, Irit. 2002. A Cross-modality Perspective on Verb Agreement. *Natural Language and Linguistic Theory* 20: 413–450.

Padden, Carol. 1988. *Interaction of Morphology and Syntax in American Sign Language.* New York: Garland.

Pfau, Roland, and Markus Steinbach. 2006. Modality-independent and Modality-specific Aspects of Grammaticalization in Sign Languages. *Linguistics in Potsdam* 24: 3–98. http://www.ling.uni-potsdam.de/lip/.

Polich, Laura. 2005. *The Emergence of the Deaf Community in Nicaragua.* Washington, D.C.: Gallaudet University Press.

Povinelli, Daniel J., Jesse M. Bering, and Steve Giambrone. 2003. Chimpanzees "Pointing": Another Error of the Argument by Analogy? In *Pointing: Where Language, Culture, and Cognition Meet,* ed. Sotaro Kita, 35–68. Mahwah, N.J.: Erlbaum.

Povinelli, Daniel J., and D. Richard Davis. 1994. Differences between Chimpanzees *(Pan troglodytes)* and Humans *(Homo sapiens)* in the Resting State of the Index Finger: Implications for Pointing. *Journal of Comparative Psychology* 108: 134–139.

Pyers, Jennie, and Ann Senghas. 2007. Reported Action in Nicaraguan and American Sign Languages: Emerging versus Established Systems. In *Visible Variation: Cross-linguistic Studies on Sign Language Structure,* ed. Pamela Perniss, Roland Pfau, and Markus Steinbach, 279–302. Berlin: de Gruyter.

Sandler, Wendy. 1999. The Medium and the Message: Prosodic Interpretation of Linguistic Content in Israeli Sign Language. *Sign Language and Linguistics* 2: 187–215.

———, and Diane Lillo-Martin. 2006. *Sign Languages and Linguistic Universals.* New York: Cambridge University Press.

Schermer, Trude. 2003. From Variant to Standard: An Overview of the Standardization Process of the Lexicon of Sign Language of the Netherlands over Two Decades. *Sign Language Studies* 3: 469–486.

Senghas, Ann. 2003. Intergenerational Influence and Ontogenetic Development in the Emergence of Spatial Grammar in Nicaraguan Sign Language. *Cognitive Development* 18: 511–531.

———, and Marie Coppola. 2001. Children Creating Language: How Nicaraguan Sign Language Acquired a Spatial Grammar. *Psychological Science* 12: 323–328.

Sexton, Amy L. 1999. Grammaticalization in American Sign Language. *Language Sciences* 21: 105–141.

Sherzer, Joel. 1973. Verbal and Nonverbal Deixis: The Pointed Lip Gesture among the San Blas Cuna. *Language in Society* 2: 117–131.

Steinbach, Markus, and Roland Pfau. 2007. Grammaticalization of Auxiliaries in Sign Languages. In *Visible Variation: Cross-linguistic Studies on Sign Language Structure,* ed. Pamela Perniss, Roland Pfau, and Markus Steinbach, 303–339. Berlin: de Gruyter.

Vos, Connie de. 2008. Compositionality in Pointing Signs. Talk presented at the Amsterdam Center for Language and Communication (ACLC), November 2008.

Wilcox, Sherman. 2004. Gesture and Language: Cross-linguistic and Historical Data from Signed Languages. *Gesture* 4: 43–73.

———. 2007. Routes from Gesture to Language. In *Verbal and Signed Languages: Comparing Structures, Constructs, and Methodologies,* ed. Elena Pizzuto, Paola Pietrandrea, and Raffaele Simone, 107–131. Berlin: de Gruyter.

Wilkins, David. 2003. Why Pointing with the Index Finger Is Not a Universal (in Sociocultural and Semiotic Terms). In *Pointing: Where Language, Culture, and Cognition Meet,* ed. Sotaro Kita, 171–215. Mahwah, N.J.: Erlbaum.

Woodward, James. 1978. The Selflessness of Providence Island Sign Language: Personal Pronoun Morphology. *Sign Language Studies* 23: 167–174.

Zhang, Niina Ning. 2007. Universal 20 and Taiwan Sign Language. *Sign Language and Linguistics* 10: 55–81.

Zimmer, June, and Cynthia G. Patschke 1990. A Class of Determiners in ASL. In *Sign Language Research: Theoretical Issues,* ed. Ceil Lucas, 201–210. Washington, D.C.: Gallaudet University Press.

CHAPTER 5

Acquisition of Topicalization in Very Late Learners of Libras

Degrees of Resilience in Language

Sandra K. Wood

INTRODUCTION

Throughout the world and even in the United States, some deaf people are still growing up with very late or limited accessible linguistic input for acquiring language. Oftentimes they develop their own gestural system (homesign), which they use with family and friends (Kegl 1994; Kegl, Senghas, and Coppola 2001; Senghas 1995, 2000; Coppola 2002; Goldin-Meadow 2005). Former homesigners often become late learners of a sign language and are typically those who have impoverished input to a spoken language and no access to a signed language until they enter a school for Deaf children at the age of five or older (Berk 2003, 2004; Lillo-Martin and Berk 2003; Bouldreault and Mayberry 2006; Newport 1990; Mayberry 1993, 1994). Although these late learners exhibit grammatical deficiencies in their grammar, they do learn much of the signed language, even well past the age of puberty, which raises questions about the strength of the critical period and about how much of the language they are able to acquire and why. Investigating the way in which these late learners (many of whom are former homesigners) acquire the structure of the linguistic systems enables us to better understand the process of language acquisition. After a quick background on the situation of the late learners in Brazil and on the critical period hypothesis, I discuss the experiment in which I studied their acquisition of language.

BACKGROUND

Deaf Adult Homesigners

In Brazil, numerous deaf adult homesigners exceed the age of twenty without significant (or sometimes any) exposure to a systematic linguistic system, either spoken/written or signed. These people typically find themselves in social and geographic isolation, which too often results in a lack of access to formal education (Fusellier-Souza 2006). Many of them eventually learn Brazilian Sign Language (henceforth Libras[1]), albeit very late (i.e., well past the age of puberty). While the first school for Deaf students in Brazil was founded in 1855 (Campello 1989) and some schools for Deaf students are thriving to this day, particularly in the south of Brazil (Skliar and Quadros 2004), many Deaf people still have not been integrated into the educational system and instead experience a kind of societal neglect and discrimination that keeps them from receiving educational and linguistic support (Campos de Abreu 1989). There has been a concerted effort to increase literacy in the Brazilian population in general, including the deaf population. However, as Ronice Müller de Quadros (personal communication, December 2006) notes, in order to increase literacy for Deaf adults, they first need to learn a formal signed language (i.e., Libras). Hence, a sizeable population of Deaf adults in Brazil, who may be former homesigners, is now learning Libras as a first language well past the age of puberty.

In this chapter I focus on two particular individuals, one who has learned Libras as a first language well after puberty and one who has learned Libras as a second language (albeit with nonnative, limited proficiency in her first language, Brazilian Portuguese). It is important to note here, however, that most Deaf people have some degree of exposure to a spoken or written language as a first language before they learn sign language simply because most deaf people have hearing parents. However, that does not always mean they achieve nativelike proficiency in their first language. They often do not achieve linguistic competence until they start learning sign language, which then becomes their primary language. This then raises the question, How late is too late? That is, is there a critical period of language acquisition that will constrain the late learner's ability to acquire Libras fluently or at near-native levels?

Critical Period Hypothesis

The premise of the critical period hypothesis as formulated by Lenneberg (1967) and Newport (1990, 1991), among others, is that language must be acquired before the onset of a specific age, which may be puberty or much earlier, to achieve a native level of fluency. If a child has not acquired a language by then, the child's fluency will be markedly decreased (i.e., never at the native level). That is, the acquisition of language is correlated with the maturational constraints imposed by the plasticity of the brain.

There are different formulations of the critical period hypothesis, but all assume a critical or sensitive period for achieving native competence.[2] If language learning takes place past this critical period, success is less certain and more variable (Bialystok and Hakuta 1999). Two types of behavioral evidence for the critical period hypothesis have been studied for the past twenty years. One set of studies focuses on those who experienced an extended delay in their exposure to their first language, most notably Deaf children, who often do not enter school until about the age of five, when they then become exposed to ASL. Many Deaf people do not learn ASL until well after puberty, but they often have varying degrees of fluency in English prior to that point (e.g., Newport 1990; Mayberry 1993, 1994). Another set of studies focuses on the acquisition of a second language either by young children or those who are well past puberty; immigrants and foreign students who move to the United States figure prominently in these (e.g., Johnson and Newport 1989; White and Genesee 1996; Birdsong and Molis 2001).

Late Learners of a First Language

Newport (1990 and other works) tested three groups of Deaf adults (ages 40–50 years): those who acquired American Sign Language (ASL) as native signers; early learners, who learned ASL at the age of four to six years; and late learners, who acquired ASL after the age of twelve. The tests comprised, among other things, a series of tasks involving the production and comprehension of complex morphology (verb agreement and verbs of motion). Compared to the native signers, the early learners had a significant decrease in accuracy on the tasks, even though many of them had been using ASL for well more than forty years. Those who acquired ASL after the age of twelve demonstrated even less accuracy on the same tasks, which showed a correlation of –0.6 to –0.7 between age of acquisition (AoA) and the test score. However, AoA was not a factor in all of the tasks. On a test involving basic word order, all three groups had an accuracy of 95 percent or better. Newport argues that this provides strong evidence for a maturational account of the critical period hypothesis, in which AoA is a factor in the acquisition of language.[3]

   Other studies done by Berk (2003, 2004) and Lillo-Martin and Berk (2003) investigate the acquisition of verb agreement in ASL by two Deaf children, MEI and CAL, who were initially exposed to ASL as a first language around the age of six. The two children were studied longitudinally, and their use of ASL verb agreement was studied intensively. They made a significant number of errors in verb agreement, compared with a two-year-old ASL Deaf native signer, and even over time these errors did not decrease. As in the Newport study, the children showed near-native fluency with the basic SVO word order for ASL and were at approximately the same stage as the two-year-old Deaf native signer. However, unlike the native signer, their production of derived word orders, such as topicalization, was limited and prone to errors.

   One would think that since MEI and CAL learned ASL well before the age of puberty, they would be closer to near-native fluency in their acquisition of verb agreement and topicalization. However, because this is clearly not the case, it may be that either the relevant critical period for these two grammatical phenomena lies well before puberty (that is, AoA is relevant for their acquisition) or these grammatical phenomena (verb agreement and/or topicalization), being language specific, are not innately constrained but must be learned by the child with sufficient input at an early age. The latter premise relates to the "resilience" of acquisition of language, which I discuss in the section called "Resilience of Language."

Late Learners of a Second Language

A classic study by Johnson and Newport (1989) involves a group of Chinese and Korean learners of English who showed an effect of AoA, in which the age of arrival correlates with decreased performance on a grammaticality judgment task. The older the student was upon arrival, the worse the student's score on the task. Furthermore, Johnson and Newport argue for a maturational account of acquisition based on finding significant correlation between young age of acquisition and performance. They found a –0.87 correlation for those who arrived before puberty and a –0.16 correlation for those who arrived after puberty. In other words, if the students/learners acquire language (either as a first or second language) during an early stage of the maturational period, they perform significantly better than those who acquire it at a later stage.

However, critical period effects have been shown to be more sensitive for first language learners than for second language learners. In a seminal study of critical period effects, two groups of language learners of ASL were studied (Mayberry and Lock 2003; Mayberry, Lock, and Kazmi 2002). One group (Deaf) learned ASL as a late first language. Another group (both Deaf and hearing) learned ASL as a second language. The ASL as a second language group did much better on the tasks than the late learners of ASL.

Also, in their study of sixty-one native speakers of Spanish who were learning English as a second language, Birdsong and Molis (2001) show a strong effect of AoA as well, extending support for Johnson and Newport's maturational account. However, in their study, they did have one participant (late learner) who was nativelike in competence, answering all of the items correctly, as the native speakers did. Moreover, thirteen participants out of sixty-one had scores of 92 percent accuracy on the test items. Birdsong and Molis state that there is "modest evidence" that near-native or nativelike competence is possible for late learners.[4]

As noted earlier, critical period effects appear to behave differently for those learning a late first language and those learning a second language. Even though there are maturational changes for second language learners, the critical period effects are much more severe for those learning a late first language. Moreover, as Johnson and Newport (1989) note, even the very late learners are able to learn ASL (without any formal instruction) and achieve some degree of fluency. They can master some aspects of grammatical constructions and morphology but just not as well as a native signer. So, now we can consider more fully the question of which grammatical constructions show AoA for only late first learners and for both late first learners and second language learners.

In the next section I demonstrate that part of the answer may have to do with how accessible these grammatical constructions are from universal grammar; that is, are some constructions innately accessible even after the critical period even though they need a quantity and quality of input for the learner to acquire them successfully? I argue that the answer lies in "degrees of resilience" evinced by certain properties of language.

Resilience of Language

Based on her seminal studies of young deaf homesigners, Goldin-Meadow (2005) suggests that language has both resilient and fragile properties. She defines "resilient properties" as those that develop regardless of the variability of the input. If the input is absent, degraded, or available, the properties will still develop in a child's communication system. In other words, resilient properties, such as constraints on word order, are present in all languages, which must have a mechanism for establishing a consistent, basic word order: SVO, OSV, SOV, and so on. Fragile properties are those that must be explicitly learned (i.e., the children must be exposed to a language model in order to acquire these properties). These fragile properties are language specific and include things like tense marking or left versus right branching, which were notably absent in the gestural system of the young homesigners that Goldin-Meadow studied. She claims that resilient properties of language are found in the linguistic gestural system of homesigners regardless of the absence of any linguistic input and further states that fragile properties, however, will not exist in their system. She does not explicitly suggest that these resilient properties are innately accessible to the child but postulates that they develop without regard to whether the input for them is available, degraded, or absent.

However, I wish to extend the notion of resilience to the innate accessibility of certain linguistic properties. I follow the same fundamental idea of resilience as Goldin-Meadow (2005) but extend it to accommodate degrees of resilience associated with levels of availability from universal grammar. First, certain resilient properties are innately available regardless of input. Second, other less resilient properties may be innately accessible but require input of some quantity or quality in order for the learner to acquire them. Moreover, other properties are not innately accessible from universal grammar but must be learned rather than innately acquired. In other words, I suggest that there are degrees of resilience that are related to the learner's innate accessibility to certain linguistic properties. Goldin-Meadow (2005) suggests that only those children who have been exposed to a language model will develop fragile properties. I propose we go one step further. According to my premise regarding degrees of resilience, native signers/speakers display fragile properties in their linguistic system, while late learners may or may not, depending on the degree of resilience of the particular linguistic property.

According to Chomsky (1981), universal grammar (UG) consists of innate principles that limit the variability of language. That is, a child knows a set of principles (rules) that apply to all languages and a set of parameters whose value can vary within a set of constraints from one language to another (Chomsky 1981; Hyams 1986; Williams 1987; Chomsky and Lasnik 1993). Basically, UG is a theory of knowledge. The internal structure of the mind cannot be understood without understanding how knowledge is acquired. As I suggested earlier, we can extend the notion of resilience, as first proposed by Goldin-Meadow, to correlate with components of UG. That is, principles are resilient properties of language, and parametric settings pertain to less resilient properties of language. There are degrees of resilience in relation to components of UG that may be more or less innately accessible (figure 5.1). The relative width of a given level in the pyramid has significance, a point I return to later.

Given the theory of UG, or the innately guided acquisition of language, what should we expect to see if we turn to a new study comparing another three sets of signers, this time homesigners, late learners, and native learners

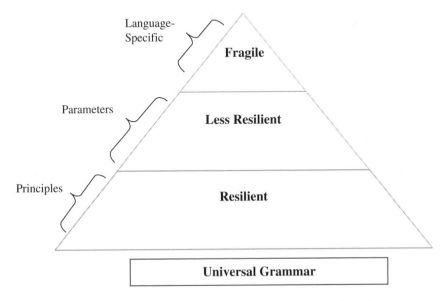

Figure 5.1. Degrees of resilience in relation to components of Universal Grammar

of a given language? Certain lexical differences would be expected since lexical information is language specific and as such would be fully learned rather than innate. Additionally, while the mechanism of syntactic movement is hypothesized to be innately available in general, properties of language, including particular types of syntactic movement that are or are not allowed, will follow from the setting of the parameters, which the child learns from exposure to the target language, so this linguistic knowledge would be less resilient. Some parameters may require more linguistic input in order to be set than others; hence, the degree of resilience comes into play. Universal principles, by hypothesis, are not required to be learned, so consistency of word order, recursion, and structural dependence are expected to be present in all linguistic systems. That is, there should be a limited set of errors with regard to resilient properties.

Previous Studies of Homesigners, Late Signers, and Native Signers of Libras

In Wood (2007), the linguistic systems of Deaf Brazilian homesigners, late learners of Libras, and native signers of Libras were studied with respect to noun-noun compounding and topicalization with an eye toward comparing the three groups in their ability to produce and/or comprehend these linguistic structures. These two phenomena were chosen for study since the first involves recursion, a more resilient property, and the second involves syntactic movement subject to a parametric setting, a less resilient property.

Previous Study: Noun-Noun Compounding

Snyder (1995, 2001) shows that noun-noun compounding illustrates properties of structural dependence and recursion, which Chomsky (1981, 1995) claims is a central component of universal grammar (see also Hauser, Chomsky, and Fitch [2002] for a deeper discussion of recursion in UG).[5] Importantly, Wood (2007) found that homesigners, late learners, and native signers of Libras were able to produce a novel, recursive noun-noun compound with at least three signs, thus providing evidence that even these participants have access to universal grammar regardless of the presence or absence of ordinary linguistic input (that is, regular exposure to natural human language). Examples are given in (1–2):[6]

(1) MOLDURA- PORCO- FOTOGRAPHIA
    frame   pig   picture
    'a picture frame with a pig on front'

(2) SAPO- CANETA- COLAR
    frog pen   necklace
    'a necklace with a pen with a frog (on its cap)'

That homesigners show evidence of recursion and structural dependence confirms that some innate mechanism is active long past any critical period and allows them to utilize noun-noun compounding in their gestural linguistic system even in the absence of ordinary linguistic input.

Topicalization

In the noun-noun compounding task discussed earlier, no significant difference was found among the three groups of signers. The second experimental task used by Wood (2007) focuses on topicalization. This time a significant difference was found among the three groups, but the late learners group revealed some interesting differences that suggest that degrees of resilience are associated with the quality and quantity of input. Moreover, topicalization is shown to be a syntactic property that can be acquired well after puberty, given the requisite linguistic input.

Topicalization in Libras is the fronting of old information (i.e., information that has already been mentioned in the discourse or is assumed to be common knowledge by the interlocutors) to the beginning of the sentence, and it is found as well in many other sign languages (Liddell 1980; Aarons 1994; Braze 2004; Lillo-Martin and Quadros 2007). In topicalization, a constituent undergoes syntactic movement as illustrated in (3–4). Libras marks topicalization with a distinctive nonmanual cue: a slight backward head tilt combined with a raised brow (Quadros 2003, Lillo-Martin and Quadros 2007), the same nonmanual cue we find in other sign languages. In (3–4) this nonmanual cue is indicated by a line above the signs it co-occurs with and the label "t."

```
                   _____t
```
(3) PERSEGUIR GATO$_i$, ROBERTO t$_i$
    chase   cat   Robert
    'As for chasing the cat, Robert did (it).'

```
     ___t
```
(4) GATO$_i$, ROBERTO PERSEGUIR t$_i$
    cat   Robert   chase
    'As for the cat, Robert chased (it).'

Recall that while syntactic movement in general is a mechanism hypothesized to be available innately (i.e., via UG), the particular instances of it that are allowed in a given language are not specified by UG but follows from individual-language parameter settings (Chomsky 1995). That is, a given language may or may not allow a specific syntactic movement (e.g., topicalization) to be utilized. Hence, signers must be provided with some systematic linguistic input in order to know whether and how their language utilizes topicalization. We therefore expect differences in use depending upon linguistic experience/circumstance.

Only a few published studies focus on the acquisition of topicalization in the context of impoverished input, but two seminal ones provide some illuminating clues as to what happens. Singleton (1989) studied a young Deaf child, Simon, and his Deaf parents, who learned ASL in their late teens. Simon's only input for ASL came from his parents, as he was mainstreamed in a public school and his parents did not associate with other Deaf members of the Deaf community. The parents thus provided Simon with degraded input, as they were neither native nor near-native in their ASL fluency. Simon outperformed his parents on several tasks of ASL morphology and syntax, one of which was topicalization. While the parents correctly interpreted sentences with topicalized subjects, they consistently misinterpreted sentences with topicalized objects and verb phrases. In contrast, Simon showed a perfect, native mastery of topicalization in ASL regardless of which constituent was topicalized despite his impoverished input with respect to topicalization from his parents.

In another study by Goldin-Meadow (2005), a young homesigner, David, showed no preference for new or old information in sentence-initial position. That is, his signing did not make the distinction found in other sign languages, where initial position (topicalization position) is typical for old information (as in ASL or Libras).

According to Goldin-Meadow's proposal that the absence of a given property of language from a homesign system indicates fragility (i.e., it is not present in all languages but must instead be learned) and my extension of the notion of fragility to UG (i.e., it is not innately accessible), we should hypothesize that topicalization, because it is less resilient, will be successfully acquired by a signer only if the signer has had systematic linguistic input from a language that utilizes syntactic movement for topicalization. In the absence of such exposure, a signer cannot be expected to perform above chance on tasks involving topicalization.

Based on what we've learned about Simon, who showed full competence in the use of topicalization in contrast to his parents, who were able to topicalize only subject noun phrases (Singleton 1989), and based further on the fact that David showed no sensitivity to a distinction between old/given information in the order of signs in his sentences (Goldin-Meadow 2005), there are two main points to consider. One is that it is possible for a child to acquire topicalization even with degraded input. Another is that topicalization is absent in the linguistic system of the young homesigners studied by Goldin-Meadow.

Extrapolating from these two points, I suggest that topicalization is not fragile as Goldin-Meadow suggests due to its absence in young homesigners. Instead, I hypothesize that the acquisition of topicalization in Libras is, as with ASL, dependent on systematic linguistic input (so David, who did not have that, showed no sensitivity to the characteristics that topicalization is sensitive to: old versus new information). Moreover, that input need not occur before the critical period (thus, Simon's parents could topicalize subjects properly even though they learned ASL as teens). That is, topicalization may be learned successfully by native and late signers of Libras, given sufficient input, but not by homesigners.

EXPERIMENT: TOPICALIZATION

In Wood (2007) I put these hypotheses to the test. I ran an experiment consisting of a comprehension task on topicalization for the three groups of homesigners, late signers, and native signers of Libras. The design of this experiment are described here, and the results are shown to diverge for two late learners of Libras. Then the results for these two late learners are discussed in more detail.

Participants

Through the assistance of a Deaf Brazilian local, Ana-Regina Campello, fourteen Deaf Brazilian adults between the ages of 23 and 53 were recruited. Campello, who is a near-native Deaf signer of Libras and a well-known member of the Deaf Brazilian community, works extensively with the Deaf community primarily in the southern and central regions of Brazil. She is also fluent in ASL and served as a consultant and coexperimenter in this project with respect to data collection and transcription. Five of the participants were native signers of Libras (ages 23–43), six were late learners of Libras (ages 23–32), and three were homesigners (ages 23, 32, and 53). One of the late learners (age 32) was a former homesigner and had been using Libras for only about a year and a half at the time of testing. Five of the six late learners had at least ten years of exposure to Libras. One late learner had been learning Libras for only three years and was fluent in spoken/written Brazilian Portuguese. The late learners and native signers had varying degrees of proficiency in Brazilian Portuguese, but most of them self-reported as not very fluent in Brazilian Portuguese. All of the late signers and native signers considered Libras to be their primary language. All of the homesigners and late learners had hearing parents. All of the native signers had Deaf parents with the exception of one, whose mother was a child of Deaf parents and also had siblings who were Deaf. All native signers were exposed to Libras from birth.

Procedure and Materials

For reasons of linguistic competence, two slightly different experiments were run: one for native and late learner signers, and a separate one for homesigners.

Each native signer and late learner was shown a picture of some activity, while the experimenter signed a sentence corresponding to the action in the picture. The participant then had to determine whether the signed sentence correctly or incorrectly matched the picture. An example of the task with a sample picture given to the native signer and late learner of Libras is presented in figure 5.2 and example (5).

$$\underline{\qquad}t$$

(5) Experimenter: GATO, CÃO MASTIGAÇÃO
                  cat   dog chew/bite
                  'As for the cat, the dog is biting (it).'

Before the task, the participants were given training in which they were asked a series of statements that would elicit the answer "correct" or "incorrect," such as pointing to the female experimenter and stating "She's a boy." Once the participants understood that they were free to correct the experimenter (that is, to say the experimenter was right or wrong), the experimental task was initiated. A total of sixteen test items were administered with each participant. Eight SVO sentences and eight OSV (topicalized) sentences were given, with four "incorrect" and four "correct" corresponding pictures in each group. For instance, the answer for example (5) would be to sign "correct."

The homesigners had difficulty answering test questions as "correct" or "incorrect," so the experimental design was revised slightly. We provided them with two contrasting pictures side by side, and the experimenter signed a sentence derived from the homesigner's gestures that corresponded to the action depicted in one of the pictures but not in the other. The participant would then choose the picture that matched the sentence. Again, half the sentences involved topicalization (OSV order), and half did not (SOV order).

Figure 5.2. Picture used in experiment: a dog is playfully biting a cat

Results

The results are illustrated in figure 5.2. A significant difference was found among the three groups using one-way ANOVA (F (2,9) = 54.67, $p < .001$). Post-hoc Tukey tests revealed that the homesigner group was significantly different from the other two groups. Indeed, the homesigners (HS) were unable to comprehend topicalized sentences, and, further, their performance on these experimental tasks was no better than chance.

In contrast, no significant difference was found between the late learners (LS) and the native signers (NS) (NS vs. LS nonsignificant; NS vs. HS, $p < .01$, LS vs. HS, $p < .05$). Late learners and native signers of Libras as a whole were able to comprehend topicalization significantly above chance.

However, two very late learners of Libras (L5 and L6) did not perform significantly above chance on the topicalization task. Because of this variance in their group, a follow-up analysis was performed. A single-sample t-test, using the mean score of the native signers (15.4 items out of 16 correct) as the baseline, showed that the homesigner group's performance was significantly below the baseline (two-tailed $p = .008$), but the late learner group's performance was not significantly different from the baseline (figure 5.3).

An analysis using an exact binomial, one-tailed test sought further differences among the participants. Each native signer performed significantly above chance ($p < .002$); all of them correctly comprehended fourteen or more of the sixteen test items. Four out of six late learners performed significantly above chance ($p < .05$). These four performed identically to the native signers. Two late learners (L5 and L6) did not perform significantly above chance: L5 was able to correctly comprehend eleven out of sixteen sentences, while L6 correctly identified nine out of sixteen. Additionally, none of the homesigners performed significantly above chance (figure 5.4).

Looking more specifically at native signers and late learners of Libras, we see that participants in both groups were clearly able to comprehend all or most instances of topicalization in the task. Individual differences were found in the late learner group, in which two participants were not able to comprehend all of the instances of topicalization.

DISCUSSION

Each of the groups performed as predicted in the topicalization task. First, the homesigners did not perform above chance, an expected outcome, since they were not exposed to systematic linguistic input. Second, native and late learners of Libras performed significantly above chance, illustrating that acquisition of topicalization in Libras is dependent on some form of linguistic input but not necessarily before the end of the critical period.

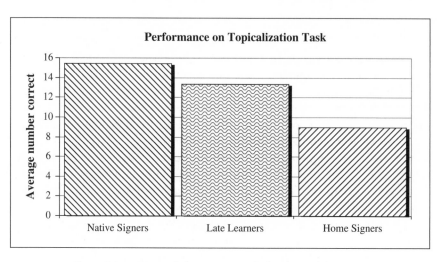

Figure 5.3. Mean performance on topicalization task by group

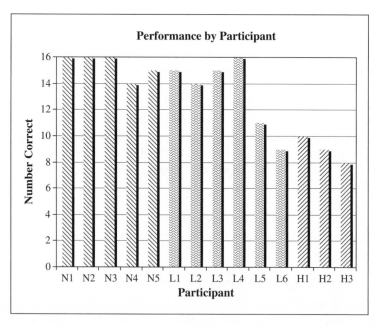

Figure 5.4. Total number of correct responses for native signers (N), late learners (L), and homesigners (H)

Further, because the premise of this chapter is that there are degrees of resilience in the acquisition of language, the results were expected to correspond to the degree of input the signer received, especially with regard to the very late learners of Libras. In fact, the results of this topicalization experiment nicely support the hypothesis that topicalization belongs on the middle level of the pyramid in figure 5.1; that is, it is less resilient.

Recall that almost all of the native signers and the very late learners of Libras performed significantly above chance in their comprehension of topicalization. However, two of the very late learners (L5 and L6) did not. I now present the details of the performance of these two signers. Participant L5 was a late learner of Libras, having learned it when she was approximately twenty-one years old. At the time of the testing, she was twenty-nine years old. She has had very limited contact with the Deaf Libras community. Her family members are all hearing, as are her husband and children. She was discouraged from socializing with the Deaf community. This relative isolation from other signers obviously affected the consistency and continuity of Libras input for her. I suggest that the requisite input she received was not of a sufficient quantity and quality to allow her to access the syntactic mechanism for topicalization in Libras. In contrast, another late learner in the group, L1, who started learning Libras at the age of eighteen and was twenty-nine at the time of testing, performed significantly above chance. Thus, L5 and L1 had very similar backgrounds and acquired Libras at around the same age. They had both been using Libras for about the same length of time. However, L1 had extensive contact with the Deaf Brazilian community, was very involved in activities and events, and maintained close relationships with other Deaf members of the community. This enabled him to receive the requisite input from the community of Libras signers on a consistent basis; his exposure had sufficient quantity and quality to allow him the access denied to L5.

The other late learner who performed by chance with topicalization was L6, a previous homesigner. At the time of testing, she had been using Libras for less than a year and a half (in contrast to most of the other late learners, who had ten years or more of experience with Libras; see the earlier section titled "Participants"). Her lexical production was predominantly Libras. However, her results in the topicalization task pattern more with the homesigners than with the other very late learners (who were, generally speaking, not previous homesigners). She was unable to comprehend instances of topicalization (as also seen with homesigners), unlike the other late learners. Since she clearly learned Libras when she was well past the age of puberty, one could conclude that her results in this experiment follow from critical period effects on acquisition. However, it seems to be more the case that input (exposure to Libras) evinces different roles for L5 and L6 for reasons that relate to the degree of resilience for topicalization.

However, given that other late learners in this study and others show evidence of understanding topicalization, it seems clear that, along with AoA being a secondary factor, the degree and length of exposure to Libras are both of crucial importance for acquisition of topicalization. In other words, the degree of resilience of certain syntactic constructions may influence the variability of the timing of acquisition, given different amounts of exposure, in the following way. The more resilient a property, the more likely it will be acquired early in the learning process, once exposure begins. If it is less resilient, then there is a greater degree of variability as to when it will be acquired in the learning process. The quantity and quality of exposure adds to the variability of acquisition. Quite possibly, only in fragile language phenomena will AoA be the most relevant (or the only) factor in language acquisition. These points are reflected by the relative width of a given level of the pyramid in figure 5.1. The wider a level is, the less important are the AoA or the quantity and quality of exposure. The narrower a level is, the more important they are.

Recall the study by Lillo-Martin and Berk (2003), in which they observed the production of topicalization utterances by two deaf children, MEI and CAL, and found it to be significantly different from that of a two-year old Deaf native signer. MEI and CAL used fewer instances of topicalized utterances and made more errors when they did use them than the native signer. Lillo-Martin and Berk spent approximately one year studying these two children (MEI 6;6–7;1 and CAL (6;10–7;4). These children pattern similarly to the former homesigner L6 in my study, who had been learning Libras for only about a year and half. In both instances, a year and half or less of exposure to their sign language as a first language is not sufficient for the acquisition of topicalization. However, based on the evidence for the late learners of Libras, my prediction is that MEI and CAL should eventually be able to use topicalization with a near-native level of competence.

As we've clearly seen in this chapter from studying late learners of Libras (and from references to other studies, such as Singleton [1989]), it is not anywhere near impossible to achieve nativelike fluency in topicalization with delayed or degraded input. To the contrary, it seems clear that topicalization can be learned with the requisite type and quantity of linguistic input; hence, topicalization is indeed less resilient but not fragile.

Less resilient properties of language will evince a variability in how well they are learned depending not only on AoA but also on the degree and quantity of linguistic input the learner receives. I venture this prediction for future research: Parameters or properties of language that are acquired later with respect to a child's age in ordinary language acquisition circumstances will turn out to be difficult for late learners to master but will be possible for the late learners to master if they are given sufficient quantity and quality of input.[7]

The implications of this chapter are significant, especially on a socioeducational level. Perhaps the most important one is that functional mastery of language is not an unreachable goal for those people whose acquisition of language has been delayed past puberty. That is, they can use the language well and master some aspects of it. However, in order for these late learners to become more fluent, they need sufficient and high-quality input on a consistent basis. It's not enough to just learn the basics, as we've seen from the results for L5. Degraded input results in deficiencies in their understanding and production of grammar. This has been evidenced by other studies as well (e.g., Newport 1990; Boudreault and Mayberry 2006; Mayberry 1993, 1994, among others). Communication is vital for human beings. The more tools at a learner's disposal, the better that learner's linguistic and communication skills will be. This is a linguistic right that every person should have irrespective of one's status in life. It is my hope that this chapter will help inform applications for teaching language to late learners of a first language.

Future research is needed to confirm the existence of degrees of resilience, and to confirm the validity of my claims in particular. More research with homesigners in other cultures will provide valuable cross-linguistic confirmation. Next on the list are follow-up studies with L6 in the near future to see whether she eventually acquires the syntactic mechanism for topicalization, as predicted by the results of this chapter. That is, I expect that, in time, she will show near-native comprehension of topicalization, assuming that she is being continuously exposed to Libras, unlike L5, who learned Libras but was not able to continue her exposure. The question is, How much time will it take for L6 to reach the point of near-native comprehension?

Another next-on-the-list project is a study of fragile properties of language, in particular, verb agreement. As noted earlier for ASL, verb agreement is extremely sensitive to errors by late language learners even when they have been using sign language for forty years or more. In contrast to topicalization, it seems that verb agreement has to be acquired before a certain age in order to be set properly. Thus, the range of resilience needs to be fully explored with other properties of language in order to understand its role within UG.

Notes

This study was supported in part by NIH, NIDCD grant #DC000183. I would like to thank Diane Lillo-Martin and William Snyder for their constructive feedback and guidance in the development of this research. I also wish to express my appreciation and gratitude to Ana-Regina Campello for assisting with the recruiting of participants and with the experiments themselves. Most of all, I extend many thanks to the Deaf Brazilian participants who willingly contributed their time to participate in the experiments and provided insight for further research and revision.

1. In the research literature, Brazilian Sign Language (Língua Brasileira de Sinais) is typically shortened to LSB. However, Deaf Brazilians refer to their sign language as Libras. In fact, many Deaf Brazilians are not even aware of the acronym LSB, nor are they aware that Libras is typically denoted as LSB outside of Brazil, especially in the research field (Ana-Regina Campello, personal communication, December 2006). This chapter uses Libras as the label of choice, respecting the designation used by the Brazilian Deaf community.

2. Some use "sensitive period," which refers to a model of acquisition that assumes acquisition is still possible after puberty. However, this terminology is also associated with the influence of outside stimuli on an organism even after the age of puberty (Kelley 1992). See Eubank and Gregg (1999) and Newport (1991) for a deeper discussion of the critical period hypothesis. For ease of exposition during this chapter, I do not make a distinction between a critical period and a sensitive period (as proposed by Eubank and Gregg [1999]) but collapse the two under the critical period hypothesis.

3. See also Boudreault and Mayberry (2006), in which late learners of ASL showed a significant decrease in mastery of certain syntactic structures, correlating with age of acquisition.

4. In fact, there is a vigorous debate among second language researchers as to whether there are actually critical period effects for second language learners. Since this is beyond the scope of this chapter, see Birdsong and Molis (2001) for a more detailed discussion of the evidence against critical period age effects for second language learners.

5. That is, noun-noun compounding has the property of a single, complex word (Snyder 1995, 2001). For instance, *cat lady* may be understood to mean a lady who loves cats or a lady who looks like a cat or a lady who is an expert on cats. Productive, recursive compounding can be illustrated by a novel three-noun compound such as *cat lady book*.

6. All instances of Libras and Brazilian Portuguese glosses are provided by Ana-Regina Campello, mentioned later in this chapter, who was a consultant and coexperimenter in this study.

7. Evidence pointing to this prediction is supported by other studies such as Newport (1990) and Mayberry (1993, 1994).

Bibliography

Aarons, Debra. 1994. Aspects of the Syntax of American Sign Language. PhD diss., Boston University.

Berk, Stephanie. 2003. Sensitive Period Effects on the Acquisition of Language: A Study of Language Development. PhD diss., University of Connecticut at Storrs.

———. 2004. Acquisition of Verb Agreement When First-language Exposure Is Delayed. In *Proceedings of the 28th Annual Boston University Conference on Language Development*, vol. 1, ed. Alejna Brugos, Linnea Micciulla, and Christine E. Smith, 62–73. Somerville, Mass.: Cascadilla.

Bialystok, Ellen, and Kenji Hakuta. 1999. Confounded Age: Linguistic and Cognitive Factors in Age Differences for Second Language Acquisition. In *Second Language Acquisition and the Critical Period Hypothesis*, ed. David Birdsong, 161–181. Mahwah, N.J.: Erlbaum.

Birdsong, David, and Michelle Molis. 2001. On the Evidence for Maturational Constraints in Second-language Acquisition. *Journal of Memory and Language* 44: 235–249.

Boudreault, Patrick, and Rachel Mayberry. 2006. Grammatical Processing in American Sign Language: Age of First-language Acquisition Effects in Relation to Syntactic Structure. *Language and Cognitive Processes* 21(5): 608–635.

Braze, David. 2004. Aspectual Inflection, Verb Raising, and Object Fronting in American Sign Language. *Lingua* 114: 29–58.

Campello, Ana-Regina. 1989. The Origin of the Deaf Community in Brazil. In *The Deaf Way: Perspectives from the International Conference on Deaf Culture*, ed. Carol J. Erting, Robert C. Johnson, Dorothy L. Smith, and Bruce N. Snider, 117–118. Washington, D.C.: Gallaudet University Press.

Campos de Abreu, Antonio. 1989. The Deaf Social Life in Brazil. In *The Deaf Way: Perspectives from the International Conference on Deaf Culture*, ed. Carol J. Erting, Robert C. Johnson, Dorothy L. Smith, and Bruce N. Snider, 114–116. Washington, D.C.: Gallaudet University Press.

Chomsky, Noam. 1981. *Lectures on Government and Binding*. Dordrecht: Foris.

———. 1995. *The Minimalist Program*. Cambridge, Mass.: MIT Press.

———, and Howard Lasnik. 1993. The Theory of Principles and Parameters. In *Syntax: An International Handbook of Contemporary Research*, ed. Joachim Jacobs, Arnim Von Stechow, and Wolfgang Sternefeld, 506–569. Berlin: de Gruyter.

Coppola, Marie. 2002. The Emergence of Grammatical Categories in Home Sign: Evidence from Family-based Gesture Systems in Nicaragua. PhD diss., University of Rochester.

Eubank, Lynn, and Kevin Gregg. 1999. Critical Period and (Second) Language Acquisition: Divide et Impera. In *Second Language Acquisition and the Critical Period Hypothesis*, ed. David Birdsong, 65–99. Mahwah, N.J.: Erlbaum.

Fusellier-Souza, Ivani. 2006. Emergence and Development of Signed Languages: From a Semiogenetic Point of View. *Sign Language Studies* 7(1): 30–56.

Goldin-Meadow, Susan. 2005. What Language Creation in the Manual Modality Tells Us about the Foundations of Language. *Linguistic Review* 22: 199–225.

Hauser, Marc D., Noam Chomsky, and W. Tecumseh Fitch. 2002. The Faculty of Language: What Is It, Who Has It, and How Did It Evolve? *Science* 298: 1569–1579.

Hyams, Nina. 1986. *Language Acquisition and the Theory of Parameters*. Dordrecht: Reidel.

Johnson, Jacqueline, and Elissa Newport. 1989. Critical Period Effects in Second Language Learning: The Influence of Maturational State on the Acquisition of English as a Second Language. *Cognitive Psychology* 21: 60–99.

Kegl, Judy. 1994. The Nicaraguan Sign Language Project: An Overview. *Signpost* 7(1): 24–31.

———, Ann Senghas, and Marie Coppola. 2001. Creation through Contact: Sign Language Emergence and Sign Language Change in Nicaragua. In *Language Creation and Language Change: Creolization, Diachrony, and Development*, ed. Michel DeGraff, 179–237. Cambridge, Mass.: MIT Press.

Kelley, Darcy B. 1992. Opening and Closing a Hormone-regulated Period for the Development of Courtship Song. *Annals of the New York Academy of Science* 662: 178–188.

Lenneberg, Eric. 1967. *Biological Foundations of Language*. New York: Wiley.

Liddell, Scott. 1980. *American Sign Language Syntax*. The Hague: Mouton.

Lillo-Martin, Diane, and Stephanie Berk. 2003. Acquisition of Constituent Order under Delayed Language Exposure. In *Proceedings of the 27th Annual Boston University Conference on Language Development*, vol. 2, ed. Barbara Beachley, Amanda Brown, and Frances Conlin, 484–495. Somerville, Mass.: Cascadilla.

Lillo-Martin, Diane, and Ronice Müller de Quadros. 2007. Focus Constructions in American Sign Language and Língua de Sinais Brasileira. In *Signs of the Time: Selected Papers from TISLR 2004*, ed. Josep Quer, 161–176. Seedorf, Germany: Signum Verlag.

Mayberry, Rachel. 1993. First-language Acquisition after Childhood Differs from Second-language Acquisition: The Case of American Sign Language. *Journal of Speech and Hearing Research* 36: 1258–1270.

———. 1994. The Importance of Childhood to Language Acquisition: Evidence from American Sign Language. In *The Development of Speech Perception: The Transition from Speech Sounds to Spoken Words*, ed. J. C. Goodman and H. C. Nusbaum, 57–90. Cambridge, Mass.: MIT Press.

———, and Elizabeth Lock. 2003. Age Constraints on First versus Second Language Acquisition: Evidence for linguistic Plasticity and Epigenesis. *Brain and Language* 87: 369–384.

———, Elizabeth Lock, and Hena Kazmi. 2002. Linguistic Ability and Early Language Exposure. *Nature* 417: 38.

Newport, Elissa. 1988. Constraints on Learning and Their Role in Language Acquisition: Studies of the Acquisition of American Sign Language. *Language Sciences* 10: 147–172.

———. 1990. Maturational Constraints on Language Learning. *Cognitive Science* 14: 11–28.

———. 1991. Contrasting Conceptions of the Critical Period for Language. In *Epigenesis of Mind: Essays on Biology and Cognition*, ed. S. Carey and R. Gelman, 111–130. Hillsdale, N.J.: Erlbaum.

Quadros, Ronice Müller de. 2003. Phrase Structure of Brazilian Sign Language. In *Cross-linguistic Perspectives in Sign Language Research: Selected Papers from TISLR 2000*, ed. A. Baker, B. van den Bogaerde, and O. Crasborn, 141–162. Hamburg: Signum.

Senghas, Ann. 1995. Children's Contribution to the Birth of Nicaraguan Sign Language. PhD diss., Massachusetts Institute of Technology.

———. 2000. The Development of Early Spatial Morphology in Nicaraguan Sign Language. In *BUCLD 24: Proceedings of the 24th Annual Boston University Conference on Language Development*, ed. S. Catherine Howell, Sarah A. Fish, and Thea Keith-Lucas, 696–707. Boston: Cascadilla.

———, and Marie Coppola. 2001. Children Creating Language: How Nicaraguan Sign Language Acquired a Spatial Grammar. *Psychological Science* 12(4): 323–328.

Singleton, Jenny. 1989. Restructuring of Language from Impoverished Input: Evidence for Linguistic Compensation. PhD diss., University of Illinois at Urbana-Champaign.

Skliar, Carlos, and Ronice Müller de Quadros. 2004. Bilingual Deaf Education in the South of Brazil. *International Journal of Bilingual Education and Bilingualism* 7(5): 368–380.

Snyder, William. 1995. Language Acquisition and Language Variation: The Role of Morphology. PhD diss., Massachusetts Institute of Technology.

————. 2001. On the Nature of Syntactic Variation: Evidence from Complex Predicates and Complex Word Formation. *Language* 77(2): 324–342.

White, Lydia, and Fred Genesee. 1996. How Native Is Near-native? The Issue of Ultimate Attainment in Adult Second Language Acquisition. *Second Language Research* 12(3): 233–265.

Williams, Edwin. 1987. Introduction. In *Parameter Setting*, ed. Thomas Roeper and Edwin Williams, vii–xix. Boston: Reidel.

Wood, Sandra K. 2007. Degrees of Resiliency in Acquisition of Language. *Nanzan Linguistics*, Special Issue 3(1): 315–330.

A Critical Period for the Acquisition of a Theory of Mind?

Clues from Homesigners

Cyril Courtin

INTRODUCTION

To what extent is it possible to develop a sense of oneself and of others without language? This may be a purely theoretical question since, fortunately, the cases of real absence of language are rare. However, as Sandra K. Wood mentions in the very first sentence of her chapter, it happens that deaf children who are born in countries where sign language is not used in schools and who have no clear Deaf community are limited to simple gestural exchanges with their caregivers, developing some kind of homesigning. In complement to Wood's inquiry about the linguistic achievement of these homesigners, a further issue is whether these few gestural exchanges during childhood or even adolescence are sufficient for the child to develop a mature cognition. The case of home-signers has seldom been addressed; here I attend to the question in the case of French deaf children, with an eye toward their developmental linguistic levels. Then I address the problem of cognitive development and extend the discussion to what currently is and is not known about the role of possible critical periods in development. Note that the deaf children addressed in this chapter are often classified as profoundly deaf; the results presented may not be the same for children with only mild hearing losses.[1] Moreover, their parents have chosen an education in either sign language or spoken language.

LINGUISTIC DEVELOPMENT OF FRENCH DEAF CHILDREN

Deaf children of Deaf parents (DoD) are often taken as an ideal example of linguistic and cognitive development. There is now a great deal of evidence that DoD children develop language milestones in sign language at the same age as hearing children in spoken language and that their cognitive levels are all well within norms (Newport and Meier 1985; Marschark and Hauser 2008). However, DoD children are quite rare, particularly when considering only those born to signing Deaf adults (Mitchell and Karchmer 2004). Besides, DoD children do not constitute a homogeneous group. For example, as noted by Meristo et al. (2007), in many countries DoD children have no choice but to attend oral schools because there is no signing school in their environment. Native signers attending oral schools demonstrate lower levels of social-cognitive development compared to DoD children attending signing schools. For cognitive development, daylong total immersion in sign language appears preferable to sign language use that is restricted to use at home.

What about signing deaf children of hearing parents (DoH)? Important variation can be seen among such children in the world. Some may appear like the homesigners described in Wood's chapter, having no contact with sign language up to their adolescence. To the contrary, other DoH children are in a very different and ameliorative linguistic environment, where, by age seven, they are reported to have benefited from several years of intensive exposure to ASL (Schick et al. 2007).

In France, deaf children have little access to sign language due to the lack of bilingual schools, as has been noticed elsewhere for Italian and Estonian children, for example (Meristo et al. 2007). Officially, most schools for deaf students are now providing courses on sign language (e.g., two hours per week) and thus claim they offer bilingual teaching. There is confusion about teaching a sign language versus teaching in sign language. Only three schools in France really teach in French Sign Language (LSF) (located in Noisiel [near Paris], Toulouse, and Poitiers). The remaining schools use, to different extents, a mixture of spoken French and sign supported systems (which may include codes closer to homesigning—schoolsigning—than to LSF) in addition to courses on LSF. This situation is far from optimal for the linguistic and cognitive development of deaf children.

There is a further complication. On February 11, 2005, the French national legislature passed Act No. 2005–102, which aims to help achieve "equal rights and chances for the disabled; for participation and citizenship." This well-intended act led to counterproductive effects, however: Deaf children now have to attend the school closest to their home, and that school has to retain LSF interpreters or cued speech interpreters in order to integrate deaf children with hearing children in the classroom. Thus, schools for deaf children now have fewer and fewer students. The overall result is that DoH children (who are the majority of deaf children) are no longer learning sign language from their deaf peers (DoD and older DoH children) or from Deaf adults and no longer have any other children with whom they can communicate easily and extensively. Deaf children are no longer confronted by and efficiently interacting with more linguistically skilled people who, in a Vygotskian point of view, would have helped them achieve higher linguistic and cognitive levels.

Thus, the proper linguistic development of signing DoH children in France cannot be guaranteed even if parents opt for a bilingual education from the very beginning of their children's life. Additionally, parents rarely make that particular choice, and children often enter signing classes only after they have gone through the oral route and failed to develop sufficient oral skills to keep attending oral schools—although some of these children may have developed a basic knowledge in the oral modality and, accordingly, may be considered second language (L2) learners of a sign language when they enter a signing environment. Their ultimate level of sign language development as adults may appear rather promising at first sight, though research discussed by Wood has shown that their sign language abilities are not as good as those of native signers and that the age at which they become fluent signers depends on many variables, including the age of first exposure and the degree and quality of exposure (for a review, see Emmorey 2002).

COGNITIVE DEVELOPMENT: THE EXAMPLE OF THEORY OF MIND

What about the cognitive development of DoH children in France? This chapter considers the case of a cognitive ability highly related to communication for its emergence and needed for proper communicative and social exchanges: the so-called theory of mind (ToM).

Definition

Theory of mind is a cornerstone of social interaction in that it concerns the development of an awareness of how mental states, such as beliefs, desires, and wishes, govern our behavior. It aims to account both for why people may act differently the second time around in the context of an apparently identical event and for why two different people may act differently in the context of an apparently identical event. Around four to five years of age, children come to understand that it is possible to have a representation of reality that is not correct, be it about perceptive entities, beliefs, or desires. Thus, by this age and owing to their ToM, children are able to predict and explain people's actions and reactions. Hence, ToM can be considered to reside at the basis of social cognition and intelligence. In addition, ToM is useful for communicative interactions since one has to consider what others know and do not know in order to correctly adapt the message one wants to transmit in order to be fully understood in any given situation.

An example of a test commonly used for assessing ToM in children is the false belief (FB) task created by Wimmer and Perner (1983), briefly presented here. After a short scenario in which two dolls are shown playing with a marble, one of the dolls puts the marble in one of two easy-to-distinguish boxes (e.g., a blue one) and leaves the scene. While the doll is gone, the other doll continues playing and takes the marble out of the box and puts it into the second box (a red one). When the first doll comes back, the child is asked, "Where will the doll look for the marble?" Before they are four to five years of age, hearing children usually fail on this task as they are unable to depart from their knowledge of reality (the marble is in the red box) in order to consider the doll's knowledge; children thus answer that the doll will look in the red box. Only around age five are children able to understand that, since the doll was out of the room and did not see that the marble was removed from the blue box, the doll thinks the marble is still in the blue box.[2]

ToM and Language

Most researchers on ToM in deaf children report that DoD children perform on par with hearing children but that signing DoH children are delayed compared to DoD and hearing children (for a review see Courtin, Melot, and Corroyer 2008). The massive failure of late signers most likely originates in the lack of early exposure to language, a point I return to later.

First, however, what about orally educated DoH children? In fact, no clear differences in performance on the FB task exist between signing and speaking DoH children in the ToM literature that has specifically addressed the issue (Courtin, 2000; Courtin and Melot 2005; Schick et al. 2007), except for Peterson and Siegal (1999), who found that oral DoH children outperformed signing DoH children. However, their oral DoH sample had moderate hearing loss, while the signing DoH sample had profound deafness, a difference that surely affected how soon these children had access to communicative interactions.

It appears that DoH children are delayed in ToM, but which part of language is involved in this delay remains unclear. It is often claimed that immersing children in a rich conversational sharing of ideas in a community of mind (Nelson 2004) should lead to an awareness of others' mental states and to a metarepresentational ToM. Nevertheless, several theories emphasize either the role of early access to communication (Peterson and Siegal 1999; Siegal 2007), the role of discussions on mental entities (Dunn 1994), or the role of grammatical skills (e.g., embedded components; see Schick et al. 2007). Thus, much remains to be done to understand how communication relates to ToM.

Age of Acquisition

No consistent age at which DoH children pass the FB task is reported; instead, particular studies' findings range from seven to sixteen years of age. This variation is explicable: Language plays a critical role in ToM development, yet the authors often do not report the age at which DoH children are confronted with a fully accessible language (sign language, or spoken language but with hearing aid/cochlear implant [CI] that is efficacious for the child). Although CIs may at first appear to some people—parents and researchers alike—as a revolutionary device for deaf children, CIs, in the end, do not change the results researchers find on tests of cognitive development, at least in France at present. Most studies of Australian or American CI children find that they do not perform better than children with ordinary hearing aids (Peterson 2004, 2007; Schick et al. 2007; but see Remmel and Peters 2009). How can we explain this apparent failure of CIs to promote cognitive development? In France, the education provided to CI children remains focused on repairing the voice and the ears rather than promoting communication. However, cognitive ToM development is not dependant on sounds and voice; instead, it relies much more on communication, the pragmatic side of language, which tends to be forgotten in oral education.[3]

Thus, it appears quite clear that language and communication are critical variables for developing ToM.

THEORY OF MIND: A CRITICAL PERIOD?

We now arrive at the crucial question: Is there a critical age for access to communication, an age that, once passed, precludes the development of a representational ToM? Isolated deaf people like the homesigners Wood addresses in her chapter seem *de facto* affected by the question. However, what about deaf children who enter signing schools late, after failing in oral education, some of whom should be considered L2 learners of sign language while others are L1 learners?

Theory of Mind Abilities in Homesigners and Late Signers

To my knowledge, only one published article on ToM in homesigners exists, and it concerns adult late signers. Morgan and Kegl (2006), in a study of 22 Nicaraguan deaf adults, all former homesigners, report that the adults who were exposed to Nicaraguan Sign Language (NSL) before age 10 tend to pass the FB test, whereas those exposed to NSL after that age fail, regardless of how many years they have been using NSL. For example, one of the adults (26 years old) who had been exposed to sign language since the age of 12 failed the FB task despite his having used sign language for fourteen years. Morgan and Kegl's results suggest that 10 years of age could be a critical point, after which introduction to an accessible language might not be sufficient to ensure success on the FB task. Even though this research is very helpful, we must be cautious in interpreting the results. Note that 4 out of the 11 adults exposed to

NSL after age 10 nonetheless passed the FB task; thus, failure is not a predictable constant. This research clearly needs replication with results for more than 11 homesigners. Adult homesigners should be tested after several years of sign language contact, with different ages of first exposure to sign language. Nevertheless, this initial research might well remain without follow-up due to the difficult requirements of the experiment.

Notice that Morgan and Kegl's findings do not mean that these adult homesigners have no access to some kind of naïve ToM or to an understanding of other's mental states but instead indicate that their understanding is more implicit than explicit. Indeed, other studies (e.g., Fusellier-Souza 2006) report that adult homesigners have rudimentary social interactions that demonstrate some implicit ToM understanding. That is, while signing, these adults may express opinions about someone else's conceptual point of view. Nonetheless, it may be difficult for them to determine what someone else specifically knows about a fact and then adapt their expression to sign all that is necessary to be understood in a particular situation. If we extend Wood's analyses of the less or more fragile properties of language to the ToM findings, we may conclude that adult homesigners have basic interpersonal communication skills (BICS), while their cognitive academic language proficiency (CALP) (which develops later) is not sufficient to enable them to pass cognitive exercises such as the FB task (for a discussion of language for communication and thinking, see Akamatsu, Mayer, and Hardy-Braz 2008). Then, naturally, the final question is what kind of ToM these homesigners develop, a question to which we return later.

One may wonder what the case is for deaf children who are enrolled in oral schools but fail to develop oral skills (comprehension/production) for any reason—refusal of oral training, rejection of hearing aids, or malfunctioning hearing aids or CIs. These children enter signing schools late, at varying ages and with varying cognitive-linguistic skills in their oral L1 (indeed, they sometimes totally lack the relevant skills). It is difficult to say whether these children, if they entered signing schools after age 10, would display results similar to those presented by Morgan and Kegl (2006). The main problem in discussing this particular point is that the issue has not been specifically addressed in studies thus far. Surely some of the participants in the signing DoH samples in the literature on ToM were former oral children whose acquisition of sign language as L1 or L2 later evolved. However, the possibility is almost never mentioned by the authors; in fact, authors may themselves not be aware of such possible cases in their samples even if they explain part of the important age differences in success rates on the FB task. For example, in Russel et al. (1998), among DoH children in total communication environments, 40 percent of the participants in the oldest age range (13–16 years) still fail the FB task. In Schick et al. (2007), signing DoH children at age 7 pass about 5.5 out of the seven tasks (thus appearing much more effective than those in Russel et al.

1998), and almost half of them pass all seven tasks, although none of them pass all seven tasks at age 6. In a study by Courtin (2000), barely 50 percent of the 8-year-old signing DoH children passed two out of three FB tasks. Thus, variation seems to be the norm, and now that language is known to be an important variable, researchers should more precisely categorize DoH children according to their age of acquisition of sign language, whether it is acquired as L1 or L2, as well as both the quantity and quality of exposure, in accordance with Wood's work. A further question, however, is how these 8- to 16-year-olds who still fail to pass the FB tasks will develop their cognition.

In fact, the question might not be correctly formulated since it addresses the mean result of a group of children instead of individual children. For example, as a group, signing DoH children are observed to fail the FB tasks up to age 8 or 9, and in several studies, their performance does not improve significantly as age increases (e.g., Courtin 2000). This may be due to the arrival of former oral DoH children who are just entering a signing environment, lowering the mean level of linguistic and cognitive development that would otherwise be observed for each age range and leading to the apparent result of nonprogression. The case may be different if one looks at the individual level or at least if one separates children into early and late DoH signers. Results of correlations between language skills and ToM scores (Remmel and Peters 2009; Schick et al. 2007) support this hypothesis. There may be a need for close control and/or categorization of which children are involved in the signing DoH samples.

It is taken for granted that, with time, children will make up for their delay in their ToM development even if they still fail at age eight, for example, but there is no clear evidence yet that this delay is, in fact, ever overcome. We do not really know, for there have been too few studies addressing ToM or ToM-like skills in older adolescents and adults. Additionally, the results reported so far appear conflicting (for a review, see Courtin, Melot, and Corroyer 2008); in the end, we have only a vague sense of later ToM development.

A Unique or Different ToM?

The age of ten might be critical for the development of a representational ToM in homesigners. At this point a further question remains. Even if deaf children—in fact sometimes adolescents—develop a ToM late, most of them nonetheless seem to develop an explicit and functional ToM (except for about 70 percent of the homesigners confronted with sign language after age ten). Is this ToM similar to that of hearing and/or DoD children, or is it different? Once again there is no agreement in the literature about this aspect of deaf children's development. In several papers Peterson (with Siegal or with Wellman and Liu) consistently report that DoH, DoD, and hearing children develop in the same way: Even if DoH children are delayed in their ToM development, the structure of their ToM is identical to that of hearing and DoD children. On the other hand, Courtin, Melot, and Corroyer (2008) report differences among these groups with respect to the cognitive structure of ToM, but with methods that differ from those of Peterson and her colleagues, so that, eventually, the two groups of researchers do not really appear in opposition. In particular, Peterson, Wellman, and Liu (2005), using five ToM tasks of differing difficulty, address the chronological order of success on these different tasks and find that the three groups of children (hearing, DoD, and signing DoH) develop in the same order—but see Remmel and Peters (2009) for a different conclusion with CI speaking DoH children.

Courtin et al. (2008) for their part focus on the FB task but ask children to justify their answers: "Why? Why does [doll's name sign] look for the marble here [pointing to the box that the child had first indicated]?" In the children's explanations, it appears that signing deaf children (DoD and DoH) are more focused on the protagonist's behaviors ("she put it here before"), while hearing children are a little more tuned in to the protagonist's mental states ("she thinks the marble is here"). It is not that deaf children do not refer to mental states or are more concrete in any sense; rather, the protagonist's mental states are invoked by deaf children as well. However, compared to hearing children, DoH and, to a lesser extent, DoD children rely much more on previous behaviors in order to—efficiently and correctly—predict and explain behaviors to come. One may think that homesigners might develop the same kind of behavioral ToM as other deaf children since observation of others' behaviors may be the only clue to understanding what happens in their surroundings. Of course, research is needed to confirm that point.

CONCLUSION

In conclusion, there exists little knowledge about possible critical ages in sign language acquisition for cognitive development. The development of a mature representational ToM may be difficult, though not impossible, when children are deprived of access to a natural and feasible communication before age ten—an age that obviously differs from that observed by Wood for linguistic development. When language is present before that time, even if access to it is delayed in young ages (due to lack of sign language or to hearing aids that do not work correctly and whose usage will eventually be stopped), ToM develops, though its structure may not be identical to that of hearing children. The ToM is nonetheless fully functional and enables children and adolescents to integrate into their social environment. When access to sign language or to effective communication via oral language and hearing aids occurs after age ten, certain cognitive development may be at risk for more than half of these children. However, much more work is needed to reach firmer conclusions.

There are also many other aspects of cognition that have not been studied. This chapter addresses ToM, but what about memory, executive functions, analogical reasoning, and so on in these homesigners who learn sign language and enter the Deaf community late?

Notes

1. The question might not now appear quite pertinent since deaf children are being implanted at a younger and younger age. However, in most studies, even implanted children are described according to their hearing abilities without their cochlear implant; additionally, their actual abilities with the cochlear implant are usually not mentioned. Thus, the way to label a deaf child would surely be a matter for discussion, whatever the choice made by the authors.

2. As in linguistics, as presented in Wood's chapter, there is debate about whether ToM is an innate competence (Leslie, German, and Polizzi 2005) or an important conceptual change (Wellman, Cross, and Watson 2001) in children's development. The debate continues (see Kovacs 2009) but I do not consider this point further as it is not essential for the present discussion.

3. The case might change in a few years in France, as some therapists and the Haute Autorité de Santé (French National Authority for Health) now suggest using LSF with young children with cochlear implants in order to facilitate the emergence of communication. However, the debate is quite acrimonious, and the suggestion may not be followed by practitioners.

Bibliography

Akamatsu, C. Tane, Connie Mayer, and Steven Hardy-Braz. 2008. Why Considerations of Verbal Aptitude Are Important in Educating Deaf and Hard-of-hearing Students. In *Deaf Cognition: Foundations and Outcomes*, ed. Marc Marschark and Peter C. Hauser, 131–169. New York: Oxford University Press.

Courtin, Cyril. 2000. The Impact of Sign Language on the Cognitive Development of Deaf Children: The Case of Theories of Mind. *Journal of Deaf Studies and Deaf Education* 5: 266–276.

———, and Anne-Marie Melot. 2005. Metacognitive Development of Deaf Children: Lessons from the Appearance-reality and False Belief Tasks. *Developmental Science* 8: 16–25.

———, and Denis Corroyer. 2008. Achieving Efficient Learning: Why Theory of Mind Is Essential for Deaf Children . . . and Their Teachers. In *Deaf Cognition, Foundations, and Outcomes*, ed. Marc Marschark and Peter C. Hauser, 102–130. New York: Oxford University Press.

Dunn, Judy. 1994. Changing Minds and Changing Relationships. In *Children's Early Understanding of Mind*, ed. Charlie Lewis and Peter Mitchell, 297–310. Hillsdale, N.J.: Erlbaum.

Emmorey, Karen. 2002. *Language, Cognition, and the Brain: Insights from Sign Language Research*. Mahwah, N.J.: Erlbaum.

Fusellier-Souza, Ivani. 2006. Emergence and Development of Signed Languages: From a Semiogenetic Point of view. *Sign Language Studies* 7: 30–56.

Kovacs, Agnes M. 2009. Early Bilingualism Enhances Mechanisms of False-belief Reasoning. *Developmental Science* 12: 48–54.

Leslie, Alan M., Tim P. German, and Pamela Polizzi. 2005. Belief-desire Reasoning as a Process of Selection. *Cognitive Psychology* 50: 45–85.

Marschark, Mark, and Peter C. Hauser, eds. 2008. *Deaf Cognition, Foundation, and Outcomes.* New York: Oxford University Press.

Meristo, Marek, Kerstin W. Falkman, Erland Hjelmquist, Mariantonia Tedoldi, Luca Surian, and Michael Siegal. 2007. Language Access and Theory of Mind Reasoning: Evidence from Deaf Children in Bilingual and Oralist Environments. *Developmental Psychology* 43: 1156–1169.

Mitchell, Ross E., and Michael A. Karchmer. 2004. Chasing the Mythical Ten Percent: Parental Hearing Status of Deaf and Hard of Hearing Students in the United States. *Sign Language Studies* 4: 138–163.

Morgan, Gary, and Judy Kegl. 2006. Nicaraguan Sign Language and Theory of Mind: The Issue of Critical Period and Abilities. *Journal of Child Psychology and Psychiatry* 47: 811–819.

Nelson, Katherine. 2004. Commentary: The Future of ToM Lies in CoM. *International Society for the Study of Behavioural Development Newsletter* 45: 16–17.

Newport, Elissa, and Richard Meier. 1985. The Acquisition of American Sign Language. In *The Cross-linguistic Study of Language Acquisition.* Vol. 1, *The Data,* ed. Dan Slobin, 881–938. Hillsdale, N.J.: Erlbaum.

Peterson, Candida C. 2004. Theory-of-mind Development in Oral Deaf Children with Cochlear Implants or Conventional Hearing Aids. *Journal of Child Psychology, Psychiatry, and Allied Disciplines* 45: 1096–1106.

———. 2007. Le développement métacognitif des enfants sourds [Metacognitive Development of Deaf Children]. *Enfance* 59: 282–290.

———, and Michael Siegal. 1999. Insight into Theory of Mind from Deafness and Autism. *Mind and Language* 15: 77–99.

Peterson, Candida C., Henry M. Wellman, and David Liu. 2005. Steps in Theory-of-mind Development for Children with Deafness. *Child Development* 76: 502–517.

Remmel, Ethan, and Kimberly Peters. 2009. Theory of Mind and Language in Children with Cochlear Implants. *Journal of Deaf Studies and Deaf Education* 14: 218–236.

Russel, Phil A., Judith A. Hosie, Colin Gray, Christine D. Scott, Norma Hunter, J. S. Banks, and Mairi C. Macaulay. 1998. The Development of Theory of Mind in Deaf Children. *Journal of Child Psychology, Psychiatry, and Allied Disciplines* 39: 903–910.

Schick, Brenda, Peter de Villiers, Jill de Villiers, and Robert Hoffmeister. 2007. Language and Theory of Mind: A Study of Deaf Children. *Child Development* 78: 376–396.

Siegal, Michael. 2007. Language Access and Theory of Mind Reasoning. *Enfance* 59: 291–297.

Wellman, Henry M., David Cross, and Julanne Watson. 2001. Meta-analysis of Theory-of-mind Development: The Truth about False Belief. *Child Development* 72: 655–684.

Wimmer, Heinz, and Josef Perner. 1983. Beliefs about Beliefs: Representation and Constraining Function of Wrong Beliefs in Young Children's Understanding of Deception. *Cognition* 13: 103–128.

CHAPTER 6

Interrogatives in Ban Khor Sign Language

A Preliminary Description

Angela M. Nonaka

INTRODUCTION: BAN KHOR SIGN LANGUAGE AND SIGN LANGUAGE TYPOLOGIES

A contribution to the nascent but growing effort to develop and conceptualize sign language typology, this chapter offers a preliminary descriptive account of interrogatives in Ban Khor Sign Language (BKSL), a relatively new and previously undescribed sign language isolate used exclusively in Ban Khor, Thailand. Although it developed only around seventy-five years ago, its use has proliferated, and today 15–26 percent of all villagers can sign (Nonaka 2007). Conservatively, the BKSL speech/sign community is three generations old and is estimated to include more than four hundred signers, of whom most are hearing (Nonaka 2007, 2009).

Ban Khor Sign Language arose de novo in Ban Khor, which has a distinctive sociolinguistic ecology, one remarkably similar to other places where indigenous (Woodward 2000) or village (Zeshan 2004b) sign languages have appeared (Kakumasu 1968; Kuschel 1973; Washabaugh 1978, 1979, 1981, 1986; Shuman 1980; Woodward 1982; Ferreiro-Brito 1983; Groce 1985; Frishberg 1987; Johnson 1991, 1994; Torigoe and Kimura 1995; Bahan and Poole-Nash 1996; Branson and Miller 1996; Kisch 2004, 2006; Sandler et al. 2005; Cumberbatch 2006; Marsaja 2006, 2008; Nyst 2006; Van den Bogaerde 2006). Found across time and space, these diverse communities share a remarkably similar sociolinguistic ecology that is characterized by (1) unusually high incidences of deafness in the population; (2) high degrees of biological and/or nonbiological kinship; (3) labor-intensive, nonindustrial local economies; (4) low intracommunity educational differentiation between deaf and hearing people; and (5) low intracommunity occupational differentiation between deaf and hearing people. Additionally, deaf-hearing sociocommunicative interactions and social relations in these societies contrast sharply with those of most other communities. In the small-scale societies where, to borrow Nora Groce's (1985) expression, (almost) *Everyone Speaks Sign Language,* language attitudes, ideologies, and practices are accommodative and inclusive of sign language and of deaf people.

It is primarily sociolinguistic context and function that currently distinguish indigenous village sign languages, like Ban Khor Sign Language, from other types of sign languages—that is, national (Woodward 2000) and/or urban (Zeshan 2006a), as well as original (Woodward 2000) varieties. Little is yet known about the characteristic linguistic features of un(der)documented indigenous village sign languages, although attempts at comparative description and analysis are beginning.

Growing awareness of the limits of our collective understanding of the true extent of sign language diversity has led to calls for more thorough linguistic survey work (Woodward 2000; Meier 2000; Nonaka 2004) and has underscored the need to develop a typology of sign languages. The effort to develop a sign language typology has been spearheaded by Ulrike Zeshan (2004a, 2004b, 2006a), who, working with international partners, has begun examining particular grammatical domains, starting with interrogative and negative constructions in more than thirty-five geographically and genetically distinct sign languages. Hers is the first large-scale, typological, cross-linguistic study of interrogatives in manual-visual languages. All of the languages save one, Kata Kolok (Marsaja 2008), however, were national or urban sign languages.

This project (see appendix) expands typological investigation of interrogatives to include a second indigenous village sign language, Ban Khor Sign Language. A foundational description of the two basic types of questions— yes/no ("polar") and wh- ("content")—is provided in the sections "Yes-no/ Polar Questions" and "Wh-/Content Questions," respectively. Another type of interrogative formation utilizing question particles is examined in the section "Question Particles and Content Questions without Words/Signs." The chapter concludes with a discussion of the implications of these findings for understanding sign language typologies.

YES-NO/POLAR QUESTIONS

Yes-no questions in Ban Khor Sign Language appear to be remarkably similar to those found in other sign languages. To date, no manual marking of polar questions has been found in BKSL. Rather, such questions are marked nonmanually through particular combinations of eyebrow movement, eye gaze, head movement, and body posture.

Nonmanual markers are critically important in all known natural human sign languages. They serve many important grammatical functions, including one analogous to prosody in spoken languages (Sandler 1999), and "in signed languages, polar questions are invariably marked by 'intonation' in the form of nonmanual signals" (Zeshan 2004b, 19). In sign languages, classic features of this "intonational" nonmanual marking of yes-no questions include direct eye contact with the recipient interlocutor; forward and/or upward body lean; slight tilting of the head (either upward, downward, or sideways); and complex manipulations of the eyebrows, often involving raised eyebrows and widely opened eyes (Baker and Padden 1978; Bergman 1984; Humphries, Padden, and O'Rourke 1985; Engberg-Pedersen 1990; Coerts 1992; Subtle Impact Software 1995; Celo 1996; Sandler 1999; Wilbur 2000; Neidle 2003; Meir 2004; Zeshan 2004b; Fischer 2006; McKee 2006; Morgan 2006; Quadros 2006; Savolainen 2006; Schalber 2006; Tang 2006; Van Herreweghe and Vermeerbergen 2006; Zeshan 2006b).

Examination of interrogatives in Ban Khor Sign Language is an ongoing endeavor, so no definitive description of the intricacies of nonmanual marking of polar questions is attempted here. Nevertheless, it is apparent that the same complex constellations of nonmanual markings described earlier also accompany yes-no questions in BKSL. For example, figure 6.1 depicts the BKSL polar question "Did you ever go to school?," which is made using the prototypical nonmanual markers of yes-no questions in sign language: raised eyebrows, widely opened eyes, direct eye contact with recipient interlocutor, and forward and/or upward tilt/lean of the head and trunk.

For purposes of transcription here, this constellation of nonmanual markers for a polar question is indicated by *pol-q* and is written above the glosses. The *pol-q* symbol's placement corresponds with the beginning and

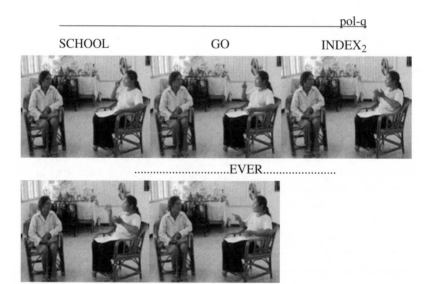

Figure 6.1. Example of a BKSL polar question expressed through nonmanual marking: "Did you ever go to school?"

ending of nonmanual activities and indicates signs encompassed by those nonmanual markers. The nonmanual markings indicate that the proposition within their scope is an interrogative.

WH-/CONTENT QUESTIONS

Whereas yes-no/polar questions are remarkably similar across sign languages, wh- or content questions exhibit considerable variability. The latter raise interesting issues related to "the size and structure of question-word paradigms, the lexical and grammatical distinctions expressed in such paradigms, related interrogative and noninterrogative uses of question words, and the syntactic position of question words in the clause" (Zeshan 2004b, 22). Again, study of the wh-system in Ban Khor Sign Language enriches our understanding of these matters.

Question Word Paradigm Size and Accompanying Nonmanual Markings

The size of question word paradigms varies dramatically across sign languages, ranging from single-word systems to multilexemic ones. Larger by one than the single question-word paradigm systems of Indo-Pakistani Sign Language (Zeshan 2004b), Kata Kolok Sign Language (Marsaja 2008), or the spoken languages of Asheninca (Cysouw 2007, Givón 2001), Kenya Swahili Pidgin (Heine, Claudi, and Hünnemeyer 1991, 57), and eighteenth-century Srnan (Muysken and Smith 1990; Bruyn 1993), Ban Khor Sign Language's wh-system is organized around two signs, which for descriptive purposes are referred to here as WH1 (figure 6.2) and WH2 (figure 6.3).

$$\frac{\text{cont-q}^1}{\text{WH1}}$$

Figure 6.2. WH1

$$\frac{\text{cont-}q^2}{\text{WH2}}$$

Figure 6.3. WH2

The first sign, WH1, is articulated by rapidly wagging the index finger back and forth and is typically accompanied by at least two distinct nonmanual markings. One, indicated by the transcription convention *cont-q¹*, involves a combination of scrunched eyebrows with forward head and/or body tilt (e.g., figure 6.2 and as shown later in figure 6.4, example 1; figure 6.4, example 3; figure 6.6, version 1; figure 6.7; figure 6.8). The second set of nonmanual markings (raised eyebrows plus forward head/body tilt), which can be used with WH1, appears in transcription as *cont-q²* (e.g., figure 6.3 and as demonstrated later in figure 6.5, example 1; figure 6.5, example 2; figure 6.6, version B; figure 6.6, version C; figure 6.8; figure 6.9; figure 6.16).

Alternatively, WH2 is made by wiggling all of the fingers on the fully extended 5 hand with the palm facing the signer. In addition, WH2 can be accompanied by either of the nonmanual markers described earlier: *cont-q¹* (e.g., figure 6.11, which appears later in this section) and *cont-q²* (e.g., figure 6.3 and subsequently in figure 6.12).

Semantics and Syntactic Patterning of WH1 and WH2

Semantically, WH1 can express several interrogative meanings, including the following:

- what?
- who?
- where?
- why?
- which?
- when?
- how?

On the other hand, WH2 is used to express just two meanings:

- How many?
- How much?

Examples of BKSL content questions using WH1 (figures 6.4–6.10) and WH2 (figures 6.11–6.12) are illustrated here.

In her discussion of generalizations about the syntactic positions of question words in sign languages, Zeshan (2006a, 3) notes "a striking preference

Example 1   Target Question: 'What's in the box?'
       Rendered Question: 'What's (in) the box?'

                         cont-q[1]
WH1   BOX   WH1

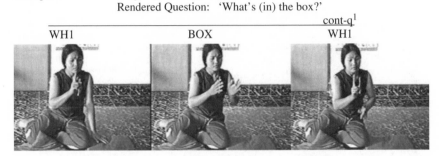

Example 2 Elicited Question: 'What did you eat for breakfast?'
      Rendered Question: 'What did you eat?'

    EAT   WH1   INDEX$_2$

Example 3   'What's that?'

                cont-q[1]
     THAT   WH1

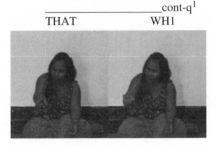

Figure 6.4. WH1 as WHAT?

for clause-peripheral positions" and states that "for question words, both clause-initial and clause-final positions are pervasive." Early investigation suggests that these patterns also apply to Ban Khor Sign Language.

The syntactic position of WH1 can vary, although it occurs most frequently at the end of utterances (e.g., figure 6.4, example 3; figure 6.5, example 2; figure 6.6, version B; figure 6.6, version C; figure 6.7, and figure 6.10). Doubling is also common, such that WH1 appears in both the initial and final positions (e.g., figure 6.4, example 1; figure 6.5, example 1; figure 6.6, version C). Sometimes

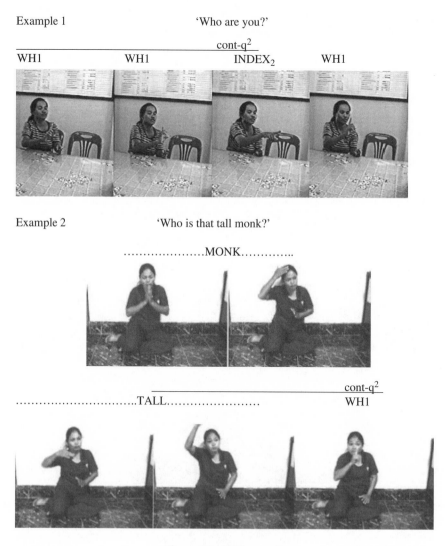

Figure 6.5. WH1 as WHO?

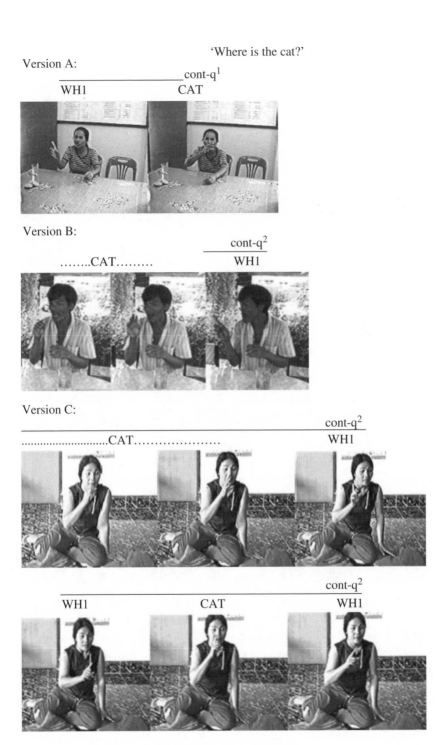

'Where is the cat?'

Version A:

_____ cont-q[1]

WH1 · CAT

Version B:

_____ cont-q[2]

.........CAT......... · WH1

Version C:

_____ cont-q[2]

............................CAT..................... · WH1

_____ cont-q[2]

WH1 · CAT · WH1

Figure 6.6. WH1 as WHERE?

'Why is the little boy crying?'

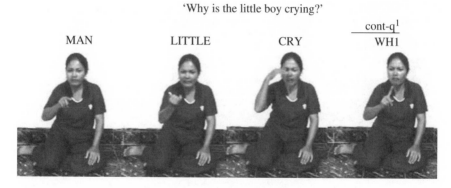

Figure 6.7. WH1 as WHY?

'Which is bigger, a water buffalo or a cat?'

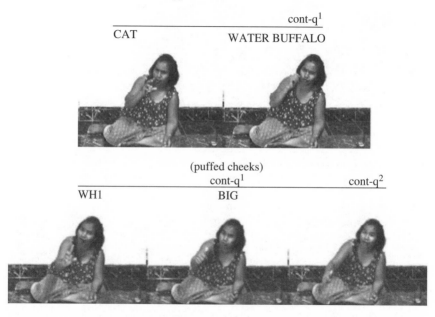

Figure 6.8. WH1 as WHICH?

WH1 occurs only at the beginning of the question (figure 6.6, version A), and occasionally the question word appears elsewhere in the utterance (e.g., figure 6.4, example 2; figure 6.8; figure 6.9).

The syntactic position of WH2, on the other hand, is consistent. It always occurs in the final position (e.g., figures 6.11 and 6.12). In addition to always appearing at the end of the question, WH2 is typically preceded by a noun or an identifier, which, when combined with WH2, operates as a countable value, a quantifiable amount, or a unit of measurement—that is, to quantify

'How will you travel to Bangkok?'

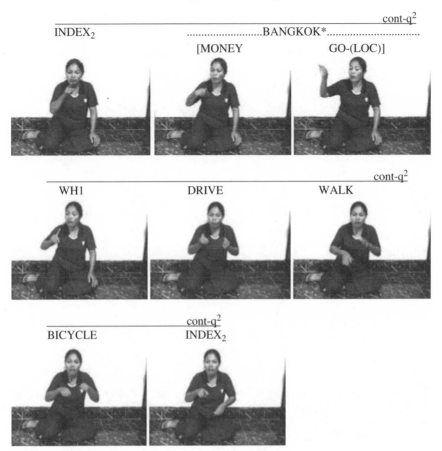

$$\text{cont-q}^2$$

INDEX$_2$ ....BANGKOK*...............................
                        [MONEY   GO-(LOC)]

$$\text{cont-q}^2$$

WH1   DRIVE   WALK

$$\text{cont-q}^2$$

BICYCLE   INDEX$_2$

Figure 6.9. WH1 as HOW (in what manner, by what means)? *In BKSL there are several place terms that can be used to refer to the Thai capital city, "Bangkok," including: (1) DRIVE-(FAR) WASH-CLOTHES WAY-OVER-THERE; (2) WASH- CLOTHES MONEY WAY-OVER-THERE; (3) or MONEY GO-WAY-OVER-THERE. The etymology of these signs derives from many Ban Khorians', especially women's, experiences working as maids in Bangkok. MONEY GO-WAY-OVER- THERE has become a prototype for the many kinds of manual labor that villagers perform as temporary migrant workers in Bangkok (Nonaka 2007).

age/number of years (figure 6.12) or to indicate time or distance from a reference point (figure 6.11).

Comparing BKSL's Wh-Question Paradigm with Selected Languages

Having outlined the basic organization of the question-word paradigm in Ban Khor Sign Language, I now compare that system with those of selected

Target Question: 'When were the three new police boxes built?'

Rendered Question: 'When were the three barrier gates built?'

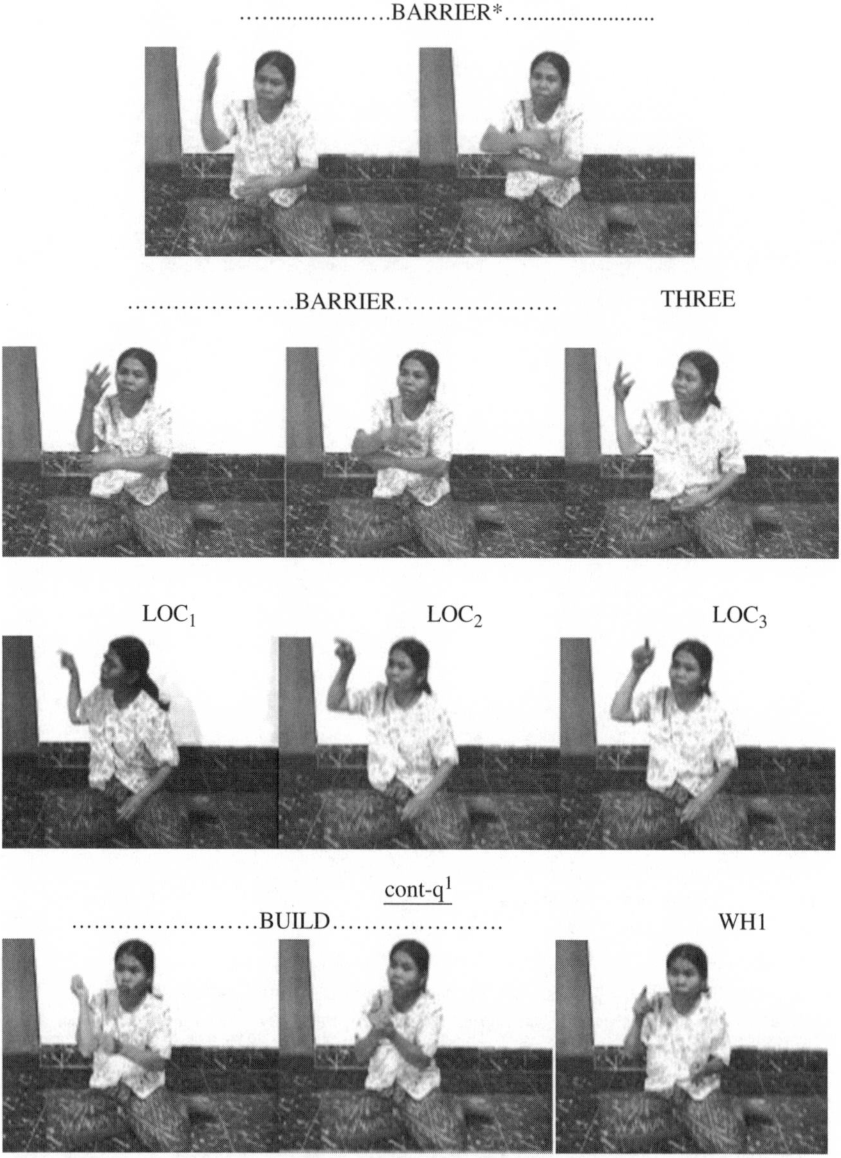

….................…BARRIER*…......................

…....................BARRIER…..................…   THREE

LOC$_1$ LOC$_2$ LOC$_3$

cont-q[1]
…....................…BUILD…....................   WH1

Figure 6.10. WH1 as WHEN? *Early in 2003 a cattle-rustling incident caused the community of Ban Khor to erect small police boxes and barrier gates at each of the three entry roads to the village. The police boxes, which were seldom if ever manned, were little more than shanty-like, lean-to huts with thatched roofing, and the barrier gates were merely large bamboo poles or tree branches with big stones or other heavy objects suspended at one end. The barrier gates moved up and down in a 90 degree arc—the motion depicted in the BKSL sign, BARRIER.

Identifier (DAY) + WH2

Target Question: When were the three new police boxes built?*

Rendered Question: How many days (ago)?

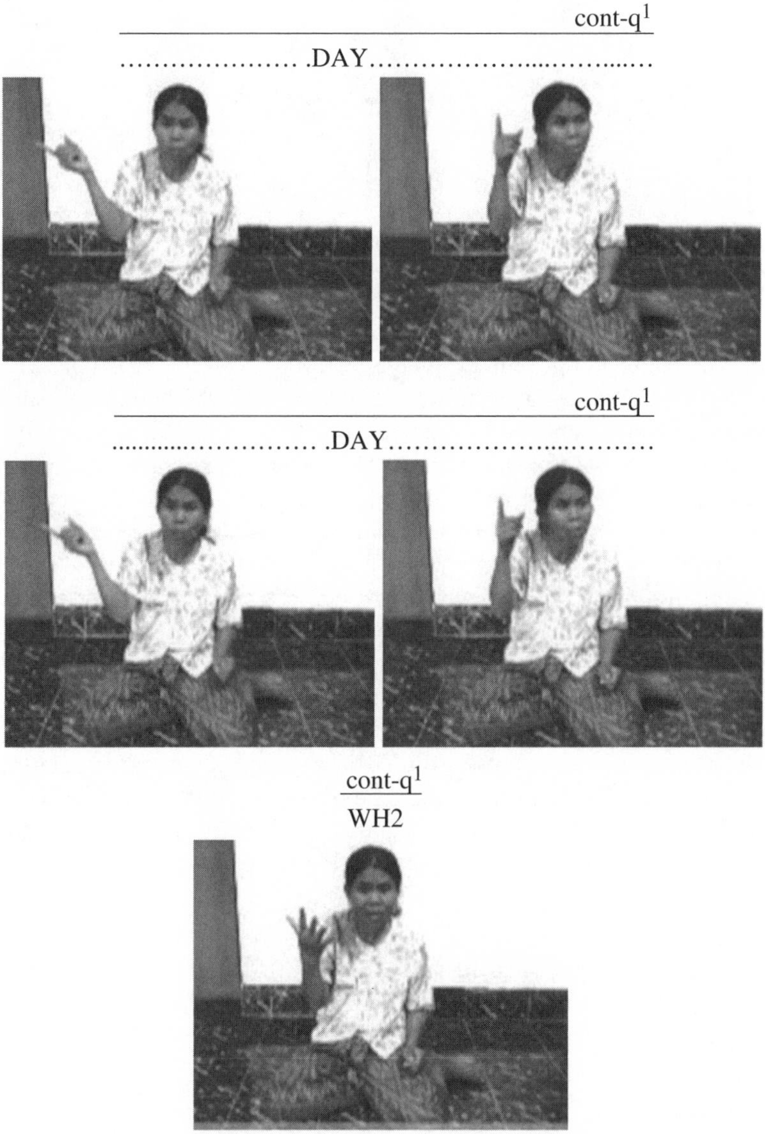

cont-q[1]

.... .DAY....................…......…....

cont-q[1]

............…............. .DAY.....................…...….…....

cont-q[1]

WH2

Figure 6.11. WH2 as HOW MANY? *Note that in the original video data from which this example is drawn, the question depicted here immediately follows the preceding one shown in figure 6.10. No explicit reference either to police boxes or barrier gates is made in this example because that information was already understood in the context of the actual flow of talk and interaction in the elicitation session.

Identifier (YEAR) + WH2

'How old are you?'

cont-q[1]

INDEX₂   YEAR   YEAR   WH2

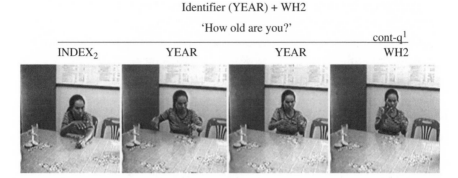

Figure 6.12. WH2 as HOW MANY?

languages, signed and spoken. In several respects, BKSL's wh-system is similar to that of Hong Kong Sign Language (HKSL). Gladys Tang (2006, 210)
reports that "there are two generic Wh-signs in HKSL, which are articulated
by the a [*sic*] 1-handshape or an open 5-handshape. The Wh-signs with a
l-handshape . . . involve a pivoting motion of the wrist," while the second generic wh-sign "is articulated by an open 5-handshape with the fingers in a
wiggling motion." In terms of their articulation, the HKSL wh-signs are identical to those of BKSL.[1]

The semantics of BKSL's two wh-signs are also similar to those of HKSL.
With just one exception (namely, "when?"), WH1 expresses the same range of
meanings in both languages. However, BKSL's WH1 occurs alone, while in
HKSL, "it is common to combine WH1 with other lexical signs to form question compounds" (e.g., PLACE + WH1 = "where?" or FACE + WH1 = "who?") or,
in the case of the "why?" content questions, to trace a question mark in neutral
signing space (Tang 2006, 210). In the case of the second wh-sign (WH1 in
BKSL or WH5 in HKSL), they are semantically identical. Both express the
meanings "how many?" or "how much?", and both are preceded by identifiers.

Thai	Nyoh
Who? ใคร Krai	Who? เผอ Phoe
What? อะไร A-rai	What? แม่นเต๋อ Man-Toe
Where? ที่ไหน The-Nai	Where? ไปกะเหลอ Pai-ka-roe
Why? ทำไม Tham-mai	Why? เช็ดเต๋อ Hed-Toe
Which? อันไหน An-nai	Which? ...เต๋อ/เหลอ ...classifier+ Toe
When? เมื่อไร Muea-rai	When? เมื่อเหลอ Muea-rer/roe
How? อย่างไร Yang-rai	How? เช็ดแบบเหลอ Hed-Bab-Rer/Roe

Figure 6.13. Comparative lists of content words in Thai and Nyoh

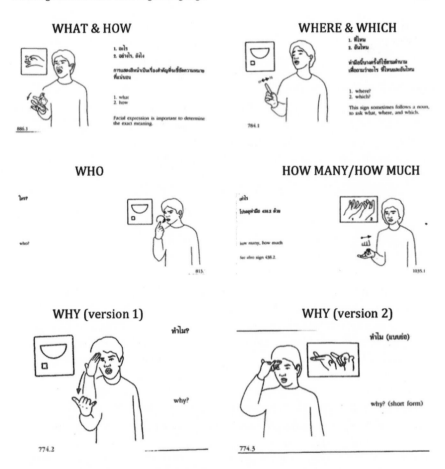

Figure 6.14. Thai Sign Language's six wh-signs. Entries from the *Thai Sign Language Dictionary* (Suwanarat et al. 1990).

There also appear to be some general similarities between the two languages' content word paradigms with regard to syntactic positioning and use of nonmanual markers, but since those are complex phenomena, it is best not to overstate the case. Conservatively, however, it is worth noting that, as in BKSL, in HKSL "wh-signs are generally clause final" (Tang 2006, 215). Moreover, accompanying "non-manual marking can be brow raise or brow furrow" (Tang 2006, 215) in HKSL, as well as in BKSL, although there appear to be differences in the scope of those nonmanual markers in the two languages.

While the many similarities between the wh-systems of BKSL and HKSL are intriguing, it is likely that the two languages are inspectionally similar but have neither an areal nor a genetic relationship. As noted at the beginning of this chapter, BKSL arose de novo after the birth of the first two deaf villagers to an ethnically Soe family that had emigrated[2] to Ban Khor, which is a predominantly[3] Nyoh-speaking Thai Lao community where, unlike other areas of Thailand, there are no Chinese residents (deaf or hearing) and little if any local Sinitic cultural influence (Nonaka 2007).

By contrast, there is no inspectional resemblance between Ban Khor Sign Language's question word paradigm and those of other languages in closest areal/geographic and sociolinguistic contact with BKSL. For example, as outlined in figure 6.13, both Thai (Juntanamalaga and Diller 1999; Iwasaki and Ingkaphirom 2005) and Nyoh,[4] two Tai-Kadai languages, have seven content words compared to BKSL's two wh-signs.

The content word paradigm of Thai Sign Language (TSL) is also very unlike that of BKSL. As shown in figure 6.14, TSL has six distinct wh-signs (Suwanarat et al. 1990), and the only similarity in articulation is between the TSL wh-sign that expresses the meanings "where" and "which" and the BKSL sign WH1. It is highly unlikely, however, that the sign is cognate in the two Thai sign language varieties, for they are genetically unrelated languages (Woodward 2000). Still, it is interesting to note that the sign—made with a 1 handshape and tremolo movement—is a content word found in numerous other sign languages, such as American Sign Language (Fischer 2006), Finnish Sign Language (Savolainen 2006), Flemish Sign Language (Van Herreweghe and Vermeerbergen 2006), Hong Kong Sign Language (Tang 2006), Japanese Sign Language (Morgan 2006), and New Zealand Sign Language (McKee 2006).

Foundational investigation of questions in Ban Khor Sign Language raises other interesting analytical issues pertaining to interrogatives in sign languages. For instance, there is evidence of the existence of at least one question particle. The next section describes that question particle, comparing it to ones found in other sign languages; considers its origins vis-à-vis spoken languages used in the community of Ban Khor; and discusses its functions, including its role in the articulation of content questions without question words/signs.

QUESTION PARTICLES AND CONTENT QUESTIONS WITHOUT WORDS/SIGNS

As explained earlier, polar questions in BKSL can be rendered solely through a constellation of nonmanual markings, *pol-q,* that co-occur with manual signs in the utterance. Wh-questions, on the other hand, utilize one of two content word signs, WH1 and WH2, that fall under the scope of two sets of nonmanual markings: *cont-q*^{1} and *cont-q*^{2}. In addition to these basic patterns, there is a third way to construct interrogatives in BKSL—through use of a question particle.

Question particles have been identified in sign languages in North America (e.g., Baker-Shenk and Cokely 1980; Neidle et al. 2000) and Europe (Celo 1996; Herreweghe and Vermeerbergen 2006; Savolainen 2006) and are suspected to occur in certain manual-visual languages in East Africa (Zeshan 2004b, 34). It is the "sign languages in East Asia," however, that are "particularly rich in question particles, which, interestingly, is also true of many spoken languages in the same region" (Zeshan 2006, 61). Whereas question particles in many spoken languages are obligatory, that is not the case in sign languages. Among sign languages with question particles, the form of those particles (e.g., manual and/or nonmanual) varies, but the primary function is the same: to signal an interrogative.

Description of the BKSL Question Particle Q^{AUH} and Its Functions

Ban Khor Sign Language evinces at least one question particle, transcribed here as Q^{AUH} (e.g., figures 6.15 and 6.16). It is a nonmanual sign articulated with a quick upward and backward nod of the head. The full grammatical functions of Q^{AUH} are not yet known, but presently at least six things are discernable about it. First, it is not obligatory. Second, it usually occurs at the end of an utterance. Although Q^{AUH} often appears after polar questions, it can also occur with content questions. The nonmanual sign falls under the scope of at least two nonmanual markings commonly associated with interrogatives: upward eyebrow movement and forward/upward head tilt. Finally, a particular mouthing, "*auh,*" always accompanies the nonmanual sign Q^{AUH}.

Elicited Question: 'Is the man sleeping?'*

(furrowed brow) Q^{AUH}

MAN   SLEEP   INDEX$_3$

Figure 6.15. Example of a BKSL polar question + Q^{AUH}. *This particular example of the question "Is the man sleeping?" implies a strong degree of disapproval that the man might be sleeping. Not all elicited examples of this question included such a negative assessment. In this instance, the implication of disapproval is made through negative facial expression that co-occurs with the signs "MAN SLEEP."

Elicited Question: 'Who ate the mandarin orange?'

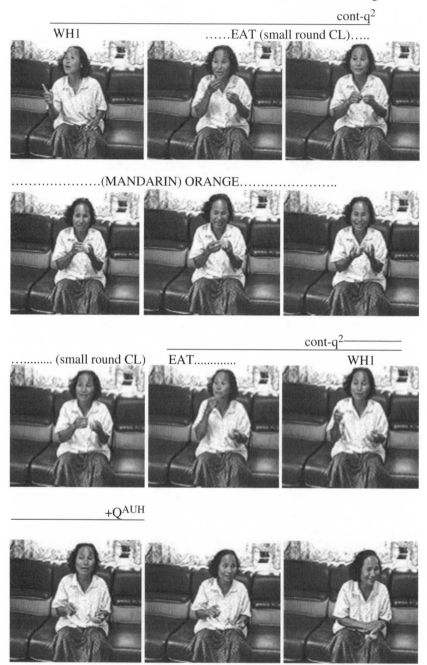

Figure 6.16. Example of a WH1 content question + Q^{AUH}

Q^{AUH}: Insights into Language Contact and Borrowing

With regard to this last point, the particular movement of the mouth characteristic of Q^{AUH} is an open mouth, which is formed in a manner consistent with the articulatory requirements for pronunciation of the sound segments *auh* (e.g., figures 6.15 and 6.16). Usually the sounds are not actually verbalized, just mouthed in BKSL. The mouthing almost certainly derives from Nyoh, the dominant spoken vernacular.

Auh, in Nyoh, is a derivative of *bauh*, a variant of *bu* (or *mai* in Thai), a negative that is used in the construction of polar questions like *gin auh* [Will you eat?] or *bai auh* [Will you go?] but never in the formation of content questions. Use of *auh* is normally accompanied by a quick upward and backward head nod. In terms of articulation, both the verbal expression and the accompanying gesture are highly visible and are used ubiquitously by Nyoh speakers.

These linguistic and paralinguistic resources appear to have been borrowed from the spoken language but then regrammaticized into Ban Khor Sign Language, so that the mouthing of *auh*, together with the nonmanual sign, now constitute a general interrogative in BKSL: the question particle, Q^{AUH}. Other instances of borrowings and regrammaticization from spoken Nyoh into Ban Khor Sign Language have also been observed, and similar phenomena are documented in other sign languages as well. For instance, Antzakas (2006) documents gestural exchange between the Deaf and hearing communities in Greece. He reports that "the use of the head movement as a hearing gesture of negation indicates that the Greek Deaf community has adopted the backward tilt of the head from the Greek hearing community," although "this gesture has been transformed by Greek Deaf people into a linguistic function and has become one of the major nonmanual negation markers in GSL" (Antzakas 2006, 269). These examples raise interesting questions about the dynamic processes of language contact and borrowing.

Content Questions without Words/Signs

There is another intriguing aspect of the BKSL question particle Q^{AUH}. Although rare in spoken languages, Zeshan found in her comparative typological study that "Across the majority of signed languages in the data, one finds content questions without question words," which are marked in two primary ways: "by facial expressions (nonmanual marking) or by mouthing, an imitation of the mouth movements of a corresponding word from the spoken language" (Zeshan 2004b, 30).

This appears to be true in Ban Khor Sign Language, too (figure 6.17). It is possible to express a wh-interrogative in BKSL without using either of the language's two content words/signs: WH1 or WH2. As the first two frame

Elicited Question: 'What's in the box?'

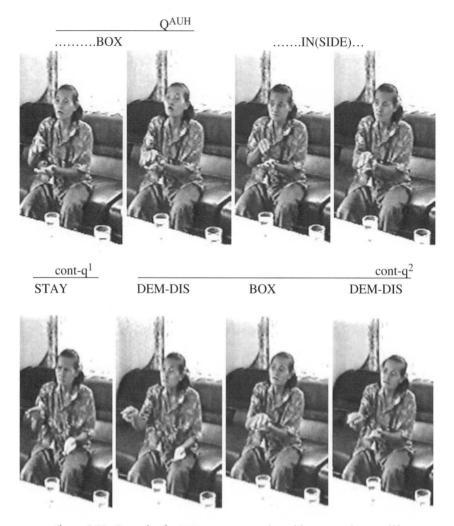

Figure 6.17. Example of a BKSL content question without question word(s)

grabs in figure 6.17 illustrate, this is achieved in large part through use of the Q^{AUH} question particle.

CONCLUSION

Documentation and description of spoken languages has been an ongoing effort for centuries. Similar work on sign languages, however, began just a few decades ago, and to date, most research has focused on a particular kind of sign language, national or urban ones, with scant attention paid to other sign language varieties. There is a pressing need to describe un(der)documented and endangered indigenous village sign languages so that we will better understand the range of variation in signed and spoken languages. This realization is now manifesting itself in concerted efforts to develop a typology of sign languages. Toward that end, this chapter has proffered a first-pass description and an analysis of interrogatives in Ban Khor Sign Language, a previously undescribed indigenous village sign language in Thailand.

Three interrogative formations are examined in the course of this chapter, beginning with yes-no/polar questions. In BKSL such questions are marked entirely nonmanually, a pattern that "occurs with great regularity in most signed languages in a very similar way" and a phenomenon akin to "the widespread use of rising intonation to mark polar questions in many spoken languages" (Zeshan 2004b, 36).

By contrast, there is significant cross-linguistic variation in sign languages with regard to wh-question formation, for "paradigms of question words can be radically different, ranging from a single general question word to large paradigms" (Zeshan 2004b, 36). With its two content words/signs, BKSL's wh-system is near the minimalist end of that continuum and is quite unlike the wh-paradigms of any other languages in close areal or interactional proximity (i.e., Thai, Nyoh, or Thai Sign Language).

Language contact is clearly implicated, however, in the case of Q^{AUH}, a question particle that can follow either yes-no or wh-questions and can wordlessly mark content questions in Ban Khor Sign Language. As described earlier, Q^{AUH} consists of two parts: a nonmanual sign articulated with the head, which is accompanied by the mouthing of *auh*. Both the sign and the mouthing derive from a gesture (an upward, backward head nod) and a spoken Nyoh word *(auh)*, both of which are widely used by hearing people in Ban Khor. The head gesture and the mouthing appear to have been borrowed into BKSL but then regrammaticized—transformed into the question particle Q^{AUH}.

Similarities (e.g., the borrowed components of the question particle Q^{AUH}) and dissimilarities (e.g., the wh-systems) between BKSL and other local languages raise an interesting issue: the impact of language contact on language structure. Zeshan has noted that "because of the sociolinguistic situation of urban sign languages as minority languages coexisting with spoken majority languages, signed-language structure is prone to interacting with and being influenced by spoken-language structure" (Zeshan 2004b, 3). Case study analysis of Ban Khor Sign Language represents an important step in a better understanding of the extent to which indigenous village sign languages are influenced by other languages in their local communities' code repertoires.

APPENDIX

This project is part of a much larger ethnographic study of Ban Khor and Ban Khor Sign Language. A decade of research has generated a robust and diverse corpus of linguistic anthropological data, including well more than one hundred hours of video recorded data, ranging from formal interviews to casual conversation. The observations and analyses presented in this chapter derive from a particular data set: a videotaped demonstration of formally elicited examples of interrogatives in BKSL.

Data were collected over the course of two fieldwork visits: a two-month trip in winter 2002 and a one-year stay in 2003. During the first visit, I used a brief, eighteen-item elicitation protocol that was administered to thirteen native BKSL signers (i.e., those who had been exposed to BKSL from birth). The same consultants and an additional five individuals were interviewed again in 2003 using an expanded elicitation protocol consisting of around fifty questions.

Both elicitation protocols were originally developed in English, translated into written Thai, and then read and audiotaped in both Thai and Nyoh. Hearing consultants listened to the audiotaped elicitations and then demonstrated the example questions in BKSL. Elicitation sessions with deaf consultants were organized differently. Because they were unable to read written Thai, the deaf consultants were paired with a hearing signer, in each case a preferred hearing family member (e.g., a sibling, cousin, child) who [had] lived in the same home with the deaf person.

In a few cases individual deaf consultants quickly caught on to the elicitation task (something quite alien to most Ban Khorians regardless of their hearing status) and, working with their hearing translators, began demonstrating the target questions in BKSL. Some deaf consultants experienced difficulty with the strict elicitation procedure. In those cases, the hearing relative typically set up a scenario and then prompted the deaf person to ask the target question. For example, a deaf consultant was successfully prompted to ask the target question "Why did the doctor go to Sakhon Nakhon?" by her hearing/signing cousin, who set up the following scenario:

> You go to the doctor's house (where there is an after-hours clinic) to buy medicine, but he's not there. So you go to the shop next door and talk to Mrs. Wan. You have a stomachache and really need to buy medicine. You talk to Wan and say . . . Then the deaf consultant would ask questions such as "Where did the doctor go?" "Why did the doctor go?" and "When will the doctor come back?"

Data were collected twice out of an abundance of caution because, frankly, I was skeptical of my own initial findings. The wh-system of BKSL was so unlike that of any sign language with which I was familiar at the time (e.g., American Sign Language, Thai Sign Language, or

Japanese Sign Language) that I assumed that my findings in 2002 were fatally flawed. Upon the advice of my dissertation committee, especially Dr. Pamela Munro, a field linguist, I was encouraged to redo the elicitations again in 2003 using the expanded elicitation protocol, which I did, only to get the same basic results: a two-question-word paradigm—results that are now unsurprising in light of the range of possible wh-systems that other researchers have documented.

After data collection was concluded, the individual signers' responses were transcribed, glossed, and compared for the purpose of data analysis. Second-phase data analysis was conducted during the summer of 2008, at which time I sat side by side with two native BKSL signing research assistants, and together we analyzed the data. This two-stage analytical process revealed the basic organization of interrogatives in BKSL, such as the size of the content question word paradigm, the syntactic position of question words, and the absence of manual marking to produce yes/no questions. That process demonstrated that question formation in BKSL is quite different from the question systems of other languages in the immediate surrounding environment (e.g., Thai, Nyoh, or even Thai Sign Language).

Notes

I wish to acknowledge the following organizations and individuals for their assistance in this project. Funding was generously provided by the National Science Foundation, the Wenner-Gren Foundation, IIE Fulbright, the Endangered Language Fund, the Explorers Club, the University of Texas Graduate Division, the UCLA Department of Anthropology, the UCLA Office of International Studies and Overseas Programs, and the UCLA Wagatsuma Memorial Fund. In addition, I extend my heartfelt gratitude to the people of Ban Khor for their hospitality. I am particularly indebted to my linguistic consultants, the deaf villagers and their families, for giving so generously of their time, energy, and expertise. The project would not have come to fruition without the hard work and invaluable help of individuals like Nipha Sukhwan, Vien Champa, Rungnapa Sornchai, Chettah Madminggao, Nutjaree Madminggao, and Amporn Jirattikorn, all of whom assisted with translation and interpretation. Generous moral support was provided by Lynn Hou, Emiliana Cruz, Tony Woodbury, Sara Stavchansky, Chiho Sunakawa, Scott Richardson, and Elena Liskova. My sincere thanks go to Pam Munro, who provided encouragement and guidance in the early phases of the fieldwork. Later in the project I also benefited tremendously from Gaurav Mathur's and Ulrike Zeshan's intellectual feedback, and any remaining analytical shortcomings are entirely my responsibility. Last but by no means least, there is Donna Jo Napoli, a gentle academic shepherd, whom I thank for her energy, enthusiasm, and dedication. She organized the stimulating conference that gave rise to this volume. For allowing us to reprint the material in figure 6.14, from *The Thai Sign Language dictionary*, rev. and exp. ed., ed. Suwanarat et al. and published by the National Association of the Deaf in Thailand, we thank Owen P. Wrigley. And for help in so many ways in procuring that permission, we thank Chip Reilly.

1. Compare WH1 and WH2 in BKSL, as shown here in figures 6.2 and 6.3, respectively, with the two HKSL signs depicted in figures 6.4 and 6.5 in Tang's article, which appears in Zeshan (2006, 210, 211).

2. According to Nonaka (2007, 62–63):

> The Ban Khorian claim that their sign language originated locally was strengthened during a research expedition to Ban Kok Muang, the village from which the Sukhwans originally emigrated around the start of the 20th century. Review of local records and interviews with village leaders and senior citizens in that community revealed no instances of "hereditary" deafness among the Sukhwan or any other surname kin group in Ban Kok Muang. Additionally, there was no evidence of any indigenous sign language (currently or formerly) used in or associated with that village. These findings from Ban Kok Muang are significant: demonstrating the unlikelihood that the Sukhwans brought either the genetic mutation for deafness or the sign language with them and thereby bolstering the case that "hereditary" deafness, and subsequently the sign language, emerged spontaneously in Ban Khor.

3. Ban Khor is highly multilingual. Other languages that are sometimes spoken in the community include Thai, Lao, Soe, and Phuthai. None of these languages is closely related to HKSL, Cantonese, or Mandarin, and, ethnically, Ban Khorians are neither Han Chinese nor members of any Chinese minority population local to the Hong Kong area.

4. The list of wh-words in Nyoh derives from original field research.

Bibliography

Antzakas, Klimis. 2006. The Use of Negative Head Movements in Greek Sign Language. In *Interrogative and Negative Constructions in Sign Languages,* ed. Ulrike Zeshan, 258–269. Nijmegen: Ishara.

Bahan, Ben, and Joan Poole Nash. 1996. The Formation of Signing Communities. In *Deaf Studies IV: Visions of the Past, Visions for the Future.* Conference proceedings, April 27–30, 1995, 1–16. Washington, D.C.: Gallaudet University College of Continuing Education.

Baker, Charlotte, and Carol A. Padden. 1978. Focusing on Nonmanual Components of American Sign Language. In *Understanding Language through Sign Language Research,* ed. Patricia Siple, 27–55. New York: Academic Press.

Baker-Shenk, Charlotte, and Dennis Cokely. 1980. *American Sign Language: A Teacher's Resource Text on Grammar and Culture.* Silver Spring, Md.: T.J. Publishers.

Bergman, Brita. 1984. Non-manual Components of Signed Language: Some Sentence Types in Swedish Sign Language. In *Recent Research on European Sign Languages: Proceedings of the European Meeting of Sign Language Research,* ed. Filip Loncke, Penny Boyes-Braem, and Ivan Lebrun, 49–59. Lisse: Swets and Zeitlinger.

Branson, Jan, and Don Miller. 1996. Everyone Here Speaks Sign Language, Too: A Deaf Village in Bali, Indonesia: An Initial Report. In *Multicultural Aspects of Sociolinguistics in Deaf Communities,* ed. Ceil Lucas, 39–57. Washington, D.C.: Gallaudet University Press.

Bruyn, Adrienne. 1993. Question Words in 18th-century and 20th-century Srana. In *Historical Linguistics 1991: Papers from the 10th International Conference on Historical Linguistics*, ed. Jaap van Marle, 31–47. Amsterdam: Benjamins.

Celo, Pietro. 1996. Pragmatic Aspects of the Interrogative Form in Italian Sign Language. In *Multicultural Aspects of Sociolinguistics in Deaf Communities*, ed. Ceil Lucas, 132–151. Washington, D.C.: Gallaudet University Press.

Coerts, Jane. 1992. Nonmanual Grammatical Markers: An Analysis of Interrogatives, Negations, and Topicalisations in Sign Language of the Netherlands. PhD diss., University of Amsterdam.

Cumberbatch, Keren. 2006. Country Sign, St. Elizabeth, Jamaica. Presented at the Workshop on Sign Languages in Village Communities. Max Planck Institute for Psycholinguistics, Nijmegen, the Netherlands, April 4–6.

Cysouw, Michael. 2007. Content Interrogatives in Asheninca Campa: Corpus Study and Typological Comparison. *International Journal of American Linguistics* 73(2): 133–163.

Engberg-Pedersen, Elisabeth. 1990. Pragmatics of Nonmanual Behaviour in Danish Sign Language. In *International Studies on Sign Language and Communication of the Deaf*, vol. 10, ed. William H. Edmondson and Fred Karlsson, 121–128. Hamburg: Signum.

Ferreiro-Brito, Lucinda. 1983. A Comparative Study of Signs for Time and Space in Sao Paolo and Urubu-Kaapor Sign Language. In *SLR 83: Proceedings of the 3rd International Symposium on Sign Language Research*, Rome, June 22–26, ed. William Stokoe and Virginia Volterra, 22–26. Silver Spring, Md.: Linstok.

Fischer, Susan D. 2006. Questions and Negation in American Sign Language. In *Interrogative and Negative Constructions in Sign Languages*, ed. Ulrike Zeshan, 165–197. Nijmegen: Ishara.

Frishberg, Nancy. 1987. Ghanaian Sign Language. In *Gallaudet Encyclopedia of Deaf People and Deafness*, ed. John V. Van Cleve, 778–779. New York: McGraw-Hill.

Givón, Talmy. 2001. *Syntax: An Introduction*, rev. ed. Philadelphia: Benjamins.

Groce, Nora Ellen. 1985. *Everyone Here Spoke Sign Language: Hereditary Deafness in Martha's Vineyard*. Cambridge, Mass.: Harvard University Press.

Heine, Bernd, Ulrike Claudi, and Friederike Hünnemeyer. 1991. *Grammaticalization: A Conceptual Framework*. Chicago: University of Chicago Press.

Humphries, Tom, Carol Padden, and Terrence J. O'Rourke. 1985. *A Basic Course in American Sign Language*. Silver Spring, Md.: T.J. Publishers.

Iwasaki, Shoichi, and Preeya Ingkaphirom. 2005. *A Reference Grammar of Thai*. New York: Cambridge University Press.

Johnson, Robert E. 1991. Sign Language, Culture, and Community in a Yucatec Mayan Village. *Sign Language Studies* 73: 461–474.

———. 1994. Sign Language and the Concept of Deafness in a Traditional Yucatec Mayan Village. In *The Deaf Way: Perspectives from the International Conference on Deaf Culture*, ed. Carol J. Erting, Robert C. Johnson, Dorothy L. Smith, and Bruce D. Snider, 103–109. Washington, D.C.: Gallaudet University Press.

Juntanamalaga, Preecha, and Tony Diller. 1999. *Beginning Thai*. Canberra: Southeast Asia Centre, Faculty of Asian Studies at the Australian National University.

Kakumasu, Jim. 1968. Urubu Sign Language. *International Journal of American Linguistics* 34: 275–281.

Kisch, Shifra. 2004. Negotiating (Genetic) Deafness in a Bedouin Community. In *Genetics, Disability, and Deafness*, ed. John V. Van Cleve, 148–173. Washington, D.C.: Gallaudet University Press.

———. 2006. The Social Context of Sign among the Al-Sayyid. Presentation at the workshop on Sign Languages in Village Communities. Max Planck Institute for Psycholinguistics, Nijmegen, the Netherlands, April 4–6.

Kuschel, Rolf. 1973. The Silent Inventor: The Creation of a Sign Language by the Only Deaf-mute on a Polynesian Island. *Sign Language Studies* 2(3): 1–28.

Marsaja, I Gede. 2006. Kata Kolok: A Village-based Sign Language in North Bali, Indonesia. Presented at the workshop on Sign Languages in Village Communities. Max Planck Institute for Psycholinguistics, Nijmegen, the Netherlands, April 4–6.

———. 2008. *Desa Kolok: A Deaf Village and Its Sign Language in Bali, Indonesia*. Nijmegen: Ishara.

McKee, Rachel. 2006. Aspects of Interrogatives and Negation in New Zealand Sign Language. In *Interrogative and Negative Constructions in Sign Languages*, ed. Ulrike Zeshan, 70–90. Nijmegen: Ishara.

Meier, Richard. 2000. Diminishing Diversity of Signed Languages (letter to the editor). *Science* 288 (June 16): 1965.

Meir, Irit. 2004. Question and Negation in Israeli Sign Language. *Sign Language and Linguistics* 7(2): 97–124.

Morgan, Michael W. 2006. Interrogatives and Negatives in Japanese Sign Language. In *Interrogative and Negative Constructions in Sign Languages*, ed. Ulrike Zeshan, 91–127. Nijmegen: Ishara.

Muysken, Pieter, and Norval Smith. 1990. Question Words in Pidgin and Creole Languages. *Linguistics* 28: 889–903.

Neidle, Carol. 2003. Language across Modalities: ASL Focus and Question Constructions. *Linguistic Variation Yearbook* 2: 71–98.

———, Judy Kegl, Dawn MacLaughlin, Benjamin Bahan, and Robert G. Lee. 2000. *The Syntax of American Sign Language: Functional Categories and Hierarchical Structure*. Cambridge, Mass.: MIT Press.

Nonaka, Angela M. 2004. The Forgotten Endangered Languages: Lessons on the Importance of Remembering from Thailand's Ban Khor Sign Language. *Language in Society* 33: 737–767.

———. 2007. Emergence of an Indigenous Sign Language and a Speech/sign Community in Ban Khor, Thailand. PhD diss., University of California at Los Angeles.

———. 2009. Estimating Size, Scope, and Membership of the Speech/sign Communities of Undocumented Indigenous/village Sign Languages: The Ban Khor Case Study. *Language and Communication* 29: 210–228. DOI 10.1016/j.langcom.2009.02.004.

Nyst, Victoria. 2006. The Sign Language of Adamarobe (Ghana). Presentation at the Workshop on Sign Languages in Village Communities. Max Planck Institute for Psycholinguistics, Nijmegen, the Netherlands, April 4–6.

Quadros, Ronice Müller de. 2006. Questions in Brazilian Sign Language (LSB). In *Interrogative and Negative Constructions in Sign Languages*, ed. Ulrike Zeshan, 270–283. Nijmegen: Ishara.

Sandler, Wendy. 1999. The Medium and the Message: Prosodic Interpretation of Linguistic Content in Israeli Sign Language. *Sign Language and Linguistics* 2(2): 187–215.

———, Irit Meir, Carol Padden, and Mark Aronoff. 2005. The Emergence of Grammar: Systematic Structure in a New Language. *Proceedings of the National Academy of Sciences* 102(7): 2661–2665.

Savolainen, Leena. 2006. Interrogatives and Negatives in Finnish Sign Language: An Overview. In *Interrogative and Negative Constructions in Sign Languages,* ed. Ulrike Zeshan, 284–302. Nijmegen: Ishara.

Schalber, Katharina. 2006. What Is the Chin Doing? An Analysis of Interrogatives in Austrian Sign Language. *Sign Language and Linguistics* 9(1–2): 133–150.

Shuman, Malcolm K. 1980. The Sound of Silence: A Preliminary Account of Sign Language Use by the Deaf in a Maya Community in Yucatan, Mexico. *Language Sciences* 2(1): 144–173.

Subtle Impact Software, Inc. 1995. Subtle Messages: American Sign Language Lessons in Non-manual Grammatical Markers. Colorado Springs: Subtle Impact Software, Inc.

Suwanarat, Manfa, Anucha Ratanasint, Vilaiporn Rungsrithong, Lloyd Anderson, and Owen P. Wrigley, eds. 1990. *The Thai Sign Language Dictionary,* rev. and exp. ed. Bangkok: National Association of the Deaf in Thailand.

Tang, Gladys. 2006. Questions and Negation in Hong Kong Sign Language. In *Interrogative and Negative Constructions in Sign Languages,* ed. Ulrike Zeshan, 198–224. Nijmegen: Ishara.

Torigoe, Takashi, and Harumi Kimura. 1995. Deaf Life on Isolated Japanese Islands. *Sign Language Studies* 24: 167–174.

Van den Bogaerde, Beppie. 2006. Kajana Sign Language, Surinam. Presented at the Workshop on Sign Languages in Village Communities. Max Planck Institute for Psycholinguistics, Nijmegen, the Netherlands, April 4–6.

Van Herreweghe, Mieke, and Myriam Vermeerbergen. 2006. Interrogatives and Negatives in Flemish Sign Language. In *Interrogative and Negative Constructions in Sign Languages,* ed. Ulrike Zeshan, 225–256. Nijmegen: Ishara.

Washabaugh, William. 1978. Providence Island Sign Language: A Context-dependent Language. *Anthropological Linguistics* 20(3): 95–109.

———. 1979. The Deaf of Grand Cayman, British West Indies. *Sign Language Studies* 31: 117–133.

———. 1981. Hearing and Deaf Signers on Providence Island. *Sign Language Studies* 24: 191–214.

———. 1986. *Five Fingers for Survival: Sign Language in the Caribbean.* Ann Arbor: Karoma.

Wilbur, Ronnie. 2000. Phonological and Prosodic Layering of Nonmanuals in American Sign Language. In *The Signs of Language Revisited,* ed. Karen Emmorey and Harlan Lane, 215–244. Mahwah, N.J.: Erlbaum.

Woodward, James C. 1982. Beliefs about and Attitudes towards Deaf People and Sign Language on Providence Island. In *How You Gonna Get to Heaven If You Can't Talk with Jesus: On Depathologizing Deafness,* ed. James C. Woodward, 51–74. Silver Spring, Md.: T.J. Publishers.

———. 2000. Sign Languages and Sign Language Families in Thailand and Vietnam. In *The Signs of Language Revisited,* ed. Karen Emmorey and Harlan Lane, 23–47. Mahwah, N.J.: Erlbaum.

Zeshan, Ulrike. 2004a. Hand, Head, and Face: Negative Constructions in Sign Languages. *Linguistic Typology* 8(1): 1–58.

———. 2004b. Interrogative Constructions in Signed Languages: Cross-linguistic Perspectives. *Language* 80(1): 7–39.

———, ed. 2006a. *Interrogative and Negative Constructions in Sign Languages.* Nijmegen: Ishara.

———. 2006b. Negative and Interrogative Structures in Turkish Sign Language (TID). In *Interrogative and Negative Constructions in Sign Languages,* ed. Ulrike Zeshan, 128–164. Nijmegen: Ishara.

Village Sign Languages

A Commentary

Ulrike Zeshan

THE IMPORTANCE OF VILLAGE SIGN LANGUAGES
FOR SIGN LANGUAGE TYPOLOGY

The beginning of the twenty-first century is a very exciting time for sign language linguistics. With a thirty-year delay in comparison with spoken language typology, we are finally beginning to see the full extent of diversity in the world's sign languages. As Angela Nonaka points out in her chapter, the newly created subdiscipline of sign language typology is at the forefront of this development.

In spoken language linguistics, the discovery and documentation of so-called exotic languages has been essential to the development of linguistic typology since the 1970s. Before then, who would have thought that a language could get by without a set of words for even the most basic numbers? Yet in the South American language Pirahã, the only way of counting involves a minimal paradigm consisting of three terms for "small quantity," "somewhat larger quantity," and "many" (Everett 2005), and similarly minimal "one-two-many" number systems have been found in other languages. Conversely, no linguist with professional training in Indo-European languages could have imagined the complexity of kinship terms found in many Australian aboriginal languages (e.g., Evans [2000] on Ilgar and Iwaidja). In these languages, the equivalents of *father, daughter,* and so on are expressed as verbs, with unusual semantic distinctions. For instance, one and the same word may designate a different kinship relation depending on whether the speaker is male or female (Evans 2000).

A similar argument about the value of data from less studied languages can now be made for sign languages, and never before have we been able to discover a similarly broad range of information about diverse sign languages in such a short span of time. For instance, it has long been assumed either implicitly or explicitly that all sign languages have complex spatial constructions with entity classifier handshapes (cf. contributions in Emmorey [2003]), where referents such as humans, vehicles, and animals are mapped onto particular handshapes, which are then moved around in signing space to create iconically motivated spatial arrays. The discovery of a village sign language in Ghana, Adamorobe Sign Language, has challenged this assumption. Not only does Adamorobe Sign Language lack entity classifier handshapes, but the entire system of spatial projection onto a horizontal plane in front of the signer simply does not exist in this language (Nyst [2007]).

In other words, recent research has already demonstrated that if we are interested in linguistic diversity in sign languages, village sign languages deserve our special attention as they are, in many respects, more different from the better-known sign languages of Europe and North America than anything else we have seen. Part of the appeal of village sign languages for sign language typology is simply that they considerably broaden our understanding of the possible range of structural diversity in sign languages. Just as any claim to linguistic universals must now pass the test of applying to sign languages, any claim to sign language universals must now pass the test of applying to village sign languages, and it is worth pointing out how recent this development has been. Although we have known for more than thirty years that sign languages exist in rural communities with hereditary deafness (cf. the references at the beginning of Nonaka's chapter), the detailed linguistic documentation of their structural properties has gained momentum only in the past few years. It is crucial that we encourage the comprehensive description of other village sign languages in the near future.

Village sign languages are also of special interest to the comparative study of sign languages for a different reason, namely their sociolinguistic setting. A signing community where the vast majority of everyday sign language users are hearing second-language users and monolingual deaf signers are in the minority and where the communication barrier between deaf and hearing people so typically experienced in urban deaf communities does not exist raises a whole range of new linguistic issues. One of these is the nature of language contact between the sign language and the spoken language in the village, as exemplified by the use of the question article Q^{AUH} in Nonaka's chapter. The diversity of such language contact situations and their differential impact on the linguistic structures of village sign languages is explored later in the section titled "Outcomes of Language Contact in Village Sign Languages." Another important issue is the stability of these sign languages, all of which are dependent on the continued presence of deaf individuals in the community. This is a precarious situation for a language to be in, and consequently, many village sign languages are in danger of dying out. In this particular case, language endangerment overlaps with much deeper philosophical questions about the nature of human language, as discussed further in the section titled "Deaf Villages and the Viability of Language Communities."

INTERROGATIVES IN SIGNED AND SPOKEN LANGUAGES

One of the most interesting aspects of Nonaka's chapter is the comparison between interrogative structures in Ban Khor Sign Language and those in other signed and spoken languages. What we find in Ban Khor Sign Language is well within the typological parameters of interrogatives in other sign languages. The only somewhat unusual feature is the question particle that has arisen as a result of contact with the local spoken language (see the next section). Rather than adding my own take on cross-linguistic comparison of sign language interrogatives along the lines of Zeshan (2004a and 2006) and discussing how the Ban Khor data fit into the overall picture, I would like to make some more general points.

First of all, we repeatedly see that identical or very similar forms can arise independently in sign languages that are in no way genetically or geographically related. For instance, a round, closed handshape (F or O handshape) combined with a variety of movement patterns (see figure 6R.1) is very common in negative particles in many sign languages (Zeshan 2004b).

The iconic basis for these forms is probably the number zero in most cases, though there are other possibilities in some instances. Similarly, an open hand with wiggling fingers, as in the Ban Khor Sign Language quantifying interrogative, is cross-linguistically very common, and finding the same sign with the same meaning in another sign language therefore means nothing in terms of the relatedness of these two languages. Again, the iconic basis of this sign, derived from counting on one's fingers, is obvious.

The iconic motivation of the other Ban Khor interrogative, the wagging upright index finger, is less obvious, but identical signs clearly exist as various question words in a number of unrelated sign languages (Zeshan 2004a). It is important to place commonalities between two sign languages in this overall context because otherwise we would start to see relationships between sign

Figure 6R.1. Signs for "none" from Turkey (with F-handshape) and from Uganda (with O-handshape). From Dikyuva and Zeshan (2008) and Lutalo-Kiingi (2008).

languages for which there is no real evidence. At the moment, we are very far from any principled approach to identifying genetic relationships between sign languages, and going into the details of theoretical and methodological problems in this area would be far beyond the scope of this chapter (for alternative views, see Padden in this volume and Woodward's response to Padden). At the very least, any lexical comparisons between sign languages that aim at identifying possible relationships between them must be careful to discount factors such as shared iconicity.[1] A large sample of cross-linguistic data that gives us an initial sense of what is and what is not common among sign languages is an essential tool in this process.

Another interesting point that is highlighted by the Ban Khor Sign Language data relates to the difference between question words that target entities (e.g., "who," "what," "where") and question words that target quantities (e.g., "how much, how many"). This distinction is exemplified particularly clearly in the two-term question word paradigm in Ban Khor Sign Language but is reflected, as well, in the structure of question word paradigms in many other sign languages, such as in the Hong Kong Sign Language examples mentioned in Nonaka's chapter. Interrogatives of quantification may form subparadigms that can be quite complex, involving spatial modification, shifting places of articulation, and the addition of a second hand. More than any other question word, interrogatives of quantification frequently have alternative noninterrogative meanings, either "many" or "number" (Zeshan 2004b), and they often form conventionalized phrases such as AGE HOW-MANY for "how old?"

However, it is not yet sufficiently clear whether the distinction between entity interrogatives and quantity interrogatives indeed has a privileged status in a substantial number of sign languages and, if so, how this would compare to data from spoken languages. In particular, it would be interesting to investigate whether the distinction between "entity" and "quantity" is important in other areas of the grammar of sign languages, just as the distinction between animate and inanimate or human and nonhuman is of crucial importance in the grammars of many languages.

OUTCOMES OF LANGUAGE CONTACT IN VILLAGE SIGN LANGUAGES

Among the range of languages that the Ban Khor data can be compared with, comparison with the main spoken language used in the same village is of particular significance. Given a sociolinguistic situation in which a sign language is created jointly by deaf and hearing people in a community, it would be easy to imagine that the spoken language used in such a deaf village should have a deep impact on the structure of the village sign language. After all, for most of the sign language users the sign language is a secondary means of communication, and, therefore, their signed utterances may well be subject to interference from their spoken language, which again would eventually be reflected in the sign language as produced by all of its users in the village, including the deaf monolingual signers. However, the reality both in Ban Khor Sign Language and other village sign languages is rather different as the influence of spoken language structures on various sign languages in rural communities is far from uniform.

Two illustrative examples from recent literature come from just such deaf villages in Bali and in Ghana. Kata Kolok (literally "deaf language" in Balinese) is used in a village in northern Bali with a group of about fifty deaf people of all ages within a total population of about twenty-five hundred, and deafness has been present in the village for generations (Marsaja 2008). Adamorobe Sign Language in Ghana, which has already been mentioned, has a similar time depth, though the number of deaf people is lower. Both of these villages have a sociolinguistic situation that is very similar to that of Ban Khor in Thailand. However, the way in which the local spoken languages have affected the linguistic structure of the sign languages is very different in both cases.

In Adamorobe Sign Language, there are many reflections of the local spoken language, Twi. Examples cited in Nyst (2007) include both the syntax (e.g., the use of serial verb constructions) and the lexicon (e.g., color terms). One of the interesting features is the use of mouth movements in the sign language that correspond to words of spoken Twi (such mouth movements are called "mouthings"; cf. Boyes-Braem and Sutton-Spence [2001]). All color terms in Adamorobe Sign Language have the same manual component with an upright, pointing index finger, a sign that could loosely be glossed as "quality." In order to differentiate between colors, signers use mouthings that correspond to color words in spoken Twi (Nyst 2007). The use of mouthings is also important in other parts of the grammar and carries a considerable functional load.

The Ban Khor interrogatives that use the question particle Q^{AUH} similarly provide evidence of the interaction between signed and spoken communication and have additional levels of complexity, as Nonaka points out. For instance, the question particle Q^{AUH} can occur with or without a manual question word; it involves a facial expression in addition to mouthing; and its syntactic distribution in polar and content questions is different from the source word in spoken Nyoh.

By comparison with these cases in Adamorobe and Ban Khor, no such influences from spoken language have been identified in Kata Kolok. The dominant spoken language in this multilingual village is the conversational variety of spoken Balinese, called Basa Biasa. Kata Kolok signers use virtually no mouthings from spoken Balinese, and the few instances that occur very occasionally, such as with the sign RICE, are in no way functionally important (Connie de Vos, personal communication, March 2009). No overlaps between the grammatical structures of Kata Kolok and spoken Balinese have been found, though we do see the influence of conventional gestures used in Bali on Kata Kolok (Marsaja 2008).

At the current stage of research, it is very important not to make premature generalizations about village sign languages. Though a generalization such as "village sign languages tend to exhibit substantial influence from the surrounding spoken language(s)" may seem logical a priori because of the sociolinguistic setting, this hypothesis is immediately defeated by data from just two village sign languages, Adamorobe Sign Language and Kata Kolok. There is no doubt that, as this line of research progresses, we will discover many more surprising facts that run counter to our acquired knowledge. In the case of village sign languages, it is particularly important that linguistic and anthropological research be brought together, and Nonaka's chapter instantiates this cross-fertilization of theoretical approaches well. It is equally important that we analyze data from individual village sign languages on their own terms first and then begin cautiously approaching inductive generalizations from these data. The current research environment in linguistics and linguistic anthropology, with our recent renewed interest in language documentation, fieldwork, and engagement with language communities, provides a good basis for this approach.

DEAF VILLAGES AND THE VIABILITY OF LANGUAGE COMMUNITIES

Most sign languages in village communities are endangered, and this adds to the urgency of documenting them. However, the situation of village sign languages is unlike that of any other group of endangered languages and raises fundamental questions about the nature of human language.

Village sign languages are endangered for two reasons. First, because they are small local languages without any official status or associated institutions, they typically come under threat immediately upon making contact with larger urban or national sign languages. For example, deaf children from a deaf village of the sort I have been discussing here might be sent to a school outside the village, where a different sign language is used. This has happened in Adamorobe village in Ghana, where the younger deaf signers now exclusively use Ghanaian Sign Language with each other (Nyst 2007). Pressure on a village sign language may also come from urban deaf communities who, well meaning but uninformed, may want to introduce the deaf villagers to what they consider to be a proper sign language. Sometimes a school for deaf children may even be set up in the village, again promoting use of the national sign language. This has happened in St. Elizabeth in Jamaica, where the original village-based Country Sign is on the verge of extinction because of the influence of Jamaican Sign Language (Zeshan 2007).

All these pressures on small minority languages are of course well known and are in no way unique to sign languages or deaf villages. However, there is another, more intriguing way in which village sign languages are endangered regardless of either external pressures or the nature of the language contact situation. In all of these village communities, the continued use of the sign language is dependent on the continued presence of deaf people in the village. This seems obvious enough, but it has profound implications for the long-term viability of these sign language communities. If and when, for any reason, deaf children are no longer born into the community, the sign language will automatically die out with the last generation of deaf people. As deafness in these village communities is usually hereditary, a change in marriage patterns can be enough to disrupt the occurrence of deafness either temporarily or for good.

Theoretically, it would of course be possible for the village community to keep using sign language even when deaf people no longer live there. The case of Australian aboriginal communities such as the Warlpiri, who use an alternate sign language under conditions of speech taboo (Kendon 1988), proves that use of a sign language is not necessarily associated with deafness. However, in the absence of other cultural factors such as speech taboos, the continued use of a sign language in a community without deaf individuals is highly unlikely. After all, all human communities have chosen to use speech rather than signing as the main mode of communication, although it would theoretically be possible for a community of hearing people to use sign language as the default option (for further discussion see the chapter by Napoli and Sutton-Spence and the response by Kendon in this volume). This, however, never happens, and the sign languages in village communities are therefore potentially endangered right from the beginning, which is an extraordinary position for a language to be in.[2] As Nonaka (2004) points out, they may arise suddenly, flourish briefly, and disappear again without a trace.

It is this fragile situation, dependent entirely on the presence of deaf individuals in sufficient number over a sufficiently long period of time, which makes village sign languages such an interesting case. For we are immediately faced with a number of deeply philosophical questions: How many individuals are actually enough for a language community to be viable? How much time depth is adequate for a language to establish itself? Which characteristics of an incipient language community have a positive or a negative impact on its viability?

A full discussion of how many individuals and how much time a language needs would be far beyond the scope of this chapter (for discussion, see the chapters in this volume by Wood and by Senghas and Coppola, as well as the response to Senghas and Coppola by Pfau). Therefore, I focus here on a single factor only in order to exemplify the kind of reasoning we may engage

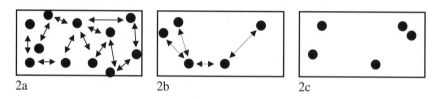

Figure 6R.2. Distribution patterns of deaf individuals in rural areas

in. Ignoring issues of time depth, I look at the geographical distribution of an incipient language community in this section.

Figure 6R.2 exemplifies three different situations with respect to the distribution of deaf individuals that we may find in a rural area. Each dot represents a deaf individual, and each arrow represents contact between individuals; for the sake of argument, the issue of time depth is largely ignored.

The diagram on the left (figure 6R.2a) shows the situation in a typical deaf village such as Ban Khor, Desa Kolok, or Adamorobe. A substantial number of deaf people are in constant contact with each other, as well as with hearing people in the village, who are not represented in the diagram. As this is a stable linguistic community, the outcome is, unambiguously, a fully functional sign language. By contrast, the diagram on the right (figure 6R.2c) shows deaf individuals who are isolated from each other. These individuals interact only with the hearing people in their environment, such as their hearing family members. Typically, they use what is known as homesign, essentially an ad hoc communication system with a low level of conventionalization. Though homesign can be a powerful communicative tool and a number of its features overlap with established sign languages, the consensus is that the linguistic status of homesign differs from that of sign languages.

The situation of special interest to us here is the intermediate situation in figure 6R.2b, which shows a number of deaf individuals who are in sporadic, unsystematic contact with each other. The size of this group of people and the frequency of their interaction is intermediate between the sign language and the homesign situation. For example, they may live in separate villages that can be reached within a day or two and might meet every couple of months during major festivals, on market days, and the like. Alternatively, they might live in the same village or vicinity but for social reasons or lack of time depth might not have had frequent and sustained contact. We could preliminarily label the signed communication that occurs in such situations "communal homesign." This communal homesign setting also seems to be the situation that initially occurs when deaf students are brought together in a newly established boarding school, such as has been described for the emergence of Nicaraguan Sign Language (Senghas 1995). I believe that, far from being something extraordinary, situations with communal homesign are actually a common occurrence, as is the emergence of new sign languages from such incipient deaf communities.

Although the social situation in figure 6R.2b is clearly intermediate between the other two, just how far the linguistic properties of communal homesign may or may not be intermediate in some way is not at all apparent. A systematic, comparative study of more than one community in diverse settings, investigating both the linguistic properties of communal homesign and the sociocultural properties of such communities, would therefore be highly instructive. In particular, where such intermediate situations occur naturally in rural areas, as opposed to engineered situations such as a newly established deaf boarding school, there may be much to learn about the human capacity for language. For example, if there is a critical period for a language to develop in individual children, is there also one for a language to develop on a communal level? If we think about grammar as continually evolving (in the sense of Hopper [1998]), where we are always moving but never arrive, could we also think of language as being emergent not only in the distant human past but also here and now? None of these questions can be answered here, but it is certain that natural laboratories, such as in Ban Khor and other rural areas with various types of signed communication, will help answer some deep philosophical questions about human language.

Notes

Figure 6R.1 is reprinted from Dikyuva and Zeshan (2008) and Lutalo-Kiingi (2008). Thanks go to Ishara Press for this permission.

1. Guerra Currie, Meier, and Walters (2002) identify a base level of lexical similarity between sign languages of around 30 percent, irrespective of whether the languages are related or not. See also the discussion of sign language varieties in the Arab world in Hendriks and Zeshan (2009).

2. One might argue that many pidgins are in a similar situation in that they are, so to speak, designed not to last beyond the first generation of users. However, in the prototypical case pidgins evolve into more stable creoles, and evolving organically into something else is clearly different from disappearing altogether.

Bibliography

Boyes-Braem, Penny, and Rachel Sutton-Spence, eds. 2001. *The Hand Is the Head of the Mouth: The Mouth as Articulator in Sign Languages.* Hamburg: Signum.

Dikyuva, Hasan, and Ulrike Zeshan. 2008. *Türk İşaret Dili, Birinci Düzey* [Turkish Sign Language, Level One]. Nijmegen: Ishara.

Emmorey, Karen, ed. 2003. *Perspectives on Classifier Constructions in Sign Languages.* Mahwah, N.J.: Erlbaum.

Evans, Nicholas. 2000. Kinship Verbs. In *Approaches to the Typology of Word Classes,* ed. Petra Maria Vogel and Bernard Comrie, 103–172. Berlin: de Gruyter.

Everett, Daniel. 2005. Cultural Constraints on Grammar and Cognition in Pirahã: An-other Look at the Design Features of Human Language. *Current Anthropology* 46(4): 621–646.

Guerra Currie, Anne-Marie, Richard Meier, and Keith Walters. 2002. A Cross-linguistic Examination of the Lexicons of Four Signed Languages. In *Modality and Structure in Signed and Spoken Languages,* ed. Richard Meier, Kearsy Cormier, and David Quinto-Pozos, 224–239. New York: Cambridge University Press.

Hendriks, Bernadet, and Ulrike Zeshan. 2009. Sign Languages in the Arab World. In *Encyclopedia of Arabic Language and Linguistics (EALL),* vol. 4, ed. Kees Versteegh, Mushira Eid, Alaa Elgibali, Manfred Woidich, and Andrzej Zaborski, 222–235. Leiden: Brill.

Hopper, Paul. 1998. Emergent Grammar. In *The New Psychology of Language: Cognitive and Functional Approaches to Language Structure,* ed. Michael Tomasello, 155–175. Mahwah, N.J.: Erlbaum.

Kendon, Adam. 1988. *Sign Languages of Aboriginal Australia: Cultural, Semiotic, and Communicative Perspectives.* New York: Cambridge University Press.

Lutalo-Kiingi, Sam. 2008. Possessive Forms and Structures in Ugandan Sign Language. In *Possessive and Existential Constructions in Sign Languages,* ed. Ulrike Zeshan and Pamela Perniss, 105–124. Sign Language Typology Series no. 2. Nijmegen: Ishara.

Marsaja, I Gede. 2008. *Desa Kolok: A Deaf Village and Its Sign Language in Bali, Indone-sia.* Nijmegen: Ishara.

Nonaka, Angela. 2004. Sign Languages—The Forgotten Endangered Languages: Lessons on the Importance of Remembering from Thailand's Ban Khor Sign Language. *Language in Society* 33(5): 737–767.

Nyst, Victoria. 2007. *A Descriptive Analysis of Adamorobe Sign Language (Ghana).* Utrecht: LOT.

Senghas, Ann. 1995. *Children's Contribution to the Birth of Nicaraguan Sign Language.* Cambridge, Mass.: MIT.

Zeshan, Ulrike. 2004a. Hand, Head, and Face: Negative Constructions in Sign Languages. *Linguistic Typology* 8(1): 1–58.

———. 2004b. Interrogative Constructions in Sign Languages: Cross-linguistic Perspectives. *Language* 80(1): 7–39.

———, ed. 2006. *Interrogative and Negative Constructions in Sign Languages.* Sign Language Typology Series no. 1. Nijmegen: Ishara.

———. 2007. The Ethics of Documenting Sign Languages in Village Communities. *Proceedings of the Conference on Language Documentation and Linguistic Theory, December 7–8, 2007,* ed. Peter K. Austin, Oliver Bond, and David Nathan, 269–279. London: SOAS.

CHAPTER 7

Sign Language Humor, Human Singularities, and the Origins of Language

Donna Jo Napoli and Rachel Sutton-Spence

INTRODUCTION

Analysis of creatively artistic sign language shows exploitation of several human singularities—that is, properties uniquely characteristic of humans as opposed to other animals and to machines. These singularities are inextricably embedded in the very nature of sign language. This finding is consistent with the claim that sign language arose at the same time as (or after) these other human singularities, but not before, and, inasmuch as that claim is correct, supports the hypothesis that sign language preceded spoken language in human evolution. In this chapter we give a quick history of the existing literature on the question of whether sign language preceded spoken language and then turn to a discussion of conceptual integration networks.

We then explain sign languages' extensive use of productive (as opposed to frozen or established) signs, which in turn depends on conceptual integration networks that coincide with other human singularities.

HISTORY OF THE LANGUAGE-ORIGIN QUESTION

Many have proposed that the first human languages were sign languages (see, for example, critique of older works in Hewes 1977, as well as Deacon 1997; Donald 1998; Rizzolatti and Arbib 1998; Gentilucci et al. 2001; Corballis 2002, 2004; Gentilucci 2003; Rizzolatti and Craighero 2004; Armstrong and Wilcox 2007; Fox 2007; Armstrong 2008). Kendon (2002) gives a critical overview of this theory throughout Western history, detailing the reasoning by which various people have come to the same conclusion, much of it having to do with the proponents' understanding of the communicative function of gestures.

Indeed, literature from a variety of disciplines that study language evolution suggests that, despite controversy on multiple issues, a considerable number of scholars today consider the default position to be a continuity of language development from gestural origins to the addition of (not supplantation by) speech over a period of hundreds of thousands of years (see several of the papers in Givón and Malle 2002; Christiansen and Kirby 2003; Pinker 1998). Johansson (2005) presents evidence of evolutionary pressure toward language more than half a billion years ago.

Many other scholars, however, argue against the gradual development from gesture to (the addition of) speech (Bickerton 2003, 2005; MacNeilage and Davis 2005a, 2005b; Emmorey 2005; Seyfarth 2005; and, for an overview, Fitch 2005). Further, many of these scholars, as well as others, espouse the alternative view that the language faculty developed recently and suddenly, which is the topic of this chapter—and they take speech to be the first language (see Hauser, Chomsky, and Fitch 2002; Fitch, Hauser, and Chomsky 2005).

We are unconvinced by either side.

Many of the arguments frequently given for the claim that sign language preceded spoken language are consistent with signs developing before spoken words, but that's all. They are far from conclusive, and they seem to us to involve a certain misunderstanding of the nature of sign languages as languages as opposed to specific individual signs that are created by manual and facial gesture. Certain motor elements in sign languages that correspond to other gestures made by natural human movements—grasping, pushing, swiping, and so on—have become conventionalized in sign languages, but that alone is not evidence that their conventionalized language form came before speech. That is, gesture alone is not language because language involves an entire system. While many websites and some popular books claim that babies learn individual signs before individual spoken words, they learn the languages (that is, the grammatical systems) at the same speed (Newport and Meier 1985). Likewise, there were signs in Britain, for example, long before there was British Sign Language (BSL) simply because Deaf people signed, but it wasn't a fully formed sign language like the one that we know now. The gestural element that matches these compressed images now shows up in sign languages as an essential component, but that does not tell us that signed languages preceded spoken ones. If it tells us that individual gestures/signs preceded individual vocalizations/spoken words, then all well and good, but for the next step we require evidence that these gestures/signs were part of sign languages (full-fledged languages) that preceded spoken ones (full-fledged languages). It's a long hop from a gesture and a vocalization to a sign language and a spoken language.

Rather, from the linguist's point of view, what we call language emerged when it emerged—that is, the language faculty in the brain evolved at some point—and whether the modality was spoken or signed is largely irrelevant. Indeed, the information that biologists present on the evolution of a so-called language gene makes no distinction between sign language and spoken language. In particular, information on the FOXP2 variant (which may have occurred more than four hundred thousand years ago in the hominoid ancestor for both Neanderthal and modern humans—see Krause et al. 2007) suggests nothing about which modality of language arose first (although it involves our ability to make speech sounds—but certainly our hands, which were busy picking fleas off our bodies, were capable of precise sign articulations long before this).

Second, an increase in human brain size occurred about one hundred thousand years ago that may well have allowed the development of language—equally either signed or spoken language (Striedter 2005). Larger brain size allowed changes in the linkage of both vocal production and visual areas to motor areas (Holloway 1995)—hence paving the way for both language modalities. Additionally, probably ninety thousand years ago or less, there was a saltation (a discrete genetic change) associated with cerebral lateralization—and this jump in genetics paved the way for the evolution of language (Crow 1998); crucially, again, this abrupt development is in no way associated with a particular language modality.

However, the crucial nature of each of these points concerning the emergence of language is disputed. Language might well have existed before the occurrence of the FOXP2 variant, depending upon one's definition of that faculty. By comparing the anatomies of living species rather than sticking solely to fossil data, one notes that the larynx descended long ago, probably at the beginning of hominoid evolution, and allowed for phonation (Fitch 2000; Nishimura et al. 2003). Further, some argue that brain linkage is not overly dependent on brain size and may have occurred at least two hundred thousand years ago (Calvin and Bickerton 2000). Finally, cerebral lateralization is found in some nonhuman primates, which certainly casts doubt on the idea that the need for language is the evolutionary impetus for lateralization (Hopkins and Vauclair forthcoming).

A cascade of biological effects led to language, but in what order they came and over how much time they occurred are open questions whose answers keep shifting as the new fossil evidence pours in and as comparative anatomical studies among living creatures are carried out. Language evolution is a field that changes not decade by decade but month by month.

However, recent findings in semantic phonology may allow us to approach the issue of language origins in a new way, and that is what we focus on here. Armstrong (2008) summarizes some of the more recent work in semantic phonology (which started with Armstrong, Stokoe, and Wilcox 1995; Stokoe 2001; Wilcox 2001) to explain how gesture can be employed to create minigrammatical units that can compose larger language utterances. Semantic phonology has its foundations in the cognitive approach to conceptual integration theory.

CONCEPTUAL INTEGRATION THEORY

Many cognitive abilities appear to be distinctively human, leading to singu-larly human activities such as art, music, dance, mathematics, and language. Among these is the ability to express metaphor, metonymy, analogy, category extensions, framing, counterfactuals, and grammatical constructions, all of which are exemplified in the next section. Conceptual integration theory (CIT) proposes that these human singularities are the product of conceptual integra-tion networks that operate dynamically (e.g., Fauconnier and Turner 2002; Fauconnier 2005; Fauconnier and Turner 2008a, 2008b). "The gist of the oper-ation is that two or more mental spaces can be partially matched and their structure can be partially projected to a new, blended space that develops emergent structure" (Fauconnier and Turner 2008a, 133).

The interesting hypothesis for us now is that the human singularities listed earlier (or, at least art, music, dance, and language) all arose at pretty much the same point in human evolution, a moment that has been dubbed the "great leap forward" (Diamond 2006, among many). As expected, the very existence of such a leap is controversial. Some say there is evidence that all sorts of human singularities, including the use of bone tools and aquatic resources, more specialized hunting, and (importantly for us), art and decoration are found in scattered sites separated by great distances and long periods of time (McBrearty and Brooks 2000; Mellars et al. 2007). Thus, they argue that these singularities developed gradually over tens of thousands of years. For the pur-poses of this chapter, we set aside the controversy and instead work with the great-leap-forward hypothesis to see what conclusions it leads us to with respect to the evolution of language.

According to Fauconnier and Turner (2008a), no one has so far been able to account for the fact (in their view) that the emergence of language was con-temporaneous with these particular human singularities, which, they argue, call for conceptual integration networks. For example, a drawing of a person hunting an animal relies on multiple correspondences: between the drawing of a person and a person in the real world, between the drawing of an animal and an animal in the real world, and also between the spatial relationship between the drawing of the person and the drawing of the animal and the spatial relationship of a person and an animal in the real world. All of those correspondences then enter into a metaphor that allows us to understand the drawing as representing that a person is hunting an animal. A general schema for conceptual integration networks of this type is given in figure 7.1. (Schemas like that in figure 7.1 are introduced in Fauconnier and Turner 1998.)

In the example we have just given of the drawing of a hunt, generic space would include mappings between certain beings and others and between cer-tain traits and others. In generic space we have all the information common to the input. We have people and animals; we have bushes and meadows; and

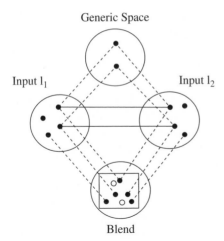

Generic Space

Input l_1

Input l_2

Blend

Figure 7.1. Conceptual Integration Networks

we have tools for hunting. But we do not have specific information about specific events. Input l_1 (location 1) would be human space, with a person hunting, hiding behind bushes, holding tools at the ready. Input l_2 (location 2) would be animal space, with the animals grazing in a meadow flanked by bushes. Blended space would be the drawing itself, in which the inputs come together to allow us to see that the drawing represents what happened in that meadow. Given that these other human singularities call for conceptual integration networks and that language emerged at the same time, Fauconnier and Turner conclude that language itself is the product of the evolution of conceptual integration networks.

Their argument is missing something crucial. Just because X happened contemporaneously with Y and because Z was crucial to X does not mean that we can conclude from that alone that Z is crucial to Y. More concretely phrased, just because the emergence of human singularities happened (as they claim) contemporaneously with the emergence of language and because conceptual integration networks were crucial to the emergence of human singularities, we cannot conclude from that alone that conceptual integration networks are crucial to the emergence of language. Language certainly calls for abstract correspondences between the phonetic shape of words and their meaning. Indeed, some scholars (looking pretty much exclusively at spoken language) have treated this kind of correspondence as the bare bones that the flesh of language is shaped upon. However, the bare bones alone cannot be taken as evidence of conceptual integration networks. Crucially, animals also express this kind of bare bones communication; animal growls, ear swivels, tail waggings, and many other things can carry meaning. While lexical items with very specific meaning (English *assassinate* or French *tour jeté* [turn while leaping], for example) seem to be limited to human language, low-information lexical items (*kill* or *run*, for example, which are highly polysemous and appropriate for a wide range of contexts) might well be part of animal communication, although, certainly, motivation in the immediate environment is essential to animal communication (Goodall 1986; Gallistel 1990), whereas it is not to human language (Chomsky 2008). What (perhaps most of all?) distinguishes human language from animal communication is the presence of syntax. Moreover, it isn't obvious that syntax need have any relationship to conceptual integration networks at all. In particular, syntax need not depend upon tropes such as metaphor or analogy; for example, even though word order often matches the order in which events happened, it need not.

However, another and at least equally important distinction between human language and animal communication is the ability to symbolize in such a way that we can evoke cognitive images and shape our understanding of reality (Chomsky 2004, referencing François Jacob). In human language, symbolism consists of the abstract correspondences between the phonetic shape of an utterance and its meaning. We needn't enter here into the question of the arbitrariness of the sound-meaning relationship, so we address only the fact that the correspondences between sounds and meanings are themselves abstractions. The question we pose is, to make those correspondences, must we appeal to metaphors and analogies?

Some have argued that metaphor is as intrinsic to language as it is to thought and that certain concepts neurally bind together (proponents point to brain-imaging technology for support; see "The Neural Theory of Language and Thought" n.d.), making metaphor a biological fact; accordingly, a language without primary metaphors is inconceivable (Lakoff and Johnson 1999; Feldman 2006). Primary metaphors are those that stem from common, shared perceptions. For example, since we visually perceive the direction "up" as connected to augmentation when we add books to a stack or liquid to a bottle, we universally (or so the claim goes) form metaphors using the direction "up" when augmentation is involved (e.g., "Prices went up").

There are problems with this approach, however. Who is to determine which metaphors are primary? Furthermore, given that there are perhaps as many as seven thousand spoken languages in the world (and who knows how many sign languages), who can verify that primary metaphors occur in all of them? However, mostly we question the reasoning behind Lakoff and Johnson's (1999) conclusion. The state of brain-imaging technology is not yet so sophisticated that it can track cognitive activity with great specificity. Nonetheless, even if future technology can show specific brain activity and even if that tracking proves that specific concepts are bound together, that still doesn't mean that language must realize that binding through primary metaphors. So, for example, the brain might bind augmentation to the direction "up" without language necessarily incorporating the word for "up" in expressions of augmentation.

In defense of this claim, we note that it is not uncommon for a language to bypass the potential for metaphor. In fact, spoken languages often do just that. For example, the time-space metaphor that we see in the use of "short" in sentences such as "It takes only a short time to drive from Boston to New York" is simply not used in Italian. Corresponding to English "short" we find Italian *breve* to modify time situations, *corto* to modify length situations, and *basso* to modify height situations. Italian certainly expresses other primary metaphors, but the point is that language can bypass these metaphors. Given that, a language without primary metaphors is therefore conceivable.

Let us back up a moment, though. What we just said needs to be qualified—and therein lies an important piece of information relevant to the origins of language: Spoken language can manage just fine without explicit or implicit analogy and with only primary metaphor (through a detached medium of typically arbitrary sounds) and without framing and counterfactuals and the other complexities mentioned earlier (though it will surely be impoverished without them)—but what about sign language? We argue in the following section that these other human singularities are essential to sign language. Hence, the emergence of sign language could not have preceded the emergence of these other human singularities; sign language must have emerged either contemporaneously with or after them.

We discuss the conclusions that follow from this observation after we have established its truth.

SIGN LANGUAGE CREATIVITY AND HUMAN SINGULARITIES

Within Deaf humor Sutton-Spence and Napoli (2009) comment extensively on a subset of sign language humor—that is, humor that plays with the linguistic structures of the language. This creativity is highly prized in the Deaf community. A prime example is a story in British Sign Language performed by Richard Carter. Here is a précis of the initial part of that story:

> It's Christmas Eve. A little girl picks up a snow globe. She shakes it and suddenly gets sucked inside—into the snow globe world. She walks through this new, snowy world and finds a house. She wipes off the window pane so she can peer inside. Father Christmas is sitting there, reading the newspaper. Time is passing—it's nearly midnight on December 24. Outside, his long-suffering reindeer is waiting, pawing the ground. The little girl hides and watches. Finally, the reindeer taps on the window, and, once he has gotten Father Christmas's attention, he signs, YOU LOOK-AT-THE-TIME! LATE COME-ON! READY WORK GET-UP. READY CHRISTMAS. WILL LATE COME-ON!" Father Christmas jumps to it and puts on his hearing aid, pockets his mobile communicator, and jumps into

his sleigh. He picks up the reins and is ready to go. The exasperated reindeer reminds him to use his magic powder. Father Christmas sprinkles some over the reindeer, whose nose starts to glow. Off goes the sleigh, flying through the sky on its way to deliver presents.

As it turns out, this simple opening of the story uses all of the human singularities related to the cognitive ability of language listed earlier: metaphor, metonymy, analogy, category extensions, framing, counterfactuals, and grammatical constructions. Let us consider each of these in reverse order.

The story is told in BSL, so, naturally, it uses grammatical constructions—that is, the language itself has a grammar.

As for counterfactuals, one normally uses that term to refer to sentences such as "If Newton hadn't proposed gravity, a contemporary surely would have" or "If pigs had wings, they'd surely be able to at least hop high." In general, a counterfactual is a statement about what would have happened if a condition had been met but, in fact, wasn't. Now consider this story: We are moving from the real world of the little girl to the world inside the snow globe, so the whole story is built on hypotheticals. In fact, since one cannot actually go inside a snow globe, the entire story is about what would happen if one could do something that one cannot do—the story itself is a giant counterfactual situation. In this sense all fiction is one giant counterfactual.

The framing in the story is clear: the familiar Christmas characters who have a familiar job to do. The meaning of a word or phrase and, in this case, a whole story is understood in relation to that frame—that is, in relation to what language users know about the context. Audiences for this story know that Father Christmas should be busy on December 24. They also know that he keeps magical reindeer that fly. We are told that the man inside the house is Father Christmas, so we understand that the reindeer outside belongs to him. When Richard Carter first mentions a reindeer, the frames for the sign REINDEER in this context are activated. When Father Christmas picks up the reins, we know they are the reins of the reindeer that will pull a sleigh through the sky. Much of the humor in this story comes from the audience members' ability to frame the meaning of the signs they see in relation to what they know. Audiences know that deaf people use sign language, wear hearing aids, and carry their mobile communicators when they go out. They thus understand that Father Christmas is Deaf (and so, probably, is the reindeer). Highly underspecified signs, such as that for picking up the reins (simply showing that Father Christmas holds something long and flat in both hands), are given full meaning through the framing, as audiences know that where Father Christmas and a reindeer are on December 24, there will also be a sleigh.

To see how the other human singularities are involved, we need only consider the fact that Father Christmas's reindeer can sign. Thus, we have extended the category of signers to include not just humans but reindeer as well. Anthropomorphization of this type is an important part of humor in both spoken and signed languages (for examples, see, among many others, Bouvet 1997 on French Sign Language; Ogawa 1999 on Japanese Sign Language; Russo 2000 and Pietrandrea 2002 on Italian Sign Language; and Emmorey 2002 on general issues in sign metaphor using American Sign Language [ASL]). Importantly, we usually find in these signed jokes and stories that nonhumans (as well as inanimate objects, such as the wings of a biplane in Bouchauveau 1994) typically sign rather than speak.

At this point a bit more information about the BSL story helps us to gain a deeper appreciation of both the creativity and the humor of the story. How on earth can a reindeer sign? After all, a reindeer has no hands, a primary articulator in signs.

Carter selects the reindeer's antlers and highlights the common understanding that they are similar in outline to hands and, thus, we are led to understand that they have a very similar shape but are intended for a very different function rather than the reality that they have neither the same biological origin nor function. Antlers are signed in BSL (as in ASL) with both hands in the 5 handshape on either side of the top of the head, giving a close visual representation of their form and location.

Richard Carter extrapolates from the homomorphism between hands and antlers, asking us to accept the less obvious but logical possibility (within this hypothetical world) that the reindeer can use his antlers to sign—and does. Carter reanalyzes the sign REINDEER so that the handshapes representing the antlers are shown to be the hands themselves, while the fingers, instead of linguistically representing bifurcating antlers, become fingers, which are then recruited to sign just as human fingers would. What could be a better example of analogy at work?

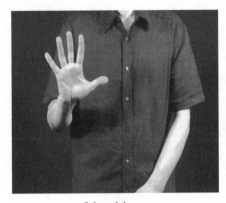

5-handshape   BSL sign REINDEER

Figure 7.2. Forms seen in Carter's poem

Carter pushes the conceit to its limit. He signs the reindeer's sentences with a consistent change in location, as all of the signs are made from the top of the head (Figure 7.3). This is, of course, because that's where the reindeer's antlers are. So Carter keeps reminding us that the reindeer is a reindeer, not a person, even as he anthropomorphizes it. The antlers are antlers, and the idea that they are hands is a particularly humorous metaphor.

The members of the audience are invited to look beyond the apparent interpretations to see the intended meaning. They can resolve the incongruity of flexible, moving antlers by reinterpreting them as hands. Here Carter is taking us into a compression (hands are like antlers in shape > hands can move > antlers can move > in particular, hands can sign > in particular, antlers can sign > hands are not anchored at the head > signs anchored at the head must be minimally modified to enable the audience to interpret them) and then back out of it. This is a remarkable example of conceptual integration networks and a lovely pushing of the counterfactual context: Reindeers don't sign, but if they did, all of these other things could follow.

The only human singularity on the list that we have not yet touched upon is metonymy. To see that, one needs to understand a linguistic characteristic of sign language: the use of classifiers. The concept of classifier handshape use in sign languages is perhaps most quickly illustrated by an example. Let's assume that we are talking about a cat. Once we've introduced the cat into the conversation and wish to give more information about its actions, experiences, or appearance, we don't move the sign CAT around in space to show what it did, nor do we alter it to show what was done to the animal. Instead, we have a range of particular handshapes to use for representing the cat as it moves through space or is acted upon by others. All the different handshapes to represent the animal and its movement are frequently termed classifiers in the discussion of sign language. Some handshapes represent the whole body of the cat, either moving or stationary. Other handshapes employ the mechanism of metonymy, indicating only a part of the body, such as the paws, the ears, or the tail, to represent the whole (Wilcox 2000).

Figure 7.3. Second part of the sign CHRISTMAS articulated at the head, rather than waist height

Richard Carter represents the reindeer at more than one point with both hands in the 5 handshape, making a walking movement at waist level to represent the hooves; the animal is reduced to hooves that paw at the ground. However, the metonymy, although it is a reduction lexically, is just the opposite visually. Focusing on the hooves allows a close-up shot like a viewfinder on a camera or a telescopic lens. It makes us empathize with the reindeer's determination to get Father Christmas into the sleigh. Carter, true to fine storytelling technique, underscores this with facial expression and body movement as part of his characterization of the reindeer.

We could have picked from dozens of other jokes and humorous stories to demonstrate that sign humor revels in these human singularities. The point, however, is not that sign humor is so very creative but, rather, that all of the things Carter does in this story and all of the sign language devices we find in other jokes and stories are typical in ordinary, daily sign language use. Examples may be seen in almost any utterance of a fluent signer.

The very lexicon of sign languages draws on metaphor, metonymy, and analogy (Russo 2000; Wilcox 2000). This, however, is not proof that sign languages must draw on these human singularities. One could definitely make up a sign language whose lexicon did not draw on metaphor, metonymy, or analogy. Indeed, even in sign languages that use analogy freely, this particular figure of speech can go only so far. Many objects are not even remotely homomorphous to (parts of) the human body, and even those that are hit brick walls quickly. For example, the V handshape is analogous to two legs, and that analogy is exploited in the sign STAND (common to many sign languages).

We can play with the V handshape and easily make other signs, such as JUMP and KNEEL, in which the movement of these two fingers mimics the

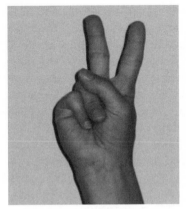

V-handshape   the sign STAND

Figure 7.4. An example of metonymy in sign language

movement of the legs. However, we can't do anything with this handshape alone (that is, unaided by additional signs or classifiers) to make the sign for the ballet movement *plié*, in which the knees bend and straighten again while the feet turn out, because the joints of the fingers do not allow that kind of movement. This argument can be further strengthened by cases in which the joints of the fingers *do* allow a certain kind of movement, but that movement is still not exploited by some sign languages to express the meaning associated with the *plié*, yet it is so exploited by other sign languages. In the case of running, the fingers of the V handshape could theoretically be made to resemble a pair of legs running, yet in ASL it is rare to see the V handshape used to express the concept of running. Rather, other classifiers must be used. In BSL, however, this V handshape may indeed be used to express the concept of running, especially if the running is not in a straight line—for example, upstairs or downstairs or around a football field. The fact that different languages elect to use certain visually motivated metaphorical signs, while some do not, demonstrates that there is no requirement to do so.

It's not surprising that mature sign languages frequently have many (indeed, probably a majority of) signs in their vocabulary for which the (phonetic) form of a sign is at least partially arbitrarily related to its meaning. That is, the motivation for a particular location, handshape, movement, orientation, or other aspect of the phonetic shape of a given sign is not obvious to a nonsigner (or even to fluent signers in many instances) without explanation. Indeed, were that not so, people who didn't know a given sign language would easily be able to guess what signers were conversing about most of the time, which they cannot. Furthermore, if that were not so, all sign languages would have pretty much the same lexicon or at least mutually comprehensible lexicons, which they do not. However, the considerably increased visual motivation of signs means that signers with a clear understanding of sign formation processes and the motivational (frequently metaphorical) processes driving them are frequently more able than nonsigners to discern the meaning of vocabulary in sign languages with which they are unfamiliar. This is further evidence to support the view that the production and understanding of sign languages requires the use of conceptual integration networks that coincide with other human singularities. When signers can apply their knowledge of metaphor, metonymy, analogy, category extensions, and so on, they are able to interpret the meaning of signs (see Pizzuto and Volterra 2000).

Nonetheless, this discussion holds only for those signs that one might find listed in a dictionary—what have been called *frozen* or *established* signs. Sign languages, however, also have productive signs not found in any dictionary (McDonald 1985; Brennan 1990; Taub 2001; Russo 2004; and others, building on the distinction in Klima and Bellugi 1979 between linguistically conventionalized and visually transparent parameters for signs). Frozen signs form the established vocabulary of any sign language and identify senses in general categories such as objects, actions, and states of being (DOG, RUN, HOT). However, they give no further indication of the specific type of dog, the way in which the running was done, or what or who is hot. Frozen signs can also convey referents (that is, which dog we are talking about or which particular event of running we want to indicate), and, again, alone they identify a referent that has no more information than the bare sense of the sign. Often frozen signs are combined with something else to add more information about the referent. For example, we might add a pointing sign to a frozen nominal to indicate the particular referent that has the sense contained in that lexical item.

Productive signs, however, do not convey a general sense and instead rely upon strong visual images behind the sign formation to indicate the specific referent under discussion. Signers will show perhaps what the dog in question looked like and how it behaved. They may show how it moved and where it went. In order to express an idea of running in this context, we may see the path taken by the dog or the manner and the duration of the running. To understand the way that the referent might be described as being hot, we could see a visual representation reflecting the dog's experience of heat or its appearance when hot.

Frozen signs, accordingly, are appropriately used in a wide range of contexts because the information they convey is so general. However, individual productive signs are appropriate in many fewer contexts because they carry a great deal of information specific to an event. Typically, a signer will articulate a frozen sign to let us know what sort of object, action, or state we're talking about and then follow it with a productive sign that might be a classifier predicate, showing the particular referent (of the type indicated by the frozen sign) performing a particular act (of the type indicated by the frozen sign). When signing about a dog, for example, the handshapes may be selected to represent the whole dog or some part of it (paws, tail, or ears), so the handshape parameter becomes a morpheme, and the hands will move to represent the manner and direction of running. Thus, movement becomes meaningful. The sign may also be combined with facial expression to show how hot the dog was at the end of the run, so facial expression also becomes meaningful by expressing information via the eyes, mouth, and head movement, which might be seen as prosodic markers or suprasegmentals, akin to intonation in spoken language (Sandler and Lillo-Martin 2006). And the sign that carried all of this meaning is not to be found in any dictionary.

Productive signs are founded on metaphor, metonymy, analogy, and categorical extensions. Signers analogize the space in front of them (where they locate the hand movements) to the space that the dog actually ran in (which might be in another city). The movement of the hands along the path are a metaphor for the dog's movement along the ground (or wherever else it ran). The hands themselves, depending on the shape they assume, can show metonymy for the dog. Wagging the hand or finger can, by extension, represent the wagging of the dog's tail. And this happens over and over and over again. In an ASL poem titled "e=mc^2," by the duo known as The Flying Words Project (Cook and Lerner 2004), the sign SNOW has a gentle, slow, primary movement of parallel hands downward in neutral space, with a secondary trill of the fingers. However, as the snow gets heavier, the movement changes: The hands push downward, showing the weight of the snow. While this duo creates art, any signer could make similar changes of the movement parameter of SNOW to show light, drifty snow or heavy, driving snow or a wild blizzard. Sign poets, comedians, and storytellers make use of devices that are already employed in everyday language.

There are many sign languages in the world; no one knows how many, though, since countries often do not include them in their census data, but surely where there are communities that have a use for signs, there are sign languages. Most of these languages have not yet been studied by linguists, but all of those on which we have any information have both frozen and productive signs. We find it impossible to imagine a sign language that does not make use of productive signs, although they may use them to different degrees. Meir et al. (2007) claim that Al-Sayyid Bedouin Sign Language (ABSL) does not exhibit some types of verb agreement that appear in many sign languages, types that might be instances of productive signs. However, other kinds of productive signs do appear in ABSL. If their findings are correct, it would be further evidence that sign languages vary in the extent to which they use productive signs. A sign language that did not make use of productive signs would be failing to exploit the very fact that sign languages are visual— and that would be absurd. Many of the items of frozen, established vocabulary in any signed lexicon probably started life as productive signs (see, for example, Johnston and Schembri 2007), so they, too, draw on this motivational source. Mature sign languages, therefore, cannot exist without metaphors, category extensions, and analogy via mimicking—the heart of productive signs. Several writers (including Bienvenu 1994 and Rutherford 1993) have observed that, in particular, humor through a mimicking use of facial expression develops early, as Deaf children learn to become expert observers of their visual world. Rutherford (1993, 108) explains that imitations "are a traditional pastime of children at the residential school and can also be seen at Deaf adult gatherings where skits or other entertainment are being performed." Imitation results from careful studying of the people around one (in Rutherford's example, the children are bored in class and have nothing better to do), and it is useful to the child to be good at it and have that skill be acknowledged and appreciated by others.

Sign languages are built on conceptual integration networks. Every time one uses a classifier handshape, one is making an analogy. Every time a classifier predicate moves through space, one is relying on overarching principles to draw comparisons between unlike objects doing unlike activities. Blended mental spaces are part of almost every sentence, as Liddell (2003) shows, since partial matchings must constantly be made. Compression is the rule in sign language.

To present a simple example, we offer the following joke, which holds in any sign language so far as we know. To appreciate it, the audience needs to understand that most signs are made with a movement of a certain size and that if the movement path of the signs is larger or smaller than expected, there is a change in the intention behind the signing. Here's the joke:

> A Deaf couple have an argument. The woman gets heated and begins moving her hands in a larger path than normal. The husband then signs, "NOT NEED YELL. I DEAF NOT BLIND."

Clearly, the husband has made a cognitively sophisticated compression. By saying that articulating a larger movement path is tantamount to yelling, he's drawing a comparison between signing and speaking, in which signing with a large movement is equivalent to speaking loudly, an equivalence that is based on a comparison between the size of a space and the intensity of a sound, which, in turn, depends on a comparison between seeing and hearing. In just two sentences, he's brought us from the production of language in two different modalities to the reception of language in two different modalities, with all of the relevant correspondences between them supporting the punch line. The important thing for us is that the joke here is not based on this sophisticated compression—but on the punch line. Indeed, in ordinary conversation, if one signs with an unusually large movement path, one might be doing the equivalent of shouting (and signing with an unusually small movement path might be equivalent to whispering). So the husband here has used a compression that is typical of daily language.

Clearly, sign language depends upon blending and compression.

CONCLUSION

Almost any sign utterance demonstrates blending of the type discussed in works on conceptual integration theory. New linguistic forms are constantly created by conceptual blends that exploit an existing grammatical apparatus as they compress and make analogies, metaphors, and category extensions, often between things as disparate as human beings and the wings of a biplane. In conceptual integration networks, sign language is a playground for mental spaces and their relationships.

Crucially, it is hard to imagine a time when sign language couldn't do such a thing. Indeed, what would sign consist of otherwise? Signs, by calling for the cooperation of so many body parts in the act of communication, beg for the signer to blend the various human singularities. It would be nonsensical to sign without them. And that means that all sign languages must be able to avail themselves of them. This means that sign language simply could not have developed in the absence of conceptual integration networks.

As we noted earlier, the particular human singularities of language (the ability to compress and to make analogies, metaphors, and categorical extensions) have all been claimed to have arisen at the same time in human evolution (Fauconnier and Turner 2008a). Thus far an account of the hypothesized coincidence is elusive. We have one giant convergence that just happened—who knows why? Since spoken languages need not avail themselves of these other human singularities (with the possible exception of primary metaphors), the emergence of spoken language could logically have preceded, coincided with, or followed the emergence of any of them.

Sign languages, however, are quite different in this regard. Sign language necessarily holds hands with these other human singularities. That means that the emergence of sign languages could logically have coincided with or followed the emergence of these other human singularities, but could not have preceded them. This point is by no means a knock-down argument that the first languages were signed. Instead, it indicates only that the hypothesized coincidence of the emergence of language with these other human singularities is somewhat less of a mystery if the first languages were signed than if they were spoken.

Note

We thank Richard Carter for his kind permission to use his story of the Snow Globe, Jami Fisher for being our ASL model, and Tim Northam for being our BSL model. We thank Gaurav Mathur for comments on an earlier draft. We also thank Maggie Tallerman for discussing with (one of) us some of the controversies about language evolution.

Bibliography

Armstrong, David. 2008. The Gestural Theory of Language Origins. *Sign Language Studies* 8: 289–314.

———, William C. Stokoe, and Sherman E. Wilcox. 1995. *Gesture and the Nature of Language*. New York: Cambridge University Press.

Armstrong, David, and Sherman E. Wilcox. 2007. *The Gestural Origin of Language*. New York: Oxford University Press.

Bickerton, Derrick. 2003. Language Evolution without Evolution. *Behavioral and Brain Sciences* 26: 669–670.

———. 2005. Beyond the Mirror Neuron: The Smoke Neuron. *Behavioral and Brain Sciences* 28: 126.

Bienvenu, Martina J. 1994. Reflections of Deaf Culture in Deaf Humor. In *The Deaf Way: Perspectives from the International Conference on Deaf Culture*, ed. Carol J. Erting,

Robert C. Johnson, Dorothy L. Smith, and Bruce D. Snider, 16–23. Washington, D.C.: Gallaudet University Press.

Bouchauveau, Guy. 1994. Deaf Humor and Culture. In *The Deaf Way: Perspectives from the International Conference on Deaf Culture*, ed. Carol J. Erting, Robert C. Johnson, Dorothy L. Smith, and Bruce D. Snider, 24–30. Washington, D.C.: Gallaudet University Press.

Bouvet, Danielle. 1997. *Le corps et la métaphore dans les langues gestuelles: À la recherche des modes de production des signes* [Body and Metaphor in Gestural Language: In Search of the Modes of Production of *Signs*]. Paris: L'Harmattan.

Brennan, Mary. 1990. *Word Formation in British Sign Language*. Stockholm: Stockholm University Press.

Calvin, William, and Derek Bickerton. 2000. *Lingua ex Machina: Reconciling Darwin and Chomsky with the Human Brain*. Cambridge, Mass.: MIT Press.

Chomsky, Noam. 2004. Biolinguistics and the Human Capacity. Presented in Budapest on May 17. http://www.chomsky.info/talks/20040517.htm.

———. 2008. The Biolinguistic Program: Where Does It Stand Today? Manuscript, May 14. Cambridge, Mass.: MIT.

Christiansen, Morten, and Simon Kirby, eds. 2003. *Language Evolution*. New York: Oxford University Press.

Cook, Peter, and Kenny Lerner. 2004. *The Can't Touch Tours 1990–2003*. Videotape anthology. Peter Cook Productions.

Corballis, Michael C. 2002. *From Hand to Mouth: The Origins of Language*. Princeton: Princeton University Press.

———. 2004. *FOXP2* and the Mirror System. *TRENDS in Cognitive Sciences* 8(3): 95–96.

Crow, Timothy J. 1998. Sexual Selection, Timing, and the Descent of Man: A Theory of the Genetic Origins of Language. *Current Psychology of Cognition* 17(6): 1079–1114.

Deacon, Terrence W. 1997. *The Symbolic Species: The Co-evolution of Language and the Brain*. New York: Norton.

Diamond, Jared. 2006. *The Third Chimpanzee: The Evolution and Future of the Human Animal*. New York: Harper Perennial.

Donald, Merlin. 1998. Mimesis and Executive Suite: Missing Links in Language Evolution. In *Approaches to the Evolution of Language*, ed. James R. Hurford, Michael Studdert-Kennedy, and Chris Knight, 46–67. New York: Cambridge University Press.

Emmorey, Karen. 2002. Mental Imagery and Embodied Cognition: Insights from Sign Language Research. *Journal of Mental Imagery* 26: 50–53.

———. 2005. Sign Languages Are Problematic for a Gestural Origins Theory of Language Evolution. *Behavioral and Brain Sciences* 28: 130–131.

Fauconnier, Gilles. 2005. Compression and Emergent Structure. *Language and Linguistics* 6(4): 523–538.

———, and Mark Turner. 1998. Conceptual Integration Networks. *Cognitive Science* 22(2): 133–187.

———. 2002. *The Way We Think*. New York: Basic Books.

———. 2008a. The Origin of Language as a Product of the Evolution of Modern Cognition. In *Origin and Evolution of Languages: Approaches, Models, Paradigms*, ed. Bernard Laks with Serge Cleuziouz, Jean-Paul Demoule, and Pierre Encrevé, 133–156. London: Equinox.

————. 2008b. Rethinking Metaphor. In *The Cambridge Handbook of Metaphor and Thought*, ed. Raymond W. Gibbs Jr., 53–66. New York: Cambridge University Press.

Feldman, Jerome A. 2006. *From Molecule to Metaphor*. Cambridge, Mass.: MIT Press.

Fitch, W. Tecumseh. 2000. The Evolution of Speech: A Comparative Review. *Trends in Cognitive Science* 4: 258–267.

————. 2005. The Evolution of Language: A Comparative Review. *Biology and Philosophy* 20: 193–230.

————, Marc D. Hauser, and Noam Chomsky. 2005. The Evolution of the Language Faculty: Clarifications and Implications. *Cognition* 97: 179–210.

Fox, Margalit. 2007. *Talking Hands: What Sign Language Reveals about the Mind*. New York: Simon and Schuster.

Gallistel, Charles R. 1990. Representations in Animal Cognition: An Introduction. *Cognition* 37: 1–22.

Gentilucci, Maurizio. 2003. Grasp Observation Influences Speech Production. *European Journal of Neuroscience* 17: 179–184.

————, Francesca Benuzzi, Massimo Gangitano, and Silva Grimaldi. 2001. Grasp with Hand and Mouth: A Kinematic Study on Healthy Subjects. *Journal of Neurophysiology* 86: 1685–1699.

Givón, Talmy, and Bertram F. Malle, eds. 2002. *The Evolution of Language out of Pre-language*. Amsterdam: Benjamins.

Goodall, Jane. 1986. *The Chimpanzees of Gombe: Patterns of Behavior*. Cambridge, Mass.: Belknap.

Hauser, Marc D., Noam Chomsky, and W. Tecumseh Fitch. 2002. The Faculty of Language: What Is It, Who Has It, and How Did It Evolve? *Science* 298: 1569–1579.

Hewes, Gordon W. 1977. Language Origin Theories. In *Language Learning by a Chimpanzee: The Lana Project*, ed. Duane Rumbaugh, 3–53. New York: Academic Press.

Holloway, Ralph L. 1995. Toward a Synthetic Theory of Human Brain Evolution. In *Origins of the Human Brain*, ed. Jean-Pierre Changeux and Jean Chavaillon, 42–60. Oxford: Clarendon.

Hopkins, William, and Jacques Vauclair. Forthcoming. Evolution of Behavioral and Brain Asymmetries in Primates. In *Handbook of Language Evolution*, ed. Maggie Tallerman and Kathleen Gibson. New York: Oxford University Press.

Johansson, Sverker. 2005. *Origins of Language: Constraints on Hypotheses*. Amsterdam: Benjamins.

Johnston, Trevor, and Adam Schembri. 2007. *Australian Sign Language (Auslan): An Introduction to Sign Language Linguistics*. New York: Cambridge University Press.

Kendon, Adam. 2002. Historical Observations on the Relationship between Research on Sign Languages and Language Origins Theory. In *The Study of Signed Languages: Essays in Honor of William C. Stokoe*, ed. David F. Armstrong, Michael A. Karchmer, and John V. Van Cleve, 35–52. Washington, D.C.: Gallaudet University Press.

Klima, Edward, and Ursula Bellugi. 1979. *The Signs of Language*. Cambridge, Mass.: Harvard University Press.

Krause, Johannes, Carles Lalueza-Fox, Ludovico Orland, Wolfgang Enard, Richard E. Green, Hernan A. Burbano, Jean-Jacques Hublin, et al. 2007. The Derived FOXP2 Variation of Modern Humans Was Shared with Neanderthals. *Current Biology* 17: 1908–1912.

Lakoff, George, and Mark Johnson. 1999. *Philosophy in the Flesh: The Embodied Mind and Its Challenge to Western Thought.* New York: Basic Books.

Liddell, Scott. 2003. *Grammar, Gesture, and Meaning in American Sign Language.* New York: Cambridge University Press.

MacNeilage, Peter F., and Barbara L. Davis. 2005a. Evolutionary Sleight of Hand: Then, They Saw It; Now We Don't. *Behavioral and Brain Sciences* 28: 137–138.

———. 2005b. The Frame/content Theory of Evolution of Speech: A Comparison with a Gestural-origins Alternative. *Interaction Studies* 6: 173–199.

McBrearty, Sally, and Alison Brooks. 2000. The Revolution That Wasn't: A New Interpretation of the Origins of Modern Human Behavior. *Journal of Human Evolution* 39: 453–563.

McDonald, Betsy H. 1985. Productive and Frozen Lexicon in ASL: An Old Problem Revisited. In *SLR '83: Proceedings of the Third International Symposium on Sign Language Research,* Rome, June 22–26, 1983, ed. William Stokoe and Virginia Volterra, 254–259. Silver Spring, Md.: Linstok.

Meir, Irit, Carol Padden, Marc Aronoff, and Wendy Sandler. 2007. Body as Subject. *Journal of Linguistics* 43: 531–563.

Mellars, Paul, Katie Boyle, Ofer Bar-Yosef, and Chris Stringer, eds. 2007. *Rethinking the Human Revolution.* Cambridge: McDonald Institute for Archaeological Research.

Neural Theory of Language and Thought, The. n.d. Online report by the Institute for Cognitive and Brain Sciences at the University of California at Berkeley. http://icbs.berkeley.edu/natural_theory_lt.php (accessed September 10, 2008).

Newport, Elissa, and Richard P. Meier. 1985. The Acquisition of American Sign Language. In *The Cross-linguistic Study of Language Acquisition.* Vol. 1, *The data,* ed. Dan I. Slobin, 881–938. Hillsdale, N.J.: Erlbaum.

Nishimura, Takeshi, Akichika Mikami, Juri Suzuki, and Tetsuro Matsuzawa. 2003. Descent of the Larynx in Chimpanzee Infants. *Proceedings of the National Academy of Sciences* 100 (12): 6930–6933.

Ogawa, Yuko. 1999. Vertical Scale Metaphors in Japanese and Japanese Sign Language. PhD diss., Gallaudet University.

Pietrandrea, Paola. 2002. Iconicity and Arbitrariness in Italian Sign Language. *Sign Language Studies* 2(3): 296–321.

Pinker, Steven. 1998. The Evolution of the Human Language Faculty. In *The Origin and Diversification of Language,* ed. Nina Jablonsky and Leslie Aiello, 117–126. San Francisco: California Academy of Sciences.

Pizzuto, Elena, and Virginia Volterra. 2000. Iconicity and Transparency in Sign Languages: A Cross-linguistic, Cross-cultural View. In *The Signs of Language Revisited: An Anthology to Honor Ursula Bellugi and Edward Klima,* ed. Karen Emmorey and Harlan Lane, 261–286. Mahwah, N.J.: Erlbaum.

Rizzolatti, Giacomo, and Michael A. Arbib. 1998. Language within Our Grasp. *Trends in Neuroscience* 21: 188–194.

Rizzolatti, Giacomo, and Laila Craighero. 2004. The Mirror-neuron System. *Annual Rev. Neuroscience* 27: 169–192.

Russo, Tommaso. 2000. Iconicità e metafora nella LIS [Iconicity and Metaphor in LIS]. PhD diss., Università degli Studi di Palermo, Italy.

————. 2004. Iconicity and Productivity in Sign Language Discourse: An Analysis of Three LIS Discourse Registers. *Sign Language Studies* 4(2): 164–197.

Rutherford, Susan Dell. 1993. *A Study of American Deaf Folklore*. Burtonsville, Md.: Linstok.

Sandler, Wendy, and Diane Lillo-Martin. 2006. *Sign Language and Linguistic Universals*. New York: Cambridge University Press.

Seyfarth, Robert M. 2005. Continuities in Vocal Communication Argue against a Gestural Origin of Language. *Behavioral and Brain Sciences* 28: 144–145.

Stokoe, William C. 2001. Semantic Phonology. *Sign Language Studies* 1(4): 434–441.

Striedter, Georg F. 2005. *Principles of Brain Evolution*. Sunderland, Mass.: Sinauer.

Sutton-Spence, Rachel, and Donna Jo Napoli. 2009. *Humour in Sign Languages: The Linguistic Underpinnings*. Dublin: University of Dublin, Trinity College Press.

Taub, Sarah F. 2001. *Language from the Body: Iconicity and Metaphor in American Sign Language*. New York: Cambridge University Press.

Wilcox, Phyllis P. 2000. *Metaphor in American Sign Language*. Washington, D.C.: Gallaudet University Press.

Wilcox, Sherman. 2001. Searching for Language: Process, Not Product. *Sign Language Studies* 1(4): 333–343.

CHAPTER 7 RESPONSE

Gesture First or Speech First in Language Origins?

Adam Kendon

INTRODUCTION

The chapter by Donna Jo Napoli and Rachel Sutton-Spence, which prompts this commentary, like many other discussions on the theme of language origins, refers to the debate about whether language began first as speech or as gesture. The authors say they are convinced of neither of these positions. However, they argue that the analysis of "creatively artistic sign language shows exploitation of human singularities," by which they mean the "distinctively human . . . ability to express metaphor, metonymy, analogy, category extensions, framing, counterfactuals, and grammatical constructions" (Napoli and Sutton-Spence, this volume). Therefore, they suggest, these singularities must have developed if sign languages were to be possible, but they are less necessary for the development of spoken language, which thus favors the hypothesis that sign language preceded spoken language in human evolution. Their disclaimer notwithstanding, they do display a bias in favor of the "gesture-first" position.

The gesture-first position is of very long standing. It is associated in the eighteenth century with scholars such as William Warburton in England, Etienne Bonnot de Condillac in France, and Giambattista Vico in Naples. It has lately undergone a modern revival and is strongly espoused by recent writers such as Hewes (1991 [1973]), Stokoe (2001), Armstrong and Wilcox (2007), Corballis (2002), and Arbib (2005). It proposes that the first language was formed from a system of symbolic or semantically significant visible bodily movements, mainly made by the hands and the face and usually referred to as "gestures" or "signs."[1] All of the writers who support this view (both early and contemporary) make some appeal to sign languages as used by deaf people. These are taken to be evidence of the idea that something recognizably linguistic can be fashioned in the kinesic medium. Since to express oneself in this medium does not (as speaking does) require any specialized anatomical equipment but can be done using motions of the hands, motions that are often apparently derived from commonplace practical actions, it seems as if using gesture is easier and somehow more natural than speaking. For this reason it is plausible to imagine that this was the first way in which people expressed themselves linguistically.[2]

The modern writers mentioned earlier all suppose that some form of sign language (or gestural language) came into being as the first form of language. Thus, Hewes (1991 [1973], 72) marshals evidence to support his argument that a "preexisting gestural language system would have provided an easier pathway to vocal language" than if this were a direct outgrowth of primate vocalizations. Armstrong and his colleagues have stated that "signed languages are the original and prototypical languages" (Armstrong and Wilcox 2007, 17), and Corballis (2002, 125) writes that "my guess is that the precursors of H. sapiens had in fact evolved a form of signed language similar in principle, if not in detail, to the signed languages that are used today by the deaf. " Arbib (2005) does not appear to go quite so far as this, for he supposes that at first there was a system, which he calls "protosign," that served as a scaffold in relation to which spoken forms of language could subsequently develop. However, he also believes that the existence of complex sign languages in modern societies supports his idea that the first form of language was gestural.

All of these writers, either explicitly or implicitly, take the view that language is a communication system to be defined in functional terms. Although they recognize that modern languages, including sign languages, have features such as phonological and morphological systems and a grammatical (e.g., phrasal and sentential) organization that can be formulated in terms of systematic syntactic rules, they do not regard these as crucial for a system if it is to deserve the label *language*. For them it is sufficient if a system can convey propositional information. The nature of the code structure by which it does so is given less discussion. On the other hand, those who suppose that language must have been spoken from the very first are much more likely to insist that the code system involved had certain formal properties. Most notably, they are likely to insist that there was a duality of patterning (hence a phonological system of some kind) and a syntactic organization that allowed for recursion (i.e., the embedding of phrases within phrases). The arbitrary nature of the form-meaning relationship is also often emphasized. Proponents of the speech-first view, in consequence, commonly tend to focus upon what might have brought about the development of these formal properties. They seem less concerned with the problem of how actions of any sort came to be able to convey meaning.

Proponents of the speech-first position advance two basic arguments. First, they point out that all modern languages are spoken. Sign languages, for them, are latter-day developments, arising in generally aberrant circumstances and developed by fully modern humans who already have all that is required to develop a language. Therefore, they can have no bearing on the issue of whether language was gestural in its first form. Second, they ask, "If an elaborate language was developed first in the modality of gesture, since modern sign languages are supposedly fully successful as languages, why was this modality ever abandoned?" They also point out that, as even a relatively superficial acquaintance with the speech apparatus will suggest, humans are anatomically and neurologically highly specialized as speaking creatures (for exemplary arguments in favor of the speech-first position, see MacNeilage 1998, 2008; and MacNeilage and Davis 2005).

Proponents of the gesture-first theory recognize the problem of explaining how and why a language of visible gestures came to be transformed into a spoken language, and they all make some effort to deal with it. Hewes, who is sympathetic to the tongue-gesture hypothesis of Sir Richard Paget (1930), also proposed by Wallace (1895) and later elaborated by Jóhanneson (1949) and Mary Le Cron Foster (e.g., Foster 1999), admits, however, that this approach "still leaves most of the postulated transformation from a gestural to a vocal language unexplained" (Hewes 1991 [1973], 70). Most others simply suppose that vocalizations somehow came to be associated with bodily actions and so, by becoming consistently associated with established forms of gesture or sign, eventually replaced them. They did so because, it is argued (for example, by Corballis 2002 and by Armstrong and Wilcox 2007), using speech for language has many advantages: It can work in the dark, it frees the hands for other activities, it works more rapidly than gesturing and perhaps is a modality in which it is possible to develop very large vocabularies of semantically contrastive forms, something that would be less likely in a gestural modality (though some of the authors who suggest this become a little uncomfortable since this implies that sign languages are inherently more limited than spoken languages, a viewpoint that is considered distasteful nowadays and is heartily rejected by most students and scholars of sign languages).

On the other hand, proponents of the gesture-first theory point out that the speech-first proponents can offer no explanation for the fact that speakers often also use gestures when they speak and that they do so in a way that suggests that such gesturing is fully integrated with the act of speaking, as if it is part of the same plan of action. The gesture-first proponents maintain that the ubiquitous coordination of gesture with speech is at least compatible with the idea that language was first established in the gestural modality and perhaps explains it, something that, according to them, the proponents of the speech-first view completely fail to do (for an early expression of this point see Kendon 1975; on the integration of gesture with speech see Kendon 1972, 1980, 2004, and McNeill 1992, 2005). The speech-first proponents, on the other hand, rarely refer to cospeech gesture, probably because they do not see why it is important. As mentioned earlier, most speech-first proponents think that something called language must have certain formal properties. For instance, the kinesic accompaniments of speaking, which are deemed paralinguistic, are not regarded as having any of these formal properties and are not considered central to language. For the speech-first proponents, then, explaining these phenomena seems a less urgent matter and perhaps not a task that is appropriate for one whose main concern is spoken language (see Bolinger 1946 for a nice discussion of the problem of where to draw the line between the linguistic and the nonlinguistic).

Rather than delving any further into the merits or demerits of either side in this debate, I suggest that the debate itself is based upon a certain view of what a language must be. If we modify this view, the debate becomes unnecessary. The idea of language that gives rise to this debate is that it must be monomodalic—it must be either completely signed or completely spoken. The possibility that something that we can call a language might utilize a mixture of modalities is not given serious consideration. However, if we allow for this possibility, we are no longer faced with the gesture-first/speech-first dilemma. Language in its monomodalic form can then be understood as a consequence of a process of specialization and differentiation from originally multimodal ensembles of action. Accounts of language origins, thus, can be recast as accounts of these processes of progressive specialization, while a discussion of language in its beginnings can focus on the behavioral systems that eventually led to language as we understand the term today. These, from the beginning, involved both vocal signaling and signaling by visible bodily action—but inextricably intertwined.

UTTERANCE CONSTRUCTION IS MULTIMODAL

When modern people engage in conversation, depending on the circumstances, they commonly draw freely on a range of expressive resources, only some of which are systematically describable in accordance with the ideals of linguistics; yet these resources can sometimes play a pivotal role in the way an utterance is constructed. This multimodal character of utterances has long been recognized in one way or another. However, only since the availability of audiovisual recording technology, which turns the fleeting flow of communicative action into inspectable objects, has this character of utterances had a chance for close study. Even now, after the more than fifty years in which this technology has been available, the implications of the multimodal character of utterance production for our conceptions of language and how it might have originated have yet to be properly grasped. The reason for this lies in part, at least, in the fact that the analysts who examine these objects start from a position that assumes that people go about utterance construction first of all as if they were writing something and then add embellishments. It may be true that sometimes people do produce utterances in this way (this is what one does when one is writing, after all), but in the contexts of a co-present interaction, participants usually do not have time. In this context, the starting point for utterance producers is some meaning that has to be expressed in the current moment. In pursuing this aim, the utterance producer will draw upon whatever resources are available at that time. Often, in describing something, for instance, rather than developing a complete description in words, which can take time to achieve, speakers will use their hands as well. These can evoke sizes, shapes, and patterns of action that can represent expressions that otherwise might have been verbally formulated.

It will be useful to look at a specific example. In the following section I present a short extract taken from a recording of a commonplace conversational occasion (Ao-Portici 1999, made in collaboration with Maria Graziano at the University of Naples "Orientale"). This extract illustrates the case of someone constructing an utterance using kinesic and spoken resources jointly. The example demonstrates that different semiotic resources can be deployed in coordination around a single aim of creating a unit of action that has complex propositional meaning.

DESCRIBING A HOME AQUARIUM

A girl who is about thirteen years old is describing her aquarium. The setting is a group of young people, a sort of informal youth group belonging to the parish of a church in Portici, near Naples, Italy. Various people in the group have been talking about their pets. Giulia (a pseudonym) says, "Ho un acquario che ci sono sei pesci" [I have an aquarium with six fish], whereupon one of the adult participants says, "Com'è fatto, quest'acquario?" [What's this aquarium like?]. In response, Giulia begins her description: "Ei ci sono le pietre piccole, poi ci sono due pietre grandi, e ci sono l'erba là" [Ei (an opening noise, similar to "um"), there are (some) little stones, then there are two big stones, and there is (some) grass there]. Immediately after she says "erba" [grass], she adds, "Non l'erba, le alghe" [Not grass, algae], thus showing that she recognized that she had made an error in saying "l'erba" and should have said "le alghe." However, to simplify our discussion, this correction is not further discussed here.

Giulia's description begins, then, with a listing some of the physical objects inside the aquarium. As she does so, however, she brings her hands into play: When she says, "Ci sono le pietre" [there are (some) stones], she lifts both her hands, which are fully open and with the fingers together and palms down, and then draws them apart in a horizontal movement (figure 7R.1A). When she says "piccole" [little (inflected for feminine plural)], she relaxes her left hand but lowers her right hand with an outward, arclike motion, at the same time holding her thumb close to (or touching) the first joint of the partially bent index finger, the other fingers folded back (figure 7R.1B). The two-handed horizontal movement is always seen by people who watch this segment as a gesture that shows that the stones are spread out horizontally.[3] The second movement of the right hand is seen as incorporating a kinesic form that expresses the concept of small, little, small amount, small size, and the like.

As Giulia says, "Poi ci sono due pietre grandi" [Then there are two big stones], she extends her arms straight in front of her and holds them steady, with each hand apparently holding an object about the size of a tennis ball (figure 7R.1C). People who see this say that she is holding out two objects, presumably showing us the two stones, which, to judge from the way she holds her hands, are positioned side by side.

When she says, "Ci sono l'erba" [There is the grass], she moves her hands rapidly up and down but in a relaxed manner, with the thumb opposed to the fingers, which are slightly curved and loosely spread (figure 7R.1D). People who see this part generally say that she is showing delicate things moving or standing upward (like flowers in a vase), and, when seen in conjunction with the words, people say she is showing the upright vegetation in her aquarium. As she says "là" [there] at the end of her phrase, she holds her hands in front of her, and her index fingers are pointing forward (figure 7R.1E). Here she appears to be pointing in conjunction with the deictic word *là* and matching a kinesic version of this word to its pronunciation, much as she matched a kinesic expression of "little" with the word *piccole* at the end of her first phrase.

Figure 7R.1 gives an idea of what these hand movements look like. Figure 7R.2 shows the exact way in which these movements are coordinated with the spoken words.

Now, if we accept these interpretations of these hand movements—that is, that they are purposefully expressive movements, the first one showing horizontalness, the second expressing the concept of little, the third showing two largish objects, and the fourth showing a plurality of delicate, upright things— we can see that, when taken in conjunction with the words uttered, the movements provide information about the spatial disposition, arrangement, and visual appearance of the objects in the aquarium well beyond anything that could be gathered from the words alone. They are an integral part of Giulia's description. The features suggested by the hand movements could equally well have been suggested by some additional words. She could have said, for example, "Ei ci sono le pietre piccole disposte orizzontalmente sul fondo dell' acquario, poi sopra ci sono due pietre grandi, una accanto all'altra, e ci sono l'erba [le alghe] là, che crescono in modo verticale [Ei! There are (some) little stones arranged horizontally at the bottom of the aquarium, then there are two big stones above, side by side, and there is (some) grass [algae] growing upward]." But she didn't. She used hand movements of a certain sort to depict some of these aspects instead.

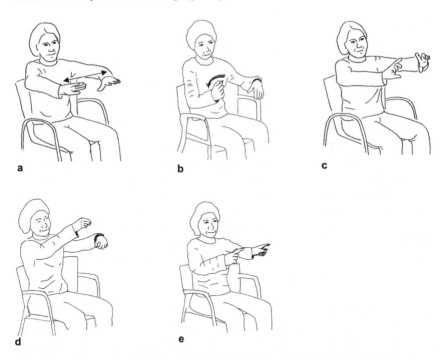

Figure 7R.1. Drawings of Giulia taken from the video-recording Ao-Portici to illustrate the hand movements described in the text. (a) The horizontal movement that coincides with "ci sono le pietre" [there are the stones]; (b) the thumb-index finger hand pose that expresses "little" that is performed as the speaker says "piccole" [little]; (c) the hand positions maintained as she says "ci sono due pietre grandi" [there are two big stones]; (d) the alternating up-down movements of the hands the speaker makes as she says "ci sono l'erba" [there is the grass]; (e) the extended index-finger hand pose (pointing) that coincides with "là" [there].

Giulia, in the turn space she is given, is to convey some idea of how her aquarium is organized, and this she does by using words to name certain objects and hand movements to say something additional about how these objects are arranged and what they look like. These hand movements are schematic devices referring to concepts like horizontalness, solid objects in space, and delicate, vertical stems. Thus, her two-handed horizontal action is a conventionalized schematic that stands in relation to the concept 'horizontal' in much the same way that the word itself does. The hand positions in the action done in relation to "due pietre" [two stones] is a widely used device to suggest a solid object, and its dynamic character here is a common kind of kinesic expression used to convey the idea of something firm in its position in space. In other words, these hand movements are kinesic schematics, constructed according to certain widely shared practices that refer to conceptual categories of shape, spatial position, and size—here I draw in part upon Cogill-Koetz's

G: Ho un acquario che ci sono sei pesci e poi…

M: E com'è fatto quest'acquario?

G: Ei ci sono le pietre piccole/ (..0.66..) poi ci sono due pietre grandi/ e ci sono l'erba là/

~~~~~~*****|***/-.-.-.-.-.-|~~~~~~~~~~~~~~~********/~~~~~********|***

   [1]   [2]   [3]   [4]   [5]

Figure 7R.2. Transcript of the first part of the aquarium from Ao-Portici showing the placement of the hand movements described in relation to speech. [1] horizontal two-handed movement; [2] the gesture coincident with *piccole* "little"; [3] two hands held forward posed as if grasping objects; [4] alternating up-down movements of the two hands; [5] the two hands held forward with index fingers extended. ~~~ preparation of the movement; *** stroke (phase of the movement which has a well defined form and which attracts a semantic interpretation); -.-.- partial recovery (hand or hands relax and move toward a rest position). For a more detailed discussion of the analysis of gesture phrases see Kendon (2004), chapter 7.

(2000) discussion of classifiers in sign languages, which develops the notion of schematic representation in the kinesic medium. To this extent they are quite like words, and, like words, they can be employed in the production of utterances. As for the movements performed as she says "piccole" [little] or "là" [there], these are not only coordinated with the pronunciation of these words but also are semantically equivalent to them and, in form, fully conventional. The gesture she makes when she says "piccole" is a conventionalized form widely used by Neapolitans in certain contexts to refer to something that is small, or to small quantities, as with words such as *piccolo* 'little,' *poco* 'a little,' and *un po'* 'a little' (see de Jorio 2000, 329–330). When she says "là" [there], as already noted, she extends her index fingers forward, as if pointing, an action that is semantically coordinate with saying "there."

A further point may now be noted. The movements associated with the words *piccole* 'little' and *là* 'there,' as I have just noted, seem to be kinesic equivalents of those specific words. Here these movements seem to have the status of individual lexical items.[4] On the other hand, the horizontal hand movement done with "ci sono le pietre" [there are the stones], the extended-arm-hand in a grasping pose done with "ci sono due pietre grandi" [there are two big stones] and the alternating upward hand movements done at the same time as "ci sono l'erba" [there is the grass] extend over several words; furthermore, they do not fit semantically with any words in the verbal component. Here their meaning adds to those expressed in the words with which they are associated. Yet, as I have suggested, these movements are kinesic schematics and refer to conceptual categories, very much like spoken words do. We can see them, then, as entering into the utterance construction as lexical items (working as adjectives or adverbs), yet, because they are kinesic forms, they can be done (as they are here) simultaneously with speaking and can, accordingly, add further semantic expression to the words. These movements do not have to alternate with words, so they do not enter into the organization of the talk sequentially,[5] but this does not seem to be a good reason to exclude them as lexical elements in the utterance. Rather, Giulia's sentences are being constructed in more than one dimension at the same time. She shows us how a speaker can engage in what have been termed simultaneous linguistic constructions.

Bencie Woll (2007) has drawn attention to the debate among philosophers of language in the eighteenth and nineteenth centuries about the extent to which linguistic expressions must be constrained to temporal linearity. It was often observed that, although the meaning of a sentence could be present all at once in a person's mind, in expressing it, the person would be constrained to conform the meaning unit, which was not exclusively linear, to the format demanded of verbal expression, which is exclusively linear. However, if we admit the possibility of using spatiovisual modes of expression as well, we can see that there may be a solution to this problem for users of spoken languages. In fact, as the example of Giulia suggests, this is commonly resorted to by speakers who, furthermore, may have at their disposal repertoires of kinesic devices that they can organize as they like in relation to the words that they are also using.

Woll wrote her discussion as a contribution to a collection of papers on the phenomenon of simultaneity in signed languages. This collection (Vermeerbergen, Leeson, and Crasborn 2007) contains many articles describing the ways in which, in signed discourse, various linguistic expressions can be performed simultaneously. This is possible because, in signing, one can make use of articulators that are spatially distributed and because one is not confined to movements inside the mouth. This suggests to Woll that we might need a three- (rather than two-) dimensional method of drawing syntactic trees.

Woll (2007, 340) describes the contrast that is often drawn between spoken language and sign language: "[T]here is general agreement that at all levels, simultaneity characterizes signed languages and linearity characterizes spoken languages, and that this is related to modality." She continues: "[In Saussure's] view, syntax exists to convert simultaneous representations to the linear ones demanded by the output system. With just one set of articulators, spoken languages have linearity; with multiple articulators (head, hands, face, etc.) signed languages have simultaneity." However, if we agree that the kinds of constructions that are illustrated in the Giulia example are commonplace among utterance producers who are using speech (and it is very easy to multiply examples to show that this is so, as in Kendon 2004), then we might come to see that spoken language, when viewed in the multimodal instantiations that speakers often provide us with in conversation, can also have simultaneity.

As the passages just quoted suggest, language is commonly viewed as mono-modalic. Such a view overlooks, however, the kind of phenomenon I have illustrated with Giulia's discourse: that when speech is used in utterance construction, this is not the only modality employed. One can, of course, dismiss Giulia's hand movements as belonging, at best, to something called paralanguage, which, from the point of view of rigorous linguistic analysis, can safely be ignored. However, when it comes to discourse in sign language, simultaneity in construction, as well as the use of space, classifiers, and other forms suspiciously similar in character to speakers' gestures, cannot be ignored. If they were (as, indeed, students of sign languages soon discovered—because for a time they did try to ignore them), the way sign languages work would be completely misunderstood. Is it possible that, by overlooking these aspects of the utterances that users of speech make, we are also in danger of misunderstanding how so-called spoken language works—how it works, that is, when it is being used by speakers in ordinary occasions of everyday talk?

Of course, when utterance producers use speech as part of what they do, they make use of words—and words can be written down. This allows us, with great ease, to carry away with us much of what was in those utterances, and it may very well be that, because of the enormous utility of writing, in fully literate cultures such as our own, we strive in our utterance productions to put as much as possible into verbal form so that it approximates what can be written down. We certainly tend to do this in any situation where what we are saying is deemed to be important, noteworthy, a contribution to a debate, and so forth. Writing has a profound and pervasive influence. It establishes a way in which language can be looked upon as an object, separated from the individual actions by which it was produced. It sets up standards for the use of words to which we are pressured to conform. It has contributed greatly to the monomodalic view of language that I have referred to. Writing, in short, has had extremely important consequences for how we use language and has ensured that so-called speaking is primarily to be thought of as a verbal form of action (Linell 2005). If, however, we were able to free ourselves of the framework in terms of which we approach language which writing has provided for us, we might be able to look in a less prejudiced way at occasions of utterance production in living conversations and see, as in the case of Giulia, how often kinesic (and other) devices are employed. Rather than view them as add-ons, useful to study, perhaps, for the light they might throw on inner cognitive processes but not worth studying for their own sake, we might come to see how they can be used as partners in the task of utterance construction and be led, in consequence, to develop a more comprehensive, even three-dimensional, account of how utterances may be structured.

It should be pointed out that the way in which kinesic action functions in Giulia's utterance is only one of the many ways speakers may use such actions. In the example, it was shown how the hands may be employed as part of a description of something, and I suggest that, in this role, they are elements in the construction of the propositional content of an utterance. However, the hands (and other parts of the body, especially the head and the face) are also employed in many other ways. For example, certain kinesic expressions indicate the type of speech act the speaker is engaging in (such as asking a question), give emphasis, mark topic in contrast to comment, offer what is being said to one's conversation partner, and the like.[6] Gestures also play a role in giving expression to a speaker's stance in interaction and in making manifest the speaker's emotions, attitudes, or commitment to what the speaker is saying, and they may also be employed directly in regulating social interaction, as in greetings, indicating where a guest is to sit down, or raising one's hand in requesting a turn at talk.

With regard to gestures that are integrated with speaking, studies of how far, to what extent, in what manner, and in what circumstances they may be important for recipients' comprehension of a speaker's utterances are rather few (see Kendon 1994 for a review of early studies). Gestures that are a part of a speaker's description, in the manner illustrated in the example, have been shown to make a difference to a recipient's understanding (see, for example McNeill, Cassell, and McCullough 1994; Beattie and Shovelton 1999), but no studies have been done on the differences to recipients of the use of so-called pragmatic or metadiscursive gestures just mentioned. That they can play an important role, however, is evidenced by the fact that gestures of this sort received a great deal of attention in the study of rhetoric and oratory, where they formed an important part of a very long tradition (Austin 1966 [1806]).

The use of gestures is neither automatic nor inevitable. They are shaped and adapted by the speaker according to communicative aim and circumstance and thus are as much a part of an utterance's design as are its words. Studies have shown that speakers adjust the kinds of gestures they employ according to whether they are in visual copresence with their interlocutor or not (Cohen 1977; Bavelas et al. 2002). It has been shown that speakers differ in how they use words to describe things, depending on whether they use gestures as a part of their descriptions (Melinger and Levelt 2004) and that, in describing objects, they shape their descriptive gestures differently according to their understanding of their recipient's informational needs (Gerwing and Bavelas 2004). It is clear that speakers vary in when and how they employ gestures, and also in the uses they make of them, according to communicative aim and circumstance.

Nevertheless, it seems that the coinvolvement of the hands (and other body parts) with speaking is a manifestation of a very deep relationship. Gesturing observed in speakers on the telephone, in those born blind (Iverson and Goldin-Meadow 2001), or in the case of IW, who, as a consequence of a neurological disease, could not monitor his hand actions kinesthetically (Cole et al. 1998), reinforces this view. It may even be that it is a manifestation of hand-mouth neurological synergies, which have their origin in the development of hand-mouth coordination in feeding, which first arose as part of an adaptation to life in an arboreal environment (Gentilucci and Corballis 2006).

Such a deep relationship, however, should not be taken to imply that one system simply is slavishly driven by the other, nor should it be taken to mean (as some have supposed) that these movements are not done for communication but for the private benefit of the speaker.[7] It means, rather, that common control systems have developed so that hand actions and mouth actions are governed together as coordinated components of the actions of the creature as it adapts what it does to the immediate and changing circumstances in which it is always immersed, as it seeks to achieve its aims. Whether these aims be those of nutrition, modification and manipulation of objects in the environment, the physical management of conspecifics, as in grooming or mating, fighting or caring for one's young, or communicative interaction, the creature's action systems work in concert. The involvement of the hands in speaking is to be understood from this point of view. In the contexts of social interaction, like the use of the voice, these movements are resources to be drawn upon and shaped by their use in the communicative process.

LANGUAGE ORIGINS AGAIN

I am suggesting that although language can approach monomodality, as it almost does when encountered in its written form,[8] this is only one version of language, and it should be understood as a very late specialization. Yet, perhaps mainly due to the influence and prestige of writing, this has come to dominate the way we think about language. Consequently, when we think about a language in another modality such as signed language, we think about this in the same way. It, too, must be pure and cleanly structured only in sign, just as spoken languages must be pure and cleanly structured only in speech—which almost always means that we tend to think of them as being whatever it is that can be written down. Then, taking this monomodalic notion of language, we project it backward onto our ancestors and wonder how they came to have such a system, as if it had to come into place at that ancient time. Then it is noticed (as it has been, at least since the seventeenth century) that language in the kinesic modality is less easily separable from forms of expression that do not seem to deserve the label *language*—continuities with pantomime and other forms of bodily expression are too obvious to be overlooked—and this means that sign languages suggest themselves as more easily understandable as something that can emerge from nonlinguistic kinds of expression. Hence the attraction of the idea that a language in the kinesic modality might have been easier to create and so must have come first in the language origins process.

As I suggested earlier, however, this gives rise to the either/or dilemma: Was language first manifested in sign (or gesture), or was it first manifested in speech? And as I have also suggested, if we get locked into this dilemma, we are at a loss to explain, on the one hand, why languages today are all spoken or, on the other hand, why speakers make any use of gesture at all. However, a look at how participants construct utterances when they are in the thick of copresent interaction, far away as they would then be from any writerly ambitions or pressures, shows that their speaking is far from monomodalic. They can often be observed to make free use of a wide range of expressive forms, including semantically significant hand movements, all of which enter into the construction of the utterance as partners in the process. Giulia's gestures could be stripped away from her utterance, but it would be at the cost of losing what she was trying to say.

I suggest that this kind of multimodal orchestration is closer to what would have been observed at the beginning, when actions of any sort first began being used symbolically, when they could be used to have reference and to convey propositional information. In those distant times, when humans (if that is what they were) first began using their communicative actions in this way, then, as now, they would have mobilized whatever might be useful in the circumstances. As the use of communication action ensembles with symbolic or referential significance became widespread, and these were, as they must always have been, components in exchanges, and as the capacity for the communication of shared meaning developed, shared systems of symbolic actions would have come about. I suggest that these would have been in various modalities, once again with an emphasis now on one, now on another, depending upon circumstance and convenience. Gradually (or perhaps not so gradually, we cannot be sure), specialization in communicative uses would have come into play, and this would probably have encouraged a tendency toward a separation of modalities. However, as modern living speakers in conversational settings attest, this separation of modalities is never complete. It has certainly been accentuated since the introduction of technologies such as writing, but this is something that began to happen many millennia after referential communication became possible. The specializations it produced, the narrow concepts of language it gave rise to, however, should not be projected backward into this distant past. To do so only creates a dilemma that cannot be resolved.

Notes

1. These terms have long been used interchangeably, and many writers use them like this today. Many who specialize in the study of signed languages, however, try to

maintain a sharp distinction between "gesture" and "sign," although, as some in the field admit, it may be quite difficult to do this in many cases (see, for example, Okrent 2002). In my view, it would be better to avoid the use of either term and instead develop a comparative semiotic treatment of the different ways in which producers of utterances, both speakers and signers, use visible bodily actions in their utterances. See Kendon (2008) for a discussion.

2. The idea that gesture (or sign) is a more natural form of expression than speaking dates at least from Quintilian, the Spanish Roman who wrote a great treatise on rhetoric in the first century AD.

3. I have solicited interpretations of the hand movements in this extract from students and others, showing it to them without sound in order to see to what extent these gestures, when seen by themselves, receive consistent interpretations. Recently, in collaboration with Mandana Seyfeddinipur of Stanford University, I have started doing this in a more formal and systematic way. See also Kendon (1978) and chapter 2 in Kendon (2004).

4. Among Neapolitans there are many gestures of this type. Elsewhere (Kendon 2004, ch. 10) I have referred to them as "narrow gloss" gestures. They may coincide, as we see here, with the pronunciation of a word that fits them closely in meaning, or they may be used simultaneously with words with different meanings, thereby working, in these cases, as components in simultaneous constructions. Because of the widely held idea (in Anglo-American gesture studies, at least) that gestures, to be worthy of study, must be spur-of-the moment creations, gestures that are notably stable in form and meaning (so-called emblems) have been very little studied. This is unfortunate, for they are of considerable interest, showing, as they do, features quite similar to what are known as frozen signs in sign languages. See Sherzer (1991), Brookes (2005), and Seyfeddinipur (2004) for exemplary studies.

5. Gestures can alternate with spoken words in sentences, of course. For examples see Kendon (2004, 183–184) and Slama-Cazacu (1976), who referred to this as "mixed syntax."

6. Bavelas et al. (1992), Müller (2004), Seyfeddinipur (2004), and Kendon (1995, 2004, 225–283) provide accounts of what have been variously referred to as interactive, metadiscursive or pragmatic gestures, or gestures with performative, parsing, and modal functions.

7. Such a view has been expressed or implied by Krauss and colleagues (e.g., Krauss, Chen, and Gottman 2000), by Kita (2000), and by Goldin-Meadow (2003), among others. Although the formulations and expressions that gestures make possible have consequences for a speaker's verbal formulations, as the work of these writers suggests, this cannot account in general for why we gesture, as some appear to suppose.

8. Even written texts are not monomodalic. We frequently encounter nonalphabetic forms, visual devices of various kinds, diagrams, and pictures, to say nothing of typographical conventions, punctuation marks, and so on—all of which may be essential to the construction of such texts as comprehensible utterances even if they are not deemed to deserve inclusion in any kind of linguistic analysis.

Bibliography

Arbib, Michael. 2005. From Monkey-like Action to Human Language: An Evolutionary Framework for Neurolinguistics. *Behavioral and Brain Sciences* 28: 105–167.

Armstrong, David F., and Sherman E. Wilcox. 2007. *The Gestural Origin of Language*. New York: Oxford University Press.

Austin, Gilbert. 1966 [1806]. *Chironomia or, a Treatise on Rhetorical Delivery*, ed. Mary Margaret Robb and Lester Thonssen. Carbondale: Southern Illinois University Press.

Bavelas, Janet B., Nicole Chovil, Douglas A. Lawrie, and Allan Wade. 1992. Interactive Gestures. *Discourse Processes* 15(4): 469–489.

Bavelas, Janet, Christine Kenwood, Trudy Johnson, and Bruce Phillips. 2002. An Experimental Study of When and How Speakers Use Gestures to Communicate. *Gesture* 1(2): 1–17.

Beattie, Geoffrey, and Heather Shovelton. 1999. Do Iconic Hand Gestures Really Contribute Anything to the Semantic Information Conveyed by Speech? An Experimental Investigation. *Semiotica* 123(1/2): 1–30.

Bolinger, Dwight. 1946. Some Thoughts on "Yep" and "Nope." *American Speech* 21: 90–95.

Brookes, Heather. 2005. What Gestures Do: Some Communicative Functions of Quotable Gestures in Conversations among Black Urban South Africans. *Journal of Pragmatics* 37: 2044–2085.

Cogill-Koetz, Dorothea. 2000. Signed Language Classifier Predicates: Linguistic Structures or Schematic Visual Representation. *Sign Language and Linguistics* 3(2): 153–207.

Cohen, Akiba A. 1977. The Communicative Functions of Hand Illustrators. *Journal of Communications* 27(4): 54–63.

Cole, Jonathan, Shaun Gallagher, David McNeill, Susan Duncan, Nobuhiro Furuyama, and Karl E. McCullough. 1998. Gestures after Total Deafferentation of the Bodily and Spatial Senses. In *Oralité et gestualité: Communication multi-modale, interaction*, ed. Serge Santi, Isabelle Guaïtella, Christian Cavé, and Gabrielle Konopczynski, 65–69. Paris: L'Harmattan.

Corballis, Michael C. 2002. *From Hand to Mouth: The Origins of Language*. Princeton: Princeton University Press.

De Jorio, Andrea. 2000. *Gesture in Naples and Gesture in Classical Antiquity: A Translation of* La mimica degli antichi investigata nel gestire napoletano (1832), *and with an introduction and notes by Adam Kendon*. Bloomington: Indiana University Press.

Foster, Mary Le Cron. 1999. The Reconstruction of the Evolution of Human Spoken Language. In *Handbook of Human Symbolic Evolution*, ed. Andrew Lock and Charles R. Peters, 747–775. Oxford: Blackwell.

Gentilucci, Maurizio, and Michael C. Corballis. 2006. From Manual Gesture to Speech: A Gradual Transition. *Neuroscience and Biobehavioral Reviews* 30: 949–960.

Gerwing, Jennifer, and Janet Bavelas. 2004. Linguistic Influences on Gesture's Form. *Gesture* 4(2): 157–195.

Goldin-Meadow, Susan. 2003. *Hearing Gesture: How Our Hands Help Us Think*. Cambridge, Mass.: Harvard University Press.

Hewes, Gordon W. 1991. Primate Communication and the Gestural Origins of Language. In *Inquiry and Debate in the Human Sciences: Contributions from Current Anthropology, 1960–1990*, ed. Sydel Silverman. *Current Anthropology* 33, special suppl.: 65–84. Chicago: University of Chicago Press. [Originally published in 1973 in *Current Anthropology* 14: 5–24.]

Iverson, Jana, and Susan Goldin-Meadow. 2001. The Resilience of Gesture in Talk: Gesture in Blind Speakers and Listeners. *Developmental Science* 4(4): 416–422.

Kendon, Adam. 1972. Some Relationships between Body Motion and Speech. An Analysis of an Example. In *Studies in Dyadic Communication*, ed. Aron W. Siegman and Benjamin Pope, 177–210. Elmsford, N.Y.: Pergamon.

———. 1975. Gesticulation, Speech, and the Gesture Theory of Language Origins. *Sign Language Studies* 9: 349–373.

———. 1978. Differential Perception and Attentional Frame: Two Problems for Investigation. *Semiotica* 24: 305–315.

———. 1980. Gesticulation and Speech: Two Aspects of the Process of Utterance. In *The Relationship of Verbal and Nonverbal Communication*, ed. Mary Ritchie Key, 207–227. The Hague: Mouton.

———. 1994. Do Gestures Communicate? A Review. *Research on Language and Social Interaction* 27: 175–200.

———. 1995. Gestures as Illocutionary and Discourse Structure Markers in Southern Italian Conversation. *Journal of Pragmatics* 23(3): 247–279.

———. 2004. *Gesture: Visible Action as Utterance*. Cambridge: Cambridge University Press.

———. 2008. Some Reflections on "Gesture" and "Sign." *Gesture* 8(3): 348–336.

Kita, Sotaro. 2000. How Representational Gestures Help Speaking. In *Language and Gesture*, ed. David McNeill, 162–185. Cambridge: Cambridge University Press.

Krauss, Robert M., Yihsiu Chen, and Rebecca F. Gottesman. 2000. Lexical Gestures and Lexical Access: A Process Model. In *Language and Gesture*, ed. David McNeill, 261–283. Cambridge: Cambridge University Press.

Linell, Per. 2005. *The Written Language Bias in Linguistics: Its Nature, Origins, and Transformations*. New York: Routledge.

MacNeilage, Peter F. 1998. Evolution of the Mechanism of Language Output: Comparative Neurobiology of Vocal and Manual Communication. In *Approaches to the Evolution of Language*, ed. James R. Hurford, Michael Studdert-Kennedy, and Chris Knight, 222–240. Cambridge: Cambridge University Press.

———. 2008. *The Origin of Speech*. Oxford: Oxford University Press.

———, and Barbara L. Davis. 2005. The Frame/content Theory of the Evolution of Speech: A Comparison with the Gestural-origins Alternative. *Journal of Interaction Studies* 6: 173–199.

McNeill, David. 1992. *Hand and Mind*. Chicago: Chicago University Press.

———. 2005. *Gesture and Thought*. Chicago: Chicago University Press.

———, Justine Cassell, and Karl E. McCullogh. 1994. Communicative Effects of Speech-mismatched Gestures. *Research in Language and Social Interaction* 27(3): 223–237.

Melinger, Alissa, and William M. Levelt. 2004. Gesture and the Communicative Intention of the Speaker. *Gesture* 4(2): 119–141.

Müller, Cornelia. 2004. Forms and Uses of the Palm Up Open Hand: A Case of a Gesture Family? In *The Semantics and Pragmatics of Everyday Gestures: Proceedings of the Berlin Conference*, ed. Cornelia Müller and Roland Posner, 233–256. Berlin: Weidler.

Okrent, Akira. 2002. A Modality-free Notion of Gesture and How It Can Help Us with the Morpheme vs. Gesture Question in Sign Language Linguistics (or at Least Give Us Some Criteria to Work with). In *Modality and Structure in Signed and Spoken Languages*, ed. Richard P. Meier, Kearsy Cormier, and David Quinto-Pozos, 175–198. Cambridge: Cambridge University Press.

Paget, Richard A. S. 1930. *Human Speech: Some Observations, Experiments, and Conclusions as to the Nature, Origin, Purpose, and Possible Improvement of Human Speech* (AMS Reprint, 1978 ed.). New York: Harcourt, Brace.

Seyfeddinipur, Mandana. 2004. Meta-discursive Gestures from Iran: Some Uses of the "Pistol Hand." In *The Semantics and Pragmatics of Everyday Gestures: Proceedings of the Berlin Conference*, ed. Cornelia Müller and Roland Posner, 205–216. Berlin: Weidler.

Sherzer, Joel. 1991. The Brazilian Thumbs-up Gesture. *Journal of Linguistic Anthropology* 1(2): 189–187.

Slama-Cazacu, Tatania. 1976. Nonverbal Components in Message Sequence: Mixed Syntax. In *Language and Man: Anthropological Issues*, ed. William C. McCormack and Stephen A. Wurm, 217–227. The Hague: Mouton.

Stokoe, William C. 2001. *Language in Hand: Why Sign Came before Speech*. Washington, D.C.: Gallaudet University Press.

Vermeerbergen, Myriam, Lorraine Leeson, and Onno Crasborn, eds. 2007. *Simultaneity in Signed Languages: Form and Function*. Amsterdam: Benjamins.

Wallace, Alfred R. 1895. The Expressiveness of Speech or Mouth-gesture as a Factor in the Origin of Language. *Fortnightly Review* 64: 528–543.

Woll, Bencie. 2007. Perspectives on Linearity and Simultaneity. In *Simultaneity in Signed Languages*, ed. Myriam Vermeerbergen, Lorraine Leeson, and Onno Crasborn, 337–344. Amsterdam: Benjamins.

Part II

SOCIAL ISSUES/CIVIL RIGHTS

CHAPTER 8

Best Practices for Collaborating with Deaf Communities in Developing Countries

Amy Wilson and Nickson Kakiri

INTRODUCTION

Millions of people worldwide find themselves marginalized from their families and communities and discriminated against by their societies just because they live with a disability. They find that national and international law does not protect them or afford them the rights to an education, appropriate health care, employment, or many other of the civil and human rights given to other family members. Unfortunately, the majority of these people with disabilities live in poverty and struggle to survive from day to day. It would appear then, that assistance from foreign organizations would be desired and appreciated, but, in Deaf communities, that at times is untrue. Jack Owiti, a deaf Kenyan, writes (Owiti 2007):

> Over the last two decades there have been several (foreign) organizations coming into Kenya and establishing "great" project ideas and visions. Sadly they have not learnt from the mistakes of their forefather—Perpetuation of the Mask of Benevolence. My opinion is that these organizations have never appreciated community entry approaches, view the Deaf as objects of benevolence and not partners in development and are "copy/pasting" foreign solutions to complex local issues. Many of these organizations have fueled the continued oppression of the Deaf Kenyans, muzzled the voices of the weak and poor while "eating the ugali [cornmeal]" in their big mansions and driving huge luxurious cars in the name of "helping" Deaf Kenyans.

We aim to make this chapter both personal and professional. In that spirit, Amy will write in the first person for the first half, and then Nickson will continue for the remainder of the chapter.

AMY WILSON

I remember bringing Harlan Lane's book *The Mask of Benevolence* as light reading for my train trip through Europe during a summer vacation from my high school teaching job in Illinois. To my surprise I found myself growing angry at Lane's negative portrayal of hearing experts as audists who "control the affairs of deaf children and adults" and "commonly do not know deaf people and do not want to" (Lane 1992, 37). How dare he insult me and label me with an ugly name like "audist" when I was helping deaf high school students be the best they could be. I had a BA in Deaf education, I knew sign language, and several of my former students were successful and had continued their studies at Gallaudet. I had a deaf friend. How could Lane say deaf people didn't have a disability and that I wasn't recognizing them as being a linguistic minority, which results in my oppressing them? He was just too much for me. He struck me as ludicrous, insulting, and profoundly ungrateful. I threw Lane's book out the train's window into a field of lavender and proceeded to forget about him.

Up to that point in my life, I had traveled in many developing countries and had often seen deaf people living in poverty. I learned that 80 percent of the world's deaf people live in developing countries (World Federation of the Deaf 2007). I felt I could make more of an impact in the world if I worked overseas rather than in the United States, so I volunteered to train teachers of deaf students for four years in northeast Brazil with the Mennonite Central Committee—an American faith-based organization. I studied Portuguese and Brazilian Sign Language (for which I use the name Libras following the practice of the deaf community in Recife; an alternative is the abbreviation LSB, as in Quadros 1999) simultaneously. I lived in a very poor Brazilian city that was also home to about twenty-five deaf people, mostly children who hadn't been exposed to much Libras, so I traveled an hour to the state capital of Recife to study Libras with two Deaf teachers. My Portuguese classes didn't meet consistently for two months, so I concentrated on Libras rather than Portuguese. To me, signing Libras differed from American Sign Language as it felt more graceful and fluid, and I picked it up quickly.

I could hardly communicate with hearing neighbors since my Portuguese was limited to "I like it" and "How much does it cost?" and even when they told me how much it cost, I couldn't understand them. I felt isolated and lonely, although my neighbors were lovely to me. For example, electricity and water were infrequent in my neighborhood, and my kind neighbors would inform me when they would be turned on so I could wash clothes, recharge batteries, or fill clay pots with water. Neighbors often brought me luscious fruits. I asked where they bought them, wanting to buy some on my own, but got lost in the Portuguese as they explained the directions. At a community meeting discussing the spreading of malaria, I mimed, drew, and explained as best I could that the open sewers and open clay pots were breeding grounds for mosquitoes, which spread diseases, and that they should wear shoes and drain or cover their pots. Everyone laughed at my "funny acting," drawings, and mangled Portuguese. Two days later barefoot neighbors poured bleach in my sewer and sprayed chemicals on my bushes. They meant well, but this wasn't what I wanted, and they were confused when I asked them to stop. My self-esteem dropped, and depression rose in correlation with my inability to communicate who I was, share my ideas and joys, or ask questions. I wondered, "Is this what deaf people experience being around hearing people who don't sign?" Consequently, I was thrilled when I traveled to Recife to see my Deaf friends. I could communicate easily with them, tell them about my neighborhood adventures, and ask them to explain Brazilian culture to me.

As my Portuguese improved, I understood my deaf friends' families referring to them as "the mute" or the "deaf-mute." Most parents had low expectations for their deaf children and didn't advocate for them to be educated. Many of my deaf friends had left school before the fourth grade because they were failing in the oral approach of education. Most were unemployed and lived with parents who usually couldn't communicate with them, although they cared for and loved them very much.

My neighbor loved her deaf son but believed he was deafened in utero by a jealous woman who gave her the "evil eye." Later I learned that the way various cultures perceive others with a disability or a difference depends on how they assign the disability or the difference to one of three major categories of social beliefs: causality, valued and devalued attributes, and anticipated role (Groce, Chamie, and Me 2000). The way in which the difference is explained in each of the three categories predicts whether the difference will be thought of as a disability and how well an individual will fare in a particular community.

Causality: Religious beliefs and folk medicine often lead to accounts of the cause of a difference. The mother mentioned earlier sensed that she had been cursed by an "evil eye" while pregnant, so she felt her deaf son was worth less than hearing children and thus had a disability. A society's belief concerning the origin of a child's disability can bring honor to one home and shame to another.

Value: Specific physical or intellectual attributes may be valued or devalued depending upon the society in which a child with a disability is born. Consequently, while some children with disabilities are embraced and loved by their families, others are abandoned.

Anticipated role: The roles individuals with disabilities are expected to play as adults in a community determine how they are accepted into their society. Will the eldest blind Japanese son be able to carry on the family business and the family name? Will an Indian daughter with diabetes bring in a substantial dowry for her parents? If they can't fulfill these roles, they may be looked upon as having a disability. If they can fulfill the roles, the difference may not disable the child at all.

Because social beliefs permeate one's culture, people with a difference can begin to believe what they hear and see; I met many brilliant deaf people who had little faith in themselves. I realized, too, that deaf people's inability to communicate easily in a hearing world kept them from learning in regular schools, from advocating for their rights, and from working in a world that denigrated their natural language. I saw how negative social beliefs led to discriminatory practices, which resulted in deaf people being uneducated, thus unemployed, hence consigning them to live in poverty. I finally understood Lane's describing the Deaf community as a language minority and not as one with a disability: It was their environment that disabled them.

Most of my deaf women friends didn't attend school and had questions about marriage, relationships, their bodies, pregnancy, and AIDS. Five women decided to form a monthly women's group, where they selected a hot topic; I researched it and then returned to share what I had learned with them. During the month the women made posters and planned activities to teach fifteen to twenty deaf women, who would then, in turn, return home and teach other deaf women. One Sunday, a hearing American visited the group. She had worked with the Deaf community for fourteen years and paid for the use of the room. I noticed her signing wasn't the fluent Libras but was choppy and difficult to read. The group was welcoming, but more deferential than friendly.

That Sunday the women discussed their bodily rights: to choose how to dress and style their hair; when and with whom to have sex, and the kind of contraceptive to use. The visitor was shocked and threatened to stop supporting them if they discussed topics related to sex. They were to talk about women's topics such as cooking or child rearing. Since these weren't issues the women were interested in discussing, the women's group slowly faded away.

This same American woman donated bus fare to members of the Sign Language Commission so they could meet in Recife to coin signs for new words, standardize signs, and draw a sign language dictionary. In my small town, a CODA interpreted in the fifth-grade classroom but often fingerspelled, as she didn't know the signs for technical words like *formula* or *photosynthesis*. Some of the students traveled with me to Recife and met with the commission to discuss signs. It was a great exchange of learning as the students taught the deaf adults new concepts, and the deaf adults taught the students new signs. Once they asked me the ASL sign for a word, and I showed them. The commission liked the ASL sign and voted to adopt it as their new sign. I was horrified, realizing I had the power to change a people's language! Subsequently, they understood and agreed they needed to develop their own language.

During a Friday night visit, the American woman noted the commission had strayed from the work she had requested—to coin biblical signs. In Signed

English she had taught them all of the Bible signs she knew, and she insisted they continue coining new name signs of biblical characters in Libras. People stopped showing up for the Sign Language Commission meetings because of lack of interest. This put a halt to the commission's continued coining of signs, work on their sign language dictionary, and the interchange between my students and the Recife Deaf adults since no one on the commission could afford the bus fare to continue to create the list of signs they wanted to use rather than the Bible words the American desired. I wondered whether this woman was changing the course of Libras in the Recife Deaf community.

The Deaf people grew angry with the American's so-called help. I could empathize a bit through my own experiences with my neighbors because their help angered me at times. I appreciated their assistance but unwillingly became dependent upon them as they held the power (via their facility with Portuguese) to know when I could bathe or turn on lights. I wanted to be able to gather this information myself. I didn't want to breathe the poison they sprayed around my house. I didn't always like the fruits my neighbors gave me, and sometimes they gave me so many they rotted.

One day, when thinking about the American woman, I realized: I've met Lane's audist here in Brazil! She didn't sign Libras—she signed Portuguese. She didn't understand Deaf culture as she never spent time in the community but rather entered and attempted to improve it according to her outsider's ideas. If she had respected the Deaf community and worked *with* its members rather than *for* them, she might have effected positive, lasting changes. Instead, many Deaf adults were dependent upon the bus fare, the food, and the small loans she parceled out.

After two years I returned to Illinois for two months and gave a presentation on my experiences in Brazil at the Illinois high school where I had taught science for twelve years. The deaf students were fascinated with my stories and also complimented me on how my ASL had improved. In some classes I was a bit uneasy as I observed that some teachers talked down to the students and did not allow the young adults an opportunity to do much independent thinking so that they could express ideas and preferences of their own. I read the Junior Association of the Deaf (JAD) schedule and learned that they were still doing the same spring activities I had decided they should do when I was a cosponsor for five years—a bake sale, volleyball, and a movie night. My deaf friend, who had taught with me, said she was thrilled at how I had changed, although I wasn't quite sure what she meant. It struck me how she was the only Deaf friend I had in the United States, whereas, in Brazil, most of my friends were deaf.

During an evening walk after I had dined with some of the teachers, I made a painful self-discovery. I had been (and maybe still partially was) an audist. I shamefully realized that when I had taught for those twelve years, I was as much of an audist as the American woman I had criticized in Brazil. I had been teaching mostly in Signed English and not ASL. Libras felt more fluid to me because I had learned it without basing it on Portuguese, and the Libras in turn informed and improved my ASL. In my teaching and in leading JAD, I had decided what was best for my students in the classroom, as well as in their leisure time. Furthermore, instead of empowering them to be independent young adults, I had protected them and held them back because I believed I knew what was better for them than they did. But, honestly, I didn't know. I never asked them, and I had never spent any time in American Deaf culture. While home, I read a quote from Peter Coleridge, a disability studies researcher in England, who wrote, "People who run institutions for disabled people, especially in the South, often see themselves as having a mission and living sacrificially in order to achieve it; the idea that they are oppressing disabled people would strike them as ludicrous, insulting, and profoundly ungrateful" (Coleridge 1993, 76).

I bought a new copy of Lane's book and, rather than tossing it out a window, now share it.

I don't relate this story proudly (but, in fact, remorsefully because I wonder whom I had hurt during my years of teaching) but to illustrate to you that most of the development assistance from foreign countries to Deaf communities in the developing world comes from people like me: people who have an earnest desire to improve the lives of deaf people but who have received no instruction in how to do it well. Not until I returned to the United States and studied international development, its history, theory, models of development, and best practices did I learn how I should have worked in Brazil.

Early Development Assistance Overseas

During their travels throughout the developing world, Christian missionaries from the North (and I am defining "North" here to mean specifically North America and northern European countries) discovered that some cultures and societies rejected their Deaf and disabled population and excluded them from social services. (Miles 2006, 2005). Services and schools for these children were established by missionaries who knew little about disability or deafness but wanted to educate and offer Christianity to this marginalized population. Their philanthropy removed the local government's obligation of offering services to deaf people and those with disabilities and left the responsibility to faith-based groups and NGOs; this continues to be the case today (Ingstad and Whyte 1995). For example, the Jamaican government relied on the goodness of foreign churches to support deaf children on the island. To this day, donations and volunteers from American church groups and foreign nonprofit groups financially support most of the schools for deaf children in Jamaica (Wilson 2001). A professional colleague who had just visited a deaf school in a developing country related angrily how the Ministry of Education stated it wouldn't support deaf schools because "deaf schools don't need it (funding) because foreign donors always give money and materials, so why should we fund it?" I asked my colleague how he had responded, thinking he'd refer them to the new UN Convention on the Rights of Persons with Disabilities or find a way to train the teachers how to advocate for adherence to their country's new national disability laws. He told me he plans to raise funds for the school in the United States. Actually, he acted as I did in the past, unaware of how we keep Deaf people dependent upon Northern charity and how that charity allows governments to delay their being accountable to people with disabilities. I found that the type of development assistance Northern groups bring to the developing world is often determined by how they conceptualize disability (Wilson 2001).

Models of Development Assistance

There are three models of development: medical, rehabilitative, and social. The *medical model* of development assistance conceptualizes disability as a sickness and focuses on that, with the result that it ignores people's spiritual, psychological, and sexual selves. A cure is sought (think of Jerry Lewis's muscular dystrophy telethon), and if no cure is found, the person with a disability is cared for and becomes dependent on others. In some countries parents see the cochlear implant as being a cure for their "defective" child. The medical model is still dominant in North America and northern European countries, and when we bring assistance to developing countries, we bring our beliefs and attitudes, too. Rather than looking at the social and political issues that oppress people with disabilities, society marginalizes those who are different, often without realizing it. Building institutions to care for people with disabilities or donating food and medicine may be helpful, but it doesn't empower people to lead independent lives.

The rehabilitative model maintains that the so-called defective person must be made (other people's idea of) normal. The rehabilitation professionals, who are seen as the experts, are more powerful than people with disabilities, and they expect that their patients will undergo treatment to become productive functioning persons in the scheme of the environment that exists. If a development organization followed the rehabilitative model with deaf individuals, it would focus on making them as hearing (so to speak) as possible and offer speech therapy, auditory training, or cochlear implants, or it might establish oral schools without the use of sign language. Deaf people might be given hearing aids and undergo years of speech therapy without the permission to use their native sign language. They might feel oppressed by the professionals, and the professionals might not understand why. As the medical model wishes to cure a "defect," the rehabilitative model wishes to make people with disabilities become more normal in order to fit into their environment.

The social model of disability appeared as people with disabilities protested previous models of disabilities, which focused on how to re-form or normalize so-called defective or disabled individuals in order for them to fit into society (Taylor 1999). The social model sees people with disabilities as possessing human differences while living in a society that disables them. Abberley (1987) says that disablism is a kind of social oppression, as are sexism, racism, homophobia, and ageism. Instead, the social mode has those who have a disability tell the helping professional how to become a resource that will help them reach their goals. The power structure would shift so that the Deaf community would have allies to work with: Native sign languages would be used in schools and recognized as formal languages, interpreters would be trained and available, and Deaf culture respected. The Deaf community could develop its own strategies for full participation in the mainstream of community life, which would lead to self-empowerment to create their own history. Making such a social model a reality, however, requires an immense paradigm shift, one that I would not have understood twenty years ago.

Perhaps you are already familiar with these different models of how non-disabled (or hearing people) view disability (or deaf people) and how people's perspective on disability can lead to behavior that either empowers or disempowers. If you're deaf, then you may know firsthand that hearing people who patronize deaf people will not empower them, while hearing people who trust your knowledge and skills will work with you to build upon your strengths. It is equally important to remember that people (deaf or hearing) from richer countries sometimes make the same mistakes that hearing people make about deaf people. People from developed countries sometimes assume this stance: "We know better, and we know more because we have more education or we do things in better ways." And then they, too, try to help poor people in ways that disempower, oppress, or cause dependency. But poor people already have the ability to help themselves. What they need are more tools, resources, and training to solve their own problems in their own ways. They also need supporting allies just like deaf people do—just like any marginalized group does.

NICKSON KAKIRI

I am Nickson Kakiri, and I came from Kenya to study at Gallaudet University, where I graduated with a BA in 2005. I am now working on my master's degree at the University of Nairobi. The Nippon Foundation awarded me a World Deaf Leadership Scholarship, which supports the education of deaf students from developing countries, who then return home and become contributing members of their society. My particular award included funding to support a research project on development assistance desired by Deaf Kenyans. I worked with

Amy Wilson to narrow down the many questions I had about this research topic. The award allowed us to travel to Kenya to conduct research to answer my questions. You might ask why we wanted and, in fact, needed to do this research.

You have to keep in mind my own background. While growing up in Kenya, I saw many organizations come to our country with big hearts and, I honestly believe, with the best of intentions. Yet, time and again, after an NGO left our country, the programs it had started quickly collapsed. This puzzled me. Why on earth would an NGO come and spend so much time, effort, and money developing a program that would collapse upon their departure? The desire to understand what made these programs fail motivated me to return to Kenya. I'll describe later some of the work I did when I returned, but first I'd like to talk more generally about Kenyan society with respect to deaf people and give a background of my own work there.

As of the time of writing this (spring 2008), there is much political upheaval in Kenya, where we see infighting and strife, particularly in the capital, Nairobi. The violence and misery touch our deaf communities in many ways. These communities are scattered across the country, but certainly many deaf people live right in Nairobi. Because unemployment is high in the country as a whole, deaf people in rural areas often wind up coming to the capital, hoping to find some kind of work so they can simply survive.

A recent survey of all of the people with disabilities in the country shows that about 4.6 percent of Kenyans experience some sort of disability (Kenya National Survey for Persons with Disabilities 2008). I cannot tell you exactly how many deaf people there are in the country, but out of a population of about 37 million people, I estimate that about 1.6 percent, or around 600,000, Kenyans are deaf. Exact figures are impossible to obtain because we do not keep accurate statistics in the country.

Even in peaceful times, however, deaf people in Kenya don't fare well. We are often asked some very bizarre questions with crude gestures—something deaf people are accustomed to in other countries, too. The mainstream of Nairobi dismisses us as lunatics when they see us signing just because they do not realize that sign language is bona fide language.

The Kenyan survey mentioned earlier reports that "Attitudes displayed by the people around them can be a bigger problem for PWDs (persons with disabilities) than the medical condition they must cope with: People living and interacting with PWDs tend to treat them differently in relation to their disabilities" (Kenya National Survey, 2008, x). People who are hard of hearing or deaf are sometimes even killed in Kenya. Deaf Kenyans have very little access to resources, and opportunities are severely limited. In all of Kenya we have only eight deaf people with university degrees and thirty deaf people who have been trained as teachers. Most deaf adults have at most a marginal elementary school education and currently are unemployed or underemployed.

We have, however, a strong deaf community that uses Kenyan Sign Language (KSL), although KSL does not find its way into the schools. Instead, we still see systems based on signing the spoken language—comparable to Signed English, for example. There are no note takers and no other auxiliary services for deaf children in the schools, so you can imagine the challenges for the deaf child. Add to this the fact that school supplies are generally lacking for all children, hearing and deaf, and you get a truly bleak picture of deaf children's education.

Amy and I conducted a research study to discover how deaf Kenyans could avail themselves of the services of foreign organizations that wanted to help improve the situation of deaf people. Many deaf people weren't aware of the existence of these organizations, but we were able to question them about how they could best participate in them.

We began with interviews in Nairobi simply because most deaf people live there. We also went to Mombasa, along the coast, and to Kisumu, in the rural area. These three places are where people travel to look for work, so it made it more likely that we'd find a substantial number of deaf communities.

We interviewed twenty-three deaf women and fifty-five deaf men from a variety of walks of life. Some participants were not affiliated with any organization, but many were associated with groups such as the Kenya National Association of the Deaf (KNAD), which is a national nongovernmental organization formed in 1986 by Deaf people; Global Deaf Connection, an international Deaf education, nongovernmental organization that works to increase opportunities for Deaf people in the world's poorest nations; the Muslim Deaf Self-help Organization; the Kenyan Sign Language Research Project, a countrywide initiative of the University of Nairobi aimed at documenting and spreading the use of KSL; and, of course, the World Federation of the Deaf. In the survey we asked many questions, but those that are pertinent to this chapter are the following:

1. Can you name an international organization that works with or for the Deaf community in Kenya? Tell us what you know about them.
   a. What are some of the positive things they do for the Deaf community?
   b. What additional assistance would you like to see international organizations provide the Deaf community?
2. What do you think are the barriers and challenges that have prevented Deaf people from advancing in society and from receiving appropriate assistance from organizations?
3. What would be appropriate assistance to the Deaf community?

The participants named a whopping thirty foreign organizations working with Deaf Kenyans. This at first baffled us. In Kenya there are only a few visible organizations—visible in the sense that you can see their offices and their representatives. However, in fact, the Internet lists numerous foreign organizations that are "helping" deaf Kenyans, yet their work and the results of it are invisible.

In naming the positive things these organizations do, people listed free food, clothing, Bibles, and other items. They also mentioned that NGOs had helped them to establish the KNAD. Actually, from our own observations, it was apparent that foreign NGOs and churches had given more assistance than the respondents mentioned, but the people on the ground saw only the few benefits they noted.

In response to the general question about the barriers that prevent progress, people had many observations to offer. They immediately said that the foreign organizations typically made many promises about what they would do, but then they would disappear from the country before the promises could be fulfilled. People were left waiting and very disappointed. They were under the illusion that they had established good friendships and relationships with these organizations—now they felt seduced and abandoned. They would try following up to see whether there were some way the promises could be kept, but no one ever answered their messages.

The money from those organizations was earmarked to help the Deaf community, but, instead, all sort of excuses were given to people about why the money couldn't be put to use for the intended purposes now that the organization through which the money was funneled had left. In general, money essentially disappears when the organizations disappear. The people we interviewed had no doubts that serious corruption was involved. In situations like this, some of them had appealed to other organizations, particularly those European groups that had originally given the money to improve the lifestyles of Kenyan Deaf people, to find out why the money was being withheld. Answers simply didn't come. These corruption charges may or may not be true, but these were the perceptions of the Deaf community.

Deaf people also reported that they were asked for favors—to withdraw from a position or to vote for certain leaders not accepted by the majority in order to get funds released to them. When they objected to these solicited favors, their complaints fell on the proverbial deaf ears. The government didn't seem to care. No one seemed to care.

At the outset, I outlined one challenge to the success of these organizations: Projects that did get funded often collapsed as soon as the funding organization left the country. Another is that the projects that were started typically demanded a constant flow of money. For the Deaf community, that meant constant dependency on some outside funding source rather than promoting independence and sustainable projects.

Deaf people objected to the limited input and involvement of deaf people in the planning of what to do with the assistance that the organizations were offering. No one seemed to recognize that the Deaf communities had their own culture, which needed to be respected, and that they consisted of competent people who longed for independence and empowerment. Indeed, the organizations themselves seemed to be part of the oppression Deaf people continually experienced rather than a relief from it. Even when decisions were made to allocate funds for something the Deaf community requested, often these decisions were reversed without consulting the community—it was clear that Deaf people really did not have a voice in the decisions after all.

Further, the efforts of the organizations were male dominated; women weren't included, and Deaf people objected to that. Often these men used the organization's funds for their own benefit. Sometimes these groups were actually operating within the country without the knowledge of the national government. For example, in 2007 an individual who had been running an organization in Kenya for many years was asked to show his permit, which he didn't have—he didn't even know he needed one. His organization's operations had been entirely unregulated.

When asked how to overcome the list of challenges and barriers they had identified, deaf Kenyans made many important suggestions. First and foremost is the need for these aid organizations to understand and respect Deaf people and their culture. This recommendation rings true to me. I recently moved to Mongolia, where I took a position with Voluntary Services Overseas (VSO), an international development charity with volunteers who are mostly skilled professionals. When I arrived in Mongolia, I had an experience that shook me. I went there willing and wanting to learn about Mongolian Deaf culture and, importantly, assuming that people would want me to learn Mongolian Sign Language. A late-deafened woman in her midthirties had told me that there was no sign language in Mongolia and that she preferred using ASL as it would be fine as a language to be incorporated into their lives. I objected, saying I preferred learning Mongolian Sign Language, but she kept pushing for ASL. With that in mind, I went to a Deaf church, where I met many Deaf people. This church had a Deaf minister and two hundred worshippers, and all of whom were using Mongolian Sign Language (MSL). I still don't understand why I was told MSL did not exist. Because these people already had their own sign language, who needed ASL? I realized I had to be careful not to go blundering in and forcing my ideas (based on misinformation, in fact) onto these people in Mongolia. I had to spend some time learning about the cultural norms and values.

Another suggestion our interviewees made was that Deaf people must be involved in the planning stages, management, and evaluation of all projects funded by these organizations. The projects cannot be imposed from the outside by people who don't understand the community's needs, values, and interests. Instead, the projects must originate within the community.

This recommendation strikes me as crucial. However, it is a very difficult recommendation to act upon. Consider the situation in Mongolia, for example. The Mongolian government is young, formed only in 1989. It was originally communist, and even today the president and the prime minister used to be members of the former Communist Party. Communism doesn't encourage the formation of civil or social organizations. In fact, it discourages them. As a result, Deaf people in Mongolia have no Deaf associations where they can get together and discuss their common needs. They don't even feel a need for such a thing because the overall atmosphere of the country simply doesn't engender such feelings. When I asked them about forming an association, they looked at me in wonder. Why would anyone need to do that? And, of course, it was my duty to explain the importance and the value of coming together in order to influence the government; that's the way people can establish and protect their rights, and that's the way you let the government know your needs. It's much more difficult to do this on an individual basis than as a group. The people I discussed this with found this argument very interesting. As of spring 2008 they are just now organizing meetings where they can share information about their experiences. The idea is spreading that they have a right to demand respect for their culture and that they should be able to decide for themselves what they need. But all of this takes time.

One thing we need to do is get the word out to the original funding sources that money should go directly to organizations made up of the people who are to receive the aid, not via broker organizations. For example, the U.S. Agency for International Development (USAID) gives much money to underdeveloped countries, but they parcel this money out to go-betweens who may know nothing about the issues surrounding deafness or about Deaf culture. The agents take control, imposing their ideas on the people who are to receive the aid. We need a more democratic management of the funds; in fact, we need Deaf people to manage the funds.

Our Kenyan interviewees also recommended that there be more training programs for Deaf people run by other Kenyans. When training comes from outside sources, as it does now, it often doesn't match the needs of the people of Kenya. Once Deaf Kenyans are trained, they will then figure out ways to solve their own problems and will know how to use the funds effectively. Further, they will find solutions that have a chance of thriving within the community. Therefore, when the foreigners leave, the projects will be sustainable, and the Kenyans will still benefit as the solutions will have been their own, thus being practical and self-perpetuating.

Another recommendation was that outside funders send Deaf staff to Kenya as they would more quickly understand the Deaf Kenyan situation and enter more quickly into smooth communication with the locals since they also use a sign language and are familiar with Deaf culture. Nonsigning hearing people that come from the outside are, frankly, a disaster: It takes a long time for them to make connections, to fully understand the needs of the community, and to work smoothly with the community they are supposed to serve.

A final recommendation was that all funding be transparent and that careful records be kept and opened to public scrutiny. Transparency is the only way to go. Any alternative invites corruption (or rumor that it exists even if it is not present), and the Deaf community loses out.

After we gathered and analyzed the data we collected, I traveled around Kenya sharing the results through public meetings of the eleven affiliates of the Kenya National Association of the Deaf, which a total of 438 deaf Kenyans attended. We have been careful to make the KSL versions accessible, regardless of level of education, so that Deaf people across the country can understand the results of this research. The results were also made available in Kiswahili and English. When we entered Kenya to undertake this research, we visited the Ministries of Education in each state to ask their permission to carry out the study, as well as to inform them of what we hoped to find. Therefore, we shared our results with these ministries, as well as with the Kenya Institute of Special Education, the Teachers Service Commission, the National Council for Persons with Disabilities, and the education attaché in the Kenyan embassy in Washington, D.C.

It is important to disclose this research with all of the Deaf communities in Kenya, as well as with the government; too often research results are not shared with the community, an omission that deteriorates the relationship between researchers and the community, who perceive this withholding of results as a form of exploitation. The community that is studied never learns the results.

That was not the case with our research. I am a member of the Deaf community of Kenya, and the results of this investigation belong to that group. Its members consented to be part of the study, and by consenting, they made the survey possible. It is their knowledge and wisdom that this study presents to the world. As we interviewed people, we wanted to make sure they felt free to express themselves fully, and part of that was assuring them that this was their study. The very act of sharing their information facilitated and fostered more of the feeling among them that they are part of a strong community. The process of conducting the research, in a way, helped to build community, and the results of the research continue to empower the people.

As our information spreads, we are seeing more and more action from civil society. The research results are discussed on blogs, where they are sometimes agreed with and sometimes disputed, but either way it is excellent for the people who write in to have their own ideas, comments, and suggestions for how they want to advance their people. The Deaf community has used the research to leverage funds to set up deaf youth projects and to send representatives to the Fifteenth World Congress of the World Federation of the Deaf in Madrid, Spain, in 2007.

CONCLUSION

Any kind of assistance brought to Deaf communities overseas must be conducted within a comprehensive social framework. Development assistance is not only about removing barriers at the individual level but also about removing physical and attitudinal barriers in society at large. Therefore, it is absolutely essential that professionals who work with the Deaf community either in their home countries or overseas be clear about their own motives, attitudes, knowledge, and perspectives. Wearing a mask of benevolence and working through a paternal model of development disempowers and worsens the situation of those you are hoping to assist.

For any positive change to occur in Deaf communities overseas, Deaf people must be empowered to make their own changes. Change must not be imposed upon them. The best way to improve the quality of life for deaf people is to focus on the community level and empowering its members, giving them a real voice in decisions that affect their lives. When people have some control over their lives, then their whole attitude toward themselves, their family, their community, and their future becomes more hopeful, and change becomes a reality. Local Deaf people must be involved in the planning and running of all aid programs, with the goal of empowering the people to improve their lives in ways that can be maintained even after funding ends. Foreign organizations must work directly with Deaf people in Kenya. Deaf workers must have training, so that they can work effectively in the Deaf community for their own benefit and empowerment. Perhaps most important of all, anyone who wants to help a community needs to be fluent in the language of its members and understand its culture. If you don't understand the culture, much will be misunderstood when you try to communicate. Our research demonstrates that the Deaf community knows itself best, and only those foreign organizations who respect this should be invited to work with them.

Bibliography

Abberley, Paul. 1987. The Concept of Oppression and the Development of a Social Theory of Disability. *Disability, Handicap, and Society* 2: 5–19.

Coleridge, Peter. 1993. *Disability, Liberation, and Development*. Oxford: Oxfam.

Groce, Nora, Mary Chamie, and Angela Me. 2000. International News and Views: Measuring the Quality of Life: Rethinking the World Bank's Disability Adjusted Life Years. *Disability World*, vol. 3. http://www.disabilityworld.org/June-July2000/International/DALY.html.

Ingstad, Benedicte, and Susan Whyte. 1995. Disability and Culture: An Overview. In *Disability and Culture*, ed. Susan Whyte and B. Benedicte Ingstad, 3–31. Berkeley: University of California Press.

Kenya National Survey for Persons with Disabilities: Preliminary Report. March 2008. http://www.ncapd-ke.org/UserFiles/File/KNSPWD/KNSPWD percent20Preliminary percent20Report.pdf (accessed June 2, 2008).

Lane, Harlan L. 1992. *The Mask of Benevolence: Disabling the Deaf Community*. New York: Knopf.

Miles, Michael. 2005. Deaf People Living and Communicating in African Histories, c. 960s–1960s. http://www.independentliving.org/docs7/miles2005a.html (accessed June 2, 2008).

———. 2006. Social Responses to Disability and Poverty in Economically Weaker Countries. Research, Trends, Critique, and Lessons Usually Not Learnt. Annotated bibliography of modern and historical material. http://www.independentliving.org/docs7/miles200603.html (accessed June 2, 2008).

Owiti, Jack. 2007. Mzee Bubu: Deaf Pride of Africa. [Internet blog]. Kenya. [cited June 3, 2008]. http://deafpride.blogspot.com/2007/09/halting-mask-of-benevolence-empowering.html.

Quadros, Ronice Müller de. 1999. Phrase Structure of Brazilian Sign Language. PhD diss., Pontificia Universidade Católica do Rio Grande do Sul.

Taylor, George. 1999. Power and Identity and Participatory Research: Using Social Action Research to Challenge Deaf and Hard of Hearing People from Minority Ethnic Communities. *Disability and Society* 14: 369–384.

Wilson, Amy T. 2001. *Development Assistance from American Organizations to Deaf Communities in the Developing World*. Gallaudet University. Dissertation Abstracts AAT 3038023.

———. 2005. The Effectiveness of International Development Assistance from American Organizations to Deaf Communities in Jamaica. *American Annals of the Deaf* 150(3) (Summer): 292–304.

World Federation of the Deaf. 2007. Deaf in Developing Countries. http://www.wfdeaf.org/pdf/fact_deafdevelop.pdf (accessed August 27, 2008).

Deaf Mobilization around the World

A Personal Perspective

Yerker Andersson

After having read "Best Practice for Collaborating with Deaf Communities in Developing Countries" by Amy Wilson and Nickson Kakiri, I have a feeling that a comparison of the old and the recent international experiences of so-called Samaritans, deaf leaders, missionaries, and past foreign aid workers, both deaf and hearing, would enrich our readers' general understanding of the issues involved. I have no intention of claiming that my own experiences are more advanced than those of other observers. Reading both old and new experiences can certainly offer a more balanced view of deaf communities in different countries. This chapter is based on my observations and reports of foreign aid activities. The reports on courses or workshops in developed and developing countries are kept in the Gallaudet archives but are not available for outsiders for protection reasons.

During the Eleventh International Games for the Deaf in Copenhagen in 1949, I was fortunate to meet several deaf leaders from various countries for the first time in my life. I became close friends with Dragoljub Vukotic, the leader of a Yugoslavian sports team, who became influential in the International Committee of Silent Sports (CISS) [in French: *Comité international des sports des sourds*] and eventually a president of the World Federation of the Deaf (WFD). We exchanged letters from 1949 until his death in 1996. Via his friendship with a deaf U.S. government administrator, Boyce Williams (in fact, the first deaf person to be employed at the federal level in rehabilitation and a founder of Professional Rehabilitation Workers with the Adult Deaf [PRWAD], which later was renamed American Deafness and Rehabilitation Association [ADARA]), Vukotic garnered grants to fund vocational training programs conducted by experts for deaf people in his country, Yugoslavia. Vittorio Ieralla, president (deaf), and Cesare Magarotto, general secretary (hearing), whom I also met, revealed that during and after World War II, the majority of deaf people in the southern part of Italy, Greece, and some parts of

Spain and Turkey never went to schools for deaf children but were, neverthe-less, able to learn sign language. The federations of deaf people in all of these countries except Turkey eventually persuaded their governments to establish and support schools for deaf youngsters. These leaders were the first after World War II to develop a worldview of deaf people. Both Ieralla and Maga-rotto were members of the *Ente Nazionale Sordomuti* [Italian Federation of the Deaf Mute], later renamed the *Ente Nazionale Sordi* [Italian Federation of the Deaf]. Ieralla later became the first president of the WFD.

Amy Wilson's observation of "many brilliant deaf people who had little faith in themselves" is not surprising. During my youth and earlier years, most deaf leaders in the world shared the same belief: Hearing was the only requirement for a successful or happy life. The deaf world (renamed the deaf community later) was regarded as an isolated social group.

When the World Federation of the Deaf was established in 1951, the leaders named earlier had for the first time expressed their concern about the diffi-culties confronting deaf people in most developing countries. However, they were unable to obtain financial support from the governments in their coun-tries. Because of their sign languages, deaf and hard-of-hearing persons have always been the last to receive attention by the governments or parliaments in virtually every country in the world. During this period, several so-called Samaritans, missionaries, and devoted teachers of deaf children were working in the colonies of Britain, France, Italy, and other countries, including the United States.

Before moving to the United States in order to enter Gallaudet College in 1955, I learned much more about deaf people and their achievements in their clubs in my native country, Sweden, and other European countries. (Addition-ally, I met many leaders of deaf clubs during my tours in seven other Euro-pean countries.) The periodicals sent by several federations of the deaf, including the National Association of the Deaf (NAD) and schools for the deaf (mostly in the United States) repeatedly published articles about the frustra-tions and achievements of deaf persons. My old friend Arthur Dimmock, a foreign news editor in the British Deaf and Dumb Association (now British Deaf Association), informed his readers about educational achievements of deaf people in developed and developing countries for more than fifty years. He called himself "deafmute" and often led groups of deaf people to visit deaf clubs and schools for deaf children in foreign countries.

During this period, most educational programs for deaf children in devel-oping countries were supported and managed by Christian missionaries from Europe and the United States. In the past, these missionaries regularly shared their experiences at international meetings on pastoral care among deaf peo-ple (see the bibliography). Most of them were more interested in the Christian protection of deaf people rather than deaf people's acquisition of human skills. Contrary to the popular belief that all schools for deaf children were oral oriented, most of these schools could, in fact, choose either the oral or the combined method, depending on governmental or parliamentary regulations in the industrialized countries. If the oral method was not required, the missionaries could either bring their acquired sign languages or adopt the native sign language of their deaf pupils. However, they usually preferred their acquired sign languages or the oral method either for the sake of convenience or because of their own inability to learn the sign language in use among the local deaf children. At that time, most non-Christian religions still were not teaching children or adults with disabilities, including deaf ones, regardless of their potential skills. During this period, teachers for deaf children had more control over their pupils' education than teachers of hearing children had over their pupils' primary and secondary schools.

With the appearance of hearing aids, the governments and business establishments in several industrialized countries began donating these devices directly to individual deaf and hard-of-hearing children in developing countries, as well as to schools for the deaf—often without understanding that batteries for hearing aids would not always be available there. Despite this change, sign languages from other countries continued to be imported in a variety of ways. For example, Swedish and Swedish-speaking Finnish teachers or missionaries had no problem adopting Swedish Sign Language at a Christian-supported school for deaf children in Eritrea (the Keren Evangelical School for the Deaf), which was supported by the Svenska kyrkan [Church of Sweden].

British Sign Language, with its two-handed alphabet, was widely used in most of the former British colonies, where it was supported by British charity societies or Christian churches. Various European sign languages and ASL were taught in non-British countries of Africa and Asia. For instance, in Japanese-occupied countries (e.g., much of Asia, particularly in the southeast, including Burma, the Dutch East Indies [now Indonesia], Korea, Malaysia, Manchuria, the Ryukyu Islands, Singapore, Taiwan, Thailand, the Philippines, and Vietnam) deaf children were trained in Japanese Sign Language. The missionaries and volunteer teachers were often not skilled in the sign languages of the developing countries. However, some of them did, in fact, attempt methods other than simply imposing the sign language of their own country, such as adopting what one might call natural sign languages, adding signs from their own country's sign language to the vocabulary of the local sign language, or allowing deaf children to retain their local sign language but requiring them to use American Sign Language (ASL) in school. This happened mostly in the western part of Africa and several countries in Asia.

The Rev. Andrew J. Foster, a black deaf graduate of Gallaudet University, established multiple schools for deaf children in Nigeria, Ghana, and Cameroon, probably more schools, in fact, than other Christian missionaries. His emphasis on ASL and Christianity in the education of deaf children in western Africa might now be considered questionable, but today deaf adults in this area still prefer ASL over the few existing tribal sign languages. During my conversation with a deaf leader from Ghana, I realized that the Ghanaian and American uses of ASL were similar, but their styles of speed, action, and repetition were not. Indeed, in later life, Reverend Foster's own ASL tended to be slow and repeating—probably influenced by the African cultural style. Deaf people in countries in eastern Africa, including Rwanda, have tended to keep their own tribal sign languages; still, those who desire further education utilize more ASL signs.

Unlike Reverend Foster, most of the Christian missionaries in Africa, Asia, and South America preferred to educate deaf children side by side with hearing children, apparently hoping that the hearing youngsters would eventually take care of the deaf ones. This was true of schools for deaf children in most European countries, too.

Even today most of the schools for deaf students in all the parts of the world vary widely in their educational requirements and in whether they allow the use of sign languages and, if so, which sign languages (local, national, foreign). The history of general education in most countries has repeatedly confirmed that academic rigor was a more important goal of schools with only hearing children in comparison to those with both deaf and hearing children. Until recently, most Christian missionaries in developing countries also had to focus on the hearing skills of deaf children of Christian parents in their schools. These Christian institutions also accepted children of non-Christian parents, provided that the youngsters adopted the Christian faith. During my school years in Sweden, Lutheran priests for deaf children went even further, persuading the non-Christian parents to allow their deaf children to join the Christian faith even while their hearing children did not. The priests argued that the deaf children would feel more isolated if they remained in their hearing parents' non-Christian faith. However, some of the deaf children later returned to their parents' religion after graduation.

Since the WFD was dominated by predominantly Christian countries in Europe during its first years, its spiritual committee had a close relationship with the WFD for many years. As national organizations of deaf people in more and more non-Christian-dominated countries joined the WFD, the spiritual committee was weakened (as it was unable to include non-Christian religious leaders). The committee was officially dissolved in 1991.

When the Peace Corps was established in 1961, the U.S. Agency for International Development (USAID) began to hire deaf and hearing Americans both to train teachers and to be teachers at deaf schools in developing countries without regard to their sign language skills. Several of the American teachers (some with and some without sign language skills) caused confusion among the deaf children by using a hodgepodge of languages and teaching methods in a school in the Philippines. In response to my complaints on behalf of the WFD, the USAID stated that its policy was to consult only Disabled Peoples International, and not national disability organizations in the United States; for this reason USAID had failed to evaluate the ASL skills of the American personnel it sent to these deaf schools. When the new regulations of the Americans with Disabilities Act of 1990 acknowledged for the first time the importance of American Sign Language in communication with deaf people, USAID finally required ASL as a skill for teacher trainers. However, whether the teachers sent by USAID were actually fluent in ASL or other sign languages used by the deaf children or adults in the various countries USAID served is still an open question. Even today USAID persists in appointing applicants from universities rather than from local or national organizations of deaf people in the United States.

Unlike USAID, foreign aid agencies in the Nordic governments have a separate council of representatives from their national disability organizations. Each of these disability organizations is instructed to choose two foreign aid workers (either with a disability or with no recognized disability) for any assignments in Africa, Asia, or South America. Depending on their skills, the deaf foreign aid workers can stay for a shorter or longer period of time in the chosen developing countries.

The first Swedish deaf foreign aid workers (one of whom came as a visitor with his wife, who was a linguist interested in deaf matters in Kenya) discovered that an American-trained deaf government official, born in Kenya, tried to instruct the existing schools for deaf children to adopt a variety of ASL instead of the tribal sign languages because the official believed that the use of ASL would speed up the deaf children's primary education. In response to a plea by the Swedish foreign aid workers, a Kenyan professor in linguistics, Okoth Okombo of the University of Nairobi, agreed to persuade the Kenyan government to retain the tribal sign languages of the deaf children and to allow the deaf children and adults to develop their tribal languages into a national language, comparable to the way national languages have evolved, spoken or signed, in many other countries.

In the chapter I am responding to, Nickson Kakiri confirms that Kenyan Sign Language (KSL) is now widely used in Kenya even though it has not found "its way into the schools." This should not come as a surprise; the failure to accept sign languages is still common in most countries. The WFD has reported that only 44 of about 120 countries worldwide have officially recognized the validity of sign languages for use in schools and other official matters. Interestingly enough, some of the states in the United States have been allowed to establish charter schools where both ASL and spoken language are equally required in classes. This is reminiscent of the social model of development mentioned in Amy Wilson's part of the chapter.

According to Swedish deaf leader Lars-Åke Wikström, the Swedish foreign aid agency Sida and its disability council were surprised when the deaf trainers were able to communicate with both literate and illiterate deaf persons in developing countries within only a few months. This kind of communication was based on a blend of easily understandable Swedish and foreign signs, and its success was probably due to the fact that the skill to observe human hand and body movements is more practiced and acute among deaf people than among hearing people. In marked contrast, the constant need for translators was time consuming for meetings between Swedish teacher-trainers and representatives of other disability organizations, which depend on hearing rather than visual skills for communication.

Again unlike USAID and the Peace Corps, Nordic disability organizations were allowed to recruit qualified persons even from foreign countries for their projects in Africa, Asia, and South America. For example, the Finnish Association of the Deaf [Kuurojen Liitto Ry] hired a deaf female leader of Tanzania to conduct a Finnish-supported project in Mozambique. The Finnish Association of the Deaf then appointed two Tanzanian evaluators, trained in general, as well as me, to evaluate its project in Tanzania. Later I was instructed to meet in Finland with those people involved in the project and discuss it further. The Danish Deaf Federation [Danske Døves Landsforbund] requested that the WFD board appoint me, with an audiologist chosen by the Danish foreign agency, Danida, to evaluate the Danish NGO umbrella for people with disabilities' [Danske Handicaporganisationer] project involving deaf people in Uganda. At a special meeting, deaf leaders from various places in Uganda, in addition to the board members of the National Association of the Deaf in Uganda, shared their experiences with the audiologist and me. The Swedish national federation of the deaf [Sveriges Dövas Riksförbund] and the Finnish Association of the Deaf agreed to hire an Australian deaf leader to manage projects in developing European countries and to conduct a workshop for deaf leaders from industrialized and developing countries on the implementation of the UN Convention on the Rights of Persons with Disabilities. All of these efforts were initiated by only Finland, Sweden, and Denmark. Such involvement of foreign aid experts in national foreign agencies outside the Nordic area remains rare.

At a conference for deaf delegates from eastern Africa and the Nordic countries, I had a chance to observe how the people from these different countries communicated with each other. Most of the delegates from the eastern part of Africa retained their tribal sign languages. Nevertheless, they still communicated with each other very well—just as we have found in European meetings of people with different sign languages. Like experienced deaf persons in industrialized countries, the people from these African countries tried different signs if their first ones were unclear instead of repeating a single sign in order to make their expressions easier to understand. If foreigners, for example, failed to understand the ASL sign for "money," a combination of signs, such as taking up a wallet, opening it, and showing money, was figured out more quickly than the same sign repeated.

National deaf social and sports organizations in the Nordic countries have maintained a working level of cooperation for more than fifty years, like other national organizations and governments and their agencies—indeed a long list of Nordic councils! Belgium, the Netherlands, and Luxembourg tried to establish a similar cooperative organization, known as Benelux, but its activities are very limited as of this point. For many years the European Union of the Deaf has maintained cooperation among the countries, thanks to financial support by the European Union. The seven regional secretariats of the WFD (South America; Mexico, Central America, and the Caribbean; Asia and the Pacific; eastern and southern Africa; Eastern Europe and Middle Asia; western and central Africa; the Arab region) receive limited financial support from the most successful national federation of the deaf in their region.

In the past, the national federations of deaf people in communist areas provided only travel support to deaf leaders in selected developing countries for attending the quadrennial World Congress of the WFD. The Nordic federations of the deaf and the national federations in a few industrialized countries have done the same since 1987. The National Association of the Deaf of the United States, because of its limited financial support, has never provided travel support to its biennial meetings for deaf leaders (except for its invited presenters) in developing countries. However, Gallaudet University has been able to invite deaf leaders and artists in developing countries for its now well-known celebrations of the Deaf way of life, Deaf Way I (in 1989, with proceedings in Erting et al. 1994) and Deaf Way II (in 2002, with proceedings in Goodstein 2002).

Furthermore, most of the federations of the deaf in developed countries, as well as universities and religious charities there, have had only a limited understanding of the cultures, languages, political structures, and natural environments of the developing countries. The result is that not nearly enough has been done to address the needs of deaf communities in these areas. Most of the national federations of the deaf in Europe were not established until cities first founded local clubs or associations, either with or without support from hearing persons. Eventually, the local clubs or associations cooperated to develop a nationwide organization, some managed by both deaf and hearing persons and others by exclusively deaf persons. Almost all the national organizations of deaf people in the capital cities of the former British colonies were established either in protest against or in cooperation with the existing British societies for deaf persons. Unlike these organizations, the old South African National Council for the Deaf, established in 1929, emerged as a new organization, now known as DEAFSA (Deaf Federation of South Africa), probably the most successful organization of deaf people in Africa. Obviously, it is a result of cooperation among deaf and hard-of-hearing people, teachers of deaf students, audiologists, and others—a cooperation still unique in the world.

Two hearing American volunteers developed an extensive sign language dictionary in Thailand with assistance from American linguists and in cooperation with its national federation of deaf people. Since the federation felt that this dictionary was too heavy to carry around, the Swedish national federation of the deaf volunteered to break it into smaller volumes. A deaf expert from Japan later advised the volunteers to establish local clubs instead of working from the top down. Several years later I had a chance to visit two of the local clubs in Thailand and was impressed by their excellent management styles, regardless of how well the national federation of the deaf was doing. Contrary to the old assumption that the growth of local clubs is essential to the establishment of a strong, nationwide organization, we now believe that the strength of any nationwide organization depends on solidarity at any level, not necessarily and uniquely at the local level.

Last spring I met two deaf individuals who had worked together for several years in Tibet. They were both from developing countries and received financial support from Handicap International in Belgium instead of from organizations of deaf people. One was a woman born in Indonesia and educated in the United States; the other was a Tibetan woman. The Indonesian was an experienced volunteer, having worked as a teacher in India before moving to Tibet. She discovered that deaf people in Tibet had no fully developed sign language but, rather, communicated through unsystematic gestures. She formed an alliance with the Tibetan woman, who happened to be fluent in Tibetan, Mandarin, and English. (Such multilingual deaf individuals are few, but not unheard of. They used to be found in many countries prior to the development of the first schools for deaf children.) These two women successfully persuaded deaf persons living in Tibet to come together socially and form a new natural sign language. Without support from any organizations, missionaries, or schools for the deaf, they appealed directly to Handicap International in Belgium for financial help. During my interview, I was clearly convinced that these two volunteers, despite their lack of organizational support, had a proper and effective understanding of the importance of local or national associations of deaf people and knew how to bring about change that would foster such groups.

Handicap International is an international, nongovernmental organization that aims to support people with disabilities in developing countries and wherever landmines, cluster bombs, or natural catastrophes pose danger. Handicap International's network consists of eight divisions, including the United States. Handicap International in the United Kingdom is the only division that gives small grants to such organizations. The organization has not yet reported the number of deaf volunteers and the number of national or local associations of persons with disabilities that it has supported in foreign aid programs.

In 2007 the Malaysian Federation of the Deaf [Persekutuan Orang Pekak] celebrated its tenth year of operation. It invited me to visit its headquarters, one of its local clubs, and a class in Malaysian Sign Language for interested hearing persons. The celebration attracted seven hundred persons, mostly deaf, from different parts of Malaysia and nearby Singapore. The federation president also brought me to the Malaysian Parliament, where the proposed laws protecting Malaysian persons with disabilities were formally presented for final consideration. These laws were approved in spring 2008. Even though Malaysia is still regarded as a developing country, very few missionaries or volunteers were involved in work with schools for deaf youngsters or the local deaf clubs.

In short, there is still room for contributions to the deaf community in several developing countries. We need schools for deaf students, national or local organizations for deaf adults, and projects for deaf children and adults. Missionaries, trainers, and other experts, whether independent or recruited by national federations of deaf people, can still help a great deal.

The three models of development assistance, as described by Amy Wilson, have occurred in both developed and developing countries. However, while deaf people in most countries now prefer the social model, persons with certain disabilities tend to favor the rehabilitative model. In fact, the membership of persons with physical and mental disabilities is more active in Rehabilitation International than in national rehabilitation associations in several countries. However, while the term *rehabilitation* has been rejected by deaf people in the Nordic countries, it is tolerated in the United States and several other countries. Nonetheless, the basic question is how national and local organizations of deaf children and adults can best cooperate with similar entities of both deaf and hearing parents of deaf children to achieve their goals. Deaf and hearing individuals desiring to work in developing countries should first join these very organizations. And everyone should strive to accomplish the objectives chosen by these organizations, including teachers, social workers, and other professionals serving deaf people. This kind of cooperation is not different from that in the hearing world. In this area, DEAFSA is probably the best example for the deaf world.

Sources of foreign aid programs for deaf people in developing countries:

www.handicap-international.org.uk
www.handicap-international.org.us
www.handicap-international.org.de (Germany)
www.handicap-international.org.be
www.handicap-international.org.fr
www.nsh.se/links.htm (a long list of Nordic councils)
www.shia.se (a list of twenty-seven member organizations)

Bibliography (and resource readings)

Albrecht, Gary L., Katherine D. Seelman, and Michael Bury, eds. 2001. *Handbook of Disability Studies*. Thousand Oaks, Calif.: Sage.

Erting, Carol J., Robert C. Johnson, Dorothy L. Smith, and Bruce D. Snider, eds. 1994. *The Deaf Way: Perspectives from the International Conference on Deaf Culture.* Washington, D.C.: Gallaudet University Press.

Goodstein, Harvey, ed. 2002. *The Deaf Way II Reader.* Washington, D.C.: Gallaudet University Press.

Mermod, Denis, ed. 1972. *Entendre avec les yeux: Extraits des actes du premier séminaire oecuménique de formation pour responsables chrétiens travaillant parmi les sourds.* [Understanding with the Eyes: Extracts from the First International Ecumenical Seminar on Pastoral Care among the Deaf]. Geneva: Editions Labor et Fides.

Rissanen, Terhi, and Eino Savisaari, eds. 1987. *Christian Responsibility in Deafwork: Proceedings of the Fourth International Ecumenical Seminar on Pastoral Care among the Deaf.* Friedberg: International Ecumenical Working Group for Pastoral Care among the Deaf.

World Health Organization. 2001. *International Classification of Functioning, Disability, and Health.* http://www.who.int/classifications/icf/en/.

CHAPTER 9

HIV/AIDS and the Deaf Community

A Conversation

Leila Monaghan and Deborah Karp

INTRODUCTION

HIV/AIDS is a significant but rarely discussed problem in the United States Deaf community. This chapter is an opportunity for us to talk about our experiences with HIV/AIDS and to provide information we think the public should know, including the impact AIDS has had on Deaf people, the way in which the lack of ASL-accessible services has hurt the Deaf community, and our belief that there should be national rather than local funding and information gathering for Deaf programs and Deaf people.

What we present here is part of our ongoing conversation in sign, speech, and writing. Many of our comments are based on notes taken during phone conversations,[1] in person or from the CART transcription from the Swarthmore conference in spring 2008, which the editors mention in the introduction to this book.

OUR CONVERSATION

Deborah: I am a Deaf activist and a former director of Maryland Deaf AIDS Project, a branch of the Family Service Foundation.

Leila: I am a hearing anthropologist and have been working on the issue of HIV/AIDS and Deaf communities from a national and international perspective. Deb and I met at the Sixteenth International AIDS Conference (AIDS 2006) in Toronto, Canada. She was visiting family in Toronto and representing the Maryland Deaf AIDS Project. I was there to give a paper on HIV/AIDS infection rates in Maryland, based upon data from Maryland's Department of Health and Mental Hygiene.

Deborah: I am Canadian, but I went to Gallaudet. I graduated in 1988 and stayed in the United States for five months after that, working as a tutor at

Gallaudet. My first experience with AIDS was when a friend from Gallaudet, Felix Vargos Ramos, asked me to visit him in the hospital. So I visited. He didn't look well. He did not admit to me that he had AIDS, and I wouldn't have understood him if he had since I didn't know anything about AIDS. He said he had cancer, and I wasn't convinced, but I tried to support him, tried to be optimistic for him. Then I found out that I wasn't allowed to stay in the United States and had to go back to Canada because of immigration laws.

Shortly after I got back to Canada, another good friend contacted me, Steve Schell. He said, "I've been diagnosed with AIDS." I still didn't know what AIDS was. He showed me the external evidence on his body—thrush, all the lumps—and he explained what the term HIV+ meant. That's when I thought back to Felix and recognized that he had AIDS as well. In 1990 Steve passed away. Before he passed away, communication was slow, but he still had some motor control, he had his mind, and he could see okay.

A little later Felix's partner contacted me: Felix was dying. So I drove from Canada to Maryland. He was completely wasted: no muscle, rail thin, but his legs were swollen. His body was destroyed, he was blind, he had no communication, his mind had shut down, he was like a vegetable. He couldn't move and had to be spoon fed. His partner, Eric, had to open his mouth so they could feed him, but he kept on clamping his mouth shut. He wasn't really swallowing. Eric said all the nerves in his neck were gone. He died twenty to thirty minutes after I last saw him.

Leila: The late 1980s and early 1990s were a time of a tremendous number of deaths. By this point, AIDS was widespread in both hearing and Deaf communities of the United States and Canada, particularly gay communities. A number of prominent members of the NY Gay Deaf community had been infected. Sam Edwards, actor, dancer, and Deaf activist, died in 1989. Broadway actor and director Bruce Hlibok had contracted AIDS but was not admitting that he had the disease (Bryan 1994, 2002). Most of the outreach at this point was being done by branches of hearing organizations. Edwards was cared for by the Gay Men's Health Crisis (GMHC) in New York, a volunteer organization that worked with a number of Deaf clients or buddies.[2] Part of the mission of GMHC and other AIDS groups of the period was to give people information about how AIDS was spread. While information about transmission and prevention was becoming common in the hearing community (Shultz et al. 1990), this information was not reaching many members of the Deaf community despite some outreach efforts by hearing organizations such as GMHC in New York (Bourquin interview 2007; Shilts 1988, Luczak 2006), and *L'Association des Bonnes Gens Sourds*, the Gay Deaf Association of Quebec (CSSQ 2007).

Deborah: Even after Felix and Steve died, I didn't know how you got AIDS. There were grapevine rumors, but I had no accurate information on how AIDS was actually transmitted. I went to NTID (National Technical Institute for the Deaf) in 1990 and did my studies, not thinking about HIV during that period. Then in 1992 I moved to Toronto. Friends there asked me if I wanted to work with AIDS outreach groups. I wasn't really interested because I didn't have information on how bad the epidemic was. Then another friend, Rodney Jameson, was diagnosed HIV+. I was startled: Why were there were so many Deaf people who were HIV+? That's when I got paranoid; I wanted to know— I needed to know—exactly how this disease was transmitted.

Then I found out it was because of unprotected sex, and that made me want to do outreach work. My friends kept dying of AIDS. I heard about so many friends from Gallaudet University, all dying. During this time I moved to Chicago, then on to Maryland, where I am now. My first job here was as an instructor for the Deaf and blind. My office was in the same building as the Family Service Foundation, which partnered with the Deaf AIDS Project, so I learned about the Deaf AIDS Project then. I met Harry Woosley at meetings in my building when he came to work with his supervisors. Harry was founder and director of Deaf AIDS and worked out of Baltimore. He then left, and the job was vacant for several months, and then I applied.

Leila: The founder of the Deaf AIDS Project, Harry Woosley, was diagnosed as HIV+ in 1992. When he first tried to find information for himself, he realized that Deaf people in general had few sources of information, so he founded the Deaf AIDS Project, which has been under the auspices of the Family Service Foundation since 1994.

Deborah: So when in 2004 the job as the Deaf AIDS Project director became available, I applied and got hired. There were so many parts to the job, and all of it involved specialized terminology. I gave out information about the agency and about HIV, I collected statistics, and I educated interpreters so they could understand enough about HIV to do their jobs adequately. One immediate problem was that the very sign PLUS (for *positive*) means good in the Deaf community—it's like a thumbs up. There was a time when people who found out they were HIV positive were relieved because they thought that was a good thing. We needed to go back and translate the English HIV+ into what that actually meant; the interpreters or whoever were signing to the patient had to learn not to sign PLUS but instead HAVE HIV.

I also did counseling sessions both for prevention and after testing, and I ran exhibits that explained the transmission and progression of AIDS. I worked with a lot of different communities, from college-educated people to teenagers—so many teenagers were being diagnosed positive. We tested people age thirteen on up. I also worked with people who had minimal education and sometimes even minimal language experience. I worked with group home residents and the developmentally delayed. I gave lectures to all these different groups, used lots of examples and lots of pictures showing what the infection looked like. Some people didn't want to see, of course, but my job was to help them understand, and to do that they needed to see what

HIV/AIDS looks like. Some of the Deaf people I worked with were HIV+, but they denied it initially. Some were aware they had it but didn't realize what the disease looked like as it progressed. Some didn't have HIV but had friends or relatives that did. And many others didn't know anybody with HIV. So this range of experience with the disease also made my job that much more challenging. The lectures changed their attitudes: People were motivated to ask questions; they wanted to be well informed.

I started developing a brochure to reach even more people but never finished it. It was hard to get approval from the Maryland AIDS Administration. We already had one when I came to the job, but it was quite sophisticated in terms of demanding a certain language and education level in order to be understood. Instead, I worked on developing a new one that would be accessible to people regardless of their language abilities or educational level. It was more pictorial, including lots of drawings about blood work, semen, nursing. We showed someone swimming—and said you couldn't get it that way. We explained that testing was confidential. Everything was very simple: lots of pictures about what you could and couldn't do, with short sentences so that people for whom English was foreign or who had only minimal language at all could still get it. One of our goals was to reach out to low-literacy groups. We found that in some group homes people didn't have basic information about sex, so we needed to explain those fundamentals to them as well. With teenagers this was particularly tricky because often the people who had authority over them didn't approve of graphic discussions. But I explained to them why it was necessary, and I was very careful with word choice with this particular age group. I showed only the most crucial pictures, I showed what herpes looked like, I explained STDs, I gave a rudimentary explanation of sex, taking care to make sure that it was sex, age, and background appropriate.

Another problem of outreach for Deaf people in particular is that they are afraid of being tested. Typically when I gave an HIV test, I did some counseling first. Sometimes a positive finding will leave a person so distraught that they don't follow up on medical services. Many of them can be hard to track, especially since they prefer not to talk to anyone about it.

Leila: Language barriers are a major reason that Deaf people don't have the information they need to protect themselves. In interviews with sixteen Deaf people in New York and Philadelphia, Elizabeth Eckhardt found that "Fourteen of sixteen individuals mentioned that HIV information must be disseminated in ASL" (2005, 39). The overall emphasis of Eckhardt's interviewees was on the importance of visual information. As one interviewee put it,

> Just lectures is not enough, there's got to be graphic pictures. I saw a picture of an STD and, man, that made an impression on me. The pictures were graphic, and it made an impression, so when you teach about AIDS, you can do the straight language narrative, but you MUST

give pictures of the potential consequences or show people a picture of someone who is healthy and has HIV, and this is what a full-blown AIDS attack can look like. There's got to be a ton of visuals . . . they need images in their mind that would make them stop, and that image needs to be done frequently. (2005, 40)

This lack of access to information about HIV/AIDS is paralleled by high rates of HIV/AIDS in Deaf communities. While the Centers for Disease Control, unfortunately (and in our opinion, wrongly), doesn't keep records, the state of Maryland's data on public testing shows Deaf people are testing HIV+ at a rate about double that of hearing people. From some data, it seems that Deaf people are being tested at higher rates than hearing people, meaning these ratios could be even higher (table 9.1).

Deborah: Just like there are no national statistics, there is no national funding for programs. We really need a national program; local funding is uneven and inadequate. The funding for the Deaf AIDS Project came from different sources. Some money came from the Ryan White Act (the U.S. government funding mechanism). That gave money to the state of Maryland, who then gave money to the University of Maryland, who then gave money to the program. We also got direct grants from various places, including Frostburg University, who gave funding for computers and for teaching sign language to the staff. One of my jobs, in fact, was to write grant applications, particularly for HIV education for our staff.

Table 9.1. Maryland 2003, 2005, 2006, and 2007 Public HIV Testing Results

Year	Hearing Status	HIV negative	Indeterminate	HIV positive	TOTAL	Percent testing HIV+	Ratio deaf to not deaf HIV+
Pre-2000	Deaf					4.3%	
2003	Deaf	794	0	38	832	4.5%	2.1
	Not deaf	37,789	0	813	38,602	2.1%	
2005[*]	Deaf	740	1	25	766	3.3%	1.9
	Not deaf	51,759	27	875	52,661	1.7%	
2006[**]	Deaf	415	0	10	425	2.4%	1.8
	Not deaf	34,181	7	458	34,646	1.3%	
2007[**]	Deaf	221	0	8	229	3.5%	2.9
	Not deaf	40,521	8	503	41,032	1.2%	

Note: These figures are from Maryland Public Testing Sites only; other testing sites in Maryland do not record information on hearing status.
[*]No figures were available for 2000–2002 and 2004.
[**]Positive figures from 2006 and 2007 include both preliminary and confirmed positives (chart adapted from figures from HRSA 2001, Monaghan 2006, and from new information provided by the Maryland Department of Health and Mental Hygiene, July 2007 and July 2008).

I've now left the Deaf AIDS Project and taken a new job as an associate consultant, a project analyst. The money is not very good, but as least there is potential for advancement. I'm not sure what's going to happen to the Deaf AIDS Project now that I've left. It is pretty stable this year; the funding has stayed the same. But for next year, no one knows what will happen with that grant. Grant contracts go year to year, making it really difficult to count on funding. Deaf programs around the country are always folding. The Centers for Disease Control and Prevention (CDC) does not recognize Deaf needs, and so it doesn't understand our funding issues. We need to document the problem for it. One big job is getting Deaf people to come into Deaf agencies for help. They instead often go into hospitals and clinics, where they're not reported as being Deaf. So documentation is elusive. Further, we need to fit into the CDC categories somehow, but that's another problem: It's not clear what category Deaf people fall under for the CDC.

When the Deaf Reach organization in Washington, D.C., had its funding for its HIV/AIDS program cut in 2007, it had to close its program temporarily. The funding was cut precisely because of the kind of misunderstanding we noted earlier. The statistics collected by the city of Washington, D.C., did not reflect an accurate picture of the number of deaf cases in Washington, D.C., so the national funding that had been made available through the Ryan White Act was cut. Deaf Reach could not show how many Deaf people were affected by HIV/AIDS, so it could not provide funding agencies with the data they needed. Unlike in Maryland, in D.C. there is no place on the form you fill out when you take an HIV test to indicate that you are deaf. What happened to Deaf Reach shows how much we need national funding for Deaf programs, not local funding, and how we need accurate tracking of Deaf infection rates just as there is for hearing groups through the CDC and the Ryan White Act.

Leila: Deaf AIDS Project and Deaf Reach are typical of Deaf outreach programs around the country: small, underfunded, and unstable from year to year. In the last couple of years projects have closed down in San Francisco, the Chicago area, New York, and elsewhere.

Part of the reason that local programs fail is a national switch in funding priorities from small programs to large programs run by hospitals (Gonzalez 2007). Further, low funding means that the Deaf programs lack the resources to coordinate with each other, making individual programs and the people working in them feel very isolated. The directorship of the Deaf AIDS Project, for example, became a dead-end job because the funding was unstable from year to year—with the ultimate result that Deborah felt she couldn't stay. The easiest place to access information on Deaf HIV/AIDS resources is POZ magazine's directory, http://directory.poz.com, under additional search options.[3] As of April 2010, it had ninety-six sites listed, up from forty-four in July 2008.

Deborah: I truly miss working for the Deaf AIDS Project. I miss helping others. I feel bad about not being part of that anymore. As I think about my own future, I am looking for ways that I can get involved in outreach again—but with a more stable situation.

Leila: We gave the original version of this chapter as part of the remarkable conference at Swarthmore College in spring 2008, like most of the chapters in this book. Ours was one of the more socially rather than linguistically oriented papers. The response of one of the audience members, however, brought home how important language and the politics of language are in this social issue:

> My husband recently passed away here in the United States, and I had problems with the hospital. My husband died because the hospital didn't provide language access to him. He didn't have interpreters and so on. After he died—he's a deaf person—I felt so so angry, and I met deaf people, and I was telling them they knew that hospital, there were problems with that hospital. . . . If everybody knows that that hospital has problems, we all should get together and do something about it. . . . The hospital and the nurses didn't know sign language. They tried to speak to him, and he didn't understand them, and he died because of stress . . .
>
> Deaf people are dying all the time because they don't know. I've had friends who died of high blood pressure because they didn't know. . . . The nurse said there are things at Wal-Mart—you can buy them there, but many people don't know you can buy your own medical equipment. It's not very expensive, and [you can] buy it and check your own blood pressure. I think about deaf people in other countries who don't know they might have diabetes or [high] blood pressure or whatever. The same thing happens with HIV and AIDS. It's still happening. It's very frustrating.

Deborah: One thing I think about in this regard is that there a new test for HIV. In the past there used to be a saliva test for people. They would send it away and wait a really long time for the results. That used to upset me because I thought of all those people who didn't know they had HIV—worrying and perhaps behaving in ways that they shouldn't if they were, in fact, infected. In Maryland, they used the old saliva test for a long time; they just stopped in June 2007. Now they're using OraQuick, an FDA-approved, rapid point-of-care fingerstick and venipuncture whole-blood test. It's a twenty-minute test, and it's provided for free. You get the results just like that—only twenty minutes. We need to let people know that test is available.

A huge advantage of getting immediate results is that you can test people and counsel them right then. You don't have to worry about them walking around uninformed and passing the disease along. The counseling is essential for those found positive. It's a major factor in controlling the epidemic.

All of this takes money: the testing, the counseling. National funding is crucial.

There are still many people who are sick and don't know it. Somehow we're hoping that out there in the world many more of these clinics with the Ora-Quick test will be set up. We hope the misunderstandings among the Deaf community will decrease. We're hoping the word will spread, and people who fear they are infected will seek HIV/AIDS services.

Leila: Any language is dependent upon its community. Sam Edwards and Bruce Hlibok were at the forefront of the development of new forms of Deaf expression, particularly Deaf theater, when they died of AIDS. Undoubtedly, some ASL expressive forms were not developed because of the shortening of the lives of those two cultural leaders.

But communities also depend on their language. When American Sign Language and other sign languages are not recognized and not utilized in a wide range of circumstances, users are made vulnerable in so many ways. In the United States, Deaf people have been cut off from HIV prevention information, accessible testing, proper treatments, and other vital health information. The Americans with Disabilities Act guarantees appropriate communication for Deaf people: "Health care providers have a duty to provide effective communication, using auxiliary aids and services that ensure that communication with people who have a hearing loss is as effective as communication with others. 28 C.F.R. S36.303(c)" (cited in NAD 2008).

Despite this, however, many aspects of our health care system do not recognize the language, the needs, and the culture of Deaf people. The state of Connecticut, for example, had to sue to get hospitals to provide proper access to interpreters. In one case, a Deaf AIDS patient died in a major hospital without ever having access to an interpreter (Harry Vrenna, interview, January 2007). In terms of keeping track of the HIV/AIDS epidemic, Deaf people don't count; the CDC keeps no statistics on deaf versus hearing infection rates.

In addition, HIV/AIDS is a problem for Deaf communities internationally. When Deb and I met at AIDS 2006 the overall consensus of the participants was that Deaf people and people with disabilities around the world were being ignored regarding this epidemic. We started a group called the Global Committee on HIV/AIDS and Disability to argue for more resources and for more information about Deaf people with AIDS. This group submitted proposals to the Seventeenth International AIDS Conference (AIDS 2008) in Mexico City. We had a number of these proposals accepted, including one for a skills-building workshop, and one for a networking zone for Deaf people and people with disabilities. Unfortunately many people who were at AIDS 2006 didn't receive scholarships to go to AIDS 2008, including Deb, Michel Turgeon from Quebec, and John Meleste from South Africa. The lack of resources at the individual and small institutional level is a barrier to raising international awareness and to building a transnational effort to fight against

HIV/AIDS in Deaf communities. Despite this, both of us will keep fighting, keep trying to get the message out about this deadly disease. The website http://hivdeaf.blogspot.com has additional information on our activities (see also Schmaling and Monaghan 2006; Monaghan 2008; Monaghan and Schmaling 2010).

Notes

We wish to thank the Maryland Department of Health and Mental Hygiene for supplying public testing site data (they provide a model for other health departments everywhere) and Douglas McLean and Forest Books for permission to print earlier data from Maryland. Our thanks also go to the enthusiastic support from Donna Jo Napoli, the guiding spirit of Gaurav Mathur, and all of our fellow participants at the remarkable "Deaf around the World" conference.

1. Deborah's side of the conversation was adapted from notes of conversations interpreted by Sorenson Video Relay Service Interpreters and CART transcriptions done by Rob Hemenway of Karasch, based on the signed and voiced interpretations by Nancy Sullivan and Rita Jo Scarcella and further edited by Donna Jo Napoli and Gaurav Mathur. The sole responsibility for this chapter, however, lies squarely on us since we have had a chance to review and revise the relevant materials.

2. Eugene Bourquin was one of Edwards's buddies with GMHC (interview, February 2007, Indiana University Human Subjects Release #06–11123); see Monaghan and Schmaling 2010 for more information.

3. Information on Deaf services can be found at http://directory.poz.com by clicking the small "Click here for additional search options" just above the search directory button and then scrolling down to "Deaf" under "Search by Service." Alternatively, go to http://hivdeaf.blogspot.com/2010/04/96-deaf-aids-clinics.html for a link to the list.

Bibliography (and resource readings)

Bryan, Anne Marie "Jade." 1994. Listen to the Hands of Our People. Video/DVD. New York: DeafVision Filmworks.

———. 2002. On and off Stage: The Bruce Hlibok Story. Video/DVD. New York: Deaf-Vision Filmworks.

Coalition Sida des Sourds du Quebéc (CSSQ). 2007. Notre historique. Website updated May 24, 2007. http://www.cssq.org/pages/accueil/historique.htm (accessed September 1, 2008).

Eckhardt, Elizabeth. 2005. An Exploration of HIV/AIDS Perceptions, Knowledge, and Beliefs among Individuals Who Are Deaf. PhD diss., New York University.

Gonzalez, David. 2007. For Smaller Fighters of H.I.V., Weapons Dwindle. March 27, 2007. http://nytimes.com (accessed January 22, 2008).

Harrington, Tom. 2004. Statistics: Deaf Population of the United States. Gallaudet University Library Deaf-related Resources, Frequently Asked Questions. http://library.gallaudet.edu/dr/faq-statistics-deaf-us.htm (accessed February 5, 2006).

Luczak, Raymond. 2006. Positive Feelings. In *HIV/AIDS and Deaf Communities. Deaf Worlds* 22(1): S77–S82, ed. Constanze Schmaling and Leila Monaghan. Gloucestershire, UK: Forest Books and Douglas McLean (http://www.ForestBooks.com).

Monaghan, Leila. 2006. Maryland 2003 HIV Infection Statistics for Hearing and Deaf Populations. In *HIV/AIDS and Deaf Communities. Deaf Worlds* 22(1), ed. Constanze Schmaling and Leila Monaghan, 83–110. Gloucestershire, UK: Forest Books and Douglas McLean (http://www.ForestBooks.com).

———. 2008. HIV/AIDS in the United States Deaf Community. In *Access: Multiple Avenues for Deaf People,* ed. Doreen DeLuca, Irene W. Leigh, Kristin A. Lindgren, and Donna Jo Napoli, 168–192. Washington, D.C.: Gallaudet University Press.

———, and Constanze Schmaling. 2010. Deaf Community Approaches to HIV/AIDS. In *At the Intersections: Deaf and Disability Studies,* ed. Alison Kafer and Susan Burch, 120–143. Washington, D.C.: Gallaudet University Press.

National Association of the Deaf (NAD). 2008. ADA Questions and Answers for Health Care Providers. http://www.nad.org/adaq&a (accessed September 1, 2008).

Schmaling, Constanze, and Leila Monaghan. 2006. *HIV/AIDS and Deaf Communities. Deaf Worlds* 22(1): 83–110. Gloucestershire, UK: Forest Books and Douglas McLean (http://www.ForestBooks.com).

Shilts, Randy. 1988. *And the Band Played On.* New York: Penguin.

Shultz, James, Rick S. Zimmerman, David Scotkin, and David Withum. 1990. Mobile AIDS Prevention Program "AIDSMOBILE": Delivery of AIDS Information and Condoms to Youth in High HIV-seroprevalence Neighborhoods. *International Conference on AIDS* (June 20–23, 1990), 6: 421 (abstract no. 3078). http://gateway.nlm.nih.gov/MeetingAbstracts/102197269.html (accessed May 21, 2008).

U.S. Census Bureau, Population Division. 2004. Annual Estimates of the Population for the Counties of Maryland: April 1, 2000, to July 1, 2003 (CO-EST2003-01-24). Release date: April 9, 2004.

CHAPTER 9 RESPONSE

HIV/AIDS and Deaf Communities in South Africa

A Conversation

John Meletse and Ruth Morgan

INTRODUCTION

We have written this chapter together sitting at the computer and conversing in South African Sign Language (SASL) while Ruth translates each SASL turn into written English.

OUR CONVERSATION

John: I am Deaf and was diagnosed HIV positive five years ago. I am thirty-three years old and very healthy. I work at Gay and Lesbian Memory in Action (GALA), where I focus on the Deaf youth HIV outreach project and have been a role model for Deaf people living with HIV as I am the only Deaf person in South Africa who has publicly disclosed his status.

   Ruth: I am hearing and HIV negative. I am also a linguistic anthropologist and have been working with Deaf communities for more than twenty years. I am affected by HIV as many people that I know are HIV positive, which is not surprising as South Africa has more than five million people infected with HIV. I met John eight years ago when he was interviewed for the Deaf culture project in South Africa, which is documented in the book *"Deaf Me Normal": Deaf South Africans Tell Their Life Stories.* He volunteered to work with me on the life-story project, and we have been colleagues and good friends since that time. I have had the privilege of witnessing his personal transformation and consequent development as an activist living with HIV over the years. I am currently working as a freelance researcher and writer. So now you know who we are, and we will continue from here, letting you eavesdrop on a conversation between us.

John: It's interesting that in the United States HIV/AIDS was seen as a gay disease in the late eighties and early nineties. I didn't know that. In South Africa HIV/AIDS has been seen as a heterosexual disease since the midnineties.

Ruth: Yes, you were probably too young to access the information about HIV and AIDS being a gay men's disease here as well in the eighties. Although in South Africa it then spread much more rapidly in the heterosexual world, so much so that by the midnineties it was no longer seen as a gay disease.

John: I saw many Deaf people who were HIV positive, but they were not disclosing their status. Some knew their status but could not talk about it due to the stigma attached to being HIV positive. I could see they had swollen glands and were losing their hair and getting very thin. Then they got sick and died without saying anything. Other Deaf people believed that they had been bewitched by *sangomas* [traditional healers], and that's why they became sick and died. They didn't believe they had AIDS-related illnesses. Due to lack of communication many Deaf people don't know about HIV/AIDS. They don't understand why the two words are used together. They only understand that HIV means that a person has a virus that will kill them. They understand that AIDS means that you are very sick and will die. Regarding HIV, they don't understand what the letters mean. They think the *H* stands for "human being," but they don't know what the *I* or *V* means or how a person gets HIV or what happens after they get it. They don't understand that it's a sexually transmitted virus. They don't know how to prevent spreading the virus. Others may not realize that they can go for treatment and instead take an HIV-positive diagnosis as a death sentence.

In my opinion the main problem here is precisely that: lack of access to information about HIV and AIDS in the Deaf community. There are many hearing organizations in the HIV sector that give written information to the public. For example, Soul City has produced many comics and pamphlets and educational materials for youth. However, such efforts often go without results. Deaf youth and adults can't understand the written pamphlets, as the literacy level is too high. At GALA (Gay and Lesbian Memory in Action), where I work, we developed an educational comic for Deaf youth which is very visual and includes illustrations of people using South African Sign Language. The comic has minimal written information. I did some work at a Deaf school called Sizwile in Soweto with this comic, and the learners understood the information.

Ruth: Yes, we developed the comic at GALA for Deaf people, so it was very visual and dealt with basic information explaining HIV and sexually transmitted infections (STIs), how they are transmitted (including a section on rape), and the use of condoms to prevent transmission. It also includes some sensitizing to and awareness raising of gay and lesbian issues and sexual orientation. We did a pilot at Sizwile School for the Deaf of Soweto using two Deaf teaching assistants and two Deaf teachers who we thought would be able to communicate most effectively with the learners. What we didn't anticipate was that the Deaf teaching assistants had internalized the need to use simultaneous communication with the learners so strongly that the learners didn't understand the information. They would mouth words in spoken English while signing what they were mouthing so they wound up using English sentence structure rather than SASL. So after the pilot we stopped using these teaching assistants, and you, John, went into the school as an outside Deaf person on a weekly basis. The Deaf teaching assistants also had a lot of myths about HIV which we spent the majority of the time dispelling so as to give them accurate information about HIV. For example, one Deaf teaching assistant believed that eating beetroot caused HIV/AIDS. She had gotten the wrong end of the story that the minister of health in South Africa at that time was espousing; the minister was encouraging HIV-positive people to eat beetroot in order to boost their immune systems and stay healthy.

John: Yes, they even believed that HIV was transmitted through kissing and sharing bath water or a glass. The problem of education about HIV is very important. Even if there is a hearing interpreter translating a speech at a school for Deaf learners, they don't have the terminology or vocabulary in SASL to convey HIV-related information accurately. For example, the speaker may be explaining STIs, and the interpreter fingerspells "STI," but the learners don't understand what an STI is since there is no sign in SASL for the concept of an STI. Therefore, I myself have invented a sign for STIs, roughly translated as INFECTION-SPREADING-UP-FROM-GENITAL-AREA-TOWARD-SHOULDERS (two fists in groin area open up into two 5 handshapes that stop at the shoulders).

This year I worked with grade 9 learners in their second year of high school, about seventeen to twenty years of age. I gave them a session every week. When I arrived at the beginning of the year, they told me that they hadn't understood a hearing presentation on HIV/AIDS with a teacher who was interpreting using simultaneous communication. They were so relieved that I had come to explain HIV to them because I was using strong SASL, and I disclosed my status and my experiences to them. They wanted me to come and work at the school as a full-time teacher. They didn't believe that I was [HIV] positive because I look so healthy and well. They expected all positive people to be thin and sickly.

They were delighted because they could understand me perfectly. In the same way that Deborah describes the importance of accurately translating the English term *HIV positive* into American Sign Language, I had to do the same. I explained to the Deaf youth the meaning of the terms *HIV positive* and *HIV negative*. In fact, "HIV positive" does not mean "well" or "good" as a PLUS sign generally means in SASL. They were shocked about this as they had always thought that the sign POSITIVE refers to a good attitude. I had to explain that the

PLUS sign means you are infected with HIV. As Deborah did, I tried using the signs HIV HAVE, but the Deaf learners didn't like that way of expressing "HIV positive," so we used the PLUS sign.

Interestingly, black hearing people have a gesture indicating the number three. It could be an SASL 3 handshape consisting of three fingers extended (pinky, ring finger, and middle finger, as in figure 9R.1) or a W handshape (ring finger, middle finger, and index finger extended, as in figure 9R.2), depending on what gesture that person uses to indicate the number three or counting on one's fingers to three. They use this gesture when gossiping about anyone who is HIV positive—they use it as part of their slang surrounding HIV, and I just found out from my hearing friends that it may be accompanied by the verbal expression *amagama amathathu* in isiZulu, which is translated as "three words/letters," referring to the three letters constituting the acronym HIV. They may also say Z3, which is a BMW model, but they use this as a shorthand way of referring to the same three letters. For example, when an HIV-positive person walks down the road, the hearing people that they pass may use this gesture with or without the accompanying verbal expression. They can also change the palm orientation of the gesture and make the sign in any location, as they usually want to avoid being seen by the target of their gossip. I was surprised to learn that hearing people use it with the isiZulu expression.

Hearing people also use this gesture when communicating to a Deaf person that someone is HIV positive or has died as a result of an AIDS-related illness.

Figure 9R.1. SASL 3-handshape for HIV-positive person

Figure 9R.2. W-handshape for HIV-positive person

Figure 9R.3. SASL sign for HIV-positive person

Black Deaf people have created an SASL sign based on this 3 handshape to refer to an HIV-positive person (note that in SASL Deaf people never use the W handshape for the number three). It is also produced with the specific orientation of palm facing inward (toward the signer). In citation form (see figure 9R.3) the location is a short distance in front of the right side of the chest. The accompanying nonmanual signal is cheeks sucked in and eyes wide open. This nonmanual signal is always used by Deaf people but never by hearing people.

Deaf people also use the sign in figure 9R.3 to gossip about another HIV-positive Deaf person who may be passing. They can then make the sign in any location, "whispering" to ensure that the Deaf person doesn't see them gossiping about them. Deaf people don't use this sign in formal situations but use it informally.

Ruth: Apart from your own work with the Deaf community around HIV education, which is mostly with learners at Sizwile School, an organization in Cape Town called the Deaf Community of Cape Town (DCCT) has been doing some interesting and important work on HIV education. For the past three years DCCT has been offering an HIV/AIDS training program in which they trained five Deaf HIV/AIDS information officers, ran an HIV/AIDS camp for Deaf youth, did outreach work with Deaf youth, and trained three Deaf lay counselors who are recognized by the Department of Health. It's a small start in the right direction, and we need to replicate this in all nine provinces of South Africa.

John: Another big problem for Deaf people when tested in South Africa at the clinics or hospitals is that Deaf persons are not given any counseling pre- or posttesting. Once the test has been done, the doctor or nurse gives the Deaf persons a sealed envelope with the results to give to their parents. The parents never disclose to them that they are positive. So these Deaf persons never know that they are HIV positive and never return for treatment. Later when they get sick, perhaps their younger brother or sister tells them that they are HIV positive, which is a big shock to them. Usually it's too late for treatment then.

Another huge problem is the stigma attached to HIV in the Deaf community. I was living in a room in the back yard of a Deaf couple's house in Soweto. The wife was first diagnosed as HIV positive. They knew I was positive and asked me for help. The doctor had been trying to respect the confidentiality of the results, so he had used different terminology when he wrote a report with her results. She didn't understand the results because nowhere in them did he use the words "HIV positive." I then went back to the hospital where she was tested and asked the doctor for the results, and he explained to me that she was, indeed HIV positive. I counseled the wife first and then later her husband. But he didn't believe that his wife was positive; he simply couldn't accept it. One night the wife wanted to hang herself, as she thought she would die soon because she was HIV positive. I had to convince her that she could still live a long time as she wasn't sick. She agreed not to commit suicide after I spent the entire night up with her. She did go for ARV [antiretroviral] treatment, but she had persistent diarrhea, as she wasn't taking her medication properly. She had a lot of pills that she didn't understand how to take. Later her husband evicted me from my room; he was angry with me for supporting his wife. He refused to accept her HIV status and feared she may have had an affair. He also refused to go for an HIV test himself.

Most Deaf and hearing people in the townships don't disclose the fact they are HIV positive due to the high levels of stigma. Unfortunately, this leads to their getting sick and dying without treatment. The Deaf community looks at me and can't believe that I am public about my status as HIV positive. They gossip about me, but I don't care at all. In the beginning all the gossip worried me a lot, but now I'm strong in who I am, and I don't let it bother me. I am still the only Deaf person who is open about my status—there is no one else who has come forth like this even though I encourage them to. I support and counsel many Deaf people who come to me and privately disclose that they are HIV positive. They are surprised that I keep their confidentiality and don't gossip about them to other Deaf people, and they are enormously relieved about that. When I was first diagnosed as HIV positive, my status was disclosed by the hearing social worker whom I had gone to for counseling at the local Deaf organization to all the people who worked there; that was very traumatic.

I want to meet with the director of the national Deaf organization so we can form a partnership in the future and work together to raise funds for a national level program. We also need to make it a priority in 2010 to raise funds to extend the project that we are already doing at Sizwile School for the Deaf to include both the adult Deaf community living in Soweto, as well as the parents of the Deaf learners.

The disability movement in South Africa also doesn't cater to Deaf people in any meaningful way—they only pay lip service to Deaf people's needs and invite me to meetings, but nothing further happens. I am never involved in planning future activities.

I was invited to attend a conference in Senegal last month for people with disabilities that are HIV positive in Africa. It was coorganized by South Africa, but I wasn't even informed; I heard about it via a Deaf person who works in Kenya. I had to organize my own funding to attend this conference. The conference aimed to develop a network of activists with disabilities to influence policy in different countries. I was encouraged to attend and was told there would be international sign language interpreters there. However, when I arrived, there were none. Some Deaf people from Mali and Senegal and Kenya had their own interpreters with them. My funders wouldn't fund a South African interpreter to accompany me as the conference [organizers] said they were providing an international sign language interpreter. As a result I couldn't participate in the conference at all because I didn't understand anything.

Ruth: It's hard to believe that what's happening on the ground is lagging so far behind all the progressive policies and legislation, which seem to be up in the clouds. The equality clause in our constitution of 1996 prevents discrimination on the basis of disability. Our constitution also ensures the rights of all South Africans to dignity and equality, especially in receiving

and imparting information, and to being able to use the language of their
choice in accessing information. We also have other protective legislation,
such as the Promotion of Equality and Prevention of Unfair Discrimination
Act of 2000. Despite all of this, Deaf people, as well as people with disabilities, are more vulnerable to HIV infection than hearing and fully abled
people and are not being reached by HIV and AIDS prevention, treatment,
and care programs due to lack of access to information in SASL. In a booklet
titled "Nothing about Us . . . Without Us! HIV, AIDS, and Disability in South
Africa," based on a 2007 report by the disability sector of the South African
National AIDS Council, we find prominent excerpts from your life story, but
there is no other specific mention of Deaf people's needs. This neglect persists despite the participation of the disability sector in South Africa
in national HIV and AIDS strategic processes and in developing specific
HIV and AIDS programs, including full participation in the current South
African National Aids Council (SANAC), which, second to the Cabinet, is
the highest national advisory body for government on all issues related to
HIV and AIDS.

John: The hearing organizations are very well organized, and I attend the
monthly meetings of the AIDS Consortium. I have to take my own interpreter
with me, which GALA has to pay for. When I go to these meetings, many
issues are discussed, but none of the organizations present are doing anything
to assist Deaf people in getting information about HIV/AIDS.

Ruth: Yes, I want to point out that one of the rights of people living with
HIV (PLHIV) from the AIDS Charter of the AIDS Consortium is that they
have the right to access information and the right to resources such as medical treatment, including ARVs in state hospitals, and a basic social welfare
grant that is given to people living with HIV. However, they won't contribute
to the cost of your interpreter when you attend their meetings. It seems that
you, John, are a lone Deaf HIV activist in quite a hostile environment most
of the time. I know you also get stressed, as you are the only support for Deaf
South Africans who are HIV positive, which is an impossible load for one
person.

John: Yes, I remember the local Deaf organization referred someone to
me for counseling. He was quite a sick man who was HIV positive. The Deaf
organization told him they couldn't help him. They told him to come see me.
He was very stressed, as he had been worrying about his condition. I had to
explain to him about getting a CD4 test. That's when I found out the horrible
fact: He had no support from the local Deaf organization. But everyone needs
that support. I was so upset. Later that very week I had to go to the clinic for
my own CD4 test and found that my count had gone down for the first time
in three years. I was desolate and had to get counseling. My counselor
explained to me that stress could cause my CD4 count to drop and not to
worry about it. It thankfully went up after the next test. I realized I have to

have debriefing after counseling someone else who is HIV positive for my own preservation.

Note

We thank Busisiwe Kheswa for taking the photos in figures 9R.1–9R.3 and John Meletse and Paul Mokgethi for serving as models in these photos.

CHAPTER 10

The Language Politics of Japanese Sign Language (Nihon Shuwa)

Karen Nakamura

INTRODUCTION

Ethnographers of Deaf communities throw around terms such as *American Sign Language* (ASL), *Irish Sign Language* (ISL), and *Japanese Sign Language* (JSL) as if there were common agreement on what constitutes these languages.[1] Powerful language ideologies (Woolard and Schieffelin 1994) motivate us to ascribe more coherence to national sign languages than may actually be the case, especially when accounting for generational, geographic, religious, or other factors. Although we may understand that language coherence is a political and social construct, we do not often take time to analyze the ways in which these processes work in the construction of local language ideologies.

Arguing against this trend to reify national sign languages, Le Master (2003) writes about the gender and age bifurcation found in Irish Sign Language as a result of having deaf boys and girls attend separate schools, while Aramburo (1995) and Lucas et al. (2001) describe elements of African American variations of American Sign Language. In both examples, external forces in the form of segregated educational institutions led to the creation of separate dialects of the national sign language. The communities themselves have had little say in the maintenance of language coherence.

In this chapter I illustrate the way in which the dominant organization of deaf people in Japan, the Japanese Federation of the Deaf (JFD), has tried to maintain active control over Japanese Sign Language, which in this chapter is referred to as Nihon Shuwa in accordance with preferred practice, through management of the lexicon and interpreter-training programs. The JFD is reacting against externalities such as the sign language news service of the national public television system, which competes in the creation of new terms. In addition, younger and more radical members of the Deaf community have begun to challenge the JFD's definition of Japanese signing, arguing for a pure Nihon Shuwa.

BACKGROUND: MAINTAINING CONTROL OVER NIHON SHUWA

In December 1997 the JFD held its year-end meeting of the Research Group for Defining and Promulgating Japanese Sign Language in a hotel located in the hot-spring resort area of Atami, just south of Tokyo. The conference room was moderately large by Japanese standards. Four long tables were arranged in a square in the middle of the room. Sowa-san, the senior JFD staff member in charge of the meeting and deaf himself since an early age, set up the AV equipment—an S-VHS video camera and a television.[2]

Funded by a government contract from the Ministry of Health and Social Welfare, the JFD's Research Group for Defining and Promulgating Japanese Sign Language was charged with creating, describing, defining, and publicizing innovative signs, usually by publishing them in a series of books called *New Signs* but also by teaching them at JFD-led teacher-training seminars across the nation.

During the year, each regional unit of the JFD was directed to coin new signs. For example, the Hokkaido unit from the northern island of Japan was responsible for new newspaper words. The members of that group scanned the daily newspapers looking for vocabulary items that were not currently in the JFD's Nihon Shuwa dictionaries, wrote them down, and brainstormed new signs. The central committee's job was to look at these suggestions and decide whether to adopt them. Rarely were the signs adopted without much discussion and modification. It was a lexicographer's dream. The staff had lugged several boxes of reference books from the JFD's Tokyo office, several rather thick Japanese language dictionaries, Nihon Shuwa dictionaries, and even a copy of an ASL dictionary.

Since 1980, the JFD had been receiving contracts from the Ministry of Health and Social Welfare to fund this research group. One of the major goals of the project was to produce new signs, and one requirement was apparently to coin at least one hundred new signs for the ministry each year. These were presented in a series of reports to the ministry and were published annually in the aforementioned *New Signs* books. The research group had to demonstrate to the ministry that it was accomplishing its three assigned tasks: coining new signs, popularizing their use, and establishing a solid foundation for Nihon Shuwa.

The leader of the Hokkaido group began his presentation. The members had been scouring the daily newspapers, looking for new words in circulation. Japanese is a voracious and adaptive language. With respect to its writing systems, Japanese has adopted kanji characters from classical Chinese, created two of its own syllabaries, and is not reluctant to use the Roman alphabet. With respect to the lexicon, Japanese has a long history of borrowings from Chinese, English, French, German, Portuguese, and other languages. New words flood into the Japanese language at an incredible pace, fueled by widespread literacy, a high educational standard, a common myth of cultural homogeneity, and powerful media companies. Words are fads in Japan: The native term *ryûkôgo* [mainstream words] refers to faddish slang terms, which, just like Chanel handbags and Eminem CDs, are enormously popular one year, coming out of seemingly nowhere, but by the next year are *shigo* [dead words].

All of Japan, apparently, is caught up in the fad of new words—everyone, except for deaf Japanese, who are not subject to the same hegemonic media assault. However, as Gramsci (1971) and various Frankfurt School theorists (Horkheimer and Adorno 1972) maintain, hegemony typically makes initial headway by appealing to desire. And in this case, it was the Deaf community's desire for these new signs, as well as the desire of the Ministry of Social Welfare not to exclude anyone.

A NEW SIGN FOR *DEJITARU* 'DIGITAL'

As an intern at the JFD, I observed the proceedings along with the other staff members, sitting near the committee members around the table. The first word chosen for a new sign was *dejitaru* 'digital.' By way of background, the late nineties marked the beginning of the digital boom in Japan, with the popularization of digital cameras, DVDs, digital video (DV) camcorders, and so on. Along with this new technological trend, the question arose as to how to sign *digital*. The Hokkaido group had previously formulated a suggestion and videotaped it: The left hand is held at chest level with the index finger pointing up (as if signing 1), while the right index finger makes a gesture like a sine wave next to it. The presenter stopped the videotape and somewhat nervously sat down. We began our discussion.

At first there was a bit of confusion since the committee members did not understand the motivation for the image of a 1-sine-wave. The group leader then explained the concepts of *analog* and *digital* and how a digital waveform approximates an analog 1, thus the *1* plus a sine wave. The other members scurried to the reference books to check. The first criticism surfaced: "It looks too much like 'Amway.'" (This was during the Nagano Winter Olympics, for which the Amway company was a major sponsor). "What does 'Amway' look like?" asked another committee member. "Amway is the D finger held up with a sine wave next to it," was the reply.[3] Since one of the goals was to create unambiguous signs, the Hokkaido 1-sine-wave suggestion was rejected as being too similar to an existing sign. We began again.

Knowing that I am somewhat of a techno nerd, the committee member sitting near me asked me what I thought *digital* looked like. I was surprised at the question since I was there just as an observer and did not think anyone would be interested in the opinion of a hearing person, but I gave it my best shot: "Well, I would sign it '10101010,'" fingerspelling the 1–0-1–0-1–0-1–0 on my right hand, right to left in the American style.

The member thought this was a great suggestion and brought it to the board's attention. In the end, the committee modified the sign, and the new sign for *digital* became the following: On the left hand, the 1 sign is made; on the right hand, the 0 sign is made. Move the 0 back and forth in front of you as if to indicate motion. I was a bit shocked. Had I just broken the prime directive of anthropology by interfering with local language politics? Regardless, my suggestion has forever been immortalized in Japanese signing (figure 10.1).

COINING NEW SIGNS IN NIHON SHUWA

In American Sign Language, a large majority of new loan words borrowed from English are simply fingerspelled, at least when initially introduced (see Brentari and Padden 2001 for a more recent view). Although the faculty and students at Gallaudet University and other colleges and universities with large numbers of deaf students coin and disseminate new signs constantly, there is not enough media or organizational hegemony in the United States to consistently spread new lexical items nationally.

The original lexicon of ASL was solidified more or less by historical factors: The first American school for deaf students was created in Hartford in 1817, with a deaf teacher in a senior position, thus enabling an immediate sign language presence. The result was that a nascent language, American Sign Language, was born from a combination of French Sign Language (LSF), initialized signs for spoken English words, and the native homesigns and sign

61 | デジタル

● 丸めた右手を人差指を立てた左手の横を通って前の方に2回動かす

Source: New Signs. The Report of the 1997 Research Group for
Standardizing Sign Language. Tokyo: Japanese Federation of the Deaf. pp. 36.
平成9年度標準手話研究所事業報告書。
東京：全日本ろうあ連盟．pp 36．

Figure 10.1. New sign for *dejitaru* [digital]

languages of Deaf people in Boston, Hartford, New York, Philadelphia, and especially Martha's Vineyard (Gallaudet University 2001).

The subsequent founding of what would later become Gallaudet University kept the language community coherent as the graduates of Gallaudet spread across the United States as teachers at schools for deaf children. The Milan Conference of 1880 ended the era of sign language use in classrooms in the United States, but by that time ASL had been firmly established as a relatively coherent language system. However, since at least the postwar period, not a single institution has exercised hegemonic control over ASL in the United States.

Furthermore, ASL has optimized fingerspelling to the point where a finger-spelled word is so fast that individual letters may not be fully articulated, and the result is as fast as a regular sign (Battison 1978). In addition, ASL signers can read fingerspelling at a tremendously fast pace, using the sign linguistic equivalents to total-word and phonemic deconstruction.[4]

In addition to fingerspelling, ASL also has a tradition of initialized signs based on the French system, whereby the handshape corresponding to the first letter of an English (or French) word is used in the sign. Many ASL words are developed using initialization, and it has become a basic means for adding new words to the lexicon. One can often figure out what an initialized sign means by breaking it down into its handshape (which indicates the first letter of the corresponding spoken language word) versus the rest of its phonologi-cal parameters, which sometimes form what's been called a family of signs (Fischer and Gough 1978) or an ion-morph (Fernald and Napoli 2000). For example, in ASL the signs for FAMILY, TEAM, SOCIETY, ASSOCIATION, GROUP, and various others differ only in handshape because they are all part of a language family that shares an ion-morph meaning 'group.'[5]

Nihon Shuwa did not have a similar base in public schools since the Minis-try of Education prohibited its use; thus, its diffusion and growth were rather limited. Such a formal institution might have supported and promoted Nihon Shuwa if fingerspelling could be used for missing lexical items. Nihon Shuwa fingerspelling is a system based on modification of the ASL manual letters to accommodate the fact that spoken Japanese uses a syllabary for loan words. So each manual letter, if you will, in Nihon Shuwa fingerspelling corresponds not to a single sound but to the onset and nucleus of a syllable (which might be a single vowel sound but is more often a consonant plus a vowel). Additionally, if a syllable has more than one element in the nucleus (that is, a long vowel) or has a coda, then we need an additional syllabary symbol for writing and, thus, for fingerspelling. In addition, Nihon Shuwa fingerspelling moves up and down, left and right, and back and forth as it compensates for the forty-seven syllables in the kana syllabary and three *dakuten* [sonant] markers. This makes for a fingerspelling technique that is relatively slower to sign and even more difficult to read.[6]

For example, six syllabary symbols (GI-YU-U-NI-YU-U) are needed to sign the two-syllable Japanese word for *milk*. Furthermore, unlike spoken Japanese, which has pitch accents, or written Japanese, which utilizes kanji (that is, borrowed Chinese characters) and two syllabaries to differentiate between homonyms of native words and foreign loan words (as well as to indicate grammatical endings), Nihon Shuwa fingerspelling cannot differentiate between native and foreign homonyms. It remains a rather cumbersome system, and although local attempts, such as the Tochigi School for the Deaf fingerspelling method, have been devised to make it more efficient, these have not caught on.

Aside from fingerspelling unknown words, Nihon Shuwa has additional methods for coining new words. One is the obvious use of compound signs. Both native Nihon Shuwa signs and the constructed kanji signs are often used for this purpose. One example is the sign for Monbushô [Ministry of Education] (figure 10.2).[7]

Japanese signers apparently do not favor compounding as a means of coining signs. While compound signs are used in proper nouns, the preference is to have a single sign rather than a compound one for common nouns.

Because Nihon Shuwa was never officially used in the classroom, initialization as a method of coining new signs has only recently been exploited in Japan. The JFD Research Group has now begun using initialization to coin new signs since it allows for families of signs, with their relative transparency of meaning. Because there has been no tradition of creating signs this way, however, there is no set of ion-morphs (such as the ASL "group" ion-morph discussed earlier) on which to overlay the initials. Thus, comprehending these new signs is more difficult than it would be if the system were more established.

That is, if you see a new sign in Nihon Shuwa, you cannot immediately do a morphemic and alphabetic deconstruction as you can in ASL. New Nihon Shuwa signs are coined in a number of ways. Some (such as the sign for *digital*) are iconic or quasi-iconic. Others take the form of the Chinese character for the word (like the sign for *kaigo* [to nurse or take care of]), which is based

Figure 10.2. Sign for *Monbushô* [Ministry of Education]

on the physical shape of the Chinese character *kai* [take care of]. Or it can be a morphemic neologism, like *hoken* [insurance], which is based on a gesture indicating 'keep or protect.'

Every time I return to Japan, I find that I must scramble to learn the new signs that have developed over the past six to twelve months because it is impossible to decode new signs from their structure alone. Only a few can be inferred accurately from the context, many fewer than can be derived in the United States from a basic knowledge of initialized signs and loan words in ASL.

WHY THE NEED TO COIN NEW SIGNS?

Why does the JFD feel compelled to coin and disseminate new signs? A bit of history will shed some light on this. In 1980 the Ministry of Welfare awarded the JFD a grant that enabled the JSL Research Group to increase the vocabulary of Nihon Shuwa signers to help ensure that they would be able to keep up with modern Japanese (both the people and the language) and to help standardize Nihon Shuwa, a boon to interpreters and deaf people alike. These are certainly laudable goals and would probably be the public reasons the JFD would give if asked.

An additional and unstated reason would be that bureaucracies exist to replicate themselves. That is, once the committee was assigned the goal of coining at least one hundred new signs a year, that in itself became the committee's raison d'être. Certainly (although no one will admit it), some of the new signs coined by the working group are fluff signs designed to meet the annual quota. This is no different from the practices of any other nonprofit organization that has to hustle at the end of the year to fulfill its contract goals.

However, there is another, more profound reason, one that is more unsettling to the JFD and one that it does not publicly discuss. For, despite saying that "Japanese Sign is . . . the type of signing used by deaf persons living in . . . Japan" (JFD 1998, 2), the JFD is very protective of Nihon Shuwa. After all, its most popular series of sign textbooks is titled *Watashitachi no Shuwa* [Our Signs]. The first-person plural possessive pronoun comes across more strongly in Japanese than in English since it is an exclusive first-person term: *Ours* means 'not yours.' When the first volume of *Our Signs* was published in 1969, Nihon Shuwa was in a considerably more marginal position in society than it is now, and the JFD was much more radical politically.

Within the last two decades, there have been two threats to the JFD's control of Nihon Shuwa, one from radical Deaf people and one from well-meaning hearing persons. With its centrist and nonexclusionary position, the JFD is caught between a rock and a hard place.

THE ROCK: D-PRO ON THE RIGHT

In 1993 a group of young deaf people who had been strongly influenced by the bicultural/bilingual model of Deaf society promoted by certain Deaf activists in the United States created D-Pro, a cultural Deaf organization in Japan (Bienvenu and Colonomos 1985). The organization explains bilingualism and biculturalism this way:

> Deaf people have two languages, spoken and written Japanese and JSL. We live in two cultures, the culture of hearing people and the culture of the Deaf. Even though Deaf people have two languages and two cultures, JSL and the culture of the Deaf have always been regarded as inferior and worthless, ignored and not respected. Even Deaf people themselves have believed themselves to be worthless and inferior.
>
> Now, Deaf people have come to understand [that] their own language, Japanese Sign Language, is as perfect a language as any other language in the world and is not inferior at all. They have realized that even if their own way of communication, activity, behavior, value, belief and so on is different from that of hearing people, who are the majority, they do not have to feel inferior and/or guilty. These differences are the result of "cultural difference." Of course, it is important for the Deaf people to acquire Japanese and the culture of hearing people. Bilingualism/ biculturalism is the philosophy that those two languages and two cultures should be equally, but separately, respected. (D-Pro n.d., 1)

One of D-Pro's central language ideologies is that there is a pure Nihon Shuwa, which is signed without mouthing or vocalizing words and has a grammar that is distinct from spoken Japanese. As a visual-spatial language, it is the true language of Japanese deaf persons. This is a fairly articulate example of Michael Silverstein's definition of a linguistic ideology: "sets of beliefs about language articulated by users as rationalization or justification of perceived language structure and use" (1979, 193).

Although some of its textbooks have begun the process, D-Pro has not yet codified this pure Nihon Shuwa grammar, but the organization's position makes one thing clear: The language used by the JFD leadership—the style of speaking while signing—is not Nihon Shuwa. The group's leaders have stated this opinion numerous times. While I was at the Tokyo office, people who had attended D-Pro lectures would come in and complain about the latest "atrocities." The leaders of D-Pro call the JFD "a hard-of-hearing-people's group." Certainly, from the outside and looking only at the leaders (many of whom admittedly were deafened late), the JFD is not "pure deaf" inasmuch as it accepts anyone with a hearing loss, regardless of one's signing capabilities or deaf heritage.

Under the D-Pro model (and the U.S. model, which D-Pro draws from), deafness has a quasi-ethnic status. The purest deaf are those who are born of deaf parents. The next purest are those who were born deaf and attended schools for deaf pupils at an early age. Those who were late deafened or did not go to schools for deaf children are often not deaf (in this model) but only hard of hearing. The only ones who can really claim to sign pure Nihon Shuwa are those who learned it from their parents.

We need to stop here a moment and tease apart the political and the linguistic. Children exposed to sign from birth (as in the case of children born to deaf parents) are native signers. Children exposed to sign before the critical age of five have a very good chance of achieving nativelike fluency in sign. However, children exposed to sign after that will probably always have some ways in which their sign is distinguishable that of from native signers. The perception that late signers (those who learned after five) don't sign "pure Nihon Shuwa" may well have its roots in the fact that they are not native signers. Still, for the D-Pro leaders to then say these people aren't "deaf but only hard of hearing" is a political labeling. Audiologically, deaf is deaf. But linguistically, native signers can be distinguished from nonnative signers. There's something ironic about not allowing people membership in the Deaf world just because they are not native signers. For those who are audiologically deaf, that may limit the worlds in which they have full membership.

The JFD leadership is shocked when a D-Pro member is heard lecturing that only people born of deaf parents know true Nihon Shuwa or when JFD members are described as hard of hearing—when they all identify as deaf. At one of these horror-story sessions, the director of the Tokyo office threw up her hands and exclaimed, "Sorewa shuwa fashizumu yo!" [That's sign fascism!]

Of course, because she was in a mixed deaf/hearing group, she spoke out loud at the same time she signed this, so, according to D-Pro, she was not signing Nihon Shuwa even in her moment of ultimate exasperation, further proving she was not really deaf but rather one of those hard-of-hearing masqueraders. Nonetheless, her claim of linguistic fascism was not far from the mark even if put in rather strident terms.

Members of D-Pro have been challenging the JFD's control of Nihon Shuwa in other areas as well. At the research group meeting mentioned earlier, one of the participants complained that he had been demonstrating new signs at a teacher-training seminar when a D-Pro member suddenly challenged him on the sign RICH-PERSON (figure 10.3).

In the JFD's dictionary (Yonekawa 1997), the illustration of the sign meaning 'rich' is best described as evoking an image of one who is fat with money, while the D-Pro member insisted that the real sign was based on the sign for 'business suit.' The JFD member was clearly disturbed by this development.

Figure 10.3. Sign for *kanemochi* [rich person]

This is very likely just a regional difference in Nihon Shuwa, although I have seen only the JFD variation and never the other variant used in the context of 'rich.' In private, many signers will compare the way they sign various words, but a public challenge is rare indeed. That the D-Pro member would challenge a JFD member (both deaf themselves) is astonishing, and that the JFD member would point out that the challenger was D-Pro is also significant. Both the D-Pro and the JFD clearly see themselves as opponents.

In one of the greatest ironies, one of the prominent leaders of D-Pro is also the head teacher at the only national, sign interpreter–training program in Japan. Funded by the Ministry of Health and Social Welfare, this program is held at the National Rehabilitation Center for the Disabled (NRCD) in Saitama prefecture, just north of Tokyo, which causes the JFD some consternation.[8] In the JFD-led interpreter courses, the interpreters not only use a grammar that closely approximates the spoken sentences they are interpreting but also learn to mouth the words at the same time (to facilitate the speechreading of unknown words). In the NRCD course (run by Harumi Kimura, the head of D-Pro), however, the interpreters work with closed mouths and use a syntax natural to sign—based largely on spatial relationships (i.e., what D-Pro calls pure Nihon Shuwa).

The victims in this case are the interpreters who complete the NRCD course. Kimura accepts only those who have relatively little sign knowledge (i.e., are not "infected" with the JFD's hard-of-hearing way of signing). They are taught through the bilingual/bicultural model (which emphasizes the differences between the Deaf and hearing cultures) and to sign in the manner described earlier.

However, once they graduate, they fall again into the domain of the JFD since that organization controls most of the interpreter dispatch centers and JFD members are the ones most likely to request interpreter services (by sheer numerical majority). The negative response to the NRCD interpreters is quite strong. Older deaf people complain that they cannot understand their signs, nor can they speechread the words since the interpreters do not mouth them. Moreover, they are unable to understand the nonlinear syntax the interpreters use. As a result, few NRCD interpreters are able to get jobs at interpreter dispatch centers unless they are retrained to sign in the more mainstream style.

The cultural divide is also quite severe. D-Pro insists that there is a separate Deaf culture that involves sign language and the embodiment of deafness, whereas the JFD leadership for the most part dismisses the idea of a separate Deaf culture. According to the JFD, signing is how they communicate, but language itself does not constitute culture. The deaf Japanese of the JFD do not see themselves as culturally apart from other Japanese. They are deaf, and they need to sign to communicate with other people, but otherwise they are the same as everyone else.

THE HARD PLACE: NHK ON THE LEFT

The JFD also finds itself at odds with another entity that threatens its control of Nihon Shuwa: the quasi-public broadcasting television network, NHK. Since 1983 NHK has been broadcasting two television shows using sign language: *Everyone's Sign* (an hour-long sign language course) and *The Sign News* (a fifteen-minute daily news show).[9]

The name of the first program is telling. The JFD's textbook series is called *Our Signs*, where *our* is clearly intended to indicate deaf people exclusively, whereas the title of NHK's show extends ownership to all Japanese.

Although it would seem that *Everyone's Sign* would be the most immediate source of threat, it is not. The level of sign language taught on the program is relatively basic, and it helps to popularize signing, so there is no issue there.

The real threat seems to be in *The Sign News* program. The producers of this eclectic program review video footage from the main news program and select the highlights, and the Nihon Shuwa newscasters (who are predominantly sign interpreters) deliver the reports. This is in contrast to similar shows in the UK and the United States (*See Hear* and *Deaf Mosaic*, respectively) that feature fluent d/Deaf signers. The producer of *The Sign News* explained to me that it uses a variety of signing styles, as well as open captions, in order to be as accessible as possible to a broad range of viewers with hearing impairments. All of the signing is both open captioned and overdubbed or simultaneously voiced.

This is where the danger lies. *The Sign News* takes the daily headlines and translates them into sign language, but new words are always popping up for which there are not yet any Nihon Shuwa signs. As a result, *The Sign News* has to work around this problem. As with most other signers, the newscasters eschew fingerspelling; in any event, one cannot fingerspell at the same speed as that in which the overdubbing voice is reading the text, so there would be no point. The newscasters therefore have to invent signs and ways of expressing new ideas.

What intensifies the problem is that the open-captioning and overdubbing make watching *The Sign News* an ideal way to learn Nihon Shuwa. It is as if you are trying to learn a foreign language and have a continuously running transliteration into your own language. The ratings for *The Sign News* are rather low, but a good number of the viewers are interpreters, who pick up any new signs that the program uses. It is also watched by foreigners, who appreciate the open-captioning and slower pace of the news.[10] (I never saw a deaf family watch *The Sign News;* most deaf people told me that it was too much of a bother.)

Until recently, most of the newscasters on *The Sign News* were hearing interpreters. The JFD's concern has been that hearing people are creating new signs on *The Sign News* without feedback from the Deaf community. Because the news must go on, the staff members of *The Sign News* are in a tough position. While a central goal of the JSL research group has been to coin new signs for use in the media, they necessarily lag behind *The Sign News*.

In 1995 NHK hired a fluent signer for *The Sign News*. Born in 1967 in Yamagata prefecture, Nasu Hideaki lost his hearing at two years of age, when he developed a high fever. He went to deaf schools for his entire elementary and secondary education and learned sign language from an older deaf person in his neighborhood. Thus, D-Pro would say he signs pure Nihon Shuwa since he does not use spoken Japanese syntax and certainly does not voice. When he signs the news, he uses typical visual-spatial language with many classifiers. Nasu would be described as using *dentôteki-shuwa* [traditional sign language] or *rôashateki shuwa* [deaf person's sign language] in contrast to *gendai no shuwa* [modern sign]. While there is open-captioning of the reports, an NHK sign interpreter voices what Nasu is saying. The reaction to him has been mixed.

Research by Shôzô Yoshizawa (1996) at the Tochigi School for the Deaf hints at certain aspects of this confusion. Yoshizawa ran a study of deaf viewers to whom he showed two clips from *The Sign News*. One clip showed a hearing interpreter who used sequential Nihon Shuwa (that is, with spoken Japanese word order), while the other showed Nasu, who used spatial Nihon Shuwa. Yoshizawa analyzed their comprehension and retention rates and came up with interesting results. For the interpreter who signed in sequential Nihon Shuwa, the deaf subjects were better able to explain in written Japanese what she had signed. In contrast, they had trouble writing down in Japanese sentences the content of Nasu's segment. However, they better understood what Nasu was talking about even if they could not write it in Japanese. Yoshizawa explains these puzzling results by pointing out that most Japanese deaf people have had many years of contact with sequential Japanese in various settings, including high school and the workplace. They are used to seeing these signs and immediately transliterating them and thus can write them down. However, they have very little comprehension of material presented in this fashion, especially if it is complex or delivered at a fast pace, such as during the news program. They are used to seeing Nasu's type of sign language because it is the informal variety that deaf people themselves use, but they have rarely seen it used in a formal setting such as on news shows. They therefore have more trouble explaining (in Japanese) what was said even if they have better comprehension at a deeper level.

This is a complicated situation, for most older deaf people will tell you that they prefer the sequential form, especially when it is used by hearing people. Situations like this are often described as *diglossic* (Hudson 1992; Errington 1991), a term that refers to the existence of both high and low forms of a language, especially in the context of colonialism. The political terrain of diglossia is just starting to emerge in Japan, but it is rapidly solidifying along territorial lines.

THE FIFTH COLUMN: STUDENTS

One emerging source of language change in Japan is the new cadre of deaf college students, especially those at the Tsukuba College of Technology (TCT) for the Deaf, the only college specifically for deaf students in Japan. Founded in 1993, TCT offers a three-year program in information and computer sciences. Many of the students at TCT attended hearing schools, so TCT provides their first occasion to meet other deaf students.

The National Association of Deaf Students and TCT have brought together this new generation of mainstreamed youth. One of the noteworthy things about this group is its playfulness in signing. For these young people, signing is a fun area of exploration and experimentation, and they mix visual and verbal puns in a complex fashion not exercised by their elders.

For example, one common signing behavior that I noticed among the students was the fingerspelling of interjections. In English, we say "oh yeah," "hmm," "whew," "wow," and so on. Spoken Japanese has a huge number of these quasi-onomatopoeic utterances, expanded even more so by the popularity of manga comics. Older signers might indicate confusion by a quizzical look, but younger signers will actually sign (using fingerspelling) HO~~~~, which is the Japanese phrase for indicating bemusement (like "hmm"). Or they will sign HEH HEH HEH HEH HEH for a confident laugh or SA~~~~~ when they are puzzled. These are all simple forms that drag across the body, just like dialogue imposed on a manga comic frame. There are also complex utterances such as O-YA or A-RE for surprise.[11]

One other new phenomenon is verbal puns in signs. For example, one popular new sign at TCT is that for indicating a pizza. The sign is made by placing the P handshape on the knee. The P handshape refers to the first letter of the English word *pizza*, while the location of the knee evokes the Japanese word for 'knee' [*hiza*]. When the handshape and the location are combined, as in P + *hiza*, the result is a sign meaning 'pizza.'

This example is similar to an ASL sign for the large department store *Sears*. The sign is made by placing both hands in the S handshape at the ears (Sutton-Spence and Napoli 2009). More common across signed languages are signs that are used to mean one thing and then are used to mean a second thing based solely on the homonymy of the corresponding spoken words. For example, in Indian Sign Language, the sign for *bindi* [a dot that some women place on the center of their foreheads] is made by pointing to the center of the forehead with the extended index finger. The sign for 'okra' (or 'ladyfinger') is the very same as the sign for *bindi* because the Hindi word for 'okra' is *bhindi*, which looks similar to *bindi* on the lips (though it sounds different).[12]

Middle-aged Nihon Shuwa signers might use fingerspelling to sign conjunctions (such as DE, which means 'and' or 'but'), but I did not see this playfulness. This habit is regionally specific. Tochigi signers will frequently use this type of conjunctive fingerspelling, but other regions use it less or not at all.

This sort of verbal witticism was developed by those who were born into a mainstream experience, were well acclimated into hearing culture, and applied their deep knowledge of spoken Japanese into a new subculture of playful punning of Japanese and Nihon Shuwa.

CONCLUSION

The centralized structure of the JFD allows it to be an active presence in creating a language ideology surrounding Nihon Shuwa. The JFD's government contracts to define and promote signing give it more say over the direction of Nihon Shuwa than the National Association of the Deaf in the United States and most other national organizations. However, even its enviable position is not unassailable, as it must fight off challenges from both the private and the public sectors.

In this chapter I have described the fragmentation that is occurring around the edges of Nihon Shuwa and the struggle for control of the language by various groups in Japan. Sign language interpreters are at the center of contending theories about Japanese signing. It is very possible to emerge from the NRCD interpreter school thinking you know and are signing so-called pure Nihon Shuwa. However, when these newly minted graduates encounter the mainstream of the Deaf community, they quickly learn that there is very little tolerance of hearing people, specifically interpreters, who use this form of signing.[13] The new community members then have to switch to a more Japaneselike Nihon Shuwa. To make matters worse, although interpreters diligently watch *The Sign News* since it is a good source of models on which to

base new signs (since it uses so many new words and comes handily captioned), they are severely criticized when they try to bring back their newfound
knowledge to interpreting sessions, for the JFD is also fighting the public
broadcasting network for control over their language.

Notes

I thank Donna Jo Napoli of Swarthmore and Gaurav Mathur of Gallaudet for their
endless good cheer and support. This chapter builds substantially from my 2006
"Creating and Contesting Signs in Contemporary Japan: Language Ideologies,
Identity, and Community in Flux" in *Sign Language Studies* 7(1): 11–29. I am grateful
to Gallaudet University Press and Project Muse for permission to reprint major parts
of that article here.

1. This chapter is based on participant-observation research of Japanese Deaf politics in Tokyo between 1997 and 2001. The study was sponsored by a Wenner-Gren
Foundation Small Grant for Dissertation Research (#6144). Sign examples used here
are courtesy of the Japanese Federation of the Deaf.

2. I sometimes use the Japanese style of the last name with an honorific (-*san*,
meaning Mr., Mrs., Ms., or Miss).

3. Here I am using ASL fingerspelling in my description. The D handshape looks
like the 1 handshape, except that in D the fingerpads of the middle finger and the
thumb come together, whereas in 1 the nonextended fingers close into a fist.

Nihon Shuwa has its own fingerspelling syllabary, which was adopted after World
War II. The system is based on American Sign Language letters, although it has been
greatly expanded to take into account the much larger syllabary in Japanese. There is
also a prewar NS fingerspelling syllabary that is no longer in current use.

4. When I took speed fingerspelling at Gallaudet University in 1995, we were taught
to recognize sequences of fingerspelled handshapes: M-A-N, E-R, P-R-O, and so forth.
Both when fingerspelling and reading fingerspelled words, signers use these as building blocks to accelerate their reading and spelling. My ASL tutor shared an anecdote
about her deaf daughter, who knew that the sign for 'refrigerator' was fingerspelled
R-E-F but was not able to connect that to the actual spelling of *refrigerator*. Other fingerspelled words (e.g., BANK, DOG) have undergone phonological rules to become bona fide
signs; that is, they've lost much or even all of their immediate association with fingerspelling. This is perhaps similar to the way in which certain loan words in Japanese
have lost their foreignness (e.g., *tempura*). Battison (1978) discusses this form of lexicalized fingerspelling and loan signs.

5. This system, which consists of a fingerspelling component that indicates the first
letter of the English word and a base ASL morpheme that indicates the class of meaning, seems remarkably similar to the way in which kanji characters are put together: a
root radical that indicates the class that the character belongs to (a category of words
related to plants, trees, humans, etc.), plus another component that indicates its pronunciation.

6. There are also many wrist motions in Nihon Shuwa fingerspelling, which
contributes to the prevalence of repetitive stress disorders among interpreters (carpal

tunnel syndrome; tennis elbow, etc.), who fingerspell the most (fingerspelling is not nearly as common in Nihon Shuwa as in ASL, however).

7. The sign images in this chapter are courtesy of the Japanese Federation of the Deaf.

8. All of the prefectural interpreter-training programs are run by JFD affiliates. It is odd that the government chose to put Harumi Kimura, a very young woman by Japanese standards (late twenties), in charge of the national interpreter program. It is even odder since the government prefers to take centrist positions, and Kimura is known for being radical. The story behind this placement is not one that I was able to elicit.

9. In addition, NHK has a program that airs issues of importance to people with disabilities, including special segments on deafness.

10. Of the fifteen-minute program, only about five minutes are dedicated to headline news. You would be better off scanning the newspaper headlines for more information. There is a complex politics as to why *The Sign News* exists. Basically NHK was pressured into it because of the international decade for persons with disabilities.

11. There are at least two equivalent forms in ASL: HA-HA-HA-HA for laughing and N-O for "no." And then there is a whole set of ASL puns, which is beyond the scope of this discussion (Sutton-Spence and Napoli 2009).

12. This is quite common in ASL, however. For example, the sign for El Paso (Texas) is the L sign held on one hand while the other hand makes an O sign that passes by the L, making "L pass O." There are myriad other examples. What is unclear is whether the students in Japan knew about the ASL puns or developed them independently.

13. Exceptions abound. I signed using a very ASL-like Nihon Shuwa, using base ASL syntax with Nihon Shuwa signs. This makes my signing very deaflike *(rôashateki)*, like Nasu-san's. However, people seemed to like it or at least to use it as a basis for assuming I was deaf myself. But then again, I was not an interpreter. Some other interpreters, especially those whose parents were deaf themselves, also sign in a very deaflike fashion, with heavy changes to the syntax (away from spoken Japanese syntax). They receive varying degrees of both positive and negative feedback. The overwhelmingly negative feedback is reserved for the NRCD graduates, although one suspects it has descended into a simple rivalry between the JFD and D-Pro at this point.

Bibliography

Aramburo, Anthony J. 1995. Sociolinguistic Aspects of the Black Deaf Community. In *Linguistics of American Sign Language*, ed. Clayton Valli and Ceil Lucas, 367–379. Washington, D.C.: Gallaudet University Press.

Battison, Robin. 1978. *Lexical Borrowing in American Sign Language*. Silver Spring, Md.: Linstok.

Bienvenu, Martina J., and Betty M. Colonomos. 1985. *An Introduction to American Deaf Culture*. Burtonsville, Md.: Sign Media.

Brentari, Diane, and Carol Padden. 2001. Native and Foreign Vocabulary in American Sign Language: A Lexicon with Multiple Origins. In *Foreign Vocabulary in Sign Languages: A Cross-linguistic Investigation on Word Formation*, ed. Diane Brentari, 87–119. Mahwah, N.J.: Erlbaum.

D-Pro. n.d. [ca. 1995] *What Is D-Pro?* Photocopied manuscript. Tokyo.

Errington, J. Joseph. 1991. A Muddle for the Model: Diglossia and the Case of Javanese. *Southwest Journal of Linguistics* 10(1): 189–213.

Fernald, Theodore, and Donna Jo Napoli. 2000. Exploitation of Morphological Possibilities in Signed Languages: Comparison of American Sign Language with English. *Sign Language and Linguistics* 3(1): 3–58.

Fischer, Susan D., and Bonnie Gough. 1978. Verbs in American Sign Language. *Sign Language Studies* 18:17–48.

Gallaudet University. 2001. History through Deaf Eyes. http://depts.gallaudet.edu/deafeyes/exhibit/.

Gramsci, Antonio. 1971. *Selections from the Prison Notebooks of Antonio Gramsci.* New York: International Publishers.

Horkheimer, Max, and Theodor W. Adorno. 1972. *Dialectic of Enlightenment.* New York: Herder and Herder.

Hudson, Alan. 1992. Diglossia: A Bibliographic Review. *Language in Society* 21(4): 611–674.

Japanese Federation of the Deaf (JFD). 1997. *Heisei 9-nendo Hyôjun Shuwa Kenkyûjo Jigyô Hôkokusho* [New Signs: A Report of the 1997 Sign Standardization Committee]. Tokyo: Japanese Federation of the Deaf.

———. 1998. Shuwa ni kansuru FAQ [Frequently Asked Questions about Sign]. *Sign Language Communication Studies* 28: 2.

Le Master, Barbara. 2003. Local Meanings of Irish Deaf Identity. In *Many Ways to Be Deaf: International Linguistic and Sociocultural Variation,* ed. Leila F. Monaghan, Constanze Schmaling, Karen Nakamura, and Graham H. Turner, 153–172. Washington, D.C.: Gallaudet University Press.

Lucas, Ceil, Alyssa Wulf, Robert Bayley, Paul Dudis, Clayton Valli, and Mary Rose. 2001. *Sociolinguistic Variation in American Sign Language.* Washington, D.C.: Gallaudet University Press.

Prime Minister's Office. 1995, 1996, 1999, 2003. *Shôgaisha Hakusho* [Disability White Paper]. Tokyo: Ministry of Finance Publishing.

Silverstein, Michael. 1979. Language Structure and Linguistic Ideology. In *The Elements: A Parasession on Linguistic Units and Levels,* ed. Paul R. Clyne, William F. Hanks, and Carol L. Hofbauer, 193–247. Chicago: Chicago Linguistic Society.

Sutton-Spence, Rachel, and Donna Jo Napoli. 2009. *Humour in Sign Languages: The Linguistic Underpinnings.* Dublin: Trinity College.

Tsukuba College of Technology Public Relations Committee. 1998. *Tsukuba Gijutsu Tankidaigaku Gaiyô* [Outline of Tsukuba College of Technology]. Tsukuba City, Japan: Tsukuba College Printing Department.

Woolard, Kathryn. A., and Bambi B. Schieffelin. 1994. Language Ideology. *Annual Review of Anthropology* 23: 55–82.

Yonekawa, Akihiko, ed. 1997. *Nihongo-Shuwa Jiten* [Japanese Language: Signing Dictionary]. Tokyo: Japanese Federation of the Deaf.

Yoshizawa, Shôzô. 1996. *Bairingaru Kyôiku, Bairingarizumu wo Kangaeru Tokino Shuwa ya Gengo no Shosokumen ni Tsuite* [Thoughts on Signing and Language in Bilingualism and Bilingual Education from the Reader's Perspective]. Manuscript.

Pluralization

An Alternative to the Existing Hegemony in JSL

Soya Mori

INTRODUCTION

Karen Nakamura's chapter clearly continues the discussion begun in her book, the by-now famous *Deaf in Japan* (Nakamura 2006). A major source of material for this extended version is her original chapter 11, titled "Language Wars and Language Policies; or, How an Itinerant Anthropologist Introduced a New Sign into the Japanese Sign Lexicon." Working from the same set of data about the Deaf community in Japan, in the present study Dr. Nakamura portrays another view of the hegemony wars in the community. This time the ideological presence of the Japanese Federation of the Deaf (JFD) in the hegemony of language politics is presented as weakened by the newer situations in Japan. I use this portrayal as a springboard for further discussion about sign language standardization and issues of hegemony, moving first to Myanmar and then back to Japan. Ultimately, my point is that pluralization has occurred as an alternative to JSL hegemony. I use the term *pluralization* to refer to the emergence of several smaller entities with power in the presence of an older, single authority. This notion describes a social/political phenomenon that is very dynamic, in contrast to *plurality*, which merely describes a static situation of several entities in place.

MYANMAR SL "STANDARDIZATION" PROJECT

I am presently (writing in the winter of 2008–2009) involved in the Myanmar Sign Language Standardization project, under the auspices of the Japan International Cooperation Agency (JICA), which is similar to USAID in the United States. The project title might appear regrettable for most Deaf Americans and sign linguists. However, we must keep in mind that JICA is a quasi-governmental organization and that its assistance projects are mainly government-to-government ones. This situation has an effect on its official framework and on the names of the projects it oversees. As is well known, the Myanmar government has a unique governing structure and system that are as highly centralized as those in China. Although there are many ethnic groups and languages in Myanmar, the official language of the country is Burmese, and most of the people in the bigger cities speak this language. Via standardization of the spoken language, the government of Myanmar can control many aspects of life in the country's major cities quite effectively despite the multiplicity of other, nonofficial languages. In fact, the government's control in Myanmar is as effective as in the United States, where English is the spoken language of the majority even outside the major cities. Indeed, spoken English hegemony in the United States (and, for that matter, in the world) is strong, so the comparison gives us an idea of the hegemony of Burmese in Myanmar.

It's no surprise, then, that the government of Myanmar would like to have a standardized sign language as in other countries. Actually, in many developed countries, the standardization process was not imposed by the government. Instead, it occurred naturally as part of Deaf community development, as in the United States and Japan. However, many developing countries do not have what could be called a national Deaf community. Rather, Deaf people are spread across the land and have little communication with each other. Often in these countries it would be hard for Deaf people to come together for a national-level meeting and to share the resources of the nationwide media because of poor infrastructure and their own livelihood situations. In these cases, most governments of developing countries feel pressured by international standards to respond to the needs of their Deaf citizens, so they try to rush the standardization process with governmental assistance. The Myanmar government turned to the Japanese government for assistance in this endeavor. The Japanese Ministry of Foreign Affairs passed the request on to JICA. Then JICA asked the Japanese Federation of the Deaf to collaborate with it because the JFD is the largest organization of deaf and hard-of-hearing people in Japan who predominantly use sign language.

JFD'S COMMITMENT AND NEW ALTERNATIVE POLICY

Through government-to-government discussions about the international cooperation involved, Myanmar Sign Language Standardization was selected as the name of the project. Taking JFD's policies about sign language in Japan as a starting point, one might have expected JFD to implement the same policies in developing countries. Initially, JFD did just that; it tried to establish the same hierarchical system in Myanmar as in Japan. With this system, a central committee has the responsibility of coining new signs, as Nakamura's chapter explains.

Delegate members of the committee then work to promote wide and effective diffusion of the new signs.

However, JFD's intentions did not meet with the success it expected. The major obstacle was the Myanmar government itself, which wanted to maintain strong control over its Deaf communities. As in Japan, JFD planned to establish a national organization of Deaf people in Myanmar as the first step in the standardization process. However, the Myanmar government officer refused to allow the formation of such an organization. While in Myanmar, as in most developing countries, some small Deaf communities are centered around Deaf schools, there is no national community and no national organization. Thus, despite the presence of these small Deaf communities, as a whole the Deaf community has no bargaining power with the hearing government.

At this point JFD asked me, as president of the Japanese Association of Sign Linguistics, to help it take another proposal to the Myanmar government for the improvement of the social welfare of Deaf people. The social welfare priority is JFD's most important policy regardless of the country it works in; indeed, this aspect of the demand-rights movement is shared by organizations of people with disabilities all over the world. Via contracts with the Japanese government, JFD works to extend its hegemony and bargaining power both within Japan and elsewhere—and civil rights is a major point to bargain for. At first, JFD proposed publishing a Myanmar Sign Language book. During the initial negotiations, the Myanmar government told JFD that it also wanted to publish a Myanmar Sign Language book. However, later JFD learned that the government had already published two authorized sign vocabulary books. At that point it was clear that JFD needed to propose an alternative project.

The policy proposal we made to the Myanmar government is as follows. We proposed that a Myanmar Sign Language textbook be published, packed with linguistic information about all aspects of the language—phonology, morphology, syntax, semantics, and culture. This text will spread the information that sign language is bona fide language and that Myanmar Sign Language, in particular, is as much a natural human language as Burmese (or any other natural human language). In this way the text will enlighten hearing and Deaf leaders and inevitably lead to greater respect of both Deaf culture and the language of Deaf communities on the part of hearing and Deaf people alike. Increased self-esteem will foster a sense of entitlement to rights and naturally lead to the internal formation of a national organization of Deaf people to demand and safeguard those rights. Therefore, the publication of such a text will, essentially and eventually, empower Deaf people in Myanmar. That is one of the tacit goals of the project: The Myanmar Sign Standardization project team expects that the wide dissemination and utilization of Myanmar Sign Language will empower Deaf people in Myanmar.

BACK TO JAPAN

This quick glance at the situation of Deaf people and of sign language in another Asian country, Myanmar, now makes obvious one of the most important benefits of the kind of hegemony found in the JFD, and that is power. The organizational hierarchy allows JFD access to national media and endeavors to secure the use of sign language in Deaf schools in each prefecture in Japan. For many years in Japan, we had no institution of higher education for Deaf youth comparable to Gallaudet University in the United States. Now we have Tsukuba University of Technology, which is the only four-year university for Deaf students in Japan. Though it has a shorter history than Gallaudet and has not yet attained the same status that Gallaudet has achieved in the eyes of American Deaf communities, it is of crucial importance to the overall situation of Deaf people in Japan. Deaf schools, from Tsukuba down to local schools throughout Japan, are reveling in sign language, and interesting linguistic phenomena, such as the verbal puns Nakamura describes, are, naturally, on the rise. The younger generation is leading the way in changing and playing with the language—just as we would expect from looking at language development in other countries. The JFD will need to follow the generational innovations and the introduction of newly coined signs and conversational styles in the future.

AN ASIDE: JSL AND INITIALIZATION

In her chapter, Nakamura writes about fingerspelling patterns in Japanese Sign Language (JSL), particularly with regard to the coining of new signs. Most of her comments are not surprising to anyone who is familiar with ASL fingerspelling. But that is not the full story. I would like to add an interesting point to that discussion since JSL differs from ASL with regard to fingerspelling in ways pertinent to the feasibility of using initialization to coin new signs.

In Japan, as Nakamura writes, we have four writing systems: Kanji (the characters), Hiragana and Katakana (two separate syllabaries), and the Roman alphabet for those who want to transliterate Euro-American words. The Katakana syllabary is used mostly to render loan words from a foreign language. However, since loan words are adapted to conform to Japanese syllable structure ((C)V—that is, an optional consonant followed by a vowel; note that only a handful of consonants can follow the vowel), very often a loan word in Japanese sounds distinctly different from the source word in English, typically having additional syllables that are absent in the English. Accordingly, many times the phonological pattern represented in the Katakana for a loan word from English does not match the phonological pattern represented in the alphabetic rendering of the word in English.

All of this is to say that as the Katakana is used for loan words in written Japanese, the Japanese fingerspelling system, which is based on a Japanese syllabary system, is employed in JSL as a loan system. So fingerspelling for Deaf Japanese is based on syllables, in contrast to the alphabetic fingerspelling that Deaf Americans use. Additionally, JSL fingerspelling is enriched by several handshapes from the ASL manual alphabet and some other features (one of which I'll discuss later)—that is, it is a manual syllabary with some extra alphabetic symbols thrown in. What this means is that any process of coining of new signs that involves fingerspelling will be different in JSL, which uses a syllabary, from that in ASL, which uses an alphabet. In particular, this means that the processes of initialization in JSL and ASL are different, but it does not mean a priori that the process need be more restricted in JSL than in ASL. However, it turns out that it is. I'd like to explain the reason for this.

Nakamura writes, "Initialization as a method of coining new signs has only recently been exploited in Japan." However, even before 1980, when JFD began inventing new signs under its contract with the Ministry of Social Welfare and Health, JSL was using several initialized signs. One example is *ri-kai* [understand], which is formed by making the sign for the syllable [ri] and then compounding it with the Nihon Shuwa sign for 'know.' This [ri] is an example of one of the few initializable fingerspellings introduced in JSL. Indeed, not many fingerspellings in JSL lend themselves to being employed in the formation of new initialized signs. This particular instance has no counterpart in ASL since ASL does not have signs that correspond to syllables (as distinct from whole words).

Other interesting questions arise when we try to render a pair of Chinese characters that have been compounded. In fact, a number of Chinese characters have infiltrated the writing system of many Asian countries to some degree, with the result that several Asian sign languages vary with respect to the characters that become rendered in the sign language. The situation is complex in that the actual compounds borrowed from Chinese vary in the written Asian languages, and which of these compounds these Asian sign languages render varies further. The result is that the distribution pattern for these compounds in the sign languages differs from those in the ambient written languages in these Asian countries. I leave this observation for future analysis.

CONCLUSION

I would like to conclude by discussing the current situation of JFD, which had hegemonic control over JSL until the 1980s. In fact, JFD was practically the only JSL lexicon book publisher in the world for a while. However, after pressure from "rocks" of the "right" and the "left" (Nakamura's terms, indicating simultaneous attacks from two sides), this situation changed drastically. Now we find a very wide range of JSL books published by private publishers, who are increasing in number—diversification of JSL resources continues. On the television network NHK, *The Sign News* program is involving more and more Deaf and CODA newscasters (as of April 2009, of the thirteen newscasters, eight are Deaf and two are CODAs) who have some relationships with D-Pro. In addition, JSL native signers have more official presence in the media than ever before. Native signer newscasters do not find it more difficult than non-native signer newscasters to convey the news. This is because they use classifiers and fingerspelling as productive vehicles for new words and technical terms. Moreover, new words and technical terms are entering the Deaf community in great number since new social and professional situations are emerging within the Japanese Deaf community. All of this predicts the demise of JFD's hegemony. An initial proof of that demise is reflected in the fact that the sales of *Watashitachi-no-Shuwa* [Our Signs] has declined rapidly, as has JFD's status in making appeals regarding the progress of social conditions of Deaf people in Japan. Now JFD has many financial problems, as well as a diminished pool of people who want to assume leadership roles. Some of JFD's exiting leaders feel a sense of crisis regarding the future of the organization. This is exacerbated by the fact that in 1991 a new organization for nonsigning deaf and hard-of-hearing people, All Japan Association of Hard-of-Hearing People, was established and is drawing potential members away from JFD.

In the United States, the National Association of the Deaf (NAD) has never had the kind of influential power over ASL that JFD has had in Japan over JSL, and JFD might well be subject to the same fate. At this moment JFD is struggling to survive. Nakamura might soon find fodder for her next study.

Note

I thank Harumi Kimura, instructor, National Rehabilitation Center for Persons with Disabilities and NHK *Deaf News* newscaster.

Bibliography

Nakamura, Karen. 2006. *Deaf in Japan: Signing and the Politics of Identity.* Ithaca, N.Y.: Cornell University Press.

CHAPTER 11

Social Situations and the Education of Deaf Children in China

Jun Hui Yang

INTRODUCTION

Let me start with a little background information about me. I was born and grew up in Beijing, China. I have been deaf since I was four and a half years old. My parents, who are hearing, invested a lot of time and money in me and treated me, their deaf daughter, much better than their hearing son. That was not customary in the Chinese culture. I attended both deaf schools and regular public schools, and I have worked as a deaf academic teacher of the deaf in Beijing for more than three years; when I was initially hired, I was the first and only such teacher at that time. I obtained a BA in Chinese language and education from Capital Normal University in Beijing in 1994, an MS degree in education from RIT in 2000, and a PhD in Deaf education from Gallaudet University in 2006. My research areas are Chinese Sign Language and deaf education. Presently I am a lecturer in Deaf studies at the University of Central Lancashire in the United Kingdom.

The main purpose of this chapter is to present an overview of social situations and educational opportunities that have influenced deaf children's and young adults' learning and language development in both Chinese Sign Language and written Chinese in mainland China.

THE SOCIAL CONTEXT IN MAINLAND CHINA

China has the largest population in the world, estimated at 1.3 billion, which is one fifth of the world's population. Of these, how many are deaf and hard of hearing? It is estimated that there are 20.57 million people, the largest deaf and hard-of-hearing population, one fourth, in the world. There have been two national censuses on disability in China, completed in 1987 and 2006. Table 11.1

Table 11.1. National Population, Percentages, and Raw Numbers

	National population	Proportion of people with disability	People with hearing impairment	D/HH children
1987	near 1.1 billion	4.9%	17.76 million (16.79% of the population with disability) 1% of the national population	younger than 14 years: 800,000
2006	more than 1.3 billion	6.43%	20.57 million (24% of the population with disability) 1.5% of the national population	younger than 6 years: 137,000 younger than 18 years: 1,820,00

Note: Hong Kong, Macau, and Taiwan are not included.
Source: www.cdpf.org.cn

displays the national population, the total estimate of people with disabilities, and the estimated population of those who are deaf and hard of hearing, including both adults and children.

The first census was less stringent than the second in that it relied more upon respondents' self-reports of their own audiological condition or their families' assessment of their deafness, which were not thoroughly verified. In contrast, the second census (in 2006) was done much more efficiently and involved audiological checks using improved technology and medical examinations by specialized practitioners. The latter figures also included a wider range of hearing loss, which is reflected in the apparently enormous rise in the percentages during the twenty years between the censuses.

The Chinese government's main focus for the entire population has been on economic development and on encouraging international exchange in business, science, technology, and education. There are gaps between developed areas, developing areas, and underdeveloped areas. Chinese families face three large challenges: health care, education, and employment. Most families with deaf or hard-of-hearing children have a heavier socioeconomic burden, especially those who seek a cure or assistive technology and training for their child's deafness and are forced to pay for hearing aids or cochlear implants, speech therapy in preschools (hearing and speech rehabilitation centers for deaf children), and other expenses. Only a very small percentage of families have received support from charities and nongovernment organizations to enable them to afford hearing aids and cochlear implants.

Modern China has experienced rapid economic development and has been in stable both politically and socially for the past twenty years. The Internet, televisions, DVD players, mobile phones, and other advanced communication technologies have been spreading rapidly throughout educational settings and society in China. Hearing aids, cochlear implants, and other devices for aural and oral training are now available in the larger cities. Many classrooms for deaf students are now equipped with computers, projectors, and multimedia equipment, some of which have been provided by charities and international organizations (e.g., UNICEF, Save the Children, PEN-International). Parents of deaf children, deaf and hearing teachers, and other deaf community members have constructed networks and support groups through Internet-based forums and extensive social activities.

More positive images of deaf people and their talents in the performance and visual arts are now being shown by the Chinese media. This has gradually changed people's attitudes toward deaf people and their language and made a significant improvement in the lives of deaf children and adults compared to the general perception of them twenty years ago. For example, on the eve of the 2005 Chinese spring festival, the most popular TV show in China featured a group of deaf dancers performing the "one-thousand handed kwan-yin," and a deaf girl taught the audience a signing sentence ("Love is our common language"); other media followed up on this with interviews and reports about deaf people and sign language. As a result, more young people are becoming interested in sign language and in getting involved in local deaf communities as volunteers. The status of sign language has improved, and many sign classes are now offered in universities and local communities.

It has been a struggle for many deaf and hearing people to understand the notion of Deaf culture in a Chinese context, where ethnic minorities and people with disabilities have traditionally been marginalized and are often at a socioeconomic disadvantage. The culture and language of the Han majority have often overshadowed the various minority groups in China. In this way the situation there is similar to that in many other countries, though perhaps more extreme than in some.

Now I wish to discuss four issues concerning the social situations and the education of deaf children in China: (i) disability vs. deaf culture, (ii) Chinese language and Chinese Sign Language, (iii) educational opportunities for deaf children and youth, and (iv) role models for deaf children. Based on these considerations, I offer, in the end, a number of recommendations for deaf education in China.

SOURCES OF DATA

The following discussion and recommendations are based on data that were collected from 2001 to 2007:

- participant observation in schools for deaf students, informal social settings, and home visits in the cities of Beijing, Dalian, Tianjin, Nanjing, Jiujiang, Shanghai, Yangzhou, Suzhou, Hangzhou, Shaoxing, and others
- field notes and semistructured interviews with deaf adults (most of whom are teachers of deaf children), hearing teachers, and parents of deaf children in signed languages and/or written Chinese. Most of the interviewees can be considered role models for deaf children.
- published books (e.g., Biggs 2004; Chen 2005) and documents, including journal entries or narratives posted by parents of deaf children and deaf people on Internet forums (e.g., www.deafchild.cn, bbs.eduol.com.cn, bbs.deafstar.net, and bbs.cndeaf.com)
- videotapes of social talks given by native CSL signers, collected for the sign language typology project at the Max Planck Institute for Psycholinguistics in 2004
- content analysis: deaf experiences in family and society, communication in varied social situations, language and literacy development, and educational backgrounds

DISABILITY VS. DEAF CULTURE

What does *deaf* mean in a Chinese context? *Deaf* or *deafness* in the Chinese written form 聋 is a combination of two characters: 龙 [dragon] on top and 耳 [ear] on the bottom, so the written form means 'Dragon cannot hear' or 'dragon ear,' depending on the interpretation. The pronunciation of the word meaning 'deaf' in Chinese is the same sound and tone as that of the word meaning 'dragon.' It is not possible to distinguish the capitalized Deaf and the lowercase deaf using Chinese characters. We can, however, indicate this concept of "big Deaf" by a phrase of multiple-character words such as 'culturally Deaf people' as opposed to 'pathologically deaf people.' There is a metaphor/ pun used in the Chinese Deaf community: Some deaf people informally refer to themselves as "dragon people" instead of "deaf people" as a way of showing their deaf pride.

Additionally, many people during interviews and in writing have quoted Helen Keller's comment: "Deafness separates people." They believe that deaf children suffer from more social isolation and discrimination than other children as a result of their partial or profound hearing loss. Successful deaf adults have testified that those barriers can be overcome if their parents and teachers make a great effort with their individualized education and reinforcement. Several deaf informants mentioned that, when they were in primary school, their parents often visited their schools, invited classmates to their home, and encouraged their deaf children to socialize with hearing peers. One father recalls his memories of his orally educated deaf daughter (who never attended a deaf school) when hearing friends were invited over: The girl did her homework quietly, while her hearing peers played with her toys and talked. Because her parents were at home, the deaf girl did not feel left out by her classmates at her home. She focused her attention on her homework and reading.

Deaf culture is a new, foreign concept in China (it is usually translated as the equivalent of *Deaf people's culture* in spoken and written Chinese languages) and is transmitted by means of workshops provided by NGOs (such as the Amity Foundation and Save the Children) and visiting exchange lecturers from Western countries; this has increased deaf people's involvement in training, and, slowly and gradually, the concept of Deaf culture is being accepted by the Deaf communities in China. For most Chinese deaf people and their families, Deafness is often first viewed as a disability, one that involves a great deal of hardship in social situations and independent living. Other Chinese minority groups who have come to take pride in themselves as a group have not had to deal with disability. Nevertheless, it is apparent that a Deaf culture can exist in China, and recent exchange visits of deaf people from foreign countries have enabled it to develop. It has been introduced through the bilingual and bicultural education pilot projects in preschools and primary schools for the deaf since 1996.

Some interviewees pointed out that they were amazed that Chinese deaf people have their own sign language, psychological characteristics, social behaviors, visual communication patterns, and social practices when seeking marriage partners, all of which are distinctly different from those of many hearing people. These components can be labeled "Deaf culture" if the public is willing to accept it; some interviewees were hesitant about whether or not deaf people should be considered an independent linguistic minority group. The Chinese government has been insistent on one national identity and one unified/standardized language in mainland China. Deaf culture has not been recognized or mentioned in the official documents issued by the Chinese Disabled People's Foundation (CDPF) and the Ministry of Education, except in the United Nations' Convention on the Rights of Persons with Disabilities (2006, Chinese version).

Deaf and hard-of-hearing children and adults have been categorized as a hearing disability group and, as such, have received some legal, humanistic, and financial support from disability organizations. The preschool education and aural-oral rehabilitation training of deaf children, as well as the secondary and postsecondary education of deaf students, were initiated by CDPF in the late 1980s because the Ministry of Education had authority only over primary schools (eight- or nine-year programs) for deaf and children with disabilities; now both work together, and CDPF provides legal and extra financial support for some special schools and three universities. Additionally, national and local associations of deaf people are controlled or funded by local governments through CDPF and its local branches. In China, deaf people from deaf families rarely serve as leaders in deaf communities or as presidents of national, provincial, or local deaf associations. Deaf families, most of whom extend no more than two generations, have suffered from socioeconomic and educational disadvantages more than other families.

Hearing rehabilitation for early deafened children, training in vocational skills, and inclusive education and employment in the mainstream society have been important parts of CDPF's goals. For all children with disabilities, the regulations on education for people with disabilities show that placement in regular schools near the children's homes is preferable to special schools, which are considered the last resort in educational options. The national agenda of the ninth, tenth, and eleventh five-year plans to improve the status and quality of the lives of people with disabilities revised the target number for early children's rehabilitation and young adults' vocational training. In these documents, Chinese Sign Language has been viewed as a communication system for the deaf and has been treated the same as Braille as a means of access to the Chinese language in different forms (e.g., the signed and the Braille forms of Chinese); however, it has not been regarded as a natural, fully developed language belonging to one of the ethnic minority language groups of China.

In China, the official names of each ethnic language are often taken from the ethnic group's name. For instance, the Chinese majority language is called the Han language, and Cantonese, for example, is categorized as a member of the Han dialects by traditional Chinese linguists; therefore, the categorizing of an ethnic identity comes first, after which the language of the ethnic group can be recognized. Deaf culture has not been widely and officially accepted or recognized. There will be a long path to travel before we gain official recognition that deaf people belong to a distinct cultural and linguistic group that has its own rights and that CSL is the language of this group, the Chinese Deaf community.

Overall, as stated in China's law on the protection of persons with disabilities, issued in 1990, deaf and hard-of-hearing people and other people with disabilities in general are expected to be useful and to contribute to the country's social and economic development and not to be burdens on their families and society.

CHINESE LANGUAGE AND CSL

Many Deaf informants believe that literacy in written Chinese is very important both in social situations and in their careers. An informant stated that "If deaf people can read and write, they are capable of participating in society." The common wisdom is that learning to read and write Chinese allows deaf children and adults to become useful members of society. The following mottos are quoted from schools for the deaf:

To be useful people. (Du Wenchang 1929, Beijing (figure 11.1, which is a photo of the gate of Beijing Second School for the Deaf)

When deaf people hear by reading text and speak by writing, none of them will be deaf anymore. (Yu Shufen 1931, Hangzhou)

When New China was established in October 1949, the illiteracy rate was 80 percent (the Chinese literacy campaign did not initially include people with disabilities and ethnic minorities; Zhang 2006; Gladney 2004). The central government initiated a literacy campaign and a language planning committee, which are now managed by the Ministry of Education, reforming the spoken and written form of Chinese, developing the Pinyin romanization (phonic spelling of sounds) system as an aid to learning pronunciation. As a follow-up, the Chinese finger alphabet has been created, making it possible to fingerspell Pinyin for the purpose of teaching deaf children how to sound out Chinese words.

Between 1959 and 1963, two volumes of the dictionary of common Chinese signs were drafted by several deaf leaders (e.g., Dai Mu and Wen Damin) in order to unify signs, construct a bridge between signs and Chinese words, and improve the Chinese literacy level of deaf people (Zhao 1999). In 1987 the term *Chinese Sign Language* was cited by Fu Zhiwei, vice president of the Chinese Association of the Deaf, and used as a title of the Chinese Sign Language

Figure 11.1. The gate of Beijing Second School for the Deaf

dictionary. This dictionary was published in 1990 and revised in 1994 and 2003. Deaf people and teachers of deaf youth in China want to promote a common sign system that can be shared nationwide. However, while the dictionary has been used to teach CSL to hearing people, many deaf adults rarely consult it; instead, they use their regional sign systems and are reluctant to give them up in favor of standardization.

There has been a long-running debate in the educational system and deaf communities on how best to use Chinese Sign Language and Chinese language (signed Chinese or a simultaneous combination of oral and manual methods) to support deaf children's learning and promote their written Chinese literacy. This study has revealed three groups with different perspectives:

(1) Hearing parents of young deaf children want their children to use hearing aids or cochlear implants to be able to hear and speak the Chinese language and to communicate orally as early as possible. They believe that early aural-oral training will help their children develop spoken language and literacy skills and provide access to better education and employment. While some of them do not object to the use of sign language, they are not willing to learn it themselves; they believe that their children will easily learn sign language on their own when they grow up.

(2) Hearing teachers of deaf students often express concern that deaf students have poor reading and writing skills. These teachers have spent a great deal of time lecturing about and revising students' writing and signing in Chinese word order but have made little progress (often with little parental involvement).

(3) Deaf adults who are concerned about meaningful interaction between teachers and deaf students also enter into this discussion. They have seen that many hearing teachers use a combination of speaking, signing, and writing on the blackboard but do not sign naturally and fluently, so their deaf students learn less than expected. Many deaf students often talk with the deaf teachers during breaks and after school. These conversations in sign language connect the classroom lessons with the deaf students' life experiences and help them integrate the academic information into an overall picture of the world. Some deaf informants indicated that the social interactions with their teachers, which occurred during the break (a ten-minute break between two classes, as well as a lunch break), were by far their best learning experiences. They vividly remember the words and information they acquired during these chats.

EDUCATIONAL OPPORTUNITIES FOR DEAF CHILDREN AND YOUTH

In 1987 less than 40 percent of the total number of deaf children were in school, but by 2006 the number had increased to 80 percent. According the

CDPF's annual report in 2006, the number of schools for deaf children and youngsters with other disabilities has increased to 1,662. More special schools will be opening in middle and western China in the coming years. Major cities have expanded educational offerings by establishing vocational and academic high school programs for deaf students. Many deaf and hard-of-hearing children attend local public schools or special classes attached to regular schools. About twenty colleges and universities offer programs in the fine arts, traditional Chinese painting, computer science, and gardening, for example, for deaf students. Teachers often sign themselves or use sign language interpreters in classes in which deaf students are enrolled. If a class has only one deaf student, the college does not always provide sign interpreter services but instead encourages hearing students to help with notetaking and volunteer tutoring (Mudgett-DeCaro and DeCaro 2006).

Some deaf and hard-of-hearing students have successfully studied with hearing peers at universities. Two hard-of-hearing informants, a man and a woman, who grew up in rural areas in the middle and western regions of China, have obtained their master's degrees and have now established careers in larger cities. They also have deaf sisters who have never attended school because they cannot hear and therefore cannot understand the lessons in a regular school in the countryside; an urban deaf school was too far away for them to attend. The deaf sisters have been working in the fields with their parents to help earn money to pay for their hard-of-hearing siblings' tuition and transportation. They are married to hearing husbands and have raised hearing children with their husbands' families, but their communications are generally limited to homesigns and gestures. They do not understand much about where their well-educated siblings live and work and cannot go to town by themselves because of their illiteracy. Deaf girls in rural settings often have less access to education than anyone else.

Children with cochlear implants can go to regular schools or to schools for deaf children. A leader of a deaf association reported that she saw some children with cochlear implants studying with children with mental disabilities in a special class where the teachers spoke very slowly because these implanted students do not fit in well with the regular classes and because their parents refused to transfer them to a school for deaf students.

International collaborations have played a key role in developing deaf education in China. Support from foreign organizations and scholars has been an important resource and a source of motivation for the development of deaf education and the training of teachers of the deaf in China (Callaway 2000; Shen, Wu and Chu 2005). The beginning of formal school-based education for deaf children in China was established by American missionaries in 1887, and other schools later opened, also with foreign missionaries' support (Dai and Song 1999). In 1957 the oral-only approach was introduced to the deaf schools by Chinese educators who had been trained in Russia. In the 1980s several

Chinese otolaryngologists traveled abroad and learned about hearing aids. Upon returning to China, they established hearing-aid clinics and speech-training centers for deaf children. In 1985, two people (one a wheelchair user and one blind) were selected by the central government as representatives of Chinese people with disabilities, and while overseas, they observed various educational and employment situations of deaf people. After returning home, they established the first special college program for deaf students and other people with disabilities in the city of Changchun in 1987 (Mudgett-DeCaro and DeCaro 2006). With financial and academic support and training by academics from the UK, Canada, the United States, Australia, and Norway, bilingual education programs in schools for the deaf have been up and running for twelve years now. The quality of education, from preschool to college, the types of educational placement, and the communicative instructional approaches in today's Deaf education in China are varied and something to be optimistic about. More academic majors and vocational programs will become available to deaf students in the future.

Levels and Types of Education Available to Deaf Persons in China

preschool (1–3 years)	oral programs, a few sign-bilingual pilot programs
primary school (9 years)	regular schools (full inclusion or special classes, a few pilot programs with sign language interpreters or interpreting teachers)

Schools for deaf students and students with special needs

high school (3 years)	few full-inclusion students in regular schools, academic programs, or vocational programs in schools for deaf or special needs students
college (3 years) or university (4 years)	a few full-inclusion and deaf-only programs (e.g., arts, computer science, gardening, interior decoration)
graduate school (MA and PhD)	very few and typically in Chinese literature and linguistics, computer science, etc.

Several schools (e.g., Suzhou, Jiujiang, Yangzhou) reinforce and celebrate the bilingual and bicultural context on campus by exhibiting colorful posters, displaying books, showing many objects in text and signing labels, requiring everyone on campus to sign, and so on.

ROLE MODELS FOR DEAF CHILDREN

Many successful stories of mainstreamed oral-deaf and hard-of-hearing people with high academic achievement have been reported by the media, and some culturally Deaf people who are sign language users have also become recognized for their excellent work in the fine arts, sports, and theater. Their stories have been collected in books, and a few have been turned into films. Recently a group of deaf activists in the Wuhan deaf association have created a film series on deaf role models, documenting their employment and social activities, such as teaching CSL classes in their spare time and playing football on weekends; they have published this on a blog. Many teachers have downloaded this material and watched it with their deaf students.

Deaf teachers in schools for deaf students are by far the most important role models for deaf students (Yang 2006). They show what deaf people can do both by example and by interacting with their students every day. They also introduce deaf guests to their students and share accounts of their struggles and successes with them. Many deaf teachers are selected as leaders of local deaf associations. A hearing principal of a school for the deaf, Fang (2004, 30), states that deaf teachers are a "gold mine" for deaf schools. As role models, they have had a powerful impact upon deaf students' linguistic, social, and academic development, raised deaf children's hopes and expectations, and built a bridge between the deaf and hearing worlds; therefore, hearing teachers cannot substitute for them. Sometimes hearing teachers have to ask deaf teachers for consultation and storytelling advice.

RECOMMENDATIONS

The discussion so far leads me to make the following recommendations for the education of deaf children in China:

1. The quality of education for deaf people depends on collaboration between families, schools, and communities. Many parents need more information about their deaf children's communication and learning needs. The social-interactive learning approach should be used in school and at home. Many deaf and hard-of-hearing students in regular schools and schools for the deaf have limited access to lectures, teacher-student interaction, and group discussions—this must change. Teachers should continually improve their signing communication and instructional skills and encourage students to engage in more investigative exercises.

2. It is necessary to increase deaf awareness training for teachers and parents, to involve the local deaf community more, and to explore Deaf

culture in a Chinese context. Some schools and parents fear that deaf students will go astray or make poor decisions during encounters with deaf adults outside of school. This overprotective attitude may actually limit the quality of these critical activities. Deaf students should have opportunities to learn from firsthand experiences in various social situations and on field trips with Deaf adults, while they continue their cultural exchange programs with regular schools; in this way they can benefit from participation in both cultures.

3. Collaboration at the international level has been effective in obtaining support and promoting the educational and social status of deaf children and adults in developing countries, so this good practice should be continued and expanded.

Note

I wish to thank Gaurav Mathur and Donna Jo Napoli for their useful comments and suggestions. I also extend my thanks to the Chinese people whom I interviewed and to Wang Ke'nan, principal of Beijing No. 2 School for the Deaf, for permission to use the school gate photo in figure 11.1. I am especially grateful to Amy Wilson for guiding me on a long academic journey of international development and Deaf empowerment from Beijing to Washington, D.C., and England. In addition, I thank the participants of the "Deaf around the World" conference in Swarthmore, Pennsylvania, for their comments.

Bibliography

Biggs, Cassie. 2004. Bilingual and Bicultural Approach to Teaching Deaf Children in China. United Nations International Children's Emergency Fund (UNICEF). http://www.unicef.org/china/Bi_Bi_Book_by_Cassie_04_ENG.pdf (accessed September 1, 2007).

Callaway, Allison. 1999. Considering Sign Bilingual Education in Cultural Context: A Survey of Deaf Schools in Jiangsu Province, China. *Deafness and Education International* 1(1): 34–46.

———. 2000. *Deaf Children in China*. Washington, D.C.: Gallaudet University Press.

Chen, Jun, ed. 2005. *Longren xuexi yuyande fangfa: Longren jiaoshi tan tenyang xuexi yuyan* [Methods for Deaf People Learning Language: Deaf Teachers Talk about Language Learning]. Beijing: Drama.

Dai, Mu, and Peng-Cheng Song. 1999. *Meng yuan yi dangnian* [When Dreams Come True, We Will Remember]. Shanghai: Education Publisher.

Fang, Hong. 2004. Longren jiaoshi de peiyang ji zuoyong [Training Deaf Teachers and Functions of Deaf Teachers]. *Journal of Nanjing Special Education* 3: 30–32.

Gladney, Dru C. 2004. *Dislocating China: Reflections on Muslims, Minorities, and Other Subaltern Subjects*. Chicago: University of Chicago Press.

Mudgett-DeCaro, Patricia A., and James J. DeCaro. 2006. Postsecondary Education for Deaf People in China: Issues, Roles, Responsibilities, and Recommendation. A

Report to the China Disabled Persons' Federation. http://www.pen.ntid.rit.edu/pdf/chinarpt06.pdf (accessed March 16, 2006).

Shen, Yulin, Anan Wu, and Chaoyu Chu, eds. 2005. *Shuangyu long jiaoyude lilun yu shijian* [Bilingual Deaf Education: Theories and Practices]. Beijing: Huaxia.

Yang, Jun Hui. 2006. Deaf Teachers in China: Their Perceptions regarding Their Roles and the Barriers They Face. PhD diss., Gallaudet University.

Zhang, Tiedao. 2006. Literacy Education in China: Background Paper Prepared for the Education for All Global Monitoring Report 2006. UNESCO. http://unesdoc.unesco.org/images/0014/001462/146208e.pdf (accessed December 16, 2007).

Zhao, Xi-An. 1999. *Zhongguo Shouyu yanjiu* [Chinese Sign Language Studies]. Beijing: Huaxia.

CHAPTER 11 RESPONSE

Social Situations and the Education of Deaf Children in India

Madan M. Vasishta

BACKGROUND

Jun Hui Yang's chapter about the social situations and education of deaf people in China is informative and enlightening. In contrast to the case of Western nations, very little written information on deafness in developing countries like China and India is available; therefore, this chapter is a welcome addition to our knowledge. In fact, as I discuss later, there are many similarities between China and India in the area of deaf education.

First, following Yang's lead, let me give a brief personal background. I was born hearing in India and became deaf at the age of eleven. After working as a farmer for nine years, I moved to Delhi, where I met deaf people and learned Indian Sign Language (ISL). I became a professional photographer and was very active with the All India Federation of the Deaf and the Delhi Association of the Deaf. I collaborated with James Woodward, Kirk Wilson, and Susan DeSantis on researching ISL in 1977; the result was the publication of the first dictionaries of regional varieties of ISL. In 1967 I learned about Gallaudet College and applied for admission. I received my PhD in special educational administration from Gallaudet University in 1983. After teaching at Kendall School, I worked as a supervisor at the Texas School for the Deaf, as assistant superintendent at the Illinois School for the Deaf, and as superintendent at the Eastern North Carolina School for the Deaf and the New Mexico School for the Deaf. At present I am a professor of administration and supervision at Gallaudet University, and I provide volunteer consultancy regarding the situation of Deaf people to a number of NGOs and government agencies in India.

In this response I give a comparative overview of India in general and of its deaf population, as well a brief history of Indian Sign Language, with a focus on the education of deaf children in India. I have been professionally and personally involved in the education and rehabilitation of deaf people in India for most of my life; therefore, some of the information in this chapter is from my own observations.

With 1.14 billion people (World Statesmen n.d.) India is second to China in population. India's population, like China's, is ethnically diverse (72 percent Aryan, 25 percent Dravidian, 3 percent Oriental). Unlike China, there are also many religious groups. Hindus (82 percent) and Muslims (12 percent) make up the majority of the Indian population. Christians (2.3 percent) and Sikhs (1.9 percent) are two minor religious groups. However, the greatest source of diversity is linguistic. There are more than four hundred languages, and, of these, twenty-two are official languages, of which Hindi and English are the main national languages (Embassy of India 2009).

According to the 2000 national census, India has about 1.26 million deaf people (UNESCO Institute for Statistics n.d.). Of these, about 200,000 are school-age children, of whom only a very small number attend schools. According to a UNESCO report (Brill 1986), only 5 percent of deaf children in India in 1986 attended school. The Ali Yavar Jung National Institute for the Hearing Handicapped (AYJNIHH) estimated that the total number of deaf children in special schools decreases gradually from grade to grade. Most students drop out after the fifth grade. Randhawa (2005) found that less than 22 percent of students in grades 1–5 went on to higher grades. Thus, about 78 percent of deaf students drop out of school after elementary education. Adenwalla (1999) has also indicated that very few deaf students finish high school.

The first research-based information on schools for the deaf was compiled in 2000 by AYJNIHH and was published in a directory format, which includes information about 431 schools (AYJNIHH 2000). Most (330) of these schools have very few students and are operated by nongovernment organizations. Three government-operated schools are large, each having about 550 students. The total number of students attending all of these schools is not available as information in the directory is sketchy. However, based on past trends and on the fact that the number of educational programs for deaf students has increased, only about 0.5 percent of deaf children attend an educational program that is in any way designed to meet their needs. The other 4.5 percent of deaf children who attend educational programs are in regular schools without any support such as interpreters, note takers, tutors, or counselors. The remaining 95 percent of deaf children receive no formal education. If we consider that 30 percent of the Indian population is of school age, the number of school-age children who are deaf in India could be nearly three million. This brings the number of children who are deaf and are receiving an education in the special programs listed in the AYJNIHH directory to about fifteen thousand (0.5 percent of three million).

Given the tendency of Indian people to hide their children with disabilities, I believe that the actual number of deaf people in India is much higher. India's population is three times that of the United States, where there are more than four million deaf people (Statistics for Country by Deafness n.d.). We can safely extrapolate that India has about fifteen million deaf people. This also means the number of deaf children who receive no educational services is much higher than cited in the preceding paragraph. Perhaps as many as nine and a half million deaf children in India are going without an education.

The past decade's economic boom in India has helped the spread of educational technology in the education of deaf children. Hearing aids, hitherto rarely used, have become more common. With its four regional centers, AYJNIHH has a major outreach program whose objective is to identify deafness and distribute hearing aids (Ali Yavar Jung National Institute for the Hearing Handicapped n.d.). However, my personal communication with many school principals indicates that use of hearing aids is severely limited due to the poor quality of Indian-made devices. Imported hearing aids cost several times more than those manufactured in India, and only a fraction of the population can afford them. This is especially true for children in rural areas.

No empirical data are available on the educational methodologies used in schools for deaf students. Data collected by AYJNIHH in 2000 indicates that the use of ISL in educational settings is sporadic. Most of these schools claim to be oral. About half of them profess to use total communication, which, loosely defined, means sign language used along with the oral approach. Only three schools for deaf children are pursuing bilingual education. However, these schools lack information about research on bilingualism in deaf education; as a result, without a theoretical base, they design their programs on whatever information is available. The first prerequisite for bilingual education is fluency in both languages—ISL and Hindi or another spoken/written language. Most deaf children arrive at school without even a rudimentary knowledge of even one language, and there they pick up ISL from the other students. The teachers should be fluent in both languages. One of these schools has a good number of teachers who are fluent in ISL. In the other two schools, most of the teachers are still learning ISL. The recognition that ISL should have a role in the education of deaf children is a fairly recent development.

Education of deaf children in public schools depends on the availability of qualified interpreters. Unfortunately, there are perhaps fewer than twenty in the whole country. There is no training program for interpreters and no organization to provide training and licenses. In 2007 the Indian National Association of the Deaf established a national interpreter organization (ASLI 2007), and AYJNIHH established another interpreter organization in November 2008 (AYJNIHH 2008).

There have been some efforts at the national level to use interpreters. One of them involved a few minutes of interpreted news on the Doordarshan (India's government-run television station). The quality of most of the interpreters, however, was very poor. Deaf people complained about it and still do. However, this effort was laudable in that it brought national exposure to ISL.

ROLE OF INDIAN SIGN LANGUAGE

As recently as 1975, most educators of the deaf in India even denied the existence of an Indian Sign Language. Vasishta (cited in Cross 1977) collected information from 117 schools for the deaf included in the directory published by the All India Federation of the Deaf (Bhat 1975). Almost all of the responding school principals denied the existence of an Indian Sign Language. However, they conceded that students used a "collection of gestures" (Cross 1977).

Linguistic work on ISL began in the 1970s. In 1977 James Woodward, Kirk Wilson, and I visited India and collected signs for linguistic analysis from four major urban centers: Delhi, Bangalore, Kolkata (formerly Calcutta), and Mumbai (formerly Bombay). Vasishta, Woodward, and Wilson (1981) established that ISL is a language in its own right and is indigenous to the Indian subcontinent. Their research and fieldwork over the five-year period resulted in the first dictionaries of ISL (Vasishta, Woodward, and DeSantis 1981). Acceptance for ISL has gradually increased and has been helped by the later work of Ulrike Zeshan (Zeshan 2000, 2003).

There is a dire need for linguistic research on ISL. To date, two linguists from Jawaharlal Nehru University (JNU) have studied ISL for their master's and doctoral-level theses. This is a great start. Unfortunately, people with political clout and no linguistic background have been calling for a standardization of ISL. A few years ago both AYJNIHH and JNU received a grant for research on ISL, and all of the efforts funded by this grant went into determining how best to standardize the language. Advice from linguists that a language becomes standard by use was neglected.

HISTORICAL

As in China, very little research on deafness in India has been either conducted or shared. Miles (2000) has compiled a historical bibliography on the education of South Asian children with handicaps. Even though the study covers a span of four thousand years, it has found only a few citations relevant to deafness and the education of deaf children. Very little information is included about deaf people in India.

With respect to schools for deaf children in India, no information was available until the late nineteenth century. Just as in many Asian and African countries, Catholic missionaries were instrumental in starting the first such schools. I now present a brief review of the history of schools for deaf children based primarily on Miles's annotated bibliography (2000), which is unfortunately incomplete and only suggestive in portions. Additional information about the founders, funding sources, curricula, methodologies, and role of deaf students in these schools would be very helpful not only from a historical perspective but also from educational and societal perspectives.

The first school for the deaf opened in 1885 in Bombay (Hull 1913) and was followed by the opening of a school in Calcutta in 1893 (Banerji 1904) and another in Palamcottah in Tamilnadu in 1896 (Swainson 1906). In 1903 there were about seventy thousand deaf children in India. Of these, only 52 (or .07 percent) were enrolled in the three schools (Banerji 1904). The figure of seventy thousand, in fact, must be a gross underestimation, given that the present number of deaf children is about ten million.

With 80 percent of the Indian population living in villages, where illiteracy in the general population was rampant until the mid-twentieth century, most deaf children likely did not attend any school. The rate of education in the urban areas is no better. Randhawa (2005) finds that most deaf children who attend school are enrolled in the primary grades, where there is a sharp decline in enrollment after the fifth grade. The number of deaf students in grades 5–8 is less than 22 percent of the total number of students in grades 1–5. Thus, about 78 percent of deaf students drop out of school after elementary education. Also, Adenwalla (1999) indicates that very few deaf students finish high school and states that a "miniscule" number of students attend university or college. India has no formal colleges for deaf students.

Discussions about starting a college for the Deaf often make the news. However, most of these talks are just that or embellishment of plans that are never realized. I am aware of a program in Pune that offers art classes to Deaf people and calls itself a "college." Recently the Ishara Foundation in Mumbai began offering classes in linguistics for the Deaf and announced the establishment of a "college" (Deafness.about.com 2008).

It is hoped that these efforts will result in a real college one day.

DEAF ORGANIZATIONS

Established in 1955, the All Indian Federation of the Deaf (AIFD) is affiliated with the World Federation of the Deaf (WFD) and was politically active throughout the 1970s. It runs a technical training school in Delhi. Unfortunately, this once-vibrant organization has been all but dormant for the past thirty years. In 2003 the vacuum created by a lack of leadership was filled by a new organization, the National Association of the Deaf (NAD), which works with other disability groups and has been very active in seeking rights for deaf people. It has a membership of more than five thousand. However, it is not affiliated with the WFD. The NAD is willing to work with AIFD, but the latter refuses to collaborate due to its belief that it is the primary Deaf organization in the country. This squabble only hurts the welfare of deaf people. In 2007 the first Indian Deaf Expo was held in Coimbatore, a small city in southern India. It was organized by a small club in town. Neither the NAD nor the AIFD was involved in the expo. This lack of a clear national leadership means that the local associations work in a vacuum, and much redundancy in work results in wasted effort.

DEAF CULTURE AND ROLE MODELS

Deaf people in India have only recently begun talking about Deaf culture, the very concept of which was imported by deaf people visiting other countries. There is no formal definition of Deaf culture within the Indian context. Some Deaf people use the term to justify aspects of their behavior as being part of "Deaf culture" when there is not always a clear connection. For example, they might hide behind "Deaf culture" to excuse certain unacceptable actions, such as being late for appointments or not doing their share of work. This causes resentment among hearing people working with deaf children. I have been asked by two magazines to step into the fray and write an article about India's deaf culture. So far I have hesitated because there just is not enough information on this topic yet.

I close with one serious problem in India. As in China, there are very few successful deaf role models. Deaf people are still not allowed to teach. At the time of writing this chapter, there are perhaps only one or two certified deaf teachers in all of India. The curriculum for deaf children—heavy on speech development and audiology—needs to be modified to enable Deaf people to acquire teacher certification. Some schools have started hiring Deaf persons as ISL teachers, who then also serve as role models for the deaf children in school. The need for this is enormous. Most deaf children in rural schools have rarely met deaf adults. In rural schools, when I have been introduced as a deaf person, I have experienced wide-eyed children staring at me.

Bibliography

Adenwalla, Dhun. 1999. Education of the Deaf in India. In *Global Perspectives on the Education of the Deaf in Selected Countries,* ed. William Brejli, 191–204. Hillsboro, Ore.: Butte.

Ali Yavar Jung National Institute for the Hearing Handicapped. 2008a. *Directory of Rehabilitation Resources for Persons with Hearing Impairment in India.* Bombay: NIHH.

Ali Yavar Jung National Institute for the Hearing Handicapped. 2008b. http://ayjnihh.nic.in/aw/news.html#4 (accessed February 2009).

————. n.d. http://ayjnihh.nic.in/aw/default.asp (accessed February 2009).

Association of Sign Language Interpreters (ASLI). 2007. http://www.signasli.org/ index.html (accessed February 2009).

Banerji, Jamini N. 1904. [Notices of Publications]. Majumdar, Mohini Mohan, 1904, *Muk-shikshâ* (Education of the Deaf and Dumb), Calcutta. 12 mo. pp. 130. *American Annals of the Deaf* 59(4): 390–391.

Bhat, R. L. 1975. *Services for the Deaf in India.* New Delhi: All India Federation of the Deaf.

Brill, Richard. 1986. *The Conference of Educational Administrators Serving the Deaf: A History.* Washington, DC: Gallaudet University Press.

Cross, Jennie. 1977. Toward a Standardized Sign Language for India. *Gallaudet Today* 8(1) 26–29.

Deafness.about.com. http://deafness.about.com/b/knowindia/india_at_a_glance.php (accessed February 2009).

Embassy of India. http://india.gov.in/knowindia/india_at_a_glance.php (accessed February 2009).

Hull, Ernest R. 1913. *Bombay Mission: History with a Special Study of the Padroado Question,* vol. 2, 1858–1890. Bombay: Examiner.

Miles, Michael. 2000. Studying Responses to Disability in South Asian History: Approaches Personal, Prakrital, and Pragmatical. *Disability and Society* 16: 143–160.

Randhawa, Surinder P. K. 2005. A Status Study of Special Needs Schools for the Deaf and Identification of Intervention Areas. PhD diss., Indian Institute of Technology at Roorkee.

Statistics by Country for Deafness. n.d. http://www.wrongdiagnosis.com/d/deafness/ stats-country.htm (accessed February 2009).

Swainson, Florence. 1906. *Report of the Deaf and Dumb and Industrial School in Connection with the Church of England Zenana Mission, Palamcottah, South India, for 1905.* Palamcottah, India: Church Mission Press.

UNESCO Institute for Statistics. n.d. http://www.uis.unesco.org/profiles/EN/EDU/ countryProfile_en.aspx?code=3560 (accessed February 2009).

Vasishta, Madan M., James C. Woodward, and Susan DeSantis. 1981. *An Introduction to Indian Sign Language: Focus on Delhi.* New Delhi: All India Federation of the Deaf.

Vasishta, Madan M., James C. Woodward, and Kirk L. Wilson. 1981. Sign Language in India: Regional Variation within the Deaf. *Indian Journal of Applied Linguistics* 4(2): 66–74.

World Statesmen. n.d. http://www.worldstatesmen.org/India.htm (accessed February 2009).

Zeshan, Ulrike. 2000. *Sign Language in Indo-Pakistan: A Description of a Signed Language.* Amsterdam: Benjamins.

————. 2003. Indo-Pakistani Sign Language Grammar: A Typological Outline. *Sign Language Studies* 3: 157–212.

CHAPTER 12

Do Deaf Children Eat Deaf Carrots?

Paul Scott

The title of my chapter—"Do Deaf Children Eat Deaf Carrots?"—is a metaphor. You know when you're trying to push a donkey along? If you put a carrot on the end of a stick, you can encourage the donkey to move. So I'm going to talk about teaching deaf children to develop their identity as deaf people and how to push them along.

So how do I push deaf children? I've been collecting a lot of deaf stories, pictures, and videos about the deaf experience. My aim is to demystify the wall for deaf children. So, for example, if you've got deaf children with hearing parents, they just can't get over that wall. If their parents are deaf, they can simply walk around that wall and get on with life. Deaf children who have hearing parents look at me as a deaf teacher, and they need to learn where their deafness comes from, so it's my responsibility to explain that to them.

I teach all about deaf identity. What it's like to be deaf. Deaf history. Deaf education. Sign language. Deaf behavior. Deaf barriers. Basic sign linguistics. Deaf storytelling. Deaf employment. The idea of a deaf village, deaf studies. Deaf schools. Deaf development. We talk about foreign sign languages and what it means to be a deaf professional. All that is split into two parts: BSL studies and deaf studies. That's my responsibility as a teacher.

Now if we talk about teaching British Sign Language (BSL), let's look at the wall as made of bricks. Let me ask you, what will happen if you take one of those bricks out? It's going to fall, right? So what you need is all of those bricks to make a good solid wall for the deaf child to learn. I'll give you three examples—directional verbs, modification, and token placement—and then I'll talk about those three bricks.

So I'm teaching children how to use BSL. They can sign fine. But we need to do language work with them to encourage them to play with the language. So I ask the children about directional verbs—for example, the signs ASK or CALL-ON-THE-TELEPHONE or LOVE or SWIM or GIVE or HELP. Then I give them some work to do and tell them to sit and work together in pairs. They have to decide whether something is a directional verb. So if you've got a sign like ASK, is it directional? If yes, you put a tick in the box. CALL-ON-THE-PHONE, yes or no? Tick. LOVE? Can you do that? No. Now, the deaf children know you can't do that. So it's a way of encouraging them to be aware of it. SWIM? Can you do SWIM? And the deaf children will say, that looks a bit strange, I've never seen that. HELP, can you do HELP? And then you can make a tick and move in both directions. Then they know how it works.

Now we've got these four different ideas related to directional verbs: location, placement, demonstration, and repetition. So, I sign ASK in one direction and again in the other direction. As for placement, I show the students that we can put ASK in lots of different places. We can use one hand. We can also use it with two hands. The children love to ask each other, "Why not sweep it around?" A lot of them think, "Wow, can you do that?" I say, "Yes, of course." So I encourage them. And the repetition—by repeating the sign ASK with facial expressions, I encourage them to play with the sign. They always love that.

Now we turn to another brick: modification. I don't usually teach children how to fingerspell the word *modification*. Instead, what we do is take the idea of something that's normally signed and then sign it less, much less, more, or to an extreme. For example, there is a sign that normally means 'sun/sunny.' If you sign it a little bit less and change your facial expression, it's less sunny, and if you sign it even less, it's not really very sunny at all. Or you can sign extreme sunniness. How would you write it? How would you write that in English? Maybe you could use capitals or bold letters (many of the deaf children don't know that). So I encourage them to think about the signs and the English words in different ways. The English teacher came to me and said, "Well, I never thought of that." I say my role is to encourage them to think differently. You can sign a bit of rain as well, or drizzling gently, or pouring, or absolutely sheeting it down. As another example, there's the normal sign HAVE. There's also I-REALLY-HAVE and OBVIOUSLY-I-HAVE. By encouraging them to think in different ways, deaf children can see how they can modify HAVE.

As for the third brick, placement, we look at tokens from various perspectives. It's very important for deaf children to understand how deaf people place things in space. Suppose you've got a fence and a tree and a flower. You can place them all relative to one another. And then there's a pond. I encourage the children to learn how to use divisional space and then to rotate things so they're looking at something from a different perspective: from the front, from the side, from behind, from above, from below. I encourage them to think, and we look at the space as a three-dimensional thing. I move the whole image through different planes, and they do that through art, as well as through signing. That's known as language play, and they love playing with language and thinking about linguistic ideas. Moreover, it's of great benefit to them.

That's what I mean by the BSL studies. Now we turn to deaf studies. People wonder what that is and what I teach about it. Again there are some bricks

Figure 12.1. Praying. Who's deaf?

in the deaf culture wall. If you take one brick out, what's going to happen? The wall comes down. So I teach them about all of the bricks. Here are three examples.

First, let's look at figure 12.1. Which of those people is deaf? Many children look at the figure and go, "Oh, right!" And I'll say, "What's wrong?" Many times when they're home and praying, they'll have one eye open, and they'll think they're the only person doing that. But now they know other people are doing that, too: They go, "Oh, they do that, too, and I thought it was just me." Who would teach them that? Nobody. They have to work that out for themselves.

In figure 12.2 we find another picture. I ask the children, "Who's deaf?" I suggest "the one who walks into the pole? Is that one deaf or hearing?" Both are deaf. If you have a deaf child with deaf parents, they'll know. However, I'm talking about deaf children with hearing parents. And they try to avoid that accident. How do you solve this issue? Like I was saying before, they're jumping up and down trying to see over this wall if they have hearing parents. If you've got deaf parents, then you understand that you might need to hold somebody and move them if they walk into a sign.

Here's a third example. Who is deaf in figure 12.3? Why am I showing you that? What's that really about? It's the ticket problem, where they call out the ticket numbers, and, of course, if you're deaf you can't hear them. You've got number seventy-six, and you have to look over somebody else's shoulder. Who has seventy-five? You're walking around trying to find out, and then you just stay behind that person. It's simply a question of who's next.

Let's look at the picture in figure 12.4. The person on the bottom is deaf. And the hearing person is being pulled down the steps because the deaf person doesn't know to stop. Now, in the future, if you think about the best jobs

Figure 12.2. Having a conversation, walking along. Who's deaf?

Figure 12.3. Standing in the ticket line at the market. Who's deaf?

Figure 12.4. Moving the couch. Who's deaf?

Figure 12.5. At a restaurant. Who's deaf?

Figure 12.6. Cover page from child's report

for deaf people, you don't think about this kind of situation. So think about that before you decide on your future job.

The last example concerning Deaf culture is in figure 12.5. Who's deaf? Again both. Obviously they can't talk with that flower arrangement between them. We know deaf people are going to move the flower arrangement to one side of the table.

Next I talk about deaf history and famous deaf people and how I teach that to the children. I have a PowerPoint presentation that I've actually taken from the work of one of the deaf children. Please remember that the child wrote this himself. I didn't help him with his English. I just let him write this on his own. Figures 12.6–12.12 show this work.

He born in La
Balme France.

It was quiet area
and mountain.

Figure 12.7. Clerc's birth in child's report

Abbe Sicard

Figure 12.8. Clerk's education in child's report

Thomas Galludeut meet
Alice Cogwell. Realise no
Deaf school in USA.

Figure 12.9. Thomas Gallaudet meets Alice Cogwell in child's report

Figure 12.10. Clerc, Gallaudet, and Sicard work together in child's report

Figure 12.11. Clerc and Gallaudet found the Hartford school in child's report

The PowerPoint presentation tells where Laurent Clerc was born—in a quiet area—and states that he went to school. It also mentions that Thomas Gallaudet met Alice Cogwell and realized there was no deaf school, so they went out to look for somebody and found Clerc. They agreed to go to the United States together. They set up the first deaf school, and Clerc stayed there until he died. The kid who wrote that story was twelve. When he finished, he presented it, and he displayed it on his shelf at home—now that's something to really be proud of.

Figure 12.12. The end of Clerc's life in child's report

Then I show the children an image of a magic carpet. They have to think about how to use their imagination. For example, they look at the government and think: What if you used your magic carpet to go to a land where nobody lived and you could set up Deafland, where you could make your own rules and your own government. How would you set up the government? Who heads the government system that's there now? What changes would you make in the new one? So we talk about human rights, for example, what deaf rights are and how they relate to human rights in general. I encourage them to open their minds and think about how that would work.

So there we are. I've told you how I teach deaf children about their identity. The children have eaten their deaf carrot. They have their deaf language and their deaf culture. Does it work? Time will tell.

Note

The cartoons in figures 12.1–12.5 are reprinted from *Deaf Culture, Our Way: Anecdotes from the Deaf Community*, ed. Roy K. Holcomb, Samuel K. Holcomb, and Thomas K. Holcomb (San Diego: DawnSignPress, 1996). I am grateful to Gallaudet University Press for this permission.

"We're the Same, I'm Deaf, You're Deaf, Huh!"

Donna West

INTRODUCTION

I am thrilled and honored to respond to Paul Scott's chapter. Paul is a friend, colleague, and coresearcher, and ten years ago we were both working in the same school for Deaf children. I left teaching to pursue research in academia, and Paul continued to work as a Deaf educator. Over the past few years I have been lucky to be invited into his classroom, to observe his teaching, and to talk to him about his work. That his work is now being published in a text such as this marks the recognition he truly deserves. Long may it continue.

In considering how I might respond to this chapter, alongside Dr. Paddy Ladd, I decided to complement Paul's work within the context of a research project I undertook as a research assistant with Dr. Ladd between 2003 and 2005 at the Centre for Deaf Studies, University of Bristol, UK. *Seeing Through New Eyes*, funded by the Leverhulme Trust, was an ethnography of Deaf educators and Deaf children that, through observation and ethnographic interviews, sought to document both the largely unrecognized work that Deaf educators (teachers, instructors, and assistants) in the UK do and the ways in which their developing, reflective, critical pedagogical practices are valued and recognized by the children they teach. Paul's description of his work, "I teach all about Deaf identity" sums up the unrecognized curriculum of many Deaf educators, when you consider all that is contained in that one paragraph.

It is the children's recognition of Deaf educators like Paul, as well as the ways in which they express this, that I would like to set down here, albeit in brief. What is special about Paul's chapter is the way in which it captures the energy of his pedagogical practice. I hope that the children's words, which I have translated from their signs, with their permission and approval, match and complement Paul's work with a similar energy.[1]

THE CHILDREN'S WORDS

Paul begins by talking about "demystifying" the wall. For the children I talked to, this leads, through storytelling, thinking strategies, and examples, to a connection of Deaf-same and to trust in their educators:

> We're the same, I'm Deaf, you're Deaf, huh! We're the same! And can sign with each other, we're the same, and we have that bond. That's right, Deaf people can relate to Deaf children, and me, I'm Deaf, good, I want more of that. Oh phew, at last! So that's why I relate to my Deaf teacher, always talk to him, always, not with hearing, no. (Kimberley)

> Well, I think that Deaf people just have more of a bond, that's why. I mean, hearing people can bond with Deaf people, but Deaf children are just more used to bonding with Deaf people, it's like they're their friends, and it means we can trust Deaf teachers. (Natasha)

From this position of Deaf-same, learning and enjoyment in learning—eating the carrot—can take place:

> One time our Deaf teacher told us, he showed us a video of real life, this person had been brought up oral, and it was awful, I couldn't believe it. And we were learning all about that, but then it was the end of the lesson, no! Come on, we don't want to stop. And the teacher laughed and said, "Sorry, end of the lesson!" so we had to wait 'til next time. And we were so excited, we'd had to wait, but then we got in there and carried on learning! (Kumar)

Paul's "teaching all about Deaf identity" is reflected in Michelle's explanation:

> We learn all about Deaf culture, you know, sign, information, all that. And it's good 'cos if we didn't have Deaf studies, we wouldn't know what Deaf means. So our Deaf teacher explains Deaf culture to us, what it means, what we need, and what our rights are, and it feels good. (Michelle)

Understanding of one's Deaf identity is also linked to children's identification with their Deaf history and a thirst for information:

> Oh, my favorite! He taught us about the Deaf people who moved to America, just to a small island, which was Deaf. And time passed, and the Deaf population got bigger and bigger, but also there were hearing people there, too, not talking, all signing, right! So they got bigger and bigger, but then they all started to move away to other parts of America, and I thought, damn! If they had stayed and were still there, then that's where I want to be, I would go there, straight away. Maybe I'd go there for a holiday and everyone would be signing—policemen, signing,

ambulance drivers signing, fire brigade, all signing, and it would be fantastic, and my eyes would pop out of my head! (Ben)

Martha's Vineyard? Is that still there? I want to move there [races through one-handed alphabet] ABCDEFGHIJKLMNOPQRSTUVWXYZ . . . yes, I will move there! (Chrissie)

Well, I heard there was a Deaf queen! Amazing! But we don't do that 'til next year, so I guess I'll have to be patient and wait 'til next year. So before, I had to wait 'til I got to be eleven, so I could have Deaf studies. Then I went through that year, and now that's finished, but there will be more next year. So I have to wait again! So step by step, slowly, patiently, and then one day finally I will get to next year! (Edwin)

We want to know who was the first ever Deaf person in the whole world, we want to know that! But nobody's researched that! (Michelle)

This learning about Deaf history, one of the bricks in Paul's identity wall, manifests itself, as Paul himself explains, in books written by the children, typed, printed, bound, and displayed on their shelves at home:

He told us the story of Helen Keller, the deaf-blind woman, and then we made our own books about her, so we could keep them and remember what we learned. So we used the Internet, found pictures and information. And he said it was to make sure we learned. And I thought that was really good and really fascinating! (Michelle)

It is worth adding that it is not only what Paul teaches but also the visual resources he develops and uses with the children that have such a big impact on their learning experiences. Here's Michelle again:

We have got a SMART Board, and it's really big, so much better, 'cos before we were all squeezed round this tiny screen, and you couldn't see properly. It was okay if there were only two of you, but there's five of us. So now the teacher can point to the screen and explain it and put all the information up there. If we use the small screen, we can only see pictures one after the other, but with the big screen, you can see it all at the same time, and so we can understand. (Michelle)

When Deaf children study Deaf history, they learn to feel pride in their heritage, to be curious, and to feel confident as young Deaf people going out into the world. Paul describes this as pushing them along. Why is Deaf history important?

It means that people realize there are Deaf people in the world. Otherwise, it seems like Deaf people are just lazy, never achieve anything in the past. Deaf history is great, we should have Deaf history. (Phoebe)

It means that people think, wow, really? Deaf people are really brave, really clever, and it will shock them. I mean, I used to think that, in the past, Deaf people didn't sign, that they were only oral, but now I know that they did have sign in the past, but they weren't allowed to sign, they had to be oral. And I thought that there were no born-Deaf people in the past. I thought they were all born hearing then became Deaf through illness. But now I know that there were Deaf people, born-Deaf people in the past. We're normal, born-Deaf, that really hit me. (Edwin)

Through history, famous Deaf people have achieved so much. And our Deaf teacher tells us that we should be proud of Deaf people's achievements in the past. And he tells us in Deaf studies that we can be proud of all those Deaf people who achieved so much so long ago. And it makes me thankful to have a connection to that history, that tradition. And because I'm Deaf, I want to tell hearing people that I am proud of who I am, and that I can achieve, too. I'm not stupid, I'm not less than you. I am the same. Deaf people can achieve the same as hearing people. And that motivates me, I am proud of my Deaf tradition, I am proud to be Deaf. And then hearing people will say, "Oh yes, Deaf, right!" 'cos they know we have a past . . . and that will be nice. (Kimberley)

And all these Deaf things happened in the past, and it's so interesting I want to know about it. It's like ideas and inventions and signing, where did they come from? Who started them? Like, whose idea was the British Deaf Association? Whose idea was the Federation of Deaf People? All these things in Deaf history are so interesting. And then it makes you feel confident that help is there, and you can have your own ideas, do things, and move on. It's like hearing history, hearing think that's important, well, Deaf history is important, too. And hearing people think that they are better, up here, and Deaf people are down there and can be brushed away, but now Deaf people are moving up! (Ben)

In demystifying the wall, children are not simply being spoon-fed information. They are also engaged with the teaching and encouraged to think for themselves, to solve problems, and to work with each other:

When we were younger, we were all sitting there, just watching, so excited! When our Deaf teacher told us stories, we were just hooked. I think he is a fantastic storyteller. (Natasha)

I remember the time he told the alarm clock story, and at the end he asked us, "So what happened? How?" and we all had to think really hard what the answer was, was it this? Was it this? And in the end he explained to us what happened in the story, and it was so funny, we were all laughing, we love that! So much fun! (Hadi)

It prepares me to feel confident. He teaches me what being Deaf is like, so when I leave school, I will be confident. I will always keep in my mind what he taught me, to be confident and strong. So like he explained to us what will happen when we leave school. And I know what being Deaf is like and that with hearing people, it can be difficult. Deaf people can teach that. (Kumar)

CONCLUSION

So there we are. Paul has explained how he teaches Deaf children about their identity. These children have certainly eaten their Deaf carrot. They have language, and they understand their Deaf culture, their Deaf heritage, and their place in the world.

Does it work? For these children, yes.

Behave well, good attitude, where from? My Deaf teacher . . . thank you very much! (Kimberley)

Note

1. Michelle (10), Ben (12), Edwin (10), Chrissie (10), Phoebe (13), Kimberley (15), Kumar (15), Natasha (14), and Hadi (13). Note that the spelling in the quotations is according to British orthography, since these are British children quoted from the context of a British study.

Deafhood and Deaf Educators

Some Thoughts

Paddy Ladd

INTRODUCTION

I too am honored to be able to respond, not only because of Paul's educational work per se but also because of his successful efforts to maintain and develop the BSL poetry tradition begun by Dorothy Miles. It is rare for an educator to be a poet, and I have observed not only the way in which he has combined the two vocations but also the profound influence of such a combination on many of the children he has taught.

My Leverhulme Trust research material (which included significant visits to two Deaf schools in the United States) is in the process of becoming a full-length book—*Seeing through New Eyes: Deaf Pedagogies and the Unrecognised Curriculum.* However, as anyone who has ever written a book while holding a full-time job knows, progress is often much slower than hoped for. The book you now hold in your hands will therefore have seen the light of day first and so represents the perfect opportunity to broaden discussion that may arise from Paul's chapter. I also want to draw on the ongoing work of Janie Goncalves (Goncalves 2009), a former PhD student at the Center for Deaf Studies, that focuses on Brazilian Deaf educators.

HOW MANY ELEPHANTS CAN FIT INTO ONE CLASSROOM?

I begin by drawing attention to the second elephant in the room of Deaf education. The first elephant has always been visible to Deaf communities, but it was only through the work of sign linguists (that is, the recognition of the sophistication of sign languages) that the degree to which Deaf children were having to struggle unnecessarily to make sense of classroom communication became more widely appreciated.

The reemergence of the second elephant after the oralist century also began with sign linguists, in their focus on Deaf people with Deaf parents as modeling the most sophisticated forms of sign languages for their research. As a consequence, in preschool education in various places around the world, Deaf families with their own Deaf children (irrespective of whether their own parents were Deaf) also began to be used as role models and advisors for hearing parents. Yet in the vast majority of Deaf educational settings, the idea that Deaf educators might actually be manifesting pedagogical strategies that could serve as models for how Deaf education itself might be conducted (and, indeed, arguably totally restructured) is still not even under consideration.

The reasons for this are of course not hard to find. Nevertheless, any layperson looking at the endless shelves of books about Deaf education written during the last two hundred years would find it a significant indictment of a system that claims to serve the best interests of Deaf children that the only texts about the contributions of Deaf educators in all that time are a handful of articles and dissertations, all from the United States and all written in the past decade.[1]

Most of us are to some degree aware that Deaf education has not been Deaf-child centered and may also be aware of some, if not all, of the reasons for this. For example, even in the nineteenth century, when there were far more Deaf educators, the philosophy of most education systems for hearing children were not child centered. Nonetheless, it is possible to speculate from the little evidence presently available (for example, Massieu's role in Clerc's education, as well as the work of other French Deaf educators, such as Berthier) that those Deaf educators were nevertheless operating from Deaf pedagogical principles and utilized Deaf pedagogical strategies.[2]

It is important to state here that Paul's chapter represents only a very small part of what he actually strives for and attains in his work. The breadth and depth of the pedagogical praxis achieved by Paul and the other Deaf educators I observed is quite remarkable. Collectively, these achievements amount to a wide-ranging, coherent set of principles and strategies, which when finally published will give important clues as to how Deaf education can be completely rethought and restructured from top to bottom. In this response I summarize the main findings, though without the data that underpin them.

TWO PRELIMINARY DIMENSIONS

Before beginning this, I want to draw attention to two dimensions that have rarely been considered with respect to their implications for Deaf education. The first is the minority education dimension. This broad field encompasses previously oppressed languages (such as Catalan) that are in fact majority languages in their own countries/regions, minorities' issues within Western nations, such as African American and Afro-Caribbean education, and indigenous education, such as Native American and aboriginal education. As Ladd, Gulliver, and Batterbury (2003) briefly illustrate, each type produces different educational challenges and imperatives, and a proper study of each of these should form a part of training syllabi for teachers of Deaf children. In most of the above minority education situations, there has been for some time an emphasis on the necessity of educating children by using their indigenous languages and cultures to develop maximally effective pedagogical strategies. Indigenous teachers are themselves seen as an indispensable cornerstone of this work. Application of these perspectives to Deaf education is urgently needed in order to improve the lives and aspirations of Deaf children all over the world.

The second involves the cultural dimensions of education. This field has not been developed to the degree necessary for modern multicultural societies, probably because of the general academic weakness of cultural studies, itself a product of the (cultural) unwillingness of societies to examine their own cultures. This worldwide pattern of ethnocentricity is exacerbated by the paucity of research on Deaf cultures themselves, so that to this day relatively little is formally known about these cultures. This has meant that the necessity of using culturally appropriate teaching strategies has rarely even been considered, let alone researched and implemented in Deaf education.

Thus, in many respects it can be said that Deaf educational thinking has barely "reached first base" in comprehending and acting upon the necessity for a Deaf-child-centered education. Inclusion of the two dimensions above is especially urgent in light of the recent "oralist backlash," which not only continues the process of denying Deaf children their bilingual, bicultural birthright, but is rolling back the gains made in the past twenty years with increasing intensity. In light of these negative developments, the work of Deaf educators like Paul takes on even greater importance.

CULTURAL HOLISM

So what can be said about Deaf pedagogical praxis as gleaned from the research? The initial analysis I produced was constructed around a concept of *cultural holism*, which seemed to underpin and inform the manner in which Deaf educators approached Deaf children. I identified six stages of development, which began with preschool and ended at the school-leaving stage.

Cultural holism in this context is a means of describing an approach to education that first of all holds societies as a whole and communities in particular within a steady gaze and is committed to understanding those "worlds." On this basis practitioners then consider how best to educate the whole child in such a way that the child can make a maximal contribution to those worlds. That contribution is at once individual, inasmuch as it encourages the academic development of individual children, and collective, inasmuch as children are given clear moral and philosophical guidance with respect to making the best possible contribution to their own communities. In the case of minority children, guidance as to how to best interact with the majority society while also maintaining a strong sense of their own collective cultural identity is also a significant feature of such pedagogical praxis.

This analysis is necessarily simplified for the purposes of this response and therefore cannot address issues such as class-related education. Similarly, the subject of what might constitute "communities" in the wider sense of the term is too complex to engage with here. However, we should note the importance of the idea—however simplistic it might be—that cultures can be viewed on a multidimensional continuum between individualist cultures and collectivist cultures, noting that Mindess (2000) situates Deaf cultures as collective cultures and that Ladd (2003) continues the process of unpacking the consequences of being collectivist cultures embedded within majority individualist cultures.

Some of the minority cultures mentioned earlier, which operate toward the collectivist end of the spectrum, also of necessity engage more intimately with aspects of culturally holistic pedagogical praxis. Many Western educational systems, as presently constructed around individualism, are still unable to grasp both the significance of collectivist cultures and the extent to which individualism disrupts or damages both collective cultural health and educational outcomes.

UNRECOGNIZED CURRICULA

Minority educators thus find themselves required to address the whole minority child in the various additional domains and dimensions mentioned earlier. The extent to which they do so can be identified and constructed as unrecognized curricula. Being thus unrecognized, they of course also receive no recompense for any additional workloads and emotional responsibilities that they bear.

And this brings us back to Deaf education. Because of the very recent reentry of Deaf educators to Deaf education, the consequent paucity of research and its absence from funding priorities, it is understandable that such use of curricula by Deaf educators around the world may as yet be unrecognized. This, however, only makes such recognition all the more urgent, especially in an era of increasing mainstreaming and ideological cochlear implantation.

THE SIX STAGES OF DEAF PEDAGOGICAL PRAXIS

The cultural holism that underpins these stages can be described as cyclic and evolutionary. Deaf collectivist cultures (when not subject to external disruption)[3] believe that what they have learned is to a significant degree the result of what has been handed down to them by older Deaf generations, including the taking on of responsibilities within those communities, adherence to certain moral principles in dealing with other community members, and a commitment to work toward a better quality of life for the communities. Thus, a member of such a community who becomes a Deaf educator is almost culturally committed to instill these values in Deaf children—including educating them to grow up to educate future generations of Deaf children.

In the process the Deaf educators also push the children toward higher aspirations and achievements within the majority cultures and encourage them to contribute to these in whichever ways they can, not least because the children's future achievements play their part in changing majority societies' negative attitudes toward Deaf communities. They begin this work at the earliest age they are permitted access to Deaf children and continue it until the children leave school (and even through to higher education if they are taught in such institutions by Deaf educators).

These six stages are presented according to the approximate chronological age when the children experience them, although it must be stressed that, as befits holistic praxis, they not only overlap but also interpenetrate each other.

Stage 1: Starting the Cognitive Engine

Although the metaphor of switching on a light might be more appropriate, the process of starting the cognitive engine begins with the youngest Deaf children, usually in preschool. An intense amount of work is involved in getting Deaf children to look at the educator in order to then focus on learning how to think, to read the world around them, to learn the importance of paying attention, to understand the concept of having names, birthdays, and parents, and so on. This extra work, which of course is one consequence of children's inability to make intellectual sense of their auditory experience, has always been underrepresented in the literature. It represents a stage Deaf educators wish to move the children through as swiftly as possible, yet it is one during which they must demonstrate tremendous patience. The wide range of strategies developed by the Deaf educators examined in our study and the manner in which these strategies were executed were both remarkable and profound.

Stage 2: Holistic Use of Modalities

Once the children begin to awake to the meaning of communication, they can be helped to quickly utilize the modalities that lie at the heart of Deaf people's modes of operation in the world. These I term the visuo-gestural-tactile (VGT) modalities. They not only encompass linguistic, paralinguistic, and (a wider interpretation of) communicative competence features but also contain much relevant cultural information. One example is the extremely sophisticated use of touch and physical contact with Deaf children, which was observed in most Deaf educators. Insofar as these modalities inform the cognitive awakening process of Stage 1, they are utilized there also.

Stage 3: Creating a Safe Deaf Space

Although "Deaf-space" creation can be found in Deaf-run preschooling, it is not until elementary school that most Deaf children are able to grasp the idea that they are Deaf in a "Hearing World" and thus can begin to appreciate that such a space has been created for them, one where they can feel psychologically safe to express themselves *as Deaf children*. Our research shows that Deaf educators used very particular strategies to help create these safe spaces, which served as refuges from negative external attitudes, behaviors, and the consequent frustrations of trying to understand how the majority society operates. More positively, these became spaces in which the importance of collective gathering and sharing of information could be made clear to the children, thus helping them to understand how to develop strategies for contending with or transcending such external challenges.

However, these spaces are not simply remedial or therapeutic. From observation, they are very much celebratory spaces, where the joy of being together as Deaf adults and Deaf children, learning to develop and perform their own VGT skills, was very visible.

Stage 4: Language Acceleration

In our study it seemed that the most rapid stage of development in the children's use of signing took place from about seven to ten years of age. In well-functioning schools, the children's signing skills were by then usually sufficiently fluent and their emotional development sufficiently under way that Deaf educators could then speed up the rate of communication and also widen the range of subjects introduced. Particular emphasis was given to helping the children to appreciate the plasticity and beauty of their language—indeed to actively understand that it is *their* language. Thus, some of the educators we observed were particularly skilled at encouraging sign play and creative signing, emphasizing the importance of storytelling[4] (which here must be understood to include something I have termed "microstorytelling"), and introducing sign linguistics. Much of Paul's work can be situated in this stage, although he utilized strategies from all six stages in his work.

Stage 5: Establishing Deaf Children's Place in the Worlds

Once communication is flowing swiftly, ranging across all kinds of subjects both far and near, the Deaf educators then begin a more formal introduction of ideas and information concerning their identity and their place in the worlds to the children.[5] I initially wondered whether this starting point would lead to negative, divisive ideas being transmitted to the children. However, it became clear that what the Deaf educators were saying in this regard was in fact confirming what the children were already thinking and feeling without having a conceptual basis available to help them work through the issues. The most obvious example is their recognition that they were fundamentally different from most other people around them in their daily lives—and that this difference could either be processed negatively (as a failing, a lack on their part) or be positively embraced and used as a basis on which to construct lives in which they could become more active agents in their own destinies.

It was already clear to the children that these issues could not easily be discussed when each was alone at home (I cannot confirm the degree to which they were able to confide in their parents), and they well knew that, in order to get together in the first place, they had to travel many miles daily through territory that, if not necessarily hostile to them, certainly left them feeling like exiles. Thus, their regular coming together already represented a space where they could collectively begin pondering the nature of their existence.

Thus, the Deaf educators who were observed worked with these existential themes to help Deaf children situate themselves positively for life in both worlds. This is not to say that the educators discouraged the children from working with the hearing world. In fact, I found the opposite—they strove to encourage the children to believe that they could achieve much within that world. Moreover, because of their own example as successful Deaf professionals, they literally embodied this to the children, in a way that is not possible for a hearing person. It is against such a background that Kimberley's and Natasha's initial comments as cited in Donna's response can be more easily understood. We can see throughout Paul's chapter how central this fifth stage is to his pedagogy and how he, like some other people, constructs this stage as being focused on what is commonly termed "identity."

Stage 6: How to Live in the Worlds

Once the children had a strong basic grasp of their own identity with respect to the worlds around them, the classroom discourses opened up further, and a significant part of the rest of their school lives with Deaf educators involved learning how best to live in these worlds. This included learning as many of the innumerable characteristics of both worlds as possible; how each world operated; what each one's strengths and weaknesses were; how to behave in each world: and where that behavior should be the same in both or modified to suit each one. Again we can see how this stage is a significant aspect of Paul's pedagogy, and this is reinforced by several of the children's quotes in Donna's response.

MINORITY CULTURAL ISSUES, PRESSURES, AND TRIUMPHS

If one takes a step back to consider a broader perspective on education in general, one can see that majority-society teachers in majority-society schools are to a large extent focused on helping children learn the innumerable characteristics of their culture, albeit for the most part unconsciously. However, they are of course rarely required to learn in any real depth about any minority cultures that their children may be part of—as typified by the "saris and samosas" critique of the limited praxis of most multicultural education. Indeed, in schools in many UK cities, the number of ethnic groups attending any one school makes any such objective extremely difficult. Given these traditional patterns, one can understand why hearing teachers of Deaf students are unaccustomed to the idea that one might actually be required to understand another culture in such depth, although this idea is not new to educators working with indigenous communities, for example.

There are deeper issues that inform the work of Deaf educators, which minority-culture educators will understand. As has been made clear already, the latter are operating as exiles in an unfriendly world and under a particular set of pressures. Having to explain and guide pupils through one culture is hard enough. Tackling two simultaneously is a huge challenge; moreover, this cannot always be done at the time and place of the educators' choosing, for distressing events taking place in the children's own daily lives both in and out of school can force some issues to the surface sooner than educators might desire.

Furthermore, Deaf educators know that one major difference between themselves and other minority educators is ethnicity—that unlike those communities where 100 percent of the children grow up with minority parents and thus have already ingested their own languages, cultures, morals, and philosophies—only 5–10 percent of Deaf children come from Deaf families with access to their own cultural equivalent.

Thus, Deaf educators realize that the Deaf school is an absolutely crucial place for Deaf children, far more so than for hearing children because they know that if the children do not pick up this crucial information while at school, most of them will likely never get it—or at least not get it until they are adults and meeting other Deaf people.[6]

So in a sense, one can say that the responsibilities and the consequent pressures on Deaf educators may be (to use a simple averaging construct) even triple those of majority-society teachers. Certainly this is one of the reasons that every Deaf classroom I entered had an underlying air of urgency—the Deaf educators had communicated all of this to the children, and the children were very much responding to it. It was during such observations that another metaphorical label, "starting the motivational engine," occurred to me, for there was no doubt that the children were generally highly motivated to make the most of the time they spent in the Deaf classrooms.

However, one should not make the mistake of thinking that this process was a fundamentally negative experience—of straightforward hard work in a kind of puritanical environment. In fact, the very opposite was true; the Deaf classrooms were very often a place of great fun and joy, giving off a very tangible underlying air of celebration. The multitude of ways in which Deaf educators interwove real life with the material they were teaching and succeeded in engaging the children in exploration and discovery were underpinned by an unstated sense of triumph against the odds. Ladd (2003) discussed the Deaf cultural concept of "1001 small victories," where each piece of information gleaned from or about the hearing world is seen as a victory in itself. This is very much what happens in many Deaf classrooms; it permeates the very air that one breathes there.

DEAF PEDAGOGICAL VALUES, SKILLS, AND STRATEGIES

Within the rubric of cultural holism, I found that Deaf educators had developed a huge number of values, skills, and strategies, and I was able to identify thirty-seven, which I grouped into six categories. Space does not permit an exposition, but I would like to draw attention to two in particular.

The first is that the Deaf classrooms were characterized by densely interwoven, multilevel activities. As the children attained true fluency in sign language, each child's individual needs could be more rapidly addressed. Information concerning the lesson at hand would flow into discussion about this or that feature of the worlds; then various children would express their own experience or thoughts, and that new information would serve as the basis for the next stage of exploration before being woven back into the official lesson plan. It seems that once certain principles are in place, then minority education can become a case of "you know that I know that you know," as it were, and thus much of what is taught can automatically operate on several levels almost simultaneously.

I was greatly encouraged to see that one school I visited in the United States had formally recognized part, if not all of the foregoing, in that it had actually designed a training program in which new hearing educators were encouraged to learn from Deaf educators. Their focus was on what they termed "classroom management," and I noticed that this reflected several of the skills manifested in stages 2–4, creating a base upon which more sophisticated multilevel education could then take place.[7]

Finally, I noted that Deaf educators in the UK, the United States, and Brazil were using similar pedagogical principles without there being any obvious contact between them—a remarkable situation. If true (and more research would be needed to establish such a claim), this not only has profound and exciting implications for the wider education field, but also raises important questions about the very nature of human existence.

I want to end by highlighting something that is not mentioned in Paul's chapter but was very clear during the research, and that is the amount of psychological energy required of Deaf educators to be able to soldier on daily in the face of such lack of recognition. In some respects, the most gratifying feature of the visits to the two schools in the States (in which around 50 percent of the educators were Deaf) came from seeing the ideas that Paul expresses here both validated and offering clues and pathways for further development. So I hope very much both that other Deaf educators will now be able to follow Paul's very valuable example by recognizing and making visible their own contributions, and that hearing educators who have observed Deaf educators' praxis will also try to make known their own observations.

Notes

1. Because I have been unable to access material not written in English, I would very much welcome any examples of texts in any other languages. Please contact me at the Centre for Deaf Studies at the University of Bristol.

2. In the book I make a distinction between Deaf and Deafhood pedagogies, but that is too complex a matter for discussion here.

3. This is extremely important because not all Deaf people make good Deaf educators, and from my observations, the reasons that some do not include the consequences of the century of disruption to that evolutionary process.

4. Space does not permit elaboration, but microstorytelling here is very different from storytelling in hearing children's education. In Deaf education it is a multilevel experience that takes place most often outside of any formal storytelling time slot and is skillfully interwoven into the minute-to-minute classroom discourse.

5. I say "worlds" in the text to indicate that, from observations, Deaf educators, no matter what country they came from (and no matter what one might think about this dualism per se) made the distinction that two worlds exist—one Deaf and one 'Hearing'.

6. In addition, given the importance of critical mass, some of the dangers of main-streaming (with the closure of the majority of Deaf schools) can be clearly viewed through this lens.

7. The subject of Deaf classroom discipline is truly fascinating and one that the book will explore more deeply.

Bibliography

Goncalves, Janie. 2009. The linguistic and cultural challenge within deaf schools in the south of Brazil: Deaf and hearing working together and the birth of cultural pedagogies. PhD diss., University of Bristol.

Ladd, Paddy. 2003. *Understanding Deaf Culture: In Search of Deafhood.* Buffalo: Multilingual Matters.

———. Forthcoming. *Seeing through New Eyes: Deaf Pedagogies and the Unrecognised Curriculum.*

———, Mike Gulliver, and Sarah C. E. Batterbury. 2003. Reassessing Minority Language Empowerment from a Deaf Perspective. *Deaf Worlds* 19(2): 6–32.

Mindess, Anna. 2000. *Reading between the Signs: Intercultural Communication for Sign Language Interpreters.* Boston: Intercultural Press.

Index